George Washington's Enforcers

George Washington's Enforcers

Policing the Continental Army

Harry M. Ward

Southern Illinois University Press / *Carbondale*

Library of Congress Cataloging-in-Publication Data
Ward, Harry M.
   George Washington's enforcers : policing the Continental Army /
Harry M. Ward.
      p. cm.
   Includes bibliographical references (p.) and index.
   1. United States. Continental Army—Military police—History.
2. United States. Continental Army—Military life. 3. Military
discipline—United States—History—18th century. 4. Washington,
George, 1732–1799—Military leadership. 5. Soldiers—United
States—Social conditions—18th century. 6. United States—
History—Revolution, 1775–1783—Social aspects. I. Title.
   ISBN-13: 978-0-8093-2688-4 (cloth : alk. paper)
   ISBN-10: 0-8093-2688-4 (cloth : alk. paper)
E259.W37   2006
973.3'4—dc22   2005027796

Printed on recycled paper. ♻

The paper used in this publication meets the minimum requirements
of American National Standard for Information Sciences—Permanence
of Paper for Printed Library Materials, ANSI Z39.48-1992. ∞

Contents

Illustrations

Following page 110

Preface

When one reflects on the hardships endured by common soldiers in the armed forces of the American War of Independence, coming to mind are the deprivations of food and clothing, the suffering from harsh winters, lack of pay, and arduous marches without much in the way of shoes. One thinks also of the duress of battle and the long periods of boredom in camp. If one were to ask an infantryman or cavalryman in the Continental army about the most objectionable aspect of service, however, the response most likely would have been the constant fear of brutal discipline.

A soldier's duty was meticulously regulated; the least infractions of rules and regulations could lead to a whipping, or worse. Soldiers were often ignorant of the military code and general rules. Fear of cruel punishment was the chief hindrance to raising new recruits. Of course, all armies require a multilayered system for implementing discipline and training. Unfortunately, in the eighteenth century, motivation for behavior among troops came almost exclusively from a negative impulse—fear of punishment—rather than from a more enlightened approach emphasizing recognition for merit.

Little is known of life in the Continental army from the point of view of the enlisted men. What diaries and journals survive mostly covered short periods of times and generally were limited to reporting movements of the army and the like. Many soldiers were illiterate, or nearly so. Seldom did the soldier-recorders express emotion, criticism of command decisions, or information relating to the interrelationship among comrades. The best information on army life during the Revolution comes from veterans recalling their youthful experiences in military service. In addition, orderly books afford, at the supreme command, division, brigade, and regimental levels, a rather thorough, ongoing summary of army routine and happenings.

Serving in the Continental army, as with all military duty, meant exchanging rights and privileges of civilian life for subordination to a strict military code. This book seeks empathy with the ragtag troops who reaped almost no gain in the long or short run, but who submitted to the thankless task of winning American independence. It probes the efforts of the army command to coerce men, many of whom were unaccustomed to any strict discipline or direction in their lives, to become competent warriors. In spite of the soldiers' reluctance to fully measure up and the unremitting, widespread desertions, by war's end, even the most severe taskmaster of them all, General George Washington, expressed pride at the upscale professionalism and ardor achieved, at long last, among the troops of the Continental army.

At the heart of maintaining order and curbing the often self-destructive tendencies of the enlisted men were the duty personnel, guardsmen, and certain individuals and units that on occasion were assigned the role of military police. With the exception of the mostly failed experiment of establishing a mounted police corps, the Maréchaussée, which did serve as a very valuable precedent for the future, there was no military police per se in the Continental army.

The Provost Marshal Department, the first step toward creating a future military police corps during the Revolutionary War, served mainly to take charge of prisoners destined for general courts-martial and to provide for implementation of capital punishment. George Washington very much wanted to have a unified military police command in the army but did not press the issue. What strides were made in developing a military police system in the Continental army were put aside after the war. During later armed conflicts, various individuals and units continued to perform the duties of military police, with the only unifying force being the establishment of a provost marshal general during the Civil War and World War I. Not until September 1941 was the Corps of Military Police created, which since has had ever-widening jurisdiction.

This book treats the varied and often overlapping means of policing the Continental army. Omitted is the custody of prisoners of war, a major function of the modern military police. This study focuses on the American soldiers and not, for instance, on the charge of captive Britons and German mercenaries, which is a large and complex subject. Most American-held prisoners of war were watched over by state militia.

The Continental army adopted almost totally the table of organization and military code of justice of the British army, with a few improvisational features here and there. On the whole, punishment in the American army was slightly more humane than in the British military system. American soldiers, like their British counterparts, often labored under the direction of ill-trained and arrogant officers. Throughout the war, the establishment and enforcement of rules and regulations and the hasty administration of military justice afforded the accused almost no due process protection. At the same time, there was the difficulty of shaping a new army and instilling in it strict discipline. The process tested the mettle of George Washington, who, as the army's chief disciplinarian, can only be judged by the dictates of military necessity as perceived at the time.

Acknowledgments

I am grateful for suggestions from those who read the manuscript of this book in whole or in part: from academia, Don Higginbotham (University of North Carolina), author on military aspects of the Revolution; David B. Mattern (University of Virginia), senior editor of the *Papers of James Madison* and biographer of General Benjamin Lincoln (1995); and Philip Ranlet (Hunter College, CUNY), author of a study of Loyalists (1986) and numerous articles on the armed forces of the Revolution; and from the military, Robert P. Davis (First Sergeant, U.S. Army, Ret.), biographer of British general William Phillips (1999); George N. Ivey (Colonel, U.S. Army, Ret.); and Lynn L. Sims (Lieutenant Colonel, U.S. Army Reserve, Ret.), Department of the Army Historian and biographer of Colonel John Lamb (1975). The author's own introduction into the military scheme of things came from two years' service in the United States Marine Corps, rising to the rank of buck sergeant; although having the dubious, rare distinction of being drafted into the corps during the Korean War, the experience left an enduring appreciation of "Semper Fi." The Army Military History Institute at Carlisle Barracks, Pennsylvania, offered guidance at the beginning of the project. Dr. Ronald E. Craig, Military Police Historian, United States Army Military Police Museum, Fort Leonard Wood, Missouri, shared with the author his files on the history of the provost marshal and the Maréchaussée Corps. Scott Houting, at the Valley Forge National Historical Park, diligently searched for illustrations. Readily available microfilm collections, including the Revolutionary War Records at the National Archives, were invaluable resources. Thanks are due collectively to the staffs of the Library of Virginia, the Virginia Historical Society, and the Boatwright Library of the University of Richmond. At the latter institution, Nancy E. Vick and Noreen Ann Cullen carried on the incessant task of securing interlibrary loans.

George Washington's Enforcers

I

Preconditions

For love of country, George Washington could tell a lie. Reporting to the British commander in chief in North America in January 1757, Washington, a colonel of the Virginia Regiment, mentioned that he and his fellow officers, during the opening round of the French and Indian War, had instilled "notions into the Soldiers (who at that time knew no better) that they were Govern'd by the [British] Articles of War"; thus, "we felt little Inconveniency." The deception was eventually rectified: "the next Campaign we were join'd with the Regulars, and made Subject to their Laws."[1]

Indeed, the experiences of the French and Indian War prepared the colonists for the later task of establishing a regular army transcending state borders. The British military system in its entirety, with the exception of certain aristocratic features, such as the buying and selling of commissions, became the model for the Continental army of the American Revolution. Unfortunately, the British emphasis on brutal punishments to maintain discipline also carried over to the early American military code and practice.

During the French and Indian War, eight thousand Americans enlisted in British military units, two of which were almost completely recruited in the colonies—the Royal American (60th) Regiment, and nine companies of Rangers, commanded by Robert Rogers.[2] Substantial numbers of Americans also served in provincial regiments comprising volunteer forces separate from the militia and enlisted for service in one campaign at a time. Thus, the first small steps were made toward creating regular military units among the colonists. Provincial regiments imitated their British counterparts. Ten companies of forty to one hundred troops each normally formed a regiment. Three field officers—a colonel, a lieutenant colonel, and a major—headed a regiment, and a captain had charge of a company. High wages, often twice the pay of British regulars, lured recruits for provincial regiments. Even then, in several colonies conscription, mainly of footloose and destitute men, was employed to fill quotas.[3]

New England, New York, and New Jersey provincials served in the campaigns of 1755–60 in upper New York. Virginia, Maryland, and North Carolina troops accompanied the Braddock expedition of 1755, and Virginia and Pennsylvania provincial regiments participated in the Forbes campaign against Fort Duquesne in 1758. One-third of the men in Massachusetts between the ages of sixteen and twenty-nine during the war saw service as soldiers in provincial regiments. From 1759 to 1762, 51,277 provincial troops were in the field: 16,835 in 1759; 15,942 in 1760; 9,296 in 1761; and 9,204 in 1762. Of all these troops, only about 2,500 stayed on during the winter.[4]

A profile of enlistees in the provincial forces resembles the makeup of the ragtag soldiery in the American armies of the Revolution. In New England, enlistees reflected the generality of civilian social status, most of them being laborers, farmers, or artisans. Many were unmarried men in their midtwenties, who considered military service supplemental employment. Outside of New England, enlistees came more from the ranks of the foreign-born and unskilled.[5] A large number of volunteers for the Virginia Regiment had not been registered as militiamen. As George Washington complained as early as March 1754, the "generality" of enlistees were "loose, Idle Persons that are quite destitute of House, and Home."[6] Non-Virginians formed more than half of the regiment, and in one company, only eight of sixty-eight had enlisted in Virginia.[7]

British officials held American-bred soldiers in contempt. Peter Wraxall, secretary for Indian affairs in New York, in 1755 declared that provincial officers were "Strangers to Military Life and most of them in no Respect superior to the Men they are put over. They are like the heads and indeed are the heads of a Mob. The Men are raw Country Men."[8] Three years later, British generals were echoing the same sentiment. Of Pennsylvania and Virginia provincial troops, General John Forbes said that most of their officers were "an extreme bad Collection of broken Innkeepers, Horse Jockeys, & Indian traders," and "the Men under them, are a direct copy of their Officers, nor can it well be otherwise, as they are a gathering from the scum of the worst of people."[9] General James Wolfe noted that "the Americans are in general the dirtiest, the most contemptible, cowardly dregs that you can conceive. There is no depending upon them in action. They fall down dead in their own dirt and desert by battalions."[10] Actually, the American common soldiers were a cut above their counterparts in the British army; and, as proved later, the misconception extended into the Revolutionary War, when the king's army discovered that determined American troops were a formidable enemy.

The colonists had little disdain for the soldiers in their provincial forces; after all, the home troops were citizen-soldiers who endured tours of duty no longer than nine months. They held, however, most unfavorable impressions of British redcoats, a view that became more pronounced when British units began performing peacetime duties as a police force in New York and Boston. The scornful attitude of Americans toward the British common soldier undoubtedly influenced them to have a somewhat similar perception of Continental army troops during the Revolution.

Recruits for the British army for the most part came from the dregs of society. For some, the army was a place of refuge, and for others, a means of livelihood. Criminals (including felons under sentence of death or deportation), debtors, and paupers were hustled off to the army by local magistrates; some recruits were forced into service upon trumped-up charges. Severe unemployment in Scotland and Ireland prompted enlistments. Often no questions were asked of recruits who were underage or failed to measure up to physical requirements. The promise of liquor rations for servicemen was an inducement in itself. As an historian of the British army has noted, typically "the recruiting sergeant, bedizened in flaunting ribbons, descanted freely—and with lies plausible, but unblushing—upon the joys of military life, and poured forth plentiful libations, till the victim in drunken enthusiasm bartered away his liberty for ever and a day."[11]

Given the large number of persons regarded as "low life" serving in the ranks of the British and provincial armies, it was considered necessary to instill harsh discipline. The dual system of military justice, wherein only the enlisted ranks faced corporal punishment and were more subject to the death penalty, mirrored the traditional distinction between "gentlemen" and the lower classes.

There was a rude awakening for men serving in the provincial regiments during the French and Indian War. The Mutiny Act voted by Parliament, receiving the king's assent on December 19, 1754, declared that American colonial troops "whenever they shall be joyned, or serve with Our Regular Forces" are "to be under the same Rules & Articles of War with them, and are to be liable to the like Paines & Penalties."[12] For troops from the northern colonies, the extreme penalties of the British military code were mostly avoided before 1757, because local commanders, elected by their men, feared that severity would cause desertion and mutiny. Provincial and British troops were not officially joined together in operations until that year. Lord Loudoun was the first commander in chief to insist on a unified command and enforcement of discipline.

The colonies did make some effort at the beginning of the French and Indian War to provide more stringent punishment for soldiers' offenses. A Massachusetts act of 1754 authorized courts-martial to inflict a death sentence for mutiny, sedition, and desertion, but the penalty had to be reviewed by the governor for approval. No mention was made of flogging in the law; thirty-nine lashes, however, was meted out by courts-martial in accordance with the civil law.[13]

At first, regulations governing the Virginia Regiment were similar to those affecting the militia. The Virginia military code of 1748 carried no death penalty, and the only corporal punishment mentioned was "tying neck and heels." Desertion, mutiny, and disobedience were subject only to fines. At the insistence of Washington and his officers, with the governor's support, the Virginia legislature in October 1755 provided the death penalty for the three above-mentioned offenses. A Virginia law of 1757, "copied from an Act of Parliament," made the distinction between provincials and militia, with the former subject to harsher penalties.[14]

George Washington expected that the Virginia military law of 1755 would arouse great fear among the common soldiers, thereby strengthening discipline. The Virginia colonel informed his second-in-command, Lieutenant Colonel Adam Stephen, in November 1755, that he should "be particularly careful in seeing that strict Order is observed among our Soldiers, as that is the Life of Military discipline—We now have it in our Power to enforce obedience . . . the Men being subject to death as in the Military Law."[15] Washington instructed his company commanders (captains) to read the 1755 act "against Mutiny and Desertion" frequently to their men and "further assure them, that if any Soldier deserts, although he return *himself*, he shall be hanged."[16]

Washington insisted on using the death penalty regularly as exemplary justice. Sergeant Nathan Lewis was sentenced to death by a court-martial of the Virginia Regiment for "retreating with a party of Men without orders and not going to the Assistance" of Captain John Mercer "when Engaged with the Indians on April 18, 1756." Governor Robert Dinwiddie forwarded a death warrant, entreating Washington to have "as many of the forces present as You can, that he may be a public Example to deter others from such like Offences." Lewis, however, was not executed.[17]

It was one thing to be convicted of cowardice and quite another for desertion. If unchecked, desertion could spread like wildfire and ruin an army. Washington soon learned, however, that the threat of death proved little deterrence to desertion. During the first half of 1757, 114 of the 400 men in the Virginia Regiment deserted at Fredericksburg and Winchester. Washington was determined to remedy this situation. He wrote British general John Stanwix in July 1757 that "I have a Gallows near 40 feet high erected (which has terrified the rest exceedingly)," and that he expected "to hang two or three on it, as an example to others."[18]

A court-martial at Fort Loudoun (Winchester), July 25–26, 1757, resulted in thirteen prisoners being sentenced to death. Actually, of the group only two were executed: twenty-year-old William Crawford and twenty-five-year-old Ignatius Edwards, who was known as a "great Dancer & Fiddler." In reporting to the governor, Washington commented, "Your Honor will, I hope excuse my hanging them. It conveyed much more terror to others, and it was for example sake."[19] Some of the deserters received as many as 1,000 lashes each. One estimate for the Virginia Regiment for mid-1757 is that the average whipping netted 613 stripes, "not much below the 1757 lash average in the British Army (731)."[20]

Northern provincials, from 1757 to the end of the war, served continually under the direction of the British army command. As historian Fred Anderson writes, American troops saw "soldiers like themselves being flogged in a daily succession, irregularly punctuated by executions. Soldiers who served in 1757 and thereafter were intensely conscious of the coercive aspects of military discipline."[21]

The British commanders in chief in North America, Lord Loudoun (1756–57) and Jeffery Amherst (1758–63), integrated a system of military justice covering both British regulars and the provincials. Only general courts-martial could order capital punishment.[22] Provincial commanders often did their best to present charges that could be tried under regimental court-martial, thus keeping culprits from the harsher penalties of a general court-martial. Gradually, punishment for provincials approximated the severity of the British military code. Regimental courts-martial did not hesitate to give the maximum sentence allowed them: five hundred lashes. Provincials tried by general courts-martial received sentences of death and whippings of up to one thousand lashes.[23] Journals kept by soldiers, which before 1757 almost never mentioned punishment, afterward frequently cited instances of cruel military justice.

At Fort Edward, provincial soldiers recorded numerous punishments. The post, on the upper Hudson River, thirteen miles south of Lake George, was the supply depot and staging area for attacking French forces along the Lake George–Lake Champlain corridor and in Canada. From May 10 to November 3, 1757, Connecticut soldier Luke Gridley noted eighty-two punishments, including seventy-one whippings and six executions.[24] From May 29 to October 4, 1759, at the fort, there were twenty floggings and eight soldiers shot or hanged.[25] In July 1760, a soldier was "whipt till the Blood Came out at the knee of his Breeches."[26] Other means of corrections were also employed. Luke Gridley's diary of 1757 mentioned that a Connecticut soldier "Run the gandtelit [gauntlet] thrugh 30 men for sleeping upon gard which Cryed Lord god have mercy on me the B[l]ood flying every stroke this was a sorrowful sight: Also one man was sintanced to Ride the wooden ho[r]se for not turning out so soon as the Rest . . . with 4 muskits tied to his feet."[27]

Provincials along with regulars were required to witness executions. Persons to be shot "had labels upon their breast which specified the crimes for which they were to die."[28] Private Lemuel Wood, seventeen years old, in July 1759 witnessed two executions by shooting. For the first, two squads of six men each performed the deed: one squad shot the condemned man through the body, and the other "blowed his head all to pieces." The second culprit refused to stay still and was therefore "tied to an old Log" and shot.[29]

Not only did American officers and soldiers learn of the brutality of the British military system, they also familiarized themselves with duties and procedures in the British army. George Washington earnestly studied British military theory and practice. During the French and Indian War, he obtained copies of the general orders of the Braddock and Forbes campaigns and of Colonel Henry Bouquet's western army.[30] For his own command, Washington relied upon information in General Humphrey Bland's *A Treatise of Military Discipline: In Which Is Laid Down and Explained the Duty of the Officer and Soldier*, then considered the bible of the British army. Washington received the book (1727 edition) from a London purchase in April

1756, though he was already familiar with it. He urged his officers to study "Blands and other Treatises."[31] By the time of the Revolution, Washington gave attention to Thomas Simes's three military dictionaries/guides, published in London and Philadelphia, copies of which he owned.[32] During his French and Indian War experience, Washington also tried to emulate British officers. As one historian has noted, "Thus he acquired their attitudes, copied their habits of command, and absorbed their prejudices to the point that he became one of them in virtually every respect but the color of his coat and the provenance of his commission."[33]

Provincial forces serving in the French and Indian War adapted to the guard system of the British army. As Fred Anderson points out, provincials had duty on five kinds of routine guard details. The quarter guard, a regimental unit consisting of about forty or more men commanded by a subaltern officer, "performed local police functions, confined prisoners awaiting regimental punishment, and patrolled the unit area at night." Also on the regimental level, a picquet (picket) guard, involving about fifty men, headed by a captain and two subalterns, could regularly be deployed to maintain outposts, protect foraging parties, and sally forth to confront forward detachments of the enemy. A main guard, consisting of a large number of soldiers drawn from one regiment, provided guards around a camp's perimeter for the purpose of external security, including protection of various property, such as the artillery park and cattle. Ordinary guards also included those details posted to attend generals and certain staff officers. Finally, a provost guard, usually commanded by a captain or subaltern, had the responsibility of general police duty, confinement of prisoners awaiting trial by court-martial, and supervision of executions and sometimes corporal punishment.[34]

The provost marshal in the British army, wrote a military authority in the seventeenth century, was "the greatest and principal gaoler of the Army." He had "the charge of all manner of *tortures* . . . and may, by his officers, use them either in case of judgment or commandment from a marshall court or otherwise upon unruliness at his own discretion; he is, by his officers, to see all places of execution prepared and furnished with engines fitting to the judgment."[35] During the French and Indian War, it was recognized that, upon authority delegated by the commanding general, the provost marshal at his discretion could "hang all stragglers and marauders."[36] Normally, he had charge of all such miscreants that were apprehended.[37]

The provost guard made the rounds of a camp looking for anyone violating general orders or any of the Articles of War. Civilians in camp also came under the guard's surveillance. In June 1758, at the siege of Louisbourg, General Amherst ordered the provost guard to destroy tents belonging to unlicensed sutlers who were selling liquor to soldiers and "to keep good order in the market, and not permit any thing to be sold there after retreat beating."[38]

The role of the provost marshal as executioner is revealed in general orders by General Amherst at Oswego, New York, on July 29, 1760. Ten prisoners under sentence of death were to be "delivered by the Provost Marshal at 8 A.M. on parade." After the prisoners were led in "devotions" by a chaplain at the site for the executions, nine of the convicted soldiers were pardoned, including John Jones of the First New York Regiment, "on condition of his serving the provost as executioner during the campaign." Then "James Ginnens of Colonel Fitch's [Connecticut] Regiment is to be executed by the Provost Marshal, or his man, hanging the prisoner James Ginnens until he is Dead." Ginnens was "to be left hanging till retreat beating, when he is to be cut down and buried by a party of the Regiment he belongs to."[39]

In addition to interior and provost guards, certain officers had responsibility relating to police functions. The adjutant (one per regiment), whose main duties involved record keeping and assisting in drill, supervised punishments at the regimental level.[40] For a period usually of twenty-four hours, officers of the day had first responsibility for attending to camp security problems, taking charge of prisoners, and checking on the guards. General orders of June 10, 1759, for General Amherst's army, consisting of regulars and provincials, in camp at Fort Edward, declared: "All Reports from the Field Officers of the Picquit and Extraordinarys that may happen in Camp are to be made to the Colonel of the Day, who will report at Orderly Time to the Commander-in-Chief. All Guards are to turn out to the Colonel of the Day. . . . He will go his Rounds, and visit all Guards and Outposts, to see that the whole are alert, and properly posted."[41]

The French and Indian War ended with the British government creating a military establishment (with the projected service of ten thousand troops) for North America. General Jeffery Amherst in 1763 relinquished the office of commander in chief of British forces in North America to General Thomas Gage, who was confirmed in that position on November 16, 1764, and served in it until 1775. Although many Americans shared a bias against standing armies that was characteristic of English Whigs and would later be vehemently opposed to the stationing of regular troops in America, during the early years after the French and Indian War, there was little sentiment against a British-imposed military establishment for the colonies. Most all of the British regulars in North America were stationed at distant or frontier posts. As long as there were no disturbing issues, such as Parliament taxing the colonists for military defense or employing troops as a constabulary force, the soldiers were welcomed as protection against Indians, foreign enemies, and domestic insurrectionists. What is significant is that the colonists had no major objection to British regulars providing for the common defense. Even Benjamin Franklin, in 1764, expressed appreciation that British troops were "necessarily posted on the Frontier. Such just and generous Actions endear the Military to the Civil Power and impress the Minds of all the Discerning with a still greater Respect for our national Government."[42]

In 1764, the Pennsylvania government called on British troops to diffuse the vigilante actions of the Paxton Boys; three companies of Royal Americans escorted friendly Indians to Philadelphia after the massacre of a group of Conestoga Indians.[43] In the same year, Colonel Henry Bouquet, solely with British troops, defeated near Pittsburgh a band of Indians involved in the Pontiac Indian uprising; Virginia kept its militia from joining the expedition.[44] In 1766 with backing from the New York Assembly, General Thomas Gage, because the "militia is not to be depended upon," ordered three hundred regular troops to quell the rent riots in Dutchess County, in the Hudson River valley.[45]

Seventy-five hundred regulars made up the British North America command in 1763. They were located at Nova Scotia, Canada; the Lake Champlain area; the Great Lakes area; Fort Pitt, South Carolina (three companies); "Louisiana and Its Dependencies"; "Florida and Its Dependencies"; and one company each in the Bahamas and Bermuda.[46] By 1767, the British army in North America consisted of 129 companies: 59 in Canada, Nova Scotia, and Newfoundland; 9 in the Great Lakes region; 12 in the Illinois country and the upper Ohio (Fort Pitt); 5 in New York City; 6 in Philadelphia; 9 in Elizabethtown and Perth Amboy, New Jersey; 3 in South Carolina; 18 in West Florida; 6 in East Florida; 1 in Bermuda; and 1 in Providence Island, Bahamas.[47]

The holding of widespread military posts had its difficulties, particularly involving discipline and frequent desertions. The effort in England to

centralize recruitment (with Major Barry St. Leger in charge) was so unproductive that convicts were being enlisted in peacetime as they were in
wartime. American colonists were even being recruited for British regular
regiments (other than for the Royal Americans). The commander in chief
for North America, Thomas Gage, complained to Major General Alexander
Mackay, in May 1769, that "men of this Country do well enough in the West
Indies" but "they generally Enlist with the Regiments in America with no
other Intent than to Desert."[48] Historian John Shy sums up the dismal situation of the British army in North America: "Postulate an army organized
to expect the worst rather than elicit the best in its soldiers; locate that army
in a rich, vast, and wild country; populate the army with its own cast-offs,
criminals, and natives of the country itself—given these elements, there was
little that could be done."[49]

Eventually, the colonists developed a great contempt for British soldiers
and officers, mostly because of their brutish and immoral ways—from service contact and civilian-military relations during the French and Indian
War. The disgust grew as the protest movement against British ministerial
tyranny took hold. It was obvious that those regulars stationed in New York
City and those brought to Boston in 1768 were intended to assist in securing public order. Although these British troops, like those in England, were
prohibited from attacking civilians unless ordered to do so by civil authorities, clashes between soldiers and the populace occurred, intermittently in
New York City between 1766 and 1771,[50] and in the famous Boston Massacre of March 1770.

Friction between civilians and the British troops (first, four regiments,
then reduced to two in 1769) quickly mounted in Boston. Clever and vi-
cious propaganda from the pens of Boston Whig leaders affected public
opinion even more adversely toward British regulars. The *Journal of the
Times*, written anonymously by Boston patriots and published widely in
colonial newspapers, from October 1768 to November 1769, was a day-to-
day account of abusive British rule in Boston. The misdeeds of soldiers
toward civilians formed a major theme. Redcoats allegedly started brawls,
caused riots at cultural gatherings, and committed robberies and rapes.[51]
Bostonians witnessed horrible scenes of British military brutality. For example, on October 6, 1768, nine or ten soldiers "were severely whipt on the
Common;—to behold Britons scourg'd by Negro drummers, was a new and
very disagreeable spectacle."[52] On October 31, all the British garrison marched

to the Common, to the "drumming of the dead beat"; a private, "dressed in white," was shot, whereupon the troops marched around the corpse, which was then buried near the site of the execution.[53] The presence of British troops in Boston stirred up considerable opposition to having a standing army. The Massachusetts House of Representatives in June 1769 resolved that the stationing of "a military force" in the colony "for the purpose of aiding and assisting the civil government" violated the "natural and constitutional rights of the people."[54]

Troops serving as a domestic police force in the colonies had a limited potential not only because of popular opposition but also because the British government did not provide a sufficient number of troops to repress widespread disturbances. Moreover, the powers of the royal governors, who could requisition troops for the purpose of law enforcement, were on the decline, and assemblies refrained from voting expenditures for British army support.[55]

During the early 1770s, the British government effected a retrenchment in the North American military establishment. Troops were removed from Boston, while some were still maintained at Castle William (an island) in Boston harbor. Although six thousand soldiers remained on the American assignment, troops of western posts between the Ohio River and the Great Lakes were withdrawn, except for Forts Niagara, Detroit, and Michilimackinac.[56] The people of Boston no longer had to worry about British troops—at least until Parliament's response to the Boston Tea Party. Anticipating resistance to the Coercive Acts, by December 1774, thirty-five hundred British soldiers had arrived in Boston and its vicinity. General Thomas Gage (now also the Massachusetts governor, for the convenience of blending civil and military authority) realized that the sizable number of troops at his command were not enough to stem a rebellion.[57]

While Americans generally opposed a standing army in peacetime, they had no qualms about a regular force of their own for wartime, even though a "national" army during war had as much potential for infringement upon liberty as did a standing peacetime army. With the outbreak of hostilities at Lexington and Concord in April 1775, Americans at first felt that the militia of citizen-soldiers could more than match the prowess of King George's regulars. The irony was that when it soon became evident a full-scale war had begun, Americans desired their own regular army of intercolonial troops. The Army of Observation around Boston, consisting of New England militia, was quickly transformed into a Continental army. Many of the new field grade and general officers in the American army had served in the last war in conjunction with British troops, either in colonial provincial corps or in the British regular army itself. A further irony was that although they showed greater tactical adaptability and improvisation than the British army, the American forces subscribed to the principles and practices of organization and discipline learned from their British counterparts.

The new American army operated chiefly outside of densely populated areas and could go its own way without provoking much military-civilian strife. Whereas Americans had once been revulsed by the barbarity of the British army during the French and Indian War and afterward, they did not exhibit similar compunctions regarding their own army and cared little about its inner workings.

2

The Common Soldier

Soldiering has always lured the young in search of adventure and glory. The armed forces provided a rite of passage, a sort of way station wherein a recruit earned his manhood, enjoyed camaraderie, became inured of discipline, received pay and sustenance, and had the satisfaction of doing his patriotic duty.

At the beginning of the Revolutionary War, a *rage militaire* spurred enlistments into the fledgling Continental army. A patriotism defined as fighting for liberty against enslavement by a tyrannical power from abroad was the overriding motivation. The thrill of war, however, among the populace, quickly wore off, and with enlistments expiring at the end of 1775, many soldiers returned home to stay.

The standard enlistment in the Continental army essentially became either a three-year stretch or the duration of the war. There were a few short-timers in service, consisting mainly of draftees. Deprivation, cruel discipline, the prevalence of disease in the camps, and the awareness that enlistees in the army exchanged liberty for a kind of slavery thwarted recruitment, and increasingly, the very poor and footloose took over the soldiering. In time, a growing sense of professionalism, unit cohesion, and pride among the common soldiers improved army morale, but the persistent hardships and suffering impaired the fighting spirit.

One irony of the Revolutionary War is the great divide between the soldiers and the civilians they were defending. The common soldiers resented that the public appeared unwilling to honor fully the enlistment contract. On the other hand, civilians generally regarded the enlisted ranks as the riffraff of society. A good citizen who served a short term of active duty absolved himself of further enlistment. The public, however, did not identify much with persons who were foolish enough to submit themselves to the army for the long haul. Not only was there no public outcry over the brutal conditions suffered by soldiers, but enlisted men themselves were relatively mute, confining themselves to grumbling in the typical soldier's fashion, although the high desertion rate and the rare attempted mutiny demonstrated the limits of their forbearance.

That many soldiers accepted conditions as they were and especially did not rise up against the cruel treatment and awful deaths inflicted on their comrades may be attributed to various factors. From a broad perspective, historian Wayne E. Lee observes that the Continental army had a great "capacity to self-censure." There were two reasons for this capacity.

> One was the clear institutional ability to punish. The other was the development of attachments, social bonds, and standards of conduct specific to the military community. The army had come to consist of longer-serving soldiers, accompanied by women and civilian support staff, supervised by the socially superior officers, all of whom became invested in the maintenance of their relations. That community could therefore self-censure.[1]

Unlike officers, enlisted men independently were without influence. The established barrier between officers and their men was unbridgeable. Washington assiduously pressed hard to curtail any fraternization between officers and the rank and file. The officer corps was essentially grounded in elitism; if it was not quite as affected by aristocratic pretensions as its European counterparts, it was every bit a caste set unto itself, separate from the common soldiers. It is true that some of the Continental army officers came from the "nonelite," such as General Charles Scott, a barely literate small farmer who, as an orphan, had been bound out as a carpenter's apprentice, or General William Maxwell, who tended a few acres in northwestern New Jersey and had long experience as a supply clerk (commissary) to a British army detachment on the frontier. But such persons as these, upon reaching the level of command, had to assume the posture of a gentleman. The entry of Scott and Maxwell into the officer corps had been made possible by their service as subalterns during the French and Indian War.

Officers were capable of acting in concert in making demands of the civil authorities; the enlisted men were not. It did little good for common soldiers to vent complaints through the noncommissioned officers, as they were also of the rank and file. Competent officers, attentive to the needs of their men, however, did not hesitate to present the needs of their soldiers to the military high command and to civilian officials as well. Still, an impenetrable wall existed between officers and the enlisted men. In the Continental army, it was difficult to rise from enlisted man to officer, although some did. No such promotions were made in the field, and generally, all company officers (subalterns and captains) were commissioned by state legislatures, and field grade officers (majors, colonels, and generals) by Congress.

The double standard of military justice kept the common soldier under tight rein. Corporal punishment or death could be inflicted on an enlisted man for almost any military transgression, while officers similarly culpable were liable for fines, reprimand, or dismissal.

Throughout the war, a strong esprit de corps among enlisted men, though often evident, was made difficult because of diverse ethnicity, recruitment from far-flung areas, resentment between short-timers and long-term enlistees, operational inactivity of the army, feeling of abandonment by the public, and lack of any recognition for merit. Not until August 1782 did Washington authorize an award for exemplary behavior by enlisted men. The Badge of Military Merit was to be conferred for "singularly meritorious action." The insignia, consisting of a purple heart of cloth or silk, "edged with narrow lace or binding," was to be worn over the left breast. Although there may have been more recipients, only three men are known to have been awarded the badge, in 1783.[2]

Many soldiers in civilian life had only had a marginal relationship with an established community and had been treated as lower-class citizens. They had been subject to corporal punishment, which was not meted out to those of a higher station. Most soldiers brought with them into service already a habit of deference. The very nature of armies requires a strict military code for submission and obedience. The Continental army, in following British and European practices, was no exception. Still, the question may arise whether, if the American forces had consistently obtained enlistees from the settled and substantial citizenry, would harsh discipline have prevailed? Given the conventional military thought of the time and the view of Washington and his officers, the influence of the French and Indian War experience, and politicians who feared a standing army with its potential to threaten civil society, inevitably discipline in the Continental army would have been severe. Especially with so many of the "lower sort" in the rank and file, it was important to exact strict military discipline by whatever means necessary.

Recruiting agents often delivered to the Continental army units enlistees of questionable physical fitness. As early as October 1775, John Adams noted that "in the Massachusetts Regiments, there are great Numbers of Boys, Old Men, and Negroes, Such as are unsuitable for service."[3] A Pennsylvania officer with the Canadian invasion force a year later had a similar observation: the New England troops were "the strangest mixture of Negroes, Indians and Whites with old men and children."[4] Certain recent historians, chiefly from examination of tax, probate, and pension records, have concluded that the common soldier of the Revolution serving after 1776 came from the poorest and most dependent levels of society, including "ne'er-do-wells, drifters, unemployed laborers, captured or deserted British soldiers and Hessians, indentured servants, and slaves."[5] Of course, the lack of wealth or community status does not necessarily mean that most enlistees were of the down-and-out type. Many probably were single, younger sons of "established" families and not yet property owners or settled citizens.[6]

A sampling of soldier profiles does reveal that the enlisted men were representative mainly of the bottom to lower-middle rungs of society. In New England, most recruits were non-property-holders,[7] and in New York and Pennsylvania, one-fourth of the soldiers had been farmers, and the others tradesmen, craftsmen, and unemployed laborers.[8] Only about half of the enlisted men in the New Jersey brigade owned any ratable property.[9] Two-thirds of Delaware's troops had been farmers, but only a few of these had owned any property.[10] Similarly, most of Maryland's and Virginia's recruits were sons of small or tenant farmers, with some enlistees being newly freed indentured servants.[11] Continentals from the Deep South also came from the poorer classes. The South Carolina Vagrant Act of March 1776 required the enlistment of all "idle men, beggars, strolling or straggling persons." As one historian states, the South Carolina "greatly understrength units" were "composed of reluctant, unpropertied, and vagrant recruits."[12]

As to be expected in any army, most Continental army troops were young. One study of the age distribution of New England soldiers finds that 9 percent were age fifteen to nineteen, 37.2 percent age twenty to twenty-nine, and 28 percent age thirty to thirty-nine.[13] For the New Jersey brigade, the number of men under age eighteen registered at 10.5 percent, age eighteen to twenty at 44.1 percent, and age twenty-three to twenty-nine at 18.7 percent.[14] A sample of Pennsylvania troops shows 11 percent were age seventeen or under, and three-fourths of all the state's Continentals were age seventeen to thirty-two.[15] The age distribution for General William Smallwood's Maryland brigade in 1782 shows that 25 percent of the men were age fourteen to nineteen, 33 percent age twenty to twenty-four, and 18 percent age twenty-five to twenty-nine.[16] An estimate for Virginia troops is that 90 percent were under age twenty-five when entering the army, with a median age of twenty to twenty-one; most troops in the fifteen-to-nineteen age bracket had joined the army as substitutes.[17]

Although there is no overall study of literacy among the troops in Washington's army, it may be estimated that at least half were illiterate. Among the population in general during the late eighteenth century, New England had an 85 percent literacy rate; Pennsylvania, 60 percent; New Jersey and Virginia, about 50 percent. In Virginia, especially among farmers and laborers, the literacy rate was well below 50 percent. With so many recruits from the lower levels of society, the literacy rate in the Continental army was undoubtedly below that for the general population.[18] A high rate of illiteracy in the Continental army is not surprising when one considers that, in World War I, one-third of draftees were illiterate.[19]

Many of Washington's troops were foreign-born. Immigration from the British Isles and Germany had been at high tide by the mid-eighteenth century. Captured German troops were allowed to enlist, as were British prisoners of war and deserters. Indentured and convict servants entered the army, many being substitutes.[20] Outside of New England, where only about 10 percent of the region's Continental troops were foreign-born, the incidence of immigrants in the army from other states is much more substantial: for example, 20 percent from New York, 70 percent from Pennsylvania, 32–52 percent from Delaware, 40 percent from Maryland, and 15 percent from Virginia. Regarding Pennsylvania, 56 percent of the foreign-born troops were from Ireland, 15 percent from Germany, and 11 percent from England.[21] By far, the greatest number of immigrants in the Continental army from all the states were Irish (including the Scots-Irish). Michael J. O'Brien, historiographer of the American Irish Historical Society a century ago, using a not fully reliable method of counting Irish names on army muster rolls, estimated that 38 percent of the Continental army was Irish (presumably, mostly immigrants).[22]

Although Congress in 1776 declared against enlisting criminals, courts nevertheless remitted sentences of convicted felons if they joined the Continental army. Such recruits generally had been found guilty of assault and battery, petty crimes, and indebtedness, although sometimes murderers and rapists were included.[23] Tories under sentence of imprisonment or death were allowed to enlist in the military forces. This was especially permissible in New Jersey. Of thirty-five persons sentenced to death for treason in Morristown, New Jersey, in November 1777, two were hanged and the other thirty-three pardoned on condition of joining the army. Convicted Tories and felons made up one-third of a regiment in the New Jersey brigade.[24]

Some 5,000 to 8,000 African Americans served in the Continental army, usually in mixed units of whites and blacks. In August 1778, 755 blacks were listed as serving in fourteen infantry brigades.[25] Although African Americans generally served as cooks, orderlies, and pioneers (unarmed laborers), New England blacks usually acted in the same capacities as white soldiers.[26] A Rhode Island regiment, commanded by Christopher Greene and consisting of about 250 blacks, existed from 1778 to 1783. Massachusetts also briefly had a black unit, the Bucks of America; and Connecticut in 1781 fielded a black company.[27] General Horatio Gates, in charge of troops in southeastern New England in July 1779, observed that blacks "make up a great Number of Soldiers . . . in this Department." Once slaves who had been sent to the army as substitutes had served their tours of duty, they often reenlisted.[28] Of the southern states, only in Maryland could slaves be enlisted into the army. In Virginia, some masters illegally sent slaves as substitutes; these recruits gained freedom after the war by legislative fiat. About 500 free blacks from Virginia served in the Continental army.[29]

Patriotism could hardly be the sole motive for enlisting in the army. Incentives had to be offered by both Congress and the states. In 1776, Congress promised a hundred acres of land to each private and noncommissioned officer at the end of the war. Seven states also gave land bounties. The states and Congress competed during the war in raising the amount of cash payments provided to recruits. Even then, there was always deficiency in army manpower.[30]

The Continental army tried aggressive recruiting, much like the British practiced. Men often enlisted on the spur of the moment, and then once inducted, the cold realization of being a soldier would set in. At first, officers were detached, sometimes for a year or two, to go into their home areas to drum up recruits. After mid-1777, recruitment was handled by local officials in enlistment districts within a state.[31] Recruiters sometimes plied potential enlistees with intoxicating drinks at taverns or at large gatherings.[32]

Typical recruiting instructions were those given to Captain Samuel Walker of Virginia. He was to accept men between the ages of seventeen and fifty, "free from lameness or other bodily infirmities, that may render them incapable of supporting the fatigues of camp."[33] Brigadier General Mordecai Gist, in Maryland in November 1780 on leave from the southern army, informed Governor Thomas Sim Lee that he was "particularly charged" with directing recruiters not to enlist anyone who was not at least five feet four inches tall and "of a good sound Constitution perfect in their Limbs, less than 50 years old."[34]

In 1776, new troops for the Third Pennsylvania Regiment were so scarce that officers and noncommissioned officers of the regiment were sent throughout Pennsylvania and also into New Jersey, Delaware, and Maryland in search of enlistees. Captain Alexander Graydon, who went out on this mission, accompanied by a lieutenant, a corporal, and a drummer, had great difficulty getting prospects to commit to military life. At a tavern, Graydon fought with a potential enlistee who said he would not join up unless the recruiting officer could whip him; soundly thrashed by Graydon, the ruffian still did not enlist but did hire himself out as a fifer to Graydon's company. In his memoirs written after the war, Graydon declared he mentioned the episode "to correct the error of those who seem to conceive the year 1776 to have been a season of almost universal patriotism." One of Graydon's few recruits found while combing Maryland's Eastern Shore was a local derelict who, a resident said, "would do to stop a bullet as well as a better man, and as he was a truly worthless dog," the "neighborhood would be much indebted to us for taking him away."[35]

To fill quotas for troops, most states, upon recommendation from Congress, resorted to conscription. The draftees, selected by lot from militia rolls, served for short periods, usually three, six, or nine months, or only for a single campaign. Bounty money was offered to the conscripts, and those remaining longer in service received the greater amount. Frequently, draftees (or their substitutes) proved to be misfits. Brigadier General John Paterson reported from West Point in March 1780 that while "we once had a respectable soldiery," all those who remain "are mostly composed of nine months' abortions, sent here with bounties . . . naked, lifeless, and dead, who never saw action" and "are now counting days, hours, and minutes they have to tarry in service."[36]

The draft weighed most heavily on the poor and the unskilled. Exemptions were widespread. Any person called up by the draft could provide a substitute. Unfortunately, many substitutes were boys, old men, or persons with impaired health. Members of certain pacifist religious groups received conscientious objector status and paid fines in lieu of service. Among exempted categories, by occupation, were lawyers, clergymen, physicians, students, millers, sailors, ferrymen, wagoners, and certain skilled craftsmen, such as blacksmiths, ship carpenters, and arms workers.

Once in the army, enduring camp life, soldiers encountered the formidable challenge of staying reasonably healthy or even alive. Almost daily there were one or several deaths, not counting those terminally ill who had been whisked away to army hospitals.[37] One problem was that the army did not thoroughly sift out new enlistees with infirmities. This neglect contrasted with later United States military forces; for example, in the 1950s and early 1960s, half of all draftees were rejected from service because of physical defects.[38]

Strength reports of the main and northern Continental armies throughout the war listed one-tenth to one-fifth of the men as "sick," unfit for duty. The largest number of sick in Washington's army was reported just before marching for winter encampment at Valley Forge.[39] Smallpox took a frightening toll; it all but decimated the northern army in summer 1776. Even inoculation, which was eventually required of all the troops, resulted in deaths because of soldiers' being weakened by fatigue and poor diet. Besides smallpox, typhus, diphtheria, dysentery, and malaria also made their deadly rounds.[40] Less-than-fatal maladies invaded the camps, such as measles, mumps, and whooping cough. The "itch," caused by lack of cleanliness and sleeping on the ground, plagued soldiers throughout the war. General Johann De Kalb wrote, "I have seen the poor fellows covered over and over with scab." Soldiers treated this condition with hog's lard or pine tar and brimstone, which produced an awful stench.[41]

Besides living with disease, soldiers had to do without pay, food, and proper clothing. Months and even years passed by without soldiers being paid. Troops under General Gates in May 1779 had pay arrears of six months, and in 1781, Virginia Continentals had not received pay in two years.[42] The certificate for overdue pay issued to soldiers at the end of the war did not have enough value to support veterans until they could find work.[43] Other than an enlistment clothing bounty they received, soldiers were expected to provide their own clothing. Supplemental food and necessities purchased from camp sutlers or nearby farmers markets came out of soldiers' pay. Price inflation and currency depreciation decreased buying power. By May 1781, Continental currency was completely worthless. Because of lack of pay and food at Valley Forge, the adjutant general reported in February 1778 that "discontent runs through the army."[44]

Periodically, Continental troops were extremely short of rations. Colonel William Malcolm, arriving at the West Point garrison in July 1778, complained that no provisions were on hand except some barrels of flour. Also, in the highlands command in November 1781, General McDougall observed that "the Troops eagerly grasped at any thing to satisfy their craving hunger."[45] At Valley Forge in February 1778, Washington regretted "the present dreadful situation of the army for want of provisions."[46] Major Ebenezer Huntington in July 1780 lamented that the army was "Week after Week" without meat and clothing. "I despise my Countrymen," he declared. "I wish I could say I was not born in America. I once gloried in it but am now ashamed of it."[47]

The worst of times occurred at the Morristown encampment in the winter of 1779–80. The men were on half-allowance of bread for six weeks, and there were very few other provisions. Washington, going against army regulations, was forced to allow troops to scour the countryside for food with impunity. The calamity was owing to waist-deep snow that hindered transportation, a drought in the fall that had lowered the water level in streams so that grist mills could not operate, and farmers refusing to sell produce to the army because of depreciation of the currency.[48] Private Joseph Plumb Martin, one of the sufferers at Morristown, recorded that "We were absolutely, literally starved. I do solemnly declare that I did not put a single morsel of victuals into my mouth for four days and as many nights, except a little black birch bark which I gnawed off a stick of wood, if that can be called victuals."[49]

Deficient clothing, including blankets, shoes, and tents, caused great suffering and was a factor in the high incidence of sickness. Soldiers rarely received all the clothing promised them upon enlistment.[50] Garments came in only three sizes. Washington complained to the clothier general in July 1757 that "the Cloaths do not wear out fairly but tear to pieces."[51] A visitor to the main army in July 1781 commented that he was impressed "not by the smart appearance, but by its destitution: the men were without uniforms and covered with rags, most of them were barefoot."[52] "Cold and nakedness," declared a group of Virginia officers to the state legislature in 1781, "have swept off four fold more of your troops than all the malice of a cruel enemy has ever been able to destroy."[53]

It is hardly an exaggeration to depict the Continental soldiers as a barefoot army. The commander in chief, in October 1977, estimated that two-thirds of his troops were barefoot.[54] Even troops in the southern army endured the same deprivation. Sergeant Major William Seymour of the Delaware regiment, serving in the southern campaign, noted that troops of the Maryland line were "obliged to march and do duty barefoot."[55] As Washington's army headed toward Valley Forge in late December 1777, Private Joseph Plumb Martin provided some protection for his feet; he made a pair of moccasins from raw cowhide, which kept his feet from "the frozen ground," although the "hard edges so galled my ankles, while on a march, that it was with much difficulty and pain that I could wear them afterwards." But the only alternative to wearing the moccasins "was to go barefoot, as hundreds of my companions had to, till they might be tracked by their blood upon the rough frozen ground."[56]

What footwear was issued to the soldiers was often poorly made. Jacob Weiss, deputy quartermaster general, responded to a regimental commander that he had three hundred pairs of "Common Mens Shoes" on hand, but they were of "such miserable Truck that the Men will scarce draw them." The soles, Weiss pointed out, "are made of Green Leather, & such as are obliged to wear them, have their feet constantly wet"; the "Sewing of the Shoes are so very Wretched, that they Rip in the course of three or four Days wear."[57]

The physical torments were bad enough. The army, in the eyes of the public, also robbed soldiers of common decency. Congressman John Adams frequently interested himself in the quality of the Continental soldiery. He complained to General Nathanael Greene in May 1777 about "the Indifference of the People about recruiting the Army." This "Melancholy" did not stem merely from the "unhappy State of our Finances," military setbacks, or the prevalence of disease in the army.

> Dissipation, Debauchery, Gaming, Prophaneness and Blasphemy, terrifies the best People upon the Continent, from trusting their Sons and other Relations among so many dangerous snares and Temptations. Multitudes of People, who with chearfull Resignation Submit their Families to the Dangers of the sword, shudder at the Thought of exposing them to . . . the more destructive Effects of Vice and Impiety.[58]

Drunkenness, as viewed by one soldier, was the primary cause of "all mischief & disorderly Conduct" in the army.[59] Alcoholic beverages flowed freely for officers and enlisted men alike. The common soldier received a daily ration of either whiskey, rum, or cider. Spirits and liquor could also be purchased at sutlers' booths in camp or at tippling houses not far away. Despite tight licensing of sutlers, individual soldiers were able to purchase large quantities of intoxicants at a time.

> Thus left to himself the Soldier as soon as he received his pay flies to the Sutler and lais it out in grog [rum mixed with water], or rather pays for what he has already drank . . . tho he may not at the time have a Shirt to his Back, or a Shoe or Stocking to his feet. The Captain Inspects his necessaries, finds his Coat & Breeches hanging in Rags about him, his Shirt, Stocking & Shoes entirely gone . . . the Soldier has not a penny to pay for mending or [to] replace them.[60]

The "Irregular Manner" by which the army often delivered alcoholic beverages—providing a large quantity of drink to make up for an amount previously allocated—was also a major cause of inebriation.[61] For the Continental soldiers, excessive drinking not only eased a drab existence; it was also, as a Revolutionary War study notes, a "defensive weapon": soldiers "were only giving back what they had received—a broken promise," whereby they could "protest against niggardly levels of support by not being in an effective condition for service."[62]

Imbibing too much led to fights, assaults, and other disorderly behavior. Lieutenant James McMichael, with Washington's army in late 1776, commented that "our soldiers drank freely of spiritous liquors"; they had a "disorder which at camp is called the 'Barrel Fever,' which differs in its effects from any other fever—its concomitants are black eyes and bloody noses."[63]

On a December afternoon in 1778, in the camp of General McDougall's division at New Milford, Connecticut, Private Joseph Plumb Martin decided to visit a sutler's "tent." There, he spotted two Irishmen soldiers; one was huge and athletic, the other was not. The two Irishmen were longtime acquaintances and talked about old times. Then suddenly, one said to the other, "Faith, Jammy, will you take a box?" The other replied, "Aye, and thank ye, too." The combatants stripped off their clothes and went outside, where a large ring was formed by spectators. Both fighters lunged after each other twice and missed both times. "The little fellow, after getting upon his feet again, as well as he could, cried out, 'I am too drunk to fight.'" Both men went back into the sutler's tent, "as bloody butchers, to drink friends again, where no friendship had been lost."[64]

Soldiers managed to evade reprimand for boxing, wrestling, or other roughhousing as long as officers did not interfere. Just about all sports activity by enlisted men was discouraged, mainly for fear that gambling would be involved. The men habitually placed bets on almost anything. Expressly prohibited were card playing, billiards, and coin-tossing games. While officers played ball games, such as cricket, wicket, shinny, "base" ball, fives (handball), and "football," there is little indication that common soldiers did the same. Swimming by enlisted men was allowed only for short periods, in early morning or late afternoon, out of concern for safety and in the belief that sun and water were a harmful combination.[65] The army's restraint on soldier recreation forced the men to improvise amusements, often involving mischievous pranks. Had Washington fostered athletic sports for his men, camp morale, health, and military effectiveness undoubtedly would have improved.

"Profane Swearing is exceedingly prevalent in the American Army," so announced general orders at Middlebrook in May 1777.[66] The commander in chief frequently condemned this vice. Foul language was a mark of the soldier's calling, and new enlistees soon "learned to swear & damn by rule." An army physician disapprovingly observed:

> Our officers & soldiers in general, are remarkably expert in the swearing way. Nothing comes more handy, or gives such power and force to their words, as a Blasphemous oath. In general the Regiment is composed of Deists, Arminians, and a few who ridicule the Bible, and everything of a sacred nature. In short they Laugh at death, mock at Hell and damnation; & even challenge the Deity, to remove them out of this world by Thunder and Lightning.[67]

The admittance of women into the encampments bolstered morale. Wives and single women earned their keep by performing services, such as washing laundry, for which the soldiers paid. The army command tried to keep out prostitutes, not always with success. Venereal disease did occur. Eventually, the army set the policy of limiting the number of women in camp and insisting on good character. Almost nothing is known of the accommodations for women, but they probably had lodgings at the edge of camp. Washington only tolerated women accompanying the army because this was a means to diminish discontent. During marches, the commander in chief prohibited women from riding in the wagons. In contrast to the women camp followers, wives of senior officers visited camp between campaigns and were treated to comfort and respect. Officers, however, occasionally associated with women of ill repute, as was evident from many officers patronizing a whorehouse near the Newburgh camp at the end of the war and when General Adam Stephen was taken to task for getting too friendly with a "strumpet."

Washington had good reason to be apprehensive about the conduct of the women camp followers. Especially, he was concerned about women coming to camp to persuade their husbands to desert or acting as agents of the enemy to do the same, as sometimes happened. Women and children at camp were kept on short rations and were in constant need. It is not surprising to find that women accompanied soldiers' plundering parties and that the main booty was women's apparel. Women also were charged with illegal activities at camp, such as selling rum. Although it was rare, women sometimes, like other civilian employees at camp, faced severe punishment, and a few were whipped or even drummed out of the camp.[68]

A common soldier might look upon a comrade as here today, gone tomorrow. Despite the threat of the lash and execution, troops deserted in large numbers, singly and in groups. Desertions were most likely to occur during the first six months of service and from December 1 to April 30, the period of greater enlistments. The growth of unit cohesion over time among long-term enlistees led to a lower frequency of soldiers taking unwarranted leave.[69] Washington considered desertion "the most pernicious vice that can possibly prevail in an Army,"[70] and he persistently required the severest punishment for deserters who were apprehended. General Horatio Gates lamented in October 1780 that "desertion, the Hospital & the Grave must soon swallow up an Army thus sent into the field in November." For lack of "Tents, & Blankets the men desert or Die."[71]

The desertion rate for the entire army during the war stood at 20–25 percent.[72] Many factors contributed to desertion: hardship caused by hunger and insufficient clothing and pay; constant fatigue; fear of battle; homesickness; family distress; and the need to return home for planting or harvesting. Those who were willing to take greater risks engaged in bounty jumping (reenlisting in a different unit) or joining the ranks of the enemy.[73]

Although small groups of soldiers collectively balked at doing duty during the war, several times full-scale mutiny erupted. In mounting their protest, soldiers discovered strength in numbers. On January 1, 1781, those Pennsylvania troops stationed near Morristown, about one thousand men, rebelled. The soldiers demanded immediate payment of arrears in pay and allowance for depreciation; receipt of clothing that had been promised; discharge of men who had served for three years and had not enlisted for the duration; and conferral of the same benefits, such as bounties, that new enlistees were receiving.[74]

Efforts by officers initially to suppress the uprising of the Pennsylvania line resulted in the deaths of two captains and the wounding of several subalterns and privates. The military rebels started for Philadelphia, where they planned to lay down their arms and appeal to Congress and the Pennsylvania government. At Princeton and Trenton, however, negotiations between representatives from Congress and the Pennsylvania Council succeeded in ending the mutiny. Those soldiers who claimed completion of enlistment were discharged; back pay and certificates for depreciation were granted. No mutineers were bound over for trial.[75] This mutiny had a rippling effect. Four months later, some soldiers in a detachment of Pennsylvania troops at York, Pennsylvania, miffed at having been paid in worthless money and still not receiving all the remuneration promised in January, gathered in protest. General Anthony Wayne ordered his officers to fire on the would-be mutineers, killing six. Wayne had another soldier bayoneted to death by a comrade; five other protesters were hanged.[76]

From January 20 to 27, 1781, five hundred men of the New Jersey brigade at Pompton, near Morristown, mutinied. They had grievances similar to those of the Pennsylvanians. The New Jersey mutineers marched to Chatham, where they collected some other members of the brigade, and returned to Pompton. This time, the commander in chief wasted no time in suppressing the mutiny. General Robert Howe and five hundred troops from West Point and vicinity marched to Pompton, where they surprised the mutineers and secured an "unconditional submission." Two of the leaders of the uprising were summarily shot.[77]

A potentially dangerous crisis erupted as the army was disbanding at the end of the war. Troops of the Pennsylvania line in Philadelphia on June 13, 1783, presented an address to Congress, demanding back pay. The secretary at war persuaded the discontents to march to Lancaster. Meanwhile, three hundred Pennsylvania troops returning from the southern campaigns arrived in Philadelphia and were joined by eighty mutineers from Lancaster. The combined group on June 21 surrounded the Pennsylvania statehouse, where for three hours they stationed guards at the doors of the room where Congress was in session. The rebellious troops then took up post at the army barracks in the city. Congress quickly adjourned and fled to Princeton. Washington responded by ordering three infantry regiments and a detachment of artillery from the New York Highlands to Philadelphia, commanded by General Robert Howe. Before an armed confrontation could occur, the mutineers marched to Lancaster, where they accepted their discharges.[78]

Delinquency among soldiers, ranging from neglect of duty to desertion and mutiny, frequently stemmed from contempt of the officer corps. As the congressional committee investigating the mutiny of the Pennsylvania line in January 1781 stated, "Indeed there Seems to be an irreparable breach between the Men and their officers, and a Total want of Confidence."[79] The problem at the start of the war was an easy fraternization between the officers and the men. Most officers had received their commissions from having been elected to a position by their men or having raised a company or regiment on their own, and they were obligated to keep the troops contented. John Adlum, a seventeen-year-old private, in 1776 commented that the officers "were a weak and shabby set, trifling characters."[80] Artillery commander Henry Knox similarly observed in September 1776 that "the bulk of the officers of the army are a parcel of ignorant, stupid men who might make tolerable soldiers, but bad officers." General Nathanael Greene wished that "the officers were as good as the Men."[81]

Unlike many officers during the early period of the war, who indulged their troops for the sake of popularity, Major General Israel Putnam knew how to be humble in order to inspire his men. A black soldier, Jacob Francis, recalled that while he and his comrades were throwing up a breastwork on Lechmere Point during the siege of Boston, the general rode up to inspect the work.

> They had dug up a pretty large stone which lay on the side of a ditch. The general spoke to the corporal who was standing looking at the men at work and said to him, "My lad, throw that stone up the middle of the breastwork."
>
> The corporal, touching his hat with his hand, said to the general, "Sir, I am a corporal."

"Oh," said the general, "I ask your pardon, sir," and immediately got off his horse and took up the stone and threw it upon the breastwork himself and then mounted his horse and rode on, giving directions.[82]

As the Continental forces adapted to military professionalism, the distinction between officers and the rank and file became more strictly observed. The quality of the officer corps improved, although courts-martial regularly ordered punishment or dismissal of officers for such offenses as theft, embezzlement, insubordination, assaults against other officers, and cowardice. Charges against officers were sometimes leveled by other officers. Complaints by enlisted men against their superiors were generally glossed over. Officially, an enlisted man could file a complaint against his company commander (with the rank of captain), but there was risk involved. The case would be tried by a regimental court-martial, and either party could then appeal the verdict to a general court-martial. If, however, "upon a second hearing, the appeal shall appear to be vexatious and groundless, the person so appealing, shall be punished at the discretion of the general court-martial."[83]

In February 1777, Jonah Holida, a soldier in Colonel Anthony Wayne's Pennsylvania regiment, stirred up grievances among his comrades. Holida was arrested for mutiny. A Captain Coe protested this action, claiming he "was of Opinion that every Soldier had a Right to deliver his Sentiments on every Occasion without being punished." Wayne responded by having Coe charged as an "Abettor of Mutiny."[84] General John Sullivan, during his campaign against the Iroquois in 1779, promised to give a fair hearing to any criticism of an officer by an enlisted man. One soldier filed a complaint against the adjutant, but after the hearing, away from Sullivan's presence, officers brutally beat the complainant.[85] The orderly books contain many instances of soldiers being sentenced to flogging for insolence and disrespect toward officers. On the rare instances when officers gave vent to their temper and struck soldiers, they did so usually with impunity. Historian Charles Royster comments that "such loss of self-control reveals these officers' preoccupation with themselves," to the detriment of the service.[86]

The army, largely due to the prompting of General Friedrich Wilhelm Augustus von Steuben, began to require general and field officers to keep closer tabs on their men—to attend parade, inspect drill, and view soldiers's living conditions. Still, the common soldier often had scant opportunity to become fully acquainted with an officer's style of command, since the officer corps seemed to have a revolving door. Resignations of officers were a continuing problem. Financial distress—from receiving inadequate pay while being required to maintain a standard of living befitting an officer and support a family—took a toll. Officers were fortunate in being able to leave the army at any time; enlisted men could not. The common soldier resented the aristocratic living of their superiors. Officers had the better food, lodging, and clothes, could keep servants, had more freedom of movement in and out of camp, and had recreational activities denied the soldiers. Transgressions by common soldiers were judged not by their peers but by officers.

Continental army officers did not sway much toward compassion when confronted with the misconduct of enlisted men. Of course, the commander in chief and other senior officers freely issued pardons and canceled punishments, but the cruel punitive measures, often far out of proportion to the degree of the offense, belied much of a sense of concern for the lowly soldier. A veteran who recalled his service as a drummer remembered one particular day when there was a series of gruesome punishments: "We would be ready almost to faint, but it was fine fun for the officers lying in the shade."[87]

The criteria for commissioning officers of South Carolina's six Continental regiments required by the legislature were that the appointees be "gentlemen of fortune and family" and have a "stake in society."[88] The same expectations generally applied to officer selection throughout the army. Not only was there a significant class differentiation in the Continental army but also a situation somewhat analogous to masters and slaves—but this, after all, was the way of premodern military service. Although, unlike slaves, soldiers served for a limited period of time, there were similarities between them and slaves. Each owed unquestioned obedience to a master, and as Caroline Cox has noted, soldiers upon enlistment "accepted punishment levels in excess of civilian norms and a system of justice that codified inequality."[89] Enlisted men of the Revolutionary War endured great peril and deprivation. They themselves had little recourse for remedy. While officers craved honor and glory, the common soldiers settled for survival.

3

Military Justice

The decision of Congress to take charge of the New England forces resisting the British military invasion seemed the logical step for American patriots. Now, resources and personnel from all the colonies could be mobilized and employed under the direction of a single command system. A large-scale federalized military establishment was viewed as a temporary expedient, one that could be reduced or even disassembled during peacetime. The grim reality, however, was that a wartime standing army required its own legal system to attend to the governance and discipline of members of the federalized armed forces. Soldiers forfeited civil liberties, and every action of an individual in military service was subject to close scrutiny.

While a well-led and disciplined army would bring victory, securing independence and liberty, it could also pose the danger of becoming so powerful as to usurp civilian authority. This was a fear shared by many patriot leaders, who yet were the very ones who supported a federal army. Congressman Samuel Adams wrote in January 1776 that a standing army "is always dangerous to the Liberties of the People. Soldiers are apt to consider themselves as a Body distinct from the rest of the Citizens." Troops under "severe" discipline become "disposed to yield implicit Obedience" to the commands of officers. "Such a power should be watched with a jealous eye."[1]

It was decided that, like civil society, the armed forces should establish a basic code that would provide guidelines for dispensing justice. An irony was that the code of rules for the Revolutionary army contained a lengthy categorization of liabilities and punishments to be incurred from misbehavior of officers and soldiers, with very slight attention given to creating a fair legal process. It was also an irony that the military code of an army fighting for American liberty was grounded in the denying of liberty in military society.

It was fitting for an emerging republic to have its military code created by congressional legislation. Historically, in Great Britain, articles of war were issued by the Crown. Parliament, however in the Mutiny Act of 1689, reserved for itself authority to establish military law during peacetime; the Crown continued to declare military rules and regulations during wartime. By a law of 1712, the Crown was given authority to extend its military code to troops abroad. Six years later, Parliament conferred on the British sovereign the responsibility of declaring articles of war for troops at home and abroad and during times of war and peace. A plenary power for establishing articles of war, however, was assumed by Parliament in 1803. The British rules and regulations for war were derived substantially from Roman practice.[2]

There is a continuum in the use of articles of war by the late colonial and American Revolutionary forces. As already noted, the American provincial regiments of the French and Indian War served under the British Articles of War. The military codes governing New England militia at the start of the Revolution were copied directly, with only minimal alteration, from the British Articles of War of 1765, and in turn, the code established by Congress for American forces during the war was mainly borrowed from the military law proclaimed by the New England states. On April 5, 1775, Massachusetts led the way in establishing a military code, followed by Connecticut and Rhode Island in May and New Hampshire in June.[3]

The fifty-three articles of the "Rules and Regulations for the Massachusetts Army" differed from its British counterpart in the severity of punishment; there were fewer death penalties, and flogging was limited to thirty-nine lashes. It was anticipated that the American troops about Boston were patriotically devoted to duty and delinquency would not be a serious problem. A death penalty under the Massachusetts code existed only for abandonment of a post under one's command, or inciting others to do so, and for revealing "the watchword to any person not entitled to receive it." For all other "crimes not capital" and "all disorders and neglects . . . not mentioned in the Articles of War," punishment was to be at the discretion of general or regimental courts-martial.[4]

Other states followed suit in duplicating the military codes of New England (and Congress). An ordinance of the Virginia Convention in July 1775 provided for a code whose only major difference was the manner of selecting members of a general court-martial. Whereas the appointment of thirteen commissioned officers to the court by the convening authority was sufficient in the other codes, the Virginia military law had the novel scheme of the commanding officer nominating twenty-four officers, from whom the offender might choose fifteen to sit on the court. A death sentence had to be argued by twelve of the fifteen members.[5] George Mason, writing to George Washington, said that the Virginia ordinance "establishing Articles of Government for the Troops" resembled the congressional Articles of War, passed shortly before the Virginia enactment, except that a court-martial "upon Life & Death is more cautiously constituted & brought nearer to the Principles of the common law."[6]

The seventy-four articles of the "Rules and Regulations of the Military Association of Pennsylvania" of April 1776 was almost entirely a copy of the Massachusetts and congressional Articles of War. One exception was the addition of a death penalty for treason. "All persons convicted of holding a treacherous correspondence with, or giving intelligence to the enemy, shall suffer death, or such other punishment as a General Court Martial shall think proper."[7] Significantly, spying by civilians came under military justice.

On June 14, 1775, the same day that it voted to raise six rifle companies from Virginia, Maryland, and Pennsylvania to join New England troops in the siege of Boston, Congress appointed a five-man committee to draft a code of military justice for the new Continental army. Comprising the committee were George Washington, Philip Schuyler, Silas Deane, Thomas Cushing, and Joseph Hewes. Washington attended only one meeting, on June 15, the day he was named commander in chief.[8]

Congress enacted the Articles of War on June 30, 1775. Most of the sixty-nine provisions repeated verbatim the Massachusetts military code of April 1775. As in the Massachusetts code, soldiers were expected to attend "divine Service" and refrain from profanity, upon penalty of a fine. No offenses involving internal army discipline were capital crimes. Only abandonment of a post and unauthorized giving away of the password merited the death penalty. Interestingly, desertion, mutiny, sedition, and treasonable activities were cited as noncapital offenses, the punishment of which was left to the discretion of courts-martial. The commander in chief could pardon culprits sentenced by a court-martial; regimental commanders could do the same for persons convicted under a regimental court-martial. Pretrial confinement was limited to eight days, or until a court-martial could be convened. Additional articles of war adopted by Congress not included in the

Massachusetts code treated such areas as furloughs, musters, and sutlers. Article 51, more explicit as to punishment than the Massachusetts code, stated "That no person shall be sentenced by a court martial to suffer death, except in the cases expressly mentioned in the foregoing articles; nor shall any punishment be inflicted at the discretion of a court-martial, other than degrading, cashiering, drumming out of the army, whipping not exceeding *thirty-nine* lashes, fine not exceeding two months pay of the offender, imprisonment not exceeding one month."[9]

Congressman Roger Sherman commented that the Articles of War did not differ much from the New England codes, "except the addition of a few, and a more particular limitation of the discretionary powers given Courts Martial."[10] The thirty-nine lashes represented the maximum sanctioned in the Bible. Richard Henry Lee wrote Washington that the Articles of War were the same as those of Massachusetts, "with very few alterations."[11]

Washington was disappointed that certain penalties had not been made more severe. Especially, he was distressed that the army's chief surgeon, Dr. Benjamin Church, discovered to be a spy for the British army, was punished only by brief imprisonment, after which he was allowed to go into exile. The commander in chief wrote Congress that Article 28, concerning any member of the army who corresponded with or gave intelligence to the enemy, should be amended.[12] A congressional committee met with Washington October 21–22, 1775, to consider revisions of the Articles of War. Following the recommendations of this conference, Congress enacted sixteen amendments on November 7. Added to the capital offenses were desertion, mutiny, sedition, corresponding with or giving intelligence to the enemy, and sleeping on guard duty.[13]

Some troops refused to "subscribe" to the Continental military code, as required by Article 1. "Their principal Objection," noted Washington, was "that it might subject them to a longer Service, than that for which they engaged, with their several provincial Establishments." Article 1 had recognized this possibility and therefore also declared that those who refused to sign the articles should either be allowed to stay in service under their state codes of military justice or be dismissed from the army, at "the Option of the Commander in chief." With the Continental army in dire straits for the remainder of 1775, Washington could hardly insist that soldiers sign the Continental Articles of War. He viewed the situation as not much of a problem, since enlistments would expire at the end of the year, and in the new army (fresh recruits and reenlistees), there would be, in effect, new contracts. Entering the new army, beginning in 1777, enlistees would pledge longer terms of service or for the duration of the war. General Philip Schuyler, commanding the northern department of the army, had the same problem as Washington, and he, too, backed away from having his men sign the articles. The draconian amendments to the Articles of War of November 1775 took effect on January 3, 1776, during the time of mustering in a new army.[14]

The harsher penalties of the amended code did little to restrain soldier misconduct. Desertion and plundering of civilian property became widespread. Executing all of the many capital offenders was not an option. The only maximum alternative was whipping, which had to be limited to thirty-nine lashes. Whipping certainly did not equal execution, and there was no middle ground between them.

Colonel Joseph Reed, the adjutant general of the army in July 1776, called to the attention of Congress that the "military system of government" was "extremely defective." The "mildness of punishment" for "crimes the most destructive to the Army, such as desertion, burglary, drink, of sleeping on guard . . . mutiny and sedition," had "made such crimes known to others [rather] than serve as examples." The American soldiers, declared Reed, equaled or even exceeded "the King's troops in all kinds of disorder and irregularity." To Reed, "alterations" were needed in the Articles of War, especially increasing the maximum of lashes in a flogging beyond thirty-nine.[15] Washington had the same view as Reed. In writing to Congress, the commander in chief said that for "the most atrocious offences" a soldier "receives no more than 39 Lashes," and these "are given in such a manner as to become rather a matter of sport than punishment."[16]

William Tudor, the judge advocate general, noted that "the infamous Desertions, the Shameless Ravages, and seditious Speeches and mutinous Behaviour which prevail" throughout the army "call in the loudest Language for a Reform. With the present Articles, the military Government, without making Soldiers, is breeding Highwaymen and Robbers."[17] Tudor believed that "an absolute Tyranny" was "essential in the Government of an Army, and that every Man who carries Arms, from the General Officer to the private Centinel, must be content to be a temporary Slave. " Only "the severest Punishments" would curtail "Practices which must ruin Us." Penalties must be stiffened because, while "Our Men are at present only Robbers," it was evident "that they will soon be Murderers, unless some are hang'd." As did Washington, Tudor favored increasing the number of lashes as punishment.[18]

On June 14, 1776, Congress decided to issue new Articles of War. The task of making changes was assigned to the Committee on Spies, whose members were John Adams, Thomas Jefferson, James Wilson, and Edward Rutledge. A draft, chiefly the work of Adams and Jefferson, was ready August 7. Debates over the document on August 19 and September 19 and 20 elicited much opposition for fear that a more stringent code might pave the way for military dictatorship. Adams argued vigorously in defense of the new document, while Jefferson remained silent during the debates. Adams boasted that he alone was most responsible for the passage of the new Articles of War. The new code, even more than the previous one, was copied from the British Articles of War; the main exceptions were deletion of some portions relating to troops abroad and the substitution of Congress for the Crown. Adams argued that the British code was derived from that of the Roman army, and therefore the Americans were borrowing from the best of military traditions.[19] It may seem odd that two champions of American liberty, Adams and Jefferson, readily supported a military system that denied basic civil liberties to soldiers and also represented an extension of the scope and severity of the military code. Military necessity trumped liberty; the former would only be temporary, the latter, enduring.

The new Articles of War passed Congress on September 20, 1776. The document contained eighteen sections, which embraced one hundred and two articles. Thirty-three new provisions were added to the old code of 1775.[20] Section 18, article 3, raised the maximum number of lashes from thirty-nine to one hundred. New capital offenses (bringing the total to sixteen) included throwing away arms or ammunition; striking a superior officer; discharging firearms or otherwise causing "false alarms in camp"; assaulting any person bringing in provisions "or other necessaries" into camp; giving "money, victuals or ammunition" to the enemy; harboring or protecting an enemy; and plundering. So faithfully was the British military code followed that one item was transferred to the American military law that appeared to have little relevance to the Continental army at the time: "Whosoever, belonging to the forces of the United States, employed in foreign parts, shall force a safe-guard, shall suffer death" (Section 13, Article 17). On this point, the codifiers may have had in mind Spanish America and the far-flung frontier.

Recommendations of a congressional committee, consisting of Samuel Adams, William Duer, and Richard Henry Lee, for amending the Articles of War passed on April 14, 1777, but no substantial change occurred. After the war, in 1786, a few were enacted.[21] The Articles of War of 1806 afforded limited protection of several procedural rights in courts-martial that existed in civilian courts. Even then, General James Wilkinson said of the 1806 code that "at best it is but a servile copy of the British articles of war."[22]

The Articles of War during the Revolution prescribed an oath of allegiance pledging obedience to the orders of Congress and superior officers. The oath (or affirmation) was to be taken before a civilian justice or magistrate within six days of enlistment; persons were inducted into a specific regiment. Some disreputable officers allowed recruits known to be bounty jumpers to enlist in their regiments despite their having taken an oath previously in joining another regiment.

One soldier, Paul Garrison, in January 1779, made it his defense against a charge of desertion that he had been permitted to reenlist in a regiment other than the one he belonged to. At the time Garrison deserted from the Third South Carolina Regiment, he met Captain George Jervey of the Fifth South Carolina Regiment, "who took me to a Tavern, and having treated me insisted that I should inlist with him." When it came time to take the oath, Garrison objected, saying that he was a soldier in the Third Regiment. Jervey then declared, "'we'll pass over that Part of the Oath,'" which was accordingly done. Garrison was "taken out by the third regiment" and "severely flogged" for desertion. While on duty again in the Third Regiment, he was arrested as a deserter from the Fifth Regiment and was sentenced to fifty lashes with switches; because of Captain Jervey's irregularity of enlisting Garrison, the sentence was remitted.[23]

For the better discipline of the army, it made sense that the troops have knowledge of the system of military justice. General orders of June 30, 1775, required that the Articles of War be read by a captain or someone he appointed in his stead to his company once a week.[24] The 1776 code stated that the Articles of War should be "read and published once every two months, at the head of every regiment, troop or company."[25] Many commanding officers neglected this requirement, and when the Articles of War, being a lengthy document, was read, the common soldiers had difficulty in comprehending and remembering all the provisions. Washington complained that the Articles of War "are read by some, only heard by others, and inaccurately attended by all, whilst by a few, they are totally disregarded."[26] Were he around today, Washington might be astonished at the degree of this neglect in the armed forces.

That soldiers were not being informed of the Articles of War or, for that matter, general orders raised a serious question: without such knowledge, to what extent was a soldier culpable for violation of the rules and regulations? A court-martial in the South Carolina line in January 1779 concluded that ignorance of military law provided no defense against a charge of misbehavior. William Fickling was prosecuted for desertion from Captain Thomas Shubrick's company in the South Carolina Fifth Regiment. At the court-martial on January 13, 1779, Shubrick testified that Fickling had enlisted in his company for three years and had been paid bounty money. Shubrick was then questioned by the court:

Q. Did you read the Articles of War to the Prisoner at the Time of his Inlistment, or at any Time after?

A. I never did, to my recollection but imagine that he had heard them read, as he belonged to the second Regiment, before he inlisted in ours.

Q. Did he at any time and when desert from your Company?

A. He deserted about the thirtieth of June last, since which time I never saw him till last Week, when he was in Camp with the sixth Regiment.

Q. What Character did the Prisoner bear?

A. He staid so short a time with the Regiment that I cannot tell.

Q. Was he sober at the Time of your paying him part of the Bounty Money?

A. He was.

Next, Lieutenant Richard Pollard of the Sixth Regiment testified that Fickling had enlisted in his unit on December 1, 1778, and apparently received $30 in bounty money for serving in place of one Wilson, a substitute who since had been discharged.

Q. Did he hear the Articles of War read?

A. He staid so short a time in the Regiment that he did not. Fickling deserted in less than three weeks. He subsequently was arrested as a deserter from the Fifth Regiment, which he denied he belonged to "in particular."

Lieutenant Isaac Weatherly of the First Regiment was then sworn in as a witness.

> Q. Do you know the Prisoner?
> A. I do. He was tried as a Deserter from the second Regiment about the Month of September 1777 at a Genl Court Martial when the Article of War against Desertion was read to him. I was a Member of that Court.

Finally the court heard from the prisoner:

> I am sorry for what I have done, and beg the Mercy of the Court. Only spare my Life now, and I declare I will always behave well, and will never drink too much Liquor in future. I beg that John Priest a Private in the same Regiment with myself may be examined to prove that I always behaved well while I was in the Regiment.

Priest and a sergeant both attested to Fickling's good behavior. The court, however, was unmoved by any extenuating circumstance or the defendant's plea and sentenced Fickling to be shot.[27]

The Articles of War for the Continental army offered scant redress for complaints against military command decisions. General Nathanael Greene rebuked a group of Pennsylvania officers who questioned a command. The officers protested Greene's reversing himself over the appointment of an officer to lead a detachment. Greene reminded the officers that "the constitution of our army and that of the civil government are uppon different principals," and "therefore to argue from analogy of the rights of men under those different governments, is confounding things that have no relation." He told the detractors to consider themselves "as officers of the Continental Army, bound by its laws and governed by military maxims."[28]

The military codes of the Revolution were meant as guidelines that had to be adhered to but had the flexibility whereby the commander in chief, other commanding officers, and courts-martial had discretion in providing implementation and further definition. Washington's commission as commander in chief, conferred by Congress, stated "you are hereby vested with full power and authority to act as you shall think for the good and Welfare of the service." Instructions to Washington three days later mentioned that since "all particulars cannot be foreseen" in the course of his military command, he should depend on his "prudent and discreet management, as occurrences may arise."[29] The commander in chief's general orders, usually issued daily, had the force of military law.

General orders and the supplementary division, brigade, regimental, and garrison orders, as Holly A. Mayer points out, were of two kinds: standing and situational. As to the former, for example, Washington issued severe prescriptions against plundering, even to the extent of permitting summary punishment and a greater number of lashes than allowed by the Articles of War. Situational orders were usually "job specific," such as regulations for a march or governing the activities of sutlers and other camp followers, wagoners, and civilians having dealings with the army. There was also the custom of war, such as army protocol and traditional army punishment (not mentioned in the Articles of War). "The custom of war," writes a nineteenth-century military authority, "is the *lex non scripta*, or common law of the army, and by the 69th article of war [code of 1806] is recognized as a guide in administering military justice." By the custom of war, company officers could order nonjudicial punishment for minor digressions from performance of duty.[30]

Like the British, the American army during the Revolutionary War period held trials in two kinds of tribunals: general court-martial, and regimental (or garrison) court-martial. A court-martial "is a lawful tribunal, existing by the same authority that any other court exists by, and the law military is a branch of law as valid as any other, and it differs from the general law of the land in authority only in this, that it applies to officers and soldiers of the army, but not to other members of the body politic, and that it is limited to breaches of military duty."[31]

General courts-martial handled the most serious crimes, such as desertion, and could inflict capital punishment, which regimental courts-martial could not do. Sometimes, it was a matter of choice which panel to use, as regimental courts-martial could order severe corporal punishment. All verdicts of a general court-martial had to be reviewed by the commander in chief, the general commanding a department, or Congress, any one of whom could order a pardon or a reduction of sentence, but never its increase; a commander of a regiment had the same authority regarding regimental courts-martial. Any of the generals who convened courts-martial could order suspension of a death sentence "until the pleasure of Congress can be known." Otherwise, there was no military appellate jurisdiction.[32] Washington frequently dispensed pardons, acting upon recommendations submitted on behalf of convicted persons. Six times, usually in conjunction with important events, such as the celebration of the Franco-American Alliance, the commander in chief issued general pardons for prisoners under sentence of death.[33]

General courts-martial consisted of thirteen general or field grade officers. Regimental courts-martial had five members, with a captain as president and the others usually of subaltern rank; on rare occasions, three members were sufficient to constitute a regimental court-martial. Decisions were made by majority vote. A death sentence from a general court-martial required the consent of two-thirds of the members. Enlisted men were at a disadvantage, being tried not by their peers but by officers. The situation was somewhat the reverse for courts-martial trials of generals. With so few generals, a trial of a general officer involved a panel of mostly field grade officers, not an enviable situation given the jealousies and politics among the officer corps, whose members were always ambitious for promotion. Examples of subordinate officers trying superiors were the courts-martial of Major Generals Alexander McDougall and Adam Stephen. Comprising the panel for McDougall were a major general, two brigadier generals, five colonels, two lieutenant colonel commandants, one lieutenant colonel, and two majors; and for Stephen, one major general, four brigadier generals, five colonels, and three lieutenant colonels. Stephen, one of the oldest generals in the army, blamed his dismissal from service on politics (Lafayette replaced him) and on being tried by officers who were much younger than him and inferior in rank.[34]

Courts-martial were more like hearings than trials. The accused was brought before what amounted to an executive board, selected by a convening authority. Members of courts-martial were both judges and jury. Due process protections were almost nil. The absence of juries, however, did not bother the judge advocate general, William Tudor, who observed that "the idea of a jury is kept up" by having thirteen members of a general court-martial, one person more than a jury.[35]

General and regimental courts-martial met almost daily. An enlisted man was indeed fortunate if he was never hauled before a military tribunal as a defendant or as a witness. An example of the scope of military justice is evident from an eleven-month span when 250 of the 316 men of the South Carolina Second Regiment were court-martialed.[36] Several cases were heard by a court-martial in a single day's session, which had to be scheduled

between the hours of 8:00 A.M. and 3:00 P.M. The lower the rank of the accused, the less attention was paid by the court. Enlisted men received short
shrift, whereas extensive proceedings were conducted for upper-ranked
officers. The trial of General Charles Lee was the longest. Prolonged because of detailed examination of many witnesses and the movement of the
army, Lee's court-martial, July 4–August 12, 1778, went through twenty-six
sessions, held successively at New Brunswick and Paramus, New Jersey, and
at Peekskill, North Castle, and White Plains, New York.[37]

The Articles of War stated that "The judge advocate general, or some
person deputed by him, shall prosecute in the name of the United States
of America."[38] Congress first appointed William Tudor, a Massachusetts
lawyer, as "Judge Advocate of the Continental Army" on July 20, 1775, and
accorded him the rank of lieutenant colonel on August 10, 1776; his successors were Lieutenant John Laurance, April 10, 1777, to June 3, 1782; Lieutenant Colonel James Innis, July 9, 1782, to September 18, 1782; and First
Lieutenant Thomas Edwards, October 20, 1782, to November 3, 1783. In
the interim between appointments, a deputy served as acting judge advocate general.[39]

The duties of judge advocate general overwhelmed Tudor during his first
year in office. He found it physically impossible to attend every general
court-martial "throughout the army," spread out for ten miles during the
siege of Boston. "Almost every Day," Tudor wrote, "a general court martial
has sit in one or other Part of the Camp." A court-martial "is no sooner
dissolved than another is ordered to sit." From July 14 to mid-August 1775,
Tudor attended twenty-seven courts-martial.[40]

Since courts-martial met in the morning and early afternoon, Tudor had
little remaining time to prepare for trials and to write reports to be submitted to the commander in chief the next day. Because of the stress, eventually a deputy judge advocate general was appointed. Lieutenant (later
Captain) John Marshall, the future chief justice, served in this capacity
intermittently from November 1777 to September 1779.[41] Also, the practice began in late 1776 of the president of each court-martial appointing
"Some proper person to act as Judge Advocate."[42]

The judge advocate general's role was more as a court administrator than
as a prosecutor seeking a guilty verdict. Although the right to counsel was
not allowed to military prisoners, a judge advocate general was expected to
present both sides of a case fairly. Later, the 1806 code stipulated that any one

serving in the capacity of a judge advocate should "consider himself as counsel for the defendant."[43] The judge advocate general arranged for the meeting of courts-martial, notified witnesses to attend, and gave orders to adjutants of regiments for bringing up prisoners. Furthermore, as Tudor noted, "In every Case where the Evidence is complicated, it is expected of me that I analyze the Evidence and state the Questions which are involved in it."[44]

Generals Lafayette and Knox were two critics of the court-martial system in the American army. Lafayette wrote Washington in January 1778 that "I am adverse to court martials." He thought they were "a very bad" English custom. In the French army, officers could punish most offenses by soldiers immediately without trial; courts-martial were held only for the most serious infractions by soldiers and officers. A primary difference between the French and American practices was that in the former a trial convened promptly. As to the American army, Lafayette asked, "How will you let an unhappy soldier be confined several weeks, with men who are to be hanged, with spies, with the most horrid sort of people, and in the same time be lost for the duty, when they deserve only some lashes?" Lafayette also criticized the overuse of courts-martial. Even if acquitted, an officer's reputation was damaged. It was better in less serious cases to reprimand an officer privately. As a case in point, Lafayette commented on the court-martial of General William Maxwell for drinking too much; Maxwell's acquittal did not dispel the view he was a drunkard.[45]

At war's end, Washington turned his thoughts toward a peacetime military establishment. He advised Congress to create a uniform military code that would cover both a standing army and state militia and would "introduce new and beneficial regulations," while expunging all "customs" that have been "unproductive of the general good."[46] In February 1783, the commander in chief set up a board of general officers to consider reforms in military law that would protect the innocent in courts-martial and also determine what "ought to be the business of a Judge Advocate, precisely delineating his duties as well with relation to the Court as with respect to the Accuser and accused."[47]

As a member of the board of general officers, General Henry Knox had specific suggestions, including the following:

> Challenges, or objections, to members of a court, without any given reason, to be admitted. . . .

General charges not to be admitted. They ought to be distinct and particular. . . .

Evidences to be allowed to put their own testimony in writing, subject to cross examination. . . .

No written testimony taken out of court, under any circumstances, to be admitted against a person in a trial of life and death. . . .

Suggestive interrogations ought not to be admitted, that is, questions which lead immediately to the fact, and which suggest an immediate answer. . . .

Courts martial should suffer nothing to be urged on the part of the prosecution or defence, but what should be pertinent to the charge. . . .

No quotations from law-authorities to be admitted in a court martial, as they would tend to involve the proceedings in endless perplexities and errors. The judge advocate must be under the immediate orders of the court. He ought impartially to bring the whole truth before the court, whether it should support the prosecution or acquit the accused. He should assist the prisoner in his defense, and in every instance govern himself by the principles of equal justice. The judge advocate is said to be the prosecutor in behalf of the United States. But if his business ends with the prosecution, the institution is unequal and unjust. An office employed on one side only, without any counterbalance, is too absurd to be tolerated.[48]

Congress made no immediate changes in the Articles of War. The May 1786 amendments, however, introduced revisions pertaining to the "Administration of Justice." The two most important provisions concerned the size of courts-martial and the holding of courts of inquiry. Although thirteen members remained the preferred number (mandated by the earlier Articles of War) for a general court-martial, now as few as five could constitute one so as not to draw officers away from important duty. For the first time, there was recognition of military courts of inquiry. During the war, courts of inquiry (each consisting of five members) were held upon demand by high-ranking officers facing accusations. The court of inquiry (derived from English military practice) functioned much like a civilian examining court or grand jury, deciding whether or not to certify charges to be tried in a court. By the Articles of War of 1786, only "one or more Officers, not exceeding three, with the Judge Advocate, or a suitable person, as a recorder," sat on a court of inquiry. Significantly, enlisted men as well as officers could seek a court of inquiry. As a precaution, the articles of 1786 state, "As Courts of Inquiry may be perverted to dishonourable purposes, and may be considered as engines of destruction to military merit, in the hands of weak and envious Commandants, they are hereby prohibited, unless demanded by the accused."[49]

Despite revisionary enactments of 1806, 1874, 1916, and 1948, the Articles of War governing the Continental army served as the core of the nation's military code until Congress established the Uniform Code of Military Justice in 1950 (becoming effective May 31, 1951).[50] This thorough revamping of the military code underwent important modification by the Military Justice Act of October 1968 (effective August 1969). These code changes and other legislation have finally removed the harsh discriminatory features and inequality that enlisted men labored under in the military justice system. One milestone along the way was a congressional enactment of August 5, 1861, that abolished flogging.[51]

Although still grounded upon congressional rather than constitutional authority, today's military justice system accords members of the armed forces most of the procedural due process guaranteed by the Bill of Rights. The notable exception is trial by jury; this shortcoming, however, has been mitigated by allowing courts-martial trials of enlisted men, upon request of the accused, to draw at least one-third of its members from the enlisted ranks (under the Articles of War, Elston Act, 1948). A military judge sits on every court.[52] There are several levels for review of court-martial verdicts, with final appellate jurisdiction belonging to the Court of Appeals for the Armed Forces.[53]

While significant gains over the years have been made to establish greater fairness in military justice, the suffering soldier of the Revolutionary army could expect scant consideration if hauled before a court-martial. The very fact he was in this situation was taken to indicate his probable guilt. In proceedings similar to the later slave trials in the South, the common soldier, with almost no guarantee of due process, answered to his superiors, whereas officers at least were tried by peers. With the multitude of cases that came before a military panel and with the army often on maneuvers, military justice for the enlisted man was disposed of swiftly. It was believed to be more important to set examples in order to maximize deterrence than to ensure a fair judicial process. Lafayette lamented, "I am sorry in seeing the less guilty being the *only one punished*."[54]

4

The Supervisors

A well-disciplined army required more than punishment of delinquents and slackers. Constant oversight was needed to maintain order and promote combat readiness. Duty officers, known as officers of the day, had as primary responsibilities during their twenty-four-hour tours of duty "handling all internal security problems" and "overseeing the performance of the interior guard."[1] Certain staff officers—adjutants, brigade majors, and inspectors—in addition to serving as channels in the flow of information and orders, had oversight in the enforcement of standards of behavior and training.

The employment of duty officers relieved the commander in chief, generals of separate armies, and unit commanders from constantly attending to many routine details of command. In effect, officers of the day acted in the stead of their commanding officers. Normally, in the assembled army, duty officers consisted of a major general and brigadier general as general officers of the day; a colonel, lieutenant colonel, and major as field officers of the day; and staff officers dovetailing their regular assignments, namely, as adjutants, brigade majors, inspectors, and quartermasters.[2]

"I am the officer of the day every fourth day," complained Major General Johann De Kalb. "Twenty-four such hours afford employment sufficient for two men," and "even in my brief leisure hours I hardly have a moment to myself, being then obliged to look after my division, and to attend the various consultations and councils of war."[3] All general and field officers had the same problem. The frequent tours as officer of the day, the incessant courts-martial, and other auxiliary obligations greatly cut into the time available for officers to exercise their command responsibilities.

General orders spelled out the duties of officers of the day. The major general of the day

> is, in some sort to represent the Commander-in-Chief—He is to give directions for all guards, parties and detachments—to receive reports of the proceedings, and of every occurrence of any importance, both in and out of camp. All deserters and prisoners, other than for common military offences, to be brought to him for examination, and disposed of by him—All detachments, or reinforcements arriving, to be reported to him immediately, on their arrival, and to take his orders—He is to superintend the regulation of the camp, and the execution of General orders; for which purpose he should visit the whole line, if not absolutely prevented by other duties; and he is to report, to the Commander in chief, what, from his observations, he may think necessary to be done, for the better regulation of the camp and army. . . . He is to make a general report next morning, to the Commander in chief, of every thing that passes worth notice on his day. Occurrences of emergency, and that require immediate attention to be reported the moment they are known by the Major General.[4]

All reports from guards and scouting parties went to the major general of the day, who also assigned duties to field officers of the day.[5] Anyone who was not a member of the army and all "suspected persons" who sought entry into an encampment were to be brought before the major general of the day "to be examined and dealt with, as he shall see fit."[6]

The brigadier general of the day

> is to be considered as the commanding officer of all the guards—He is to receive his orders in the morning from the Major General. He is to attend the Grand parade, to see every thing conducted with propriety—to assign the posts and give all necessary directions—to visit them after they arrive, & see that they have taken post right; have followed the rules prescribed them; taken proper precautions to secure themselves and avoid surprize; and to give his orders accordingly—On an alarm he is to perform all the essential duties of commanding officer of the guards—He is to make a general report of every thing relating to them, to the Major General.[7]

In attending the grand parade at guard mounting, usually held at 8:00 or 10:00 A.M., the brigadier general of the day had to see that guard details were "regularly made up" and "properly posted," appoint the schedule for field officers of the day to make their rounds in visiting guard posts, and make sure that while the troops were on the parade field they were properly exercised in "maneuvers and Evolutions [changes in disposition of troops, especially in close order drill]," according to the "Regulations for the discipline of the Army."[8] General orders of January 31, 1780, stipulated that the brigadier general of the day, along with a field officer of the day, "will as usual superintend the police of the camp and the service of the guards."[9] The brigadier general of the day could be held accountable for holding prisoners. Major General Alexander McDougall, commander of American troops in the New York highlands, ordered that the brigadier general of the day should "examine into the State, Condition and manner of treating the Prisoners in Provost, and obtain a Return of them"; those prisoners who were "triable by Regimental Courts Martial" were to be sent to the quarter guards of their respective regiments, "specifying their Crimes and the names of Witnesses."[10]

The field officers of the day were to

> attend the Grand parade, and assist the Brigadier; and follow such directions, as he shall think proper to give, respecting the guards— They are to visit them at night, by way of *grand rounds*, escorted by a small party of horse—to see if they are alert and upon the watch, and if the sentries are well stationed and instructed, and do their duty— They are to receive an evening report from the officers, of the state of their guards, and of what unusual occurrences may have happened, and to give directions accordingly. Every thing extraordinary to be reported to the Brigadier, as soon as their tour is over, or sooner, if necessary—They are to receive morning reports from the several guards, when relieved, and digest them in a general one for the Brigadier.[11]

The brigadier general of the day assigned separate rounds to the field officers of the day so that there was "a constant Succession of visiting Officers."[12] A field officer of the day, in making his rounds, was assisted by a party consisting of a sergeant and not more than six men.[13] Other duties of the field officer of the day included sending out scouts and patrols,[14] keeping an eye on camp sutlers (with authority to confiscate wares belonging to unlicensed sutlers),[15] and punishing immediately any soldier causing "wanton and unnecessary destruction" of civilian property "in the vicinity of the camp."[16]

Field officers of the day provided the essential service of constant surveillance of measures relating to camp security. This military practice allowed regular line officers periodic assignments to attend to broad responsibilities at the brigade level rather than to problems of immediate command. Because, in the process, field officers of the day and officers in the regular chain of command were one and the same, the double duty widened experience.

For officers below field rank, there were also important duty assignments. Late in the war, a captain of the day was appointed for each division, whose chief duty was "to visit the camp guard of the division to which he belongs"; reports of his findings were to be sent to an officer of the day, with the material "to be digested in the General report to the Commander in Chief." Obviously, the duties of the field officer of the day overlapped with those of the captain of the day. One way to distinguish the two was to have a field officer of the day visit camp guards in the daytime and the captain of the day to make his rounds at nighttime.[17] A regimental officer of the day, usually a lieutenant, kept tabs on all the men in camp; he reported those absent from the rolls and could confine those soldiers returning to camp after being away without leave.[18] Also on the regimental level, a captain or subaltern was appointed on a daily and rotating basis to superintend camp police (see chapter 11).

Certain staff personnel took turns as duty officers. The brigade major of the day performed much in the same capacity as in his normal routine. According to orders, the brigade major of the day

> is also to attend the parade—to receive the detachments that are to compose the guards, and compare them with the detail—to inspect their arms, accoutrements, ammunition and dress—to count off the guards and assign the officers their posts by lot—to march them from the Grand parade, and do every other requisite duty, agreeable to the orders of the Brigadier. He is to give each commanding officer of a guard the parole [password] and countersigns before he march off; and is to attend the Brigadier frequently through the day, to receive his further occasional orders.[19]

The brigade major of the day also was expected to check at headquarters for any special orders, which he was to distribute to the brigadier generals.[20]

It became a "standing rule, without particular invitation," for the generals and field officers of the day to join Washington for dinner at 3:00 P.M., after their tours of duty. The occasions afforded Washington an opportunity to become better acquainted with the personal and leadership qualities of his senior officers. Normally, Washington's dinner guests consisted of the seven to nine aides, the major and brigadier generals of the day, two lieutenant colonels (field officers of the day), and a brigade major of the day, sometimes with other officers as guests. At Valley Forge, Captain Caleb Gibbs, Lieutenant George Lewis (Washington's nephew), and General Steuben and several of his aides frequently attended the dinners. At the dinner table, seated near Washington, one of his aides made the servings and passed out the wine bottles. Invariably for dessert, guests reached into a bowl of hickory nuts.[21]

As the war progressed, there were slight changes in the officer of the day roster. For a while, a "picquet major of the day" replaced a brigade major of the day, though presumably they were much the same. Rarely, brigade and regimental adjutants of the day are mentioned. Starting in March 1783, shortly before disbandment of the army, inspectors or captain inspectors of the day were assigned to "superintend the Police of their respective Brigades."[22] A quartermaster of the day was introduced by general orders of September 7, 1782. "The responsibilities of this duty officer were to make sure

> the regulations for the order and Discipline of the troops are duly attended to, and that all dead carcasses and every other nuisance in the environs of camp be removed. He must see that good communications be opened between the guards and picquets of the Camp and have a general superintendence of all fatigues ordered for general purposes in or near camp, he may call on the Adjutant General for such fatigue parties as he finds necessary and draw tools from the Quarter master general occasionally but he must before he is relieved return the tools. . . . The Quartermaster of the day will attend the grand parade every morning and report to the General officer of the day.

On the day that he was relieved from duty, the quartermaster of the day was expected to join the other officers of the day for dinner with the commander in chief.[23]

Three staff officers—adjutants, brigade majors, and inspectors—often shared similar responsibilities in matters relating to army personnel. There was no general staff system to coordinate functions of staff departments. The problem of overlapping duties, however, was not so great in the areas of logistics and supply, where new departments were regularly created to ease the burdens of the Quartermaster Department; for example, the Commissary of Issues, the Commissary of Purchases, the Wagon Department, and the Forage Department.

The primary duties of adjutants were to keep tabs on the personnel of units and to promulgate orders. In practice, adjutants also assisted in the training, inspection, and fatigue assignments of troops and, on the regimental level, oversaw the implementation of court-martial sentences.

On the day after Congress named George Washington commander in chief, it also established the office of adjutant general. One day later (June 17, 1775), Congress elected Brigadier General Horatio Gates to that position.[24] Gates's successors were Colonel Joseph Reed (June 5, 1776, to January 22, 1777); Brigadier General Arthur St. Clair (January to February 19, 1777); Brigadier General George Weedon (February 19 to March 1, 1777); Major Isaac Budd Dunn (March 1 to April 9, 1777); Lieutenant Colonel Morgan Conner (April 18 to June 18, 1777); Colonel Timothy Pickering (June 18, 1777, to January 13, 1778); Colonel Alexander Scammell (January 5, 1778, to January 1, 1781); and Brigadier General Edward Hand (January 8, 1781, to November 3, 1783).[25] Unlike most staff officers, the adjutant general, who received pay and rations as a brigadier general, held rank and a commission in the line and therefore could return to duty as a regular officer.[26] The adjutant general was entitled to two assistants, also appointed from the line, with the pay and rations of a lieutenant colonel, and one clerk, who served at the level of a captain.[27]

A deputy adjutant general was appointed for both the northern and southern armies.[28] Colonels Edward Fleming (August 1775 to June 1776) and William Malcolm (June to October 1778) served in this capacity in the northern army;[29] and for the southern army, Captain Edmund Hyrne (1778–81), Colonel Otho Williams (1781), and Colonel Josiah Harmar (1782).[30]

It may be said simply that the chief job of the adjutant general was to keep track of the number and whereabouts of troops. He was "charged with the general detail of the army."[31] The adjutant general certified muster rolls, pay rolls, and "weekly Returns or Returns of any other kind."[32] He received reports on guards after guard mounting and reported daily on "the situation of all posts placed for the safety of the army."[33] The adjutant general himself or through an aide delivered general orders and also the parole and countersign to the brigade majors for proper distribution.[34] In June 1779, Congress imposed upon the adjutant general additional duties as assistant inspector general.[35] Alexander Scammell, after three years as adjutant general, finally resigned, effective January 1, 1781, due to being overburdened. He returned to the command of a New Hampshire regiment and was mortally wounded at the siege of Yorktown.[36]

Of the staff personnel officers, the regimental adjutants had the toughest assignments, providing accountability at the basic level. Adjutants of regiments received the pay and rations of a captain and had the rank of a first lieutenant.[37] General Steuben's *Regulations for the Order and Discipline of the Troops of the United States* outlined the primary duties of a regimental adjutant, who was chosen from among the most experienced subalterns by the field officers of a regiment.

> He must keep an exact detail of the duty of the officers and non-commissioned officers of his regiment, taking care to regulate his roster in such a manner as not to have too many officers or non-commissioned officers of the same company on duty at the same time.
>
> He must keep a book, in which he must every day take the general and other Orders . . . assemble the first serjeants of the companies, make them copy the orders, and give them their details for the next day.
>
> He must attend the parade at the turning out of all guards or detachments, inspect their dress, arms, accoutrements and ammunition, form them into platoons or sections, and conduct them to the general or brigade parade.
>
> When the regiment parades for duty or exercise, he must count it off, and divide it into divisions and platoons, and carry the orders of the colonel where necessary.[38]

General orders in November 1777 made it the responsibility of both adjutants and brigade majors to "bring no man to the parade" who did not have a "decent" appearance, "having his beard shaved, hair combed, face washed and cloaths put on in the best manner in his power."[39] The regimental adjutant appointed the guard and work (fatigue) details at the grand parade, made weekly returns of "the strength" of his regiment, made sure that sergeants called rolls, saw that field officers exercised the troops, required that all orders reach the enlisted men and officers, and had the parole and countersign delivered to all regimental guards in and out of camp.[40]

Adjutants of regiments brought arrested soldiers to court-martial. Once, an officer of the day inquired of a prisoner, Thomas Fletcher, by whom had he been confined, and the reply was "Adjutant Devil—Damn him!" For this declaration, Fletcher was sentenced to five days of the hardest labor to be ordered by the adjutant.[41] An undesirable duty of the adjutant was to superintend punishments ordered by regimental courts-martial. No wonder the whipping post was called the "Adjutant's Daughter." Typically, in reference to a whipping, a regimental order read, "the Adjutant will see it executed this Evening at Roll call in presence of the Regiment."[42]

The sergeant major, writes Lawyn C. Edwards, "served as the primary assistant to the regimental adjutant" in the Continental army. He aided in the "administration, discipline, and drill, and he paid strict attention to the conduct and behavior of the soldiers."[43] The priority of the sergeant major in Washington's army was serving more as "the eyes, the ears, and the voice" of a commanding officer than, as he would later, "the enlisted conscience among the brass." The sergeant major in the Continental army made sure that company orderly sergeants delivered to the adjutant all required returns and reports.[44]

The brigade majors of the Continental army may be viewed as deputy adjutant generals or as brigade adjutants. As the chief staff officer of a brigade, the brigade major attended to administration affecting personnel and served as an intermediary between regimental adjutants and the adjutant general. The adjutants of the usual six or so regiments in a brigade answered to the brigade major, who in turn reported to the adjutant general. Congress permitted Washington and commanders of separate armies to appoint brigade majors from officers in the line holding the rank of major or, in certain instances, captain. Like most staff members, brigade majors had to give up their status as a line officer, although they could return to the line if all the officers of their respective regiments approved.[45] Brigade majors received the same pay as assistants to the adjutant general.[46]

Generally, as one writer notes, the brigade major "was responsible for organizing daily work and guard parties, inspecting equipment, supervising drills, overseeing discipline, and making returns."[47] Essentially, he performed the same duties for a brigade as did adjutants of regiments. "In Action," a brigade major assisted his brigade commander "in the Formation, Manoeuvres &c. of the brigade."[48] He convened brigade-level courts-martial.[49] The brigade major received and examined weekly returns of manpower and equipment in the regiments, making inquiries regarding any discrepancy found when compared to the previous returns; the brigadier general certified the final results.[50] Brigade majors were required to drop by the orderly office punctually at 11:00 A.M. to receive general orders for distribution.[51]

A primary function of the brigade major was to superintend the daily guard detachments. The process started when a regimental adjutant delivered troops selected for guard duty over to the brigade major at the grand parade.[52] The brigade major made sure that the soldiers going out on guard duty measured up to standards of personal appearance and dress and that they were adequately prepared with arms and accoutrements.[53] He made up the guard details at the grand parade and also assigned fatigue parties, meanwhile keeping a duty roster for all noncommissioned officers and officers of the brigade. The brigade major submitted a "return of all the Guards, where mounted and number of Sentries furnish'd by each guard," and he had "to be very careful that the Guards are properly relieved."[54] The parole and countersign were supplied to all guards by the brigade major.[55]

When brigade inspectorships were created in 1778, it was soon apparent that their duties were similar to those performed by the brigade majors. General Steuben noted that in this situation there were "two different analogous departments between which there is no certain line drawn."[56] Congress on February 18, 1779, determined that a brigade inspector in the future would be one of the majors of a brigade and that his office was "annexed" to that of the brigade major. The commander of a brigade would appoint the brigade inspector and major. The former brigade majors did not become unemployed; they would now serve as aide-de-camps to the brigadier generals.[57]

The duties of the brigade inspector and major were essentially those that had been assigned to the brigade major. Upon receiving general orders, the new staff officer was to communicate them to the brigade and the regiments through the regimental adjutants and to all officers of the brigade. The brigade inspector and major was also "to inspect the police of the camp, the discipline and order of the service." He was exempt from "common" camp and garrison duty.[58]

In early August 1777, the new commander of the German regiment, Colonel Henry Leonard Philip, the Baron d'Arendt, formerly of the Prussian army, wrote Washington stating the necessity of establishing the office of "Inspector General of Infantry," which would introduce "Principles of regular Discipline, uniform and essential Manoeuvres" and serve "many other purposes."[59] Already, Congress on July 8, 1777, had appointed Lieutenant

Colonel Mottin de la Balme "inspector general of the cavalry of the United States of America" and on August 11, 1777, named Philippe Charles Jean Baptiste, Tronson du Coudray, "inspector general of ordnance and manufacture" at the rank of major general. Coudray soon made a quick exit, drowning in the Schuylkill River on September 15, 1777.[60]

On recommendation of the Board of War, Congress adopted d'Arendt's proposal on December 13, 1777. While providing for two inspector generals, Congress only appointed one for the time being: Major General Thomas Conway, a French army veteran. Unfortunately, the inspector general reported directly to the congressional Board of War, thereby bypassing Washington. With the commander in chief treating him coolly, and becoming implicated with alleged intrigue seeking the removal of Washington from command, Conway resigned from the inspectorship on April 28, 1778.[61]

Congress had a twofold purpose in creating the post of inspector general: "the promotion of discipline in the American army" and "the reformation of the various abuses which prevail in the different departments." On the personnel side, inspectors were to conduct periodic reviews of the troops, to make sure that soldiers were properly instructed in drill and, most important, to see that "the rules of discipline are strictly observed, and that the officers command their soldiers properly, and do them justice." Furthermore, inspectors were to file returns with Congress on such matters as clothing, arms and accoutrements, recruits, casualties, desertions, and pay and rations. One "return" was to evaluate "all the officers of each regiment, with observations upon the behaviour, capacity and assiduity of every individual." In conducting reviews, inspectors should make contact with all the troops, "attending to the complaints and representations of both soldier and officer, and transmitting to Congress what petitions and grievances he shall think worthy of notice."[62]

The inspector generalship languished, with General Conway not pursuing his duties aggressively and Congress not appointing a second inspector general. The situation changed, however, with the coming of Baron Friedrich Wilhelm Augustus von Steuben. Though Steuben (with the aid of Benjamin Franklin) duped the Americans into thinking that he had been a Prussian general, he nevertheless had ample experience as a staff officer in the Prussian army. Arriving at Valley Forge on February 23, 1778, Steuben set about assisting in the inspection of troops, without holding a commission. Impressed by Washington's and other officers's recommendations,

Congress on May 5, 1778, named Steuben a major general and inspector general of the army.[63]

The danger that the Board of War could regulate the army without Washington's participation was short-lived. Washington himself stepped in to prevent a competition between the commander in chief and the inspector general. In general orders of June 15, 1778, Washington stated that Steuben was responsible for preparing regulations for the army upon approval of the commander in chief.[64] Congress subsequently acknowledged that Washington had direct command over the inspector general, although the inspector general still reported to the Board of War on deficiencies in matériel and, "with the approbation of the Commander in Chief," also on suggestions for any improvements of the Articles of War relating to discipline.[65]

Steuben quickly instituted reforms in drill, maneuvering exercises, and marching. With a model company, consisting mostly of members from Washington's Life Guard, Steuben personally taught the new practices to be adopted by all the army. The Prussian drillmaster set an "excellent example" for all army officers, wrote an aide to Washington in March 1778, by "descending to the functions of a drill-Sergeant."[66] Steuben insisted that officers be more concerned with the welfare of their soldiers; he himself visited the sick and sought out complaints from enlisted men, which he tried to have redressed.[67]

In March 1779, Congress had printed three thousand copies of Steuben's military manual and ordered that the "Regulations" therein be observed by the whole American army. The *Regulations* contained twenty-five chapters relating to varied aspects of army duty, organization, and drill. Exact scrutiny was given to a soldier's movements. For example:

> At attention: Position of a Soldier without Arms
>
> He is to stand straight and firm upon his legs, with the head turned to the right as far as to bring the left eye over the waistcoat buttons; the heels two inches apart; the toes turned out; the belly drawn in a little, but without constraint; the breast a little projected; the shoulders square to the front, and kept back; and the hands hanging down the sides with the palms close to the thighs.[68]

General Steuben "has two ranks of Inspectors under him," Washington wrote to the president of Congress.[69] There were assistant inspectors, one of whom was the adjutant general, and the others each tended to a division (equivalent to two or three brigades). Subinspectors were the brigade inspectors. Assistant inspectors, who were required to be native-born, could substitute for the inspector general in conducting reviews and, in separate armies, exercised the full authority of an inspector general. Congress appointed the assistant inspectors, and Washington named the subinspectors.[70] A scale for added compensation voted by Congress in December 1780 precisely identifies the "officers in the inspector's department":

> To the adjutant general, as assistant inspector, thirty five dollars per month;
> To an assistant inspector in a separate army, thirty dollars per month;
> To a lieutenant colonel, as inspector of a division, twenty five dollars per month;
> To a major, as inspector of a brigade [subinspectors], twenty five dollars per month.[71]

In addition to infantry brigades, artillery and cavalry units and the West Point garrisons were supposed to have their own subinspectors.[72] Among the division inspectors were Lieutenant Colonels Ebenezer Sprout and Francis Barber and Majors Nicholas Fish and William Scott.[73] Lieutenant Colonel Jean Baptiste Ternant, a French engineer, served as the assistant inspector general for Generals Robert Howe and Benjamin Lincoln's southern army, from fall 1778 until the surrender of American forces at Charleston in May 1780.[74]

Steuben managed to place all functions for inspection of troops under his department. Besides grafting the adjutant general's office and the brigade majors into the inspectorate, he secured the abolition of the mustermaster general (also known as the commissary general of musters). A mustermaster general, existing since the beginning of the war in July 1775, had charge of all the muster rolls of the army and inspected troops and equipment.[75] These duties duplicated those of the inspector general. Frequently, the mustermaster general was criticized for not having the army "more generally mustered."[76] In November 1778, the Mustermaster General Department suffered extreme humiliation, when a half-dozen Tory banditti abducted the mustermaster general and his deputy, along with the muster rolls of the whole Continental army (see chapter 6).[77] It was hardly a surprise that a council of general officers on July 26, 1779, voted to put an end to the Mustermaster General

Department. Washington gave his endorsement, and on January 12, 1780, Congress terminated the office.[78]

The Inspector General Department succeeded so well that there was little need for Steuben to devote full attention to it. The regulations were firmly in place, and all that was now required was for the various inspectors to hold periodic reviews and report on their findings. Steuben took leave of his post for a year (November 1780 to November 1781), commanding troops in Virginia during the British invasions of that state, from January to June 1781, and one of the three Continental divisions at the siege of Yorktown.

Considering that the inspector generalship had accomplished "the principal object" of introducing "a uniform discipline" throughout the army,[79] Steuben, upon returning from field duty, proposed that his department be reestablished at a more modest level. Congress concurred and on January 10, 1782, reduced the personnel to the inspector general, his secretary, and one inspector for each of the separate armies. Reviews for "every denomination of service" were to be conducted once a month, with inspection of "the number and condition of the men and horses, the discipline of the troops, the state of their arms, accoutrements, ammunition, cloathing and camp equipage." The inspector general and inspectors of a separate army were "subject only to the orders of Congress, the Secretary at War, Commander in Chief, or commanding officer of a seperate army."[80] Under the new system, the assistant inspector generals and subinspectors were eliminated. The adjutant general was once again independent of the inspector general, and the office of brigade major was revived.[81]

Under the reorganization of January 10, 1782, Colonel Walter Stewart served as inspector for the northern army, and since Washington's army during the final year of the war was stationed in the New Jersey–New York highlands, Stewart performed some of the inspections of units in the main army.[82] Colonel Jean Baptiste Ternant, released from his prisoner of war status in January 1782, resumed his post as inspector for the southern army.[83]

Steuben stayed on as inspector general. His main task was to preside over the reduction of the army. In summer 1782, Steuben wrote Washington, asking if "the Department of Inspector General" had been "necessary in the Army" and had "this Department been conducted during the Course of five years agreeable to your wishes?" Washington answered that the inspector generalship had been "of the utmost utility," especially "for having Established one uniform System of Manoeuvres and regulations" in the army.[84]

Steuben resigned his office, effective April 15, 1784, and his longtime aide-de-camp, Major William North, succeeded him, serving as inspector general to the minuscule peacetime army from April 15, 1784, to June 25, 1788.[85]

During the war, the constant attention given to the common soldier by duty and staff officers contributed to military proficiency and the making of a professional soldier. By the gradual clearing of lines of responsibility, soldiers more quickly responded to measures for self-improvement and acquired individual and unit pride.

5

Washington's Life Guard

The idea of having his own life guard appealed to George Washington. A life guard, doubling as body and honor guard, had been customary in European practice for the purpose of serving sovereigns and commanding generals. The French army had the Gardes Françaises; and the British army had its Horse Guards and Horse Grenadiers. Household regiments provided security for the British royal family; and in Prussia, Frederick William I (1713–40) and Frederick William II (1786–97) maintained a palace guard consisting of giant-size soldiers.[1] During the American Revolution, guards drawn from the British royal household infantry served in America.[2]

To George Washington, a life guard would be an elite outfit, made up of the most physically fit and best performing soldiers. The guardsmen would exemplify soldiering traits to be envied by their comrades in arms. In a republican army, Washington was smart enough not to seek a life guard so exclusive as to be seen as abetting dictatorial ambition. The commander in chief had a pragmatic view: to establish a life guard not only for the protection of his person, headquarters, documents, and personal property but that he could also employ in various activities, ranging from carrying dispatches to assisting in providing household service to the Washingtons and the extended "family" of aides.

On March 11, 1776, a few days before the British evacuation of Boston, Washington issued general orders that read:

> The General being desirous of selecting a particular number of men, as a Guard for himself, and baggage, the Colonel, or commanding Officer, of each of the established Regiments, (the Artillery and Riffle-men excepted) will furnish him with four, that the number wanted may be chosen out of them. His Excellency depends upon the Colonels for good Men, such as they can recommend for their sobriety, honesty, and good behaviour; he wishes them to be from five feet,

eight Inches high, to five feet, ten Inches; handsomely and well made, and as there is nothing in his eyes more desireable, than Cleanliness in a Soldier, he desires that particular attention may be made, in the choice of such men, as are neat, and spruce.

Furthermore, the soldiers sent to Washington should be "perfectly willing, and desirous, of being of this guard. They should be drill'd men."[3]

The following day, the guard was organized, with fifty enlisted men. Captain Caleb Gibbs, adjutant of a Massachusetts regiment, was named commandant of the unit. Gibbs, age twenty-eight, was a native of Rhode Island but was living in Massachusetts at the start of the war. Lieutenant George Lewis, a nephew of George Washington, was named second-in-command.[4] Successive commandants of the Life Guard were Second Lieutenant (later First Lieutenant and then Captain) William Colfax, January 1, 1781, to September 5, 1783 (assigned to the Life Guard on March 18, 1778); and First Lieutenant (later Captain) Bezaleel Howe, September 5 to December 20, 1783. Other officers serving in the Life Guard were First Lieutenant John Nicholas, May 1 to June 1, 1777; First Lieutenant Robert Randolph, May 1, 1777, to September 26, 1778; First Lieutenant (Captain, as of December 4, 1778) Henry Phillip Livingston, June 2, 1777, to March 26, 1779; Surgeon Samuel Hanson, son of a future president of Congress, March 19, 1778, to March 26, 1779; First Lieutenant Benjamin Grymes (or Grimes), March 19, 1778, to March 26, 1779; and Second Lieutenant (later First Lieutenant) Levi Holden, June 23, 1781, to November 3, 1783.[5] From March 1779 to the end of the war, the unit was allowed only two officers.

Captain (Major, as of July 29, 1778) Gibbs, as commandant of the commander in chief's guard for four and a half years, bore a host of responsibilities. Besides commanding the guard, he served as a supplemental aide-de-camp to Washington from May 16, 1776, to January 1, 1781. Gibbs supervised Washington's headquarters household. It was he who purchased food and other supplies. He was the cashier, in charge of all the accounts, and made disbursements. He kept an eye on the domestic staff, including an elderly housekeeper. On occasion, members of the guard were employed at headquarters as purveyors, bakers, cooks, and hostlers, for which they received a monthly allowance in addition to their regular pay. Washington cautioned Gibbs not to engage for household duty "a mere greenhorn."[6]

Just looking after the dining fare for Washington, his headquarters staff, and numerous guests proved an enormous drain on Gibbs's time. Typical of the countless requisitions he made to the Commissary of Provisions office was one of February 1780: "We are out of Beer, you will please send on a large Quantity as soon as possible. A barrell of Cranberries are much wanted."[7] A soldier noted in his diary about the same time, "Maj. Gibbs made a feast to his excellency Gen'l. Washington, Gen'ls. Howe, Paterson & numerous field & commissioned officers."[8] Gibbs was noted for his congeniality. A Virginia lady visiting at camp said of Gibbs that he was "a good natured Yankee who makes a thousand Blunders in the Yankee stile and keeps the Dinner table in constant Laugh."[9]

To Washington, no duty of his Life Guard was more important than moving and guarding his own and headquarters's baggage. Once the commander in chief berated Gibbs for half filling a trunk.[10] To a French officer, the Chevalier de Chastellux, in November 1780, it was a most impressive sight to see "the battalion of the General's guards encamped within the precincts of his house; nine wagons destined to carry his baggage, ranged in his yard," amidst "a great number of grooms holding very fine horses belonging to the general officers and their aides-de-camp."[11]

The Life Guard provided a headquarters security detachment. Customarily, in camp two sentries were assigned to the front and two in back of Washington's residence day and night. Arrangements were made that in case of emergency, guards would enter the house and barricade the doors and position themselves with muskets at the windows. Rarely did Washington use members of the Life Guard for personal escort.[12]

Soldiers in the commander in chief's guard sported a flashy uniform, consisting of a dark-blue coat with buff trim, a single-breasted red vest, buckskin breeches strapped into black boots, white bayonet and body belts, a black cocked or round hat with a binding of white tape, and gilt buttons. Officers, besides the epaulets, wore a blue and white feather in their hats.[13] After the British evacuation of Boston in March 1776, the Life Guard accompanied the Continental army to New York City, where an enemy invasion was expected. The guardsmen were situated around army headquarters at Varick and Charlton Streets.[14] Washington had a rude awakening in the discovery that not all of his security was trustworthy.

On June 16, 1776, a prisoner in the New York City jail wrote a letter to the New York Provisional Congress that two other prisoners, Sergeant Thomas

Hickey and William Green, a drummer, both British deserters who had enlisted in the American army and were members of Washington's Life Guard, had joined others in a treasonous plot, led by Gilbert Forbes, a gunsmith. The conspirators allegedly intended to assist British forces in the capture of American forts and to blow up magazines and assassinate Washington and other generals. The royal governor of New York, William Tryon, made small monetary payments to the plotters through the mayor of New York City, David Mathews. A special investigative committee of the New York Provincial Congress turned up fourteen supposed conspirators, including Hickey and Mayor Mathews. Eight of the accused were members of the commander in chief's guard.[15]

For some reason, Hickey became the scapegoat for hatching the plot. Tried by a court-martial, he was convicted of mutiny, sedition, and "holding a treacherous correspondence" with the enemy. Hickey was hanged in a field near Bowery Lane on June 28, 1776, before a throng of twenty thousand spectators.[16] Despite the comment of William Eustis, a surgeon in the American army, in a letter of June 28, that "we are hanging them as fast as we find them out," it appears that all the other alleged conspirators were imprisoned in Connecticut, and all escaped, making their way to British lines.[17] Hickey became the first American executed for treason against the United States.[18] As a result of the Hickey affair, starting in October 1776, British deserters were not allowed to join the Continental army—and certainly not Washington's Life Guard.[19]

Others of Washington's guardsmen caused trouble. Two members were court-martialed in September 1776. Sergeant Peter Richards, for "Abusing and striking" Captain Gibbs, was sentenced to a whipping of thirty-nine lashes and reduction in rank.[20] A Sergeant Clements was convicted of neglect of duty and sentenced to reduction in rank and forced to rejoin his regiment.[21]

Most army enlistments expired at the end of 1776. Some of the discharged men resumed military service. Because of this turnover, the commander in chief's Life Guard was dissolved in February 1777. To avoid the disloyalty and misbehavior manifested by certain members of the original Life Guard, Washington planned that future guardsmen should be Virginians. In April 1777, he contacted the Virginia regimental commanders to furnish men for a new guard "company." Washington asked the colonels to be "extremely cautious" in making a selection, because "it is more than probable that in the Course of the Campaign, my Baggage, Papers, & other Matters of great public Import may be committed to the sole Care of these Men." The new recruits for the Life Guard should be five feet nine inches to five feet ten inches in height, "sober, young, active & well made," and also "of good Character," and "possess the pride of appearing clean & soldierlike." For security reasons, it was best that the new guardsmen be "Natives, & Men of some property." Actually, Washington was showing his preference for Virginians. He pleaded with the colonels, however, not to divulge his desire for only "Natives," so as not "to create any invidious Distinction between them & the Foreigners."[22]

The reformed Life Guard had a rank and file of four sergeants, four corporals, a drummer, a fifer, and fifty privates, for a total of sixty men. Captain Caleb Gibbs resumed his command, assisted by two Virginia lieutenants, Robert Randolph and John Nicholas; Nicholas lasted only a month, and on June 2, 1777, was replaced by Lieutenant Henry Phillip Livingston of New York.[23] The Life Guard was allotted one or several women camp followers. On August 16, 1777, Lieutenant Livingston sent a requisition to the Commissary Department: "Let the bearer have 1 Days provision for 48 Men & 1 Woman of His Excellency's Guard."[24]

The practice then began of detaching cavalry troops from time to time to act in conjunction with the Life Guard. These dragoons remained on the muster lists of their assigned units and when serving with the guardsmen were designated as being "on command." Thirty-eight men from the Third Regiment of Continental Dragoons were detached to the Life Guard from May 1, 1777, to September 26, 1778; George Lewis, now a captain, and Lieutenant Robert Randolph were the officers in this dragoon detachment.[25] Subsequently, other detachments from dragoon units were assigned to the Life Guard, as needed and particularly in battle situations.[26] Elisha Sheldon's Second Continental Light Dragoons, who were, as one French officer reported, "the best troops on the continent," provided a bodyguard and escort for Washington during summer 1781.[27]

The arrival of Baron von Steuben at Valley Forge on February 23, 1778, led to an additional role for the Life Guard. Steuben asked permission of Washington to set up a special drill company that would serve as a model for the rest of the army. On March 17, 1778, general orders authorized one hundred "chosen men" to be annexed to the commander in chief's guard for the purpose of serving as the model unit for implementing new drill instructions: "as the Generals guard is composed intirely of Virginians the one hundred draughts are to be taken from the troops of the other States." The additional guardsmen were to be between five feet eight inches and five feet ten inches tall, twenty-eight to thirty years old, of "robust constitution and Limbs well formed and of excellent character well established for Sobriety and fidelity."[28] Members of Steuben's personal guard were included in the added quota. The Life Guard was thus expanded to 151 men: 1 captain, 3 lieutenants, 1 surgeon, 4 sergeants, 3 corporals, 2 drummers, 1 fifer, and 136 privates. The new officers (joining Captain Gibbs and Lieutenant Livingston) were First Lieutenant Benjamin Grymes and Second Lieutenant William Colfax; Samuel Hanson served as surgeon. Thirty-six members of the Life Guard were exempted from the drill detachment in order to perform duty at headquarters.[29]

One young Massachusetts private, Elijah Fisher, who joined the new commander in chief's guard, said that the duty was "much better" than being in his regiment because the guardsmen were allowed to "go where they would."[30] Steuben made the commander in chief's guard into his own "military school."[31] Training started March 19 and lasted for six weeks. Steuben personally oversaw the drilling. For initial instruction, the guards were divided into fourteen squads, with Steuben in charge of one, and his subinspectors, the others.[32]

With the end of the training period, the guard was now free to be deployed on special assignments. From May 18 to 20, 1778, one hundred members of the Life Guard joined General Lafayette's twenty-four-hundred-man reconnaissance expedition. At Barren Hill, on the Schuylkill River, eleven miles from Philadelphia, the American force met up with General William Howe's troops, six thousand in all. Although caught between two enemy flanking forces, Lafayette miraculously extricated his men and returned to Valley Forge.[33]

Captain Gibbs, Lieutenant Grymes, four sergeants, four corporals, and seventy-two men of the guard joined Colonel Daniel Morgan's vanguard on June 22, 1778, to harass the British army as they retreated across New Jersey, heading for New York City. Morgan's detachment did not fight in the battle of Monmouth, June 28, but after the engagement, gave hot pursuit of the enemy. The rest of the Life Guard had charge of the headquarters baggage.[34] During the Rhode Island campaign of July–August 1778, Captain Gibbs served as an aide-de-camp to General Nathanael Greene.[35]

It was still a problem to find all good men for the commander in chief's guard. Like the Hickey tragedy two years before, gross misdeeds by guardsmen occurred in October 1778. Private Elijah Fisher, returning from furlough on October 6, was surprised to discover "an alteration in the Dress of my mates." He asked Private John Herrick about the sudden change. Herrick replied that his father had sent him some money. Fisher reminded Herrick that, in that case, he should pay him the $16 that Herrick had borrowed from him. Then "in comes one or two more. I Said have you had money sent you from home, I fear that you have taken some other way to git it than that." Herrick then came clean and related to Fisher what had really happened. The whole affair had begun when Private John Herring was sent into the countryside to buy

> things for the General's Famely and he had a horse and a pass to go
> where he Could git such things. . . . he Come to an old Tory's house
> and they would not Let him have any thing and he sees several things
> that he wanted so when he Come home he gos to his messmates and
> tales them and they gos and robed him of several things. I said that
> Whether he be a tory or not If it should be found out (which such
> things as Robery selim is) some or all of you will be hung which
> surprized them Vary much but there was no more heard about it.

Despite efforts to conceal the crime, four guardsmen were arrested: John Herring, John Herrick, Moses Walton, and Elias Brown. These miscreants were also linked to another house robbery several days after the first crime. Actual identification was difficult because the robbers had blackened their faces. Stolen deerskin breeches were found on Walton, and Herrick, who claimed that he had been a member of the robbery group under duress, "turned State's Evedence against the others." A court-martial on October 22, 1778, condemned Herring, Walton, and Brown to be hanged and Herrick to receive a hundred lashes. Execution of each sentence was to take place at a different location: Brown to be hanged before General Alexander McDougall's division at New Milford, Connecticut; Herring before General Johann De Kalb's division stationed fourteen miles northeast of Fishkill; and Walton before General Horatio Gates's division stationed at or near West Point. Herrick was to receive his one hundred lashes at army headquarters at Fredericksburg, New York. Herring was hanged, and Herrick received his punishment; Brown and Walton, however, escaped. Brown, who had been a fifer in the Life Guard, showed up later as a mechanic in the army under an assumed name. His father, Ephraim Brown, of Windsor, Connecticut, wrote Washington in May 1779, asking a pardon for his son, which was granted, and Elias Brown rejoined his original unit, a Connecticut regiment, where he won promotion to fife major.[36]

As if members of the Life Guard committing capital offenses were not enough, other instances of delinquent behavior also surfaced in fall 1778. The Life Guardsmen prided themselves as the elite group in camp. Then, all of a sudden, there was a new privileged corps—the mounted police, commanded by Captain Bartholomew Von Heer (see chapter 13). The guardsmen resented Von Heer's men, who occasionally did guard duty similar to that expected of the Life Guard; especially irksome was that most of the mounted police were of German extraction and could arrest and confine at their discretion any soldier for wrong-doing, even members of the Life Guard.

On the evening of October 7, Von Heer's police arrested some guardsmen for violating regulations. Soon, guardsmen—Henry Despestet, Daniel Thompson, John Kidder, John Cole, Asa Adams, Samuel Wortman, Jonathan Moore, Davis Brown, and Edward Wiley—put on their sidearms and went looking for members of the mounted police corps. Before there was any confrontation, they, too, were arrested. This led to more guardsmen going out to seek revenge. The group—Sergeant William Roach, Corporal Joshua Forbes, and Privates John Smith, Solomon Townshend, William Palmer, Lewis Flemister, Henry Perry, and William Jones—accosted Corporal Wingler of Von Heer's police, and all the offenders were arrested. At courts-martial on October 15 and 16, all the guardsmen who had been apprehended were acquitted, with the exception of Privates Smith and Townshend. Smith was convicted of calling Corporal Wingler a "Hessian Bourgre [Bugger]"; and Townshend was found guilty of striking Wingler. Both Smith and Townshend were deemed "guilty of swearing and unsoldierly behaviour after being in Custody of Capt. Van Heer"; their punishment, however, was set at time already served in confinement. In an unrelated case, Private Joseph Timberlake of the Life Guard was found guilty for "knocking down Lieutt. David Ziegler [of a Pennsylvania regiment] when he was in the way of duty." Timberlake was sentenced to a whipping of one hundred lashes.[37]

There appears to have been sustained discontent among some of the Life Guard. During the course of the war, 30 of the 330 known guardsmen deserted, most of them doing so during their tenure with the Life Guard.

Several of the deserters went aboard privateers, and a few were later taken back in the army. None faced execution.[38]

The relationship between Major Gibbs and Washington was strained in fall 1779. The exact cause is not known. A letter from Washington to Lieutenant William Colfax is the only indication of the rift. Gibbs, said Washington, "has been guilty of a piece of disrespect . . . and because I would not suffer my orders to be trampled on, a supercilious and self-important conduct on his part is the consequence." The commander in chief told Colfax "that I consider you as the instrument, not the cause of disobedience to my orders respecting the Tent."[39] Headquarters at this time was at West Point. On September 16, the Life Guard had been responsible for setting up a marquee, in which an elaborate dinner was held in honor of the visiting French minister, the Chevalier de la Luzerne.[40]

The troop strength of the Life Guard again dwindled. During 1779 and early 1780, a number of guardsmen were discharged. To replenish the rank and file (numbering sixty in 1779) and to expand the size of the Life Guard, Washington on March 19, 1780, ordered a draft from the line: "Two trusty soldiers from each regiment of Infantry and a good active serjeant from each brigade with their Arms Accoutrements, Blankets, Packs &c. are to assemble on the grand parade tomorrow morning at troop beating. The officers of the day will have them formed into Platoons and the Brigade Major of the day will march them to Head Quarters where they are to join His Excellency's Guards 'till further orders."[41] The height requirements remained the same, five feet eight inches to five feet ten inches. The new guardsmen were to be listed as being "on command" from the regiments from which they were drafted and thereby would still be members of their regiments.[42] The March draftees stayed in the Life Guard until mid-July, when they were replaced by a similar process. The size of the Life Guard was now raised to 180 men.[43] The practice began of daily calling up soldiers to form "the Picquet Guard at Headquarters," drawn on a rotating basis from each of the divisions at camp. Whether this group was used for headquarters security or sent to outpost duty is not known. One time, a subaltern, a sergeant, a corporal, and twenty-one privates were ordered from a Pennsylvania brigade "to mount at Head Quarters immediately."[44] In any event, the Life Guard lost some of its elitism, with soldiers being detailed directly from the ranks on a rotating basis.

Since the Life Guard was now formed by soldiers on temporary assignment, Washington had less compunction about sending this unit into battle.

The Life Guard most distinguished itself during the British invasion of New Jersey in June 1780. General Wilhelm von Knyphausen, acting commander of British troops in New York while General Henry Clinton was laying siege to Charleston, South Carolina, landed near Elizabethtown, New Jersey, on June 7, 1780, with five thousand men, in expectation of marching on the American encampment at Morristown. Knyphausen was counting on reports that Washington's troops were mutinous. As the British army moved toward Morristown, Washington sent troops to the Springfield–Short Hills area. The American vanguard consisted of General William Maxwell's New Jersey brigade, the commander in chief's guard, and local militia. As the British came up to the village of Connecticut Farms, the American forward troops made a stand. The commander in chief's guard, commanded by Major Caleb Gibbs, assisted by Lieutenant William Colfax, "gave the Enemy the first charge." This was a rare instance when American soldiers made good use of bayonets. Gibbs informed General Maxwell the next day, "I had the happiness to give the Hessian lads a charge just before sunsett & drove them Thoroughly. We gave them after they gave way, about eight rounds. I have lost 3 kild as many wounded & as many missing."[45] Maxwell himself reported that this engagement was "the closest action I have seen this war."[46]

The British burned houses at Connecticut Farms and then retreated toward Elizabethtown. Gibbs's guard, along with Maxwell's brigade and militia, harassed the enemy on their march. The Life Guard stayed in the field for a week before they were called off the lines. The guards were not involved in the battle of Springfield, June 23, when the enemy came out one more time.[47]

Washington continued to draw his guard from the divisions on a rotating basis; only the two officers—Gibbs and Colfax—had permanent tenure with the guard. General orders for September 7, 1780, requisitioned a captain, a subaltern, three sergeants, three corporals, one drummer, one fifer, and forty privates from General Alexander McDougall's division to join the commander in chief's guard.[48] On April 8, 1781, Washington wrote General William Heath to send him a subaltern, a sergeant, two corporals, and twenty privates "to reinforce my Guard. This party is to be relieved once a Week."[49]

On January 1, 1781, Major Gibbs was transferred to the Second Massachusetts Regiment, and in August, to a light infantry unit. Wounded at the battle of Yorktown, he was soon breveted a lieutenant colonel. He ended his service in Colonel Henry Jackson's infantry regiment on June 20, 1784, being one of the few officers retained in the army after the end of the war. Gibbs became a Boston businessman, and in December 1794, obtained a clerkship at the Boston Navy Yard at Charlestown, a position he retained until his death on November 6, 1798.[50]

Lieutenant William Colfax, twenty-four years old, succeeded Gibbs as commandant of the commander in chief's guards. Technically, he was transferred to a Connecticut regiment and served in the guard "on command." Colfax retired from the army on November 3, 1783, having been promoted to captain in April of that year. During the War of 1812, he returned to the army and served as a brigadier general. Colfax had a gregarious personality and was considered a favorite of Martha Washington. He is described as having "dark hair, always well powdered and worn in a queue, a clean shaven face, a clear, florid complexion, and beautiful blue eyes dancing with expression."[51] Colfax assumed all the duties of supervising Washington's headquarters household, including keeping accounts and making purchases, as had Gibbs.[52] The only difference was that Colfax did not stand in as a part-time aide-de-camp.

On July 3, 1781, the Life Guard, detached with some of General Benjamin Lincoln's troops as part of a projected attack upon British outposts north of New York City, met up unexpectedly with a fifteen-hundred-man British foraging party near Kingsbridge, a British post at the northern tip of Manhattan Island. A heated skirmish ensued, and the Americans were forced to retreat back to Washington's army, now at Valentine's Hill, four miles away. During the engagement, Lieutenant Colfax was wounded, along with a sergeant and fourteen soldiers of the guard (three of whom later died).[53]

The Life Guard accompanied Washington to Yorktown and presumably saw no action, being stationed adjacent to headquarters at the rear of the allied forces. On November 5, 1781, the guard left with Washington overland and reached Philadelphia on November 26. While the main army was posted at Morristown and the New York Highlands, Washington established headquarters at the Benjamin Chew house in Philadelphia, with the guard stationed nearby. On March 22, 1782, Washington and the guard moved to Newburgh, New York, while the army was scattered at various places in the Highlands. As the last cantonment of the main army, troops took up post at New Windsor along the Hudson River, on October 22, 1782, with Washington and his guard staying at Newburgh, two miles above New Windsor.[54]

During the last year of the war, the size of the Life Guard was kept to the minimum of the rank and file: forty-one in May, sixty-five in August, and fifty-nine in December 1782.[55] Congress on May 26, 1783, ordered the commander in chief to furlough all soldiers who had enlisted for the duration of the war and to discharge them upon the signing of the peace treaty. Washington announced the furlough policy on June 2. Only a very few troops were retained in the army: some New England soldiers, several artillery companies, and for the time being, a light infantry unit for bringing order to Westchester County, New York.[56] On June 6, all but one (Sergeant John Phillips) of the sixty-four rank and file of the Life Guard (all the members had enlisted for the war) were furloughed, along with Lieutenant Levi Holden. Lieutenant Colfax, who was continued as commandant, went on furlough in July, whereupon an orderly sergeant looked after the guard until Lieutenant Bezaleel Howe was appointed commandant of the guard on September 5, 1783. Howe, from a New Hampshire regiment, stayed on until his discharge on December 20.[57]

With the army disintegrating, Washington was somewhat uncertain what to do about replacing his guard. In early June 1783, he first ordered that to fill the void left by the furloughed guardsmen, one subaltern and thirty-eight rank and file "be taken from the three years men in the Massachusetts Line"; he reversed this order the next day by requiring the guard "be furnished daily" from the regiment "which gives the other Guards."[58] Finally, on June 16, 1783, it was decided that thirty-eight men selected from the New Hampshire line, including twelve mounted troops, would have the honor of forming the Life Guard until the total dismantling of the army.[59]

The last Life Guardsmen probably did not wear the distinctive uniform since they served but a short while. The twelve mounted guardsmen, however, undoubtedly wore blue coats "faced with white" as was standard for all units of mounted infantrymen. The white silk flag of the Life Guard, probably introduced in the latter part of the war, depicts a guardsman in light infantry attire: "a blue coat with white facings, white waistcoat and breeches, black half-gaiters, and a cocked hat with a blue and white feather." The guardsman on the flag is holding the reins of a horse while receiving a banner from the Genius of Liberty (a woman resting her hand on the Union Shield), with an eagle adjacent to the shield. The motto above the scene reads "Conquer or Die."[60]

Leaving the army under the acting command of Major General Henry Knox, Washington on August 19, 1783, left Newburgh for Princeton, New Jersey, where he would consult with Congress on the present and future state of the army. He resided at a house in Rocky Hill, four miles from Princeton, with the Life Guard encamping in tents on the lawn. Washington relied upon the twelve mounted infantry of the Life Guard for primary headquarters security. All of these men, like the rest of the guard, were from New Hampshire: Sergeant Nehemiah Stratton, Corporals Joel Holt and Asa Redington, and Privates Stephen Ames, William Batchelder, James Blair, Ebenezer Coston, Abraham Currier, William Ferguson, David Morrison, Benjamin Pierce, and Luther Smith.[61] On October 6, Congress authorized Washington "to reward the diligence and fidelity of the twelve horsemen, who have acted as his guard at headquarters, by presenting them with their horses and accoutrements on their discharge." Four days later, Congress awarded Bezaleel Howe, the guard's commandant, a commission as brevet captain.[62]

On November 9, Washington headed northward to attend to the final chapter of the war, the British evacuation of New York City. He sent all of the guard, except for Howe and the twelve mounted guardsmen, to West Point, "under the care of a good Sergeant." At West Point, these men rejoined their regiments, with some staying on in what was left of the army, a unit that became known as the American Regiment.

Captain Howe and the twelve mounted guardsmen had one final assignment: to deliver the commander in chief's baggage to Mount Vernon. Along the way, the escort was to drop Washington's "Accounts" at the office of the superintendent of finances, Robert Morris, in Philadelphia. Washington was especially concerned about protecting the contents of the six baggage wagons on their journey. Howe was told that "the Waggons should never be without a Sentinel over them; always locked and the Keys in your possession." Washington warned against ferrying across the major rivers when winds were strong. After accomplishing the mission, Howe and the escort guardsmen went to West Point, New York, where they were mustered out of the army on December 20, 1783.[63]

The commander in chief's Life Guard for seven and a half years provided the essential services of headquarters security, bodyguard for Washington, and, especially when the army was in transit, cover for Washington's baggage and command documents and papers. The guardsmen were elitist only in that they were assigned to the commander in chief, exempted from camp duty, and were of a certain size, young, and exemplary soldiers. The eventual rotation of members from different state lines made the guard more representative of the army at large. That the guard had members early on who were disloyal and prone to rowdy behavior discouraged Washington from making the unit into one of personal attachment. By and large, the quality of the guard was high, and it fought with distinction in several battles.

The Life Guard ceased as the army disbanded. There was never any possibility for it to develop into a power base, with Washington eschewing any dictatorial tendencies, the postwar army having no commander in chief, and there being no head of state for the national government.

6

Generals' Guards

Generals of the Continental army could claim the services of a personal guard. The creation of these guards often posed a problem because of the drain of manpower from an already depleted rank and file. Not unlike the commander in chief's guard, a general's guard provided security for his person and for brigade or division headquarters and other services, such as watching over baggage, running errands, and carrying dispatches. Most generals, however, did not avail themselves of a full complement of guardsmen, and some, from time to time, declined having a guard unit altogether. Generals had ample assistance from their aides-de-camp and staff personnel, including adjutants and brigade majors; and like other officers, they were allowed to keep servants who were generally drawn from the ranks.

The employment of senior officers' guards had been a long-standing practice in European armies. A marshal of France in the early eighteenth century had a guard retinue of a captain, a lieutenant, an ensign, and fifty men.[1] Usually, in the British army, a lieutenant general kept a guard of about thirty-three men; a major general, twenty-three; and a brigadier general, fifteen.[2] During the French and Indian War, Major Generals Edward Braddock and Jeffery Amherst, both of whom commanded military campaigns in America, each had a guard consisting of a lieutenant and thirty men, who were supplied from regiments on a rotating basis.[3]

A contingency standard existed for the size of guards for generals in the Continental army, although the number of soldiers involved varied according to availability, circumstance, and the desire of individual generals. A major general was entitled to a guard of one or two subalterns, one or two sergeants, one or two corporals (or drummers), and twenty privates. Normally, a brigadier general's guard consisted of a sergeant, a corporal, and twelve privates. The quartermaster general and adjutant general had the same prerogative as a brigadier general; other staff department heads could retain four to seven men as a guard, usually one corporal and the rest privates.[4]

General De Kalb complained that "the generals never think of sparing their men. They take the full complement of guards to which their rank entitles them. The general of the highest grade has a lieutenant with thirty men, the brigadier a sergeant, with twelve men to watch him, and the remaining staff officers in proportion." De Kalb said his setting "a good example" by reducing his guard was "by no means imitated."[5] At least two major generals did create guards with an excessive number of men. Major General John Sullivan, still in Rhode Island in early 1779 after his unsuccessful campaign against the British there, had a "Life Guard" consisting of a captain, a first lieutenant, a second lieutenant, an ensign, ten noncommissioned officers, and sixty-one privates.[6] In August 1780, Major General Benedict Arnold's "life guard consisted of one hundred men." Arnold, commandant at West Point, resided at the Beverley Robinson house, on the east side of the Hudson River, opposite and below West Point. A member of the guard recalled that two men were drafted "out of each company to form General Arnold's life guard." Members of the guard lived in tents and barracks around the Robinson house. "Their business was to stand guard and sentry" and "to go on errands to different places and was all the time under arms."[7]

The major generals usually had their twenty-four- to twenty-six-man guard, from whom sentinels were assigned to watch over the quarters, three by day and four by night. Occasionally, major generals took a larger-than-standard guard; for example, Horatio Gates, thirty-two (late 1777); and Benjamin Lincoln, forty-five (May 1777). Congress assigned a forty-three-man bodyguard to General Steuben in 1779; his guard numbered only fourteen by May 1782. Sometimes, major generals kept only the number of guards allotted to brigadier generals; for example, Israel Putnam (May 1776), Lord Stirling (September 1779), and Robert Howe (October 1780 and January 1781).[8]

Brigadier General Louis Le Bègue de Presle Duportail, a Frenchman serving as the army's chief engineer, as befitting his rank kept a guard of one sergeant, one corporal, and twelve privates, usually furnished from the sappers and miners in his corps.[9] Orders for Brigadier General William Woodford's brigade of May 26, 1777, at Middlebrook stipulated that one sergeant, one corporal, and twelve privates should "mount immediately as a Guard at General Woodford's Quarters. The Brigade Major will not receive any

Soldier for this Guard, or any other but what is Clean & dress'd in a Soldier like manner."[10] Standing guard for Woodford may not have been a satisfying experience. A disgruntled orderly sergeant signed off division orders of November 20, 1779, with "Beau Woodford Commander of the Virg Divis and the Damndest Partial Rascal on this earth without exception."[11]

Besides having the privilege of keeping a personal guard, generals and other officers as well were allowed to retain soldiers as servants. Those officers of means sometimes hired civilians as servants, and a few also had slaves to attend them. Civilian servants were entitled to army-issued rations and clothing.[12] The practice of using soldiers as officers' servants threatened to be a serious problem. Sometimes, wrote Brigadier General Otho Williams, the officers "detain Soldiers as waiters without permission."[13] Dr. Benjamin Rush, physician general for the Middle Department, in 1777 observed that "there are nearly as many Officers as men in our Army." Officers rode up to headquarters "with Soldiers behind them in the capacity of Servants." Even the surgeon and two mates of a regiment each had a "Servant drawn from ranks to attend them," who are "always exempted on this Account from camp and field duty."[14] An inspection report by General Steuben of Connecticut troops in 1779 indicated that of the "364 Men of these two Brigades Scattered about in small Detachments," more "than half of them are Employ'd as Waiters to the Staff Officers in and out of the Line."[15] A soldier in General Lachlan McIntosh's army in the Fort Pitt sector commented in October 1778 that "above one 20th part of our little army are employed as officers servants."[16]

Washington preferred that soldiers acting as servants should bear arms, especially when battle was impending. On September 20, 1777, general orders required that "all soldiers who wait on officers, be armed, and do the duty of soldiers on any emergency, particularly that the fire of so many men be not lost in a day of action."[17] Servants bearing arms were exempt from sentry and other camp duties but were expected to appear at parades and monthly inspections. For army servants not bearing arms, their only military obligation was to attend inspections.[18] Probably most soldiers in this category were very young and not adept at military skills; using them as servants removed nuisances from combat units. To limit a siphoning off of troops from the army, only field officers of regiments and corps could "take a Servant with them on Furlough."[19] At times, no officers' servants were permitted to leave camp.[20]

During 1780–82, orders went out restricting the number of servants that an officer could have. Relating to "Infantry, Artillery and all Corps serving on foot," a colonel was entitled to two servants without arms; a lieutenant colonel and a major, two each—one with arms and one without; and all other officers, surgeons, and mates, one each with arms. The regulations were almost the same for cavalry officers. There were no stipulations regarding major and brigadier generals of the line. Staff officers "belonging to Corps" had the following allocation: major and brigadier generals, four servants each, and all other officers, one each—all without arms. No one among the "civil staff" was allowed "to take a Soldier as a Servant."[21]

At an encampment, hundreds of soldiers did duty as sentries, guarding army storehouses, installations, and the quarters of the generals. As the army came upon a projected campsite, the scene resembled a "land rush" as generals and officers and staff department heads sent men forward to claim the use of local houses. Almost all the residences in the countryside or nearby village were selected for some kind of army use.[22]

"Plans of quarters are unknown," wrote General De Kalb. "The quarter-masters-general provide quarters for the commander-in-chief and for themselves, but for nobody else. The other generals, even some of the officers, take their quarters where and as they please and can. For this purpose thousands are often to be seen hastening on in advance of the army."[23] Some field officers wound up living in huts or tents. Competition developed over attempts to secure adequate quarters. Near Morristown, in late December 1779, General William Maxwell was miffed that two Pennsylvania officers, Colonel William Butler and Major Thomas Church, had appropriated living space that Maxwell expected to occupy. Maxwell requested General Nathanael Greene, the quartermaster general, "to order my quarters to be cleared as soon as possible." The New Jersey general mentioned that he had been living in one room, eighteen feet by fourteen feet, "where the Brigade Chaplain, my Aid De Camp and myself eat, drink, sleep and keep our baggage."[24]

On the morning of December 19, 1777, as Washington's army was marching the last few miles before reaching Valley Forge, Brigadier General George Weedon, a tavern keeper and now commander of a Virginia brigade, dispatched an officer to find quarters. Abijah Stephens, a Quaker, and his family were startled when the officer came up to their home along Trout Run in Tredyffrin Township and wrote on the door "General George Weedon." The visitor said that the general and his guard would arrive later in the day.

Although not having anticipated the army would settle in their neighborhood, the Stephens family began to prepare to receive hungry soldiers. They baked buckwheat cakes and concocted a large amount of beef broth by boiling "scraps, shins and other pieces of beef"; to the liquid were added the buckwheat cakes and vegetables. Soon, chilled and hungry soldiers appeared and were invited into the Stephens house, where they were rewarded with hot nourishment. Unfortunately, before the soldiers had finished eating, General Weedon arrived, and furious that riffraff had invaded his new quarters, ordered the soldiers out of the house. Mrs. Stephens, not to be deterred from feeding the soldiers, invited them to return and fed them out on the lawn.

While Weedon stayed at the Stephens home, his soldiers cut down trees and fences, which were used for fuel and construction of huts. Utensils and other property were stolen. Weedon kept a "strong guard" at his quarters. Even on "the most inclement nights," the guardsmen walked around in the yard. Often in the night, members of the Stephens family, from the second floor (Weedon occupying the first), threw out food to the men on watch.[25]

To a young enlisted man, another general seemed uncaring for his troops. Corporal Lemuel Roberts observed that, in June 1780,

> On our arrival near Morristown, general M'Dougal requesting a guard to escort him in, I turned out as one, and we marched with him nearly ten miles, where he put up with a militia Col. leaving his guard to shift for themselves, in the open air, and this too after having trotted a considerable part of the way on his horse, and consequently having kept his guard in smart motion.

In the evening, Corporal Roberts found himself as a

> sentry at the general's door, and feeling resentful for his unfeeling conduct, I kept such a stamping on the loose boards of the stoop, as to prevent his sleeping, and at length he sent the colonel out to still me: This gentleman, judging rightly of the existing facts, came out with a case bottle of whiskey, which he left with me for the service of the sentries on the stand, with a request that they would be as still as possible, and his politeness very much favored the churlish general's repose.[26]

A detail of men serving as a guard for a general was expected to present a smart appearance. This, however, was not always the situation. In January

1778, General Anthony Wayne, accompanied by his guard, went to Lancaster, Pennsylvania, site of the clothier general's department, in hopes of securing clothing for his troops. Lieutenant Colonel William S. Smith, commandant of the barracks at Lancaster, noted that in "passing by" Wayne's quarters he "observed the Guard stationed at the Generals Door, without their Uniform Coats & Hats on . . . absolutely disgracing the Regiments they belong to."[27]

General Nathanael Greene was one general who did not always keep a full guard. While serving as quartermaster general, however, he had a standard-size guard. In September 1779, the asthmatic Rhode Islander's ire was raised when he learned that the sergeant of his guard had been arrested and jailed on a complaint of Captain Andrew Irvine, adjutant of a Pennsylvania regiment. The cause of the action was owing to two members of Greene's guard, in a "Breach of a Division order," performing "in a Meniel office by Carrying Beef from the Commissary's."[28] The soldiers had simply served on a detail under staff rather than line authority. Greene took to task the regimental commander, Colonel Walter Stewart, for permitting interference with his command. "No order given an inferior can affect a superior," said Greene, "every Guard sent to a General Officer is entirely under his command, and [is] to obey his orders until relievd."[29]

There was one instance of a brigadier general refusing to supply a guard to his superior, a division commander. Major General Stirling complained to Washington that bad blood existed between himself and his second-in-command, Brigade Commander Thomas Conway. Stirling considered that Conway had a habit of "behavior unbecoming an Officer." As the main army made its way southwest of Philadelphia about September 1, 1777, to engage the enemy, Stirling complained to Washington that Conway had forbidden the brigade major, Captain William Barber, to obey any order from Stirling unless approved by Conway. When Barber relayed Stirling's request for Conway to provide Stirling with a general's guard of one sergeant and twelve men, "the Answer was, 'Tell my Lord I do refuse the Guard.'" Shortly afterward, when "a like written order" was submitted, Conway "put it in his pocket without paying the least attention to it." Stirling told the commander in chief that Conway showed "determination to disobey my orders."[30] It is not known how the Stirling-Conway impasse was resolved. In defense of Conway, about this time he had been given temporary command of Stirling's division by Washington because Stirling was suffering from a bad case of rheumatism.[31] With the army about to do battle, Conway was concerned about drawing any further manpower from his feeble brigade because a number of his men had just been transferred to a light infantry unit.[32]

To spare the use of prime soldiers, sometimes mostly boys made up a general's guard. The Connecticut regiment of Colonel Return Jonathan Meigs was ordered in November 1778 to furnish General Alexander McDougall's guard a "Sober Sergt. 2 Corporals and 24 Privates Small Boys Such as are least able to endure the winter Cold."[33] At Newburgh, New York, in July 1782, General Edward Hand, the adjutant general, wrote Colonel Walter Stewart that

> Baron Steuben has lately selected me a Guard of Boys, who being too young and small to do duty in the line . . . he has drawn a sergeant from the 2d Connecticut regt. and referred me to you for a corporal. . . . he should be one who is in some measure incapable of Field duty— he at the same time should be a sober steddy man to keep the boys in order & if he be capable of instructing them in reading and writing it may contribute to the good of the Service.[34]

On the basis of its impracticality, Washington sometimes intervened to deny or reduce a general's guard. As General Charles Lee, who had been organizing defenses in New York City, was about to set off to assume command of the Southern Military District in March 1776, he was told by Washington to leave his guard behind. Washington, with his headquarters still at Cambridge, Massachusetts, was looking forward to moving the army to New York City. "You mention nothing of the Guard that went with you from hence," wrote Washington. "As it will create great confusion in the Regimental Accounts, and they can be of no great Service to you—I must beg you will let them remain in New York where they will be soon join'd by their respective Regiments."[35]

In November 1782, General McDougall, after being relieved of the command at West Point, though still in charge of a division, suffered a flare-up of his rheumatism while staying at his headquarters at the Robinson house across from West Point. Washington could see no reason for McDougall to keep a full general's guard. The commander in chief wrote General Henry Knox, then commandant at West Point, that although "it will not be best to withdraw" the guard entirely, the size of the guard could be lessened.

Washington asked Knox to arrange with McDougall "in a friendly manner" for a guard made up of a small detachment of Connecticut soldiers or invalids.[36]

Colonel Moses Hazen, who commanded a Canadian regiment of brigade size, thought he was entitled to a general's guard. While in charge of the army post and supply center at Fishkill, New York, in January 1780, he sought to establish his own guard. This action Washington vetoed: a "Colonel's guard of a serjeant and twelve" was "contrary to regulations."[37]

A breach in security by a guard could put a general's safety in peril. In June 1776, with American forces being pushed out of Canada by a strong British offensive, General John Sullivan with his newly arrived brigade waited at Chambly, across the St. Lawrence River on the Richelieu River, not far from Montreal, expecting soon to link up with the retreating rebel force. General Benedict Arnold, withdrawing from Montreal, sent eighteen-year-old Captain James Wilkinson to Sullivan's camp to warn of impending attack by the enemy. Wilkinson came into Sullivan's camp during a heavy rainstorm at night and discovered all of Sullivan's troops sleeping, and no sentinels posted anywhere. Sullivan was at an unguarded headquarters in conference with his chief subordinates.[38]

On the morning of December 13, 1776, Major General Charles Lee had the misfortune of being captured by a scouting party of thirty light dragoons led by Lieutenant Colonel William Harcourt. Washington had been urging Lee and his three-thousand-man force to move from the Highlands and link up with the main army, which had retreated across the Delaware River. Lee delayed but at last began his march. With his own troops bivouacked three miles away, Lee took overnight quarters at the house of a widow at Basking Ridge, New Jersey, a short distance from Morristown.

As he and the army prepared to move on, Lee lingered to finish a letter to General Gates. All of a sudden, Major James Wilkinson, who had dropped by to bring a dispatch from General Gates, called out to Lee, "Here, Sir are the British Cavalry." Lee responded, "Where is the guard? Damn the guard, why don't they fire?" Turning to Wilkinson, he said, "Sir, see what has become of the guard." Looking out the window, Lee saw the guard, which had been quartered in an outbuilding and was totally surprised by the attack, being driven "in different directions." Two of the guardsmen were killed and two wounded. With Harcourt threatening to burn down the house, Lee surrendered. His legs and arms pinioned to a horse, Lee was delivered to a jail at the British post at New Brunswick, and on January 1, 1777, was confined at the prison in city hall, New York City.[39] Although he could have been charged with treason, having been on a British army pension, he was given prisoner of war status and was exchanged in May 1778. Presumably, some members of Lee's guard escaped.

Another daring raid succeeded in overcoming a general's guard. A group of Loyalist refugees, consisting primarily of Wiert C. Banta, Nathaniel Biggs, John Mason, James and Richard Smith, and Thomas Ward, all experienced banditti, were sent out by the British command in New York City to rob the Continental army mails. Instead of mere mail robbery, the band pulled off one of the boldest feats of the war. Banta and his five associates (others in the party refused to press on) crept into the American encampment located at Kakiat and vicinity, Orange County, New York. The intruders were originally looking for mail allegedly delivered to the Harding house in Kakiat. They learned from a Tory, however, that the mail had not arrived but that General Sullivan was staying at the Harding house. As the banditti came near the house, they spotted a sergeant and twelve soldiers, members of a general's guard, "making themselves merry," and were able to disarm them. Inside the house, the intruders found, not General Sullivan, but Colonel Joseph Ward, mustermaster general of the Continental army, and the deputy mustermaster general, Colonel William Bradford. The two American officers were made prisoners, and acting upon information provided by a servant, Banta and his associates went out to the barn where they seized the muster rolls of the army. Mounted on horseback, the invaders and their two prisoners rode hastily out of camp into the woods and finally reached a boat that had been hidden in a creek that emptied into the Hudson River. The captors, a scant moment ahead of their pursuers, navigated across the river and brought their prisoners and the important papers to British authorities in New York City.[40]

There may have been other instances of a general's guard being assaulted by the enemy. But if posted inside camp, there was not much likelihood of having to fend off an attack. The makeup of a general's guard was improvisational, usually with soldiers answering the call for this duty. For battle action, guardsmen returned to their line units. From brief service in a general's guard, soldiers did not gain any special identity or status privileges.

7

Camp and Quarter Guards

"The camp and quarter guards," noted Baron von Steuben in his *Regulations*, "are for the better security of the camp, as well as for preserving good order and discipline."[1] These guards, ordinary and interior, in contrast to those who were extraordinary and exterior, were but a part of the extensive guard system that at any given time involved the service of more than one-fourth of the Continental army.

There were also numerous "detached Guards," who watched over all kinds of army property, such as commissary stores, livestock, horses, quartermaster supplies, magazines, artillery, and installations. Guards protected officers and escorts and secured American soldiers under arrest and prisoners of war. Many of the guards were pickets—soldiers posted near and far from the camp for the purposes of early warning and sounding an alarm in the event of any contact with the enemy, helping to police the countryside, and guarding access routes, such as roadways and bridges.[2]

Most of the soldiers who went on detached guard duty first had to assemble as the main guard, which may be defined as "the principal guard from which the necessary details for minor or special guards are made."[3] Each brigade had a main guard, usually consisting of one captain, two subalterns, two or three sergeants, two or three corporals, one drummer, and forty to fifty privates. Usually, the brigade main guards of a single division joined together to form the main guard of the camp, with rotation daily by division. The main guard, therefore, was quite large. When a division was detached from the rest of the army, it had its own main guard. General Benjamin Lincoln's division, posted at four locations in the vicinity of Bound Brook, New Jersey, on May 13, 1777, had a main guard of 289 men.[4]

Soldiers drawn for detached guard duty were formed daily on the regimental parade ground and inspected by the regimental adjutant, and then they were conducted to the brigade parade ground, where they were reviewed by the brigade major. Finally, they were sent to form the main guard on the grand parade ground, where they were reviewed by the brigadier general of the day and field officers of the day. At the grand parade, the new guards were exercised in various elements of their drill before being separated into different guard detachments. "One Man of each Detail Guard" was "sent to the Grand Parade to Pilot the New Guards to the Relief of the Old ones."[5] At the end of each grand parade, the parole and countersign were given to all the guards.[6] Frequently, guards were equipped with a half-pike, a round wooden pole, six feet six inches long, with an iron blade ten inches long, pointed and flat, at one end; the blade was sharpened all around. This spear, similar to the officer's spontoon, had a sling attached so that it could be carried from the shoulder.[7]

Sometimes, a grand parade for changing of the detached guards was not held. Major General De Kalb, commanding a division at Valley Forge, refused to call a grand parade. Writing to the Comte de Broglie, De Kalb said that he would "never unnecessarily increase the troubles of the soldiers, nor keep them under arms to no purpose." The assembling and the mounting of the guard "is done so slowly, that it generally consumes two hours." De Kalb described a grand parade:

> When the troops are drawn up in order, the officers of the guard and those commanding the pickets post themselves opposite the line on horseback. The drummers then march solemnly down the front from left to right, beating the drums all the time. Then they make a wide detour, and repeat the performance in the rear of the troops, until they halt on the right of the line. At this moment the command to march is given, and the troops pass in review before the officers. You must understand that the whole parade, headed by the general, makes a circuit around the little cluster of horsemen, and then, before setting out to mount guard, range themselves again on the ground from which they started, a march which occupies at least three-quarters of an hour. How sad, that troops of such excellence and so much zeal, should be so little spared and so badly led.[8]

A house or hut was set aside for use of the main guard, to shelter reserves waiting to be assigned or those returning from guard duty. There were other guardhouses as well, for the use of those serving as regimental or brigade guards. A guardhouse, sometimes more than one building, was also used as a place of detention for arrested soldiers. Guardhouses were often notoriously unclean. General orders for July 24, 1775, reported that "the main Guard room is kept abominably filthy and dirty." In General McDougall's division, stationed at Peekskill in summer 1777, "much Damage" was "done by the Main Guard to the House in which it is kept, by Cutting the Pillars of the Piaza" and "cutting up the Floor." McDougall issued orders that "strictly enjoins . . . the Main Guard & every other Guard to take Special Care not to injure the Houses in which they keep or the adjacent Buildings under severe Penalties." "Old" guards had to clean the premises of a guardhouse before being relieved by a "new" guard; officers of the day were also required to make sure the guardhouses were kept clean.[9]

Private Daniel Granger, merely thirteen years old, stood his first guard while serving with troops besieging Boston in December 1775. He was "marched off to the Main Guardhouse," where he awaited his turn as a sentry. After standing guard from 10:00 P.M. to midnight on a hill "where the Wind blew extremely cold," he was relieved and went back to the guardhouse for respite before standing guard again. There "was a good fire, & as soon as I got warm, I wrapped my Blanket round me, lie down on the cold wet floor, my Pack for a Pillow, and then slept, but some scuffled and wrassled all night rather than to sleep on a wet floor."[10] Washington became exasperated at the "unsoldierlike" appearance of so many men who showed up for guard mounting. General orders stressed that the new guardsmen should be shaven and have clean hands and faces, hair combed and powdered, and clean clothes.[11]

The camp guard was not detailed from the main guard; rather, it was posted after being drawn up on the brigade parade ground. It served "to keep good order and discipline, prevent desertions, and give the alarm."[12] The camp guard provided the chain of sentinels stationed around an encampment.[13] The camp guard was formed by combining brigade camp guards, each of which normally consisted of a subaltern, one or two sergeants, one or two corporals, one drummer, and twenty-seven to thirty-six privates.[14] Officers of the day jointly with the adjutant general decided on the number of sentries needed to be drawn "from each Regiment sufficient to keep up the Chain."[15] Whenever a gap existed between brigade camp guards in the chain, the major general commanding the division was to order up additional camp guards.[16]

The chain of camp guard sentinels surrounded a camp at the distance of three hundred paces. These guards were stationed within the hearing of each other.[17] According to regulations, "a Captain from the Division" was "to be appointed daily as officer of the day for the Camp Guards," who should "visit them by day and go the rounds by night."[18] Also, field officers of the day, with an escort not to exceed a sergeant and six men, were to pass the chain of sentinels and make the "grand rounds" (from midnight to dawn) to check on pickets and other outguards. There were also "visiting rounds" conducted "at intermediate periods between sunset and sunrise." All guards were expected to challenge anyone approaching by demanding that the countersign be given.[19]

For the camp guard (chain of sentinels) as well as other guards, the officer of the guard, every half hour after the beating of the tattoo until reveille, was to call out to a sentry, "All's Well!" The "Sentry next him" then passed the call "to the next Sentry on the right & so on from Sentry to Sentry till the whole have cryed All's-Well!"[20] The alternative to repeating this call was to sound the alarm. Captain Enoch Anderson reported one humorous situation. He had established a chain of sentinels about a town, instructing the sentinel on the right to cry "All's Well!" every half hour, with the other guards following suit. When Anderson returned to his quarters, he could not "sleep a wink." Instead of crying "All's Well!" every half hour, the sentinels "began to cry it every ten minutes, and at last constantly on, which made a constant bellowing and a great noise." Eventually, Anderson sent soldiers to relieve the sentinels, giving them the same order to give the call every half hour. But the new guards "were worse than the others! Suffice it to say, that throughout the whole night this bawling of 'all's well' was kept up by these young soldiers."[21]

A fifteen-year-old private in a Connecticut regiment had a close call in 1776 while serving in a chain of sentinels of nearly two hundred men.

> I was upon my post as sentinel about the middle of the night. Thinking we had over-gone the time in which we ought to have been relieved, I stepped a little off my post towards one of the next sentries, it being quite dark, and asked him in a low voice how long he had been on sentry. He started as if attacked by the enemy and roared out, "Who comes there?" I saw that I had alarmed him and stole back to my post as quick as possible. He still kept up his cry, "Who comes

there?," and receiving no answer, he discharged his piece, which alarmed the whole guard, who immediately formed and prepared for action and sent off a non-commissioned officer and file of men to ascertain the cause of alarm.

They came first to the man who had fired and asked him what was the matter. He said that someone had made an abrupt advance upon his premises and demanded, "How comes you on, sentry?" They next came to me, inquiring what I had seen, I told them that I had not seen or heard anything to alarm me but what the other sentinel had caused. The men returned to the guard, and we were soon relieved, which was all I had wanted.[22]

Private Joseph Plumb Martin recalled another incident while serving on camp guard in 1777. "We kept a considerable chain of sentinels," said Martin. During the night an officer, "attended by a small escort" went on "visiting rounds." The officer examined all the sentinels. He found one sentry "who had stowed himself away snugly in an old papermill; another had left his post to procure a draught of milk from the cows in a farmer's yard, and others were found, here and there, neglecting their duty." All the delinquents were arrested and held for courts-martial. When the officer came up to Private Martin, the young Connecticut soldier demanded from him the countersign, which was given, and the officer moved on. Martin congratulated himself for properly doing his duty. The next morning, Martin was "posted at the colonel's marquee door" when the officer who had inspected the sentinels the night before went into the tent and, with Martin eavesdropping, told the colonel that during his rounds he had come upon a sentinel "who challenged me like a man." But, the officer continued, although he thought he had "found a soldier after detecting so many scoundrels," no sooner had he given the man (Martin) the countersign than "the puppy shouldered his piece, and had I been an enemy I would have knocked his brains out." Martin was devastated by the officer's remark but realized that the "admonition" had made him a better soldier.[23]

Penalties became more severe for dereliction of duty while on sentry duty. Death was meted out for sleeping and desertion while on guard duty.[24] A sentry quitting his post without orders or retreat of the army was "to be instantly Shot down."[25] Sitting or leaning on a post while on guard duty brought a whipping of at least twelve lashes.[26] Allowing a person to approach without giving the countersign also could lead to corporal punishment of the negligent sentry.[27]

"The privileges of guards and especially of sentries," noted Washington, "are very extensive in every Army, and it is necessary for the sake of order and security that they should be held inviolable," but "at the same time any disorders they commit are doubly culpable and ought to be more severely punished in a legal course." In May 1779, at the Middlebrook encampment, Washington disapproved of the court-martial acquittal of two army captains who had beaten several sentries while they were on duty. "Inflicting personal punishment for personal insult," Washington said, would establish a precedent "subversive of all military discipline."[28] However, he did not order a retrial.

Sentinels in the camp guard spelled each other for six-hour shifts during a twenty-four-hour period. General Steuben's *Regulations* describe the manner for changing of the guard. When the relief guard arrives at its destination, both it and the old guard present arms. The officers of both guards meet and then return to their guards. All sentinels are then ordered to "*Shoulder—Firelocks!*" The noncommissioned officers of both guards then "advance in front of the new guard." The sergeant of the new guard

> tells off as many sentinels as are necessary; and the corporal of the new guard conducted by a corporal of the old guard, relieves the sentinels, beginning by the guard house.
>
> When the sentinel sees the relief approach, he presents his arms, and the corporal halting his relief at six paces distance commands, *Present—Arms! Recover—Arms!*
>
> This last command is only for the sentinel relieving, and the one to be relieved; the former immediately approaching with the corporal, and having received his orders from the old sentry, takes his place; and the sentry relieved marches into the ranks, placing himself on the left of the rear rank.
>
> *Front—Face!* Both sentries face to the front. The corporal then orders *Shoulder—Firelocks! Support—Arms! March!* and the relief proceeds in the same manner till the whole are relieved.
>
> If the sentries are numerous, the serjeants are to be employed as well as the corporals in relieving them.
>
> When the corporal returns with the old sentinels, he leads them before the old guard, and dismisses them to their ranks.

The officer of the old guard then forms his guard in the same manner as when he mounted, and marches them in order to camp.

As soon as he arrives in the camp, he halts, forms the men of the different brigades together, and sends them to their respective brigades, conducted by a non-commissioned officer, or careful soldier.

When the old guard march off, the new guard present their arms, till they are gone, then shoulder, face to the left, and take the place of the old guard.[29]

The sentinels of the camp guard had to be constantly vigilant to prevent enlisted men without passes from leaving or entering camp. Sentries allowing such a breach were to be punished for disobedience of orders.[30] Local inhabitants with passes were permitted access to camp until 10:00 P.M.[31] Because "many suspicious persons" were "frequently seen lurking in and about Camp," general orders in April 1780 required guards "to take up and examine all Strangers" who entered camp or its vicinity without passes or other authorization and "send them to the Officers of the Day for particular examination who will either dismiss or confine them as circumstances may require."[32] During daytime, when soldiers were not on duty and there was no impending enemy attack, they were usually allowed to roam to a distance of one mile from camp. Marauding in the countryside continued throughout the war as a major problem and was met by stern measures. Sentinels were expected to be always on the alert to intercept soldier-plunderers. For example, in August 1781, general orders stated that "Camp guards are to stop, & critically examine all Soldiers coming into Camp with ears of Corn," and "when a satisfactory account is not given that it was honestly obtained, confine & report them."[33]

Efforts were made from time to time to curtail soldiers from "Continually Strolling from their Encampment." Frequent roll calls were the main solution. General Horatio Gates's orders of June 3, 1778, which insisted that regular roll calls be conducted and that absentees be "strictly" punished, cautioned, "Ruine dwells next door to Security."[34] The roll calls lightened the burden of the soldiers in the chain of sentinels, with fewer men leaving camp. Gates also ordered, in November 1782, that "if a commanding Officer of a regiment suspects that soldiers have left their companies in the night to go marauding, he will order a Catch roll to be called, turning all the men out upon the regimental Parade." Those who were absent were "to be punished at Troop beating."[35]

While the camp guard had the responsibility of guarding the perimeter of an encampment, the quarter guard attended solely to internal security. "The Design of a Quarter-Guard," according to British practice, similar to that of the Americans, "is rather for preserving the Peace and Tranquillity within the Regiment, by quelling all Disputes that may arise, either between Officer and Officer, or amongst the Soldiers, than for a Security against the Enemy." The quarter guard, however, should be on the alert for any enemy parties that might try to penetrate the camp.[36]

The quarter guard did not participate in the guard mounting at the grand parade. Sentries of a quarter guard stood watch five to six hours during a twenty-four-hour period. Every regiment had a quarter guard. Although General Steuben's *Regulations* favored a quarter guard of one corporal and nine privates, the normal composition was one subaltern, one or two sergeants, one or two corporals, a fifer and drummer, and eighteen to twenty-seven privates.[37] Quarter guards stood about eighty yards in front of each regiment, "directly opposite to the Center of their own Regiments, facing them."[38]

During nighttime, about ten men of the guard were posted at the rear of the regiment. These soldiers were to make sure that the sutlers' booths were closed and to guard horses, wagons, and other equipment belonging to the regiment and any nearby storehouses.[39] An hour after the sounding of retreat, the officer of the quarter guard sent a sergeant and six men to see that soldiers had extinguished all lights. Such a patrol checked on sentries one hour after a change of guard, which meant, with a tour of guard duty being two hours, sentries were visited every hour; this arrangement lasted until dawn. The quarter guard was to quell any "Noise or Disturbance in the Regiment" and to apprehend any soldier going away without leave or who was drunk or was caught selling or wasting supplies or equipment.[40] The officer of the quarter guard, or in his stead a sergeant or corporal, each morning sent a report to the "officer of the Camp Guard," who then answered to the brigade commander.[41]

Several enlisted men described their experiences while performing duty in the quarter guard. Private Simeon Lyman, on November 4, 1775, in the American lines before Boston, commented:

> I was on quarter guard, and I stood 6 hours[,] 2 hours at once, and there was one that was drunk and they put him under guard, and I had to keep him 2 hours and he would try to get out, and I stood with my gun and bayonet and he would crowd on it, and I pricked him

and he would swear, and the sergeant told me to keep him in the house, and he would not go, and I pushed him down and bid him to stand, and he would swear and damn us all, and, about 10 o'clock he [I?] was relieved.

Three days later, Lyman also recorded in his diary, "I come on quarter guard and it rained all day, and I stood 3 times 2 hours in the night."[42]

One summer night in 1781, Joseph Plumb Martin, with Washington's army in the New York Highlands, and at last having been promoted to corporal, found himself in charge of a small quarter guard. Martin had not slept for more than twenty-four hours. He was allowed, therefore, to get some rest in between the relief of sentries. During the night, a sentry stopped several officers who were passing by.

The sentry called me up, and I took the strangers to our officers, where they went through an examination and were then permitted to pass on. I returned to my guard and lay down till called up again to relieve the sentinels. All this time I was as unconscious of what was passing as though nothing of the kind had happened, nor could I remember anything of the matter When told of it the next day, so completely was I worn down by fatigue.[43]

The quarter guard served as an interior chain of sentinels, complementing the camp guard. Quarter guardsmen were expected to pick up any unauthorized strangers in camp and to prevent soldiers from being away from their huts, tents, or barracks at nighttime. John Adlum, a seventeen-year-old soldier stationed at Fort Lee, New Jersey, in November 1776 had duty in a quarter guard that had to deal with officers who "were in the habit of going into the country after night afrolicking," contrary to orders of Brigadier General James Ewing. "The officer commanding the quarterguard (which was a subaltern's) would not stop or take them up on their return to camp." Major General Nathanael Greene had just arrived to assume command of the troops at Fort Lee. Ewing feared that Greene would blame him for the misconduct of the officers and therefore ordered the adjutant to solve the problem. The adjutant went to Private Adlum and said that Adlum would be promoted to corporal if he agreed to take charge of a quarter guard and apprehend the officers who were going out at night and hold them until "the brigadier disposes of them." No officer would be assigned to the quarter guard, and Adlum would have full authority. Adlum agreed and picked to go with him four well-seasoned soldiers who had deserted from the British army—two Englishmen and two Irishmen; these recruits "heartily despised" the officers and "would glory in having the opportunity" to arrest them.

The officers congratulated Adlum on his appointment and said they expected Adlum not to interfere with their coming and going. Despite Adlum's warning, several officers "went into the country." On their return, Adlum had them detained and took away their swords. One officer tried to resist arrest, and Adlum had him thrown into the guardhouse. When General Ewing came up, the arrested officer yelled to be let out. When the door was opened, the officer complained of "his hard treatment" and being robbed of his sword. All of the detained officers said in their defense that they thought that General Ewing's orders pertaining to leaving the camp applied only to enlisted men. Ewing replied that that was obviously not the case and told the officers that they should set a good example for their soldiers; it was intimated that any further such disobedience of orders would result in court-martial and being cashiered out of the army. Adlum did not want to release the most offending officer, threatening that he would complain to General Greene should this be done; but upon prompting by General Ewing, the culprit begged Adlum's pardon and said that he was thankful that he was not bayoneted when resisting arrest—an apology that the undaunted corporal accepted.[44]

The quarter guards, spread throughout a camp, established a police presence. Although the sentries of a quarter guard were stationed on the site of their respective regiments, the linkage of quarter guards made for a web in which a soldier would be ensnared if he wandered off the grounds that his unit occupied. At nighttime, at least, it was almost impossible for soldiers out drinking or bent on mischief or for unauthorized civilians to go very far before being challenged by guards. Even then, the camp and quarter guards were but parts of the police-security system.

8

Picket Men and Safeguards

Vigilance had to be exerted outside an army encampment not only as a protective shield to absorb the first shocks of enemy incursions but also to secure the adjoining countryside: to prevent spying, round up stragglers, thwart desertion, and protect citizens from marauding soldiers.

"Guards stationed at isolated areas contiguous to camps were called picket men," writes one historian.[1] The terms *picket* and *outguard* were often used interchangeably. More specifically, picket men were stationed close to camp, being concerned mainly with detecting and detaining deserters, stragglers, and other suspicious persons. Outguards, as such, were stationed further away, with their chief task being to watch for movements of the enemy.[2]

Large numbers of soldiers were "drawn out daily" as pickets. Understandably, as battle became imminent, many soldiers were actively engaged as pickets or outguards or held in readiness to relieve those on this duty. Thus, on September 10, 1777, the day before the battle of Brandywine, eight hundred men from four Continental divisions and four hundred troops from a militia division were called up as pickets/outguards. On September 15, as Washington's army prepared to confront the enemy at Warren Tavern, Pennsylvania, six hundred men were ordered to serve as out-of-camp guards, with each brigade contributing to this force "in proportion to its strength." At "every new incampment," the out-of-camp guards were posted by the major general of the day and the quartermaster general, "aided by other officers of the day."[3]

Unlike the sentinels of the camp guard who ringed a camp, a soldier who served as a picket/outguard was one of a group, from which individual sentries fanned out. A typical picket guard manning an outpost was nearly company size, consisting of a captain, one or two subalterns, two to four sergeants, two to four corporals, a drummer, a fifer, and fifty privates.[4] The picket groups were usually placed about a half mile from each other, with their sentries patrolling the distance in between.[5]

Steuben's *Regulations* set guidelines for picket duty.

> During the day, the sentinels on the out-posts must stop every party
> of men, whether armed or not, till they have been examined by the
> officer of the guard.

> As soon as it is dark, the countersign must be given to the senti-
> nels of the picquets and advanced posts, after which they are to chal-
> lenge all that approach them; and if any person, after being ordered
> to stand, should continue to approach or attempt to escape, the sen-
> try, after challenging him three times, must fire on him. . . .

> Whenever a sentry on an out-post perceives more than three men
> approach, he must order them to stand, and immediately pass the word
> for the serjeant of the guard; the officer of the guard must immediately
> parade his guard, and send a serjeant with a party of men to examine
> the party: The non-commissioned officer must order the command-
> ing officer of the party to advance, and conduct him to the officer of
> the guard: who, in case he is unacquainted with his person, and does
> not choose to trust either to his cloathing or to his knowledge of the
> countersign, must demand his passport, and examine him strictly; and
> if convinced of his belonging to the army, must let him pass.[6]

One soldier during the time of the Valley Forge encampment recalled
an unusual experience:

> One dark night he was on picket duty next to a thicket following the
> hard packed path left in the snow by the previous pickets, when he
> heard a noise in the thicket. He called out a challenge and on the third
> challenge he fired his gun. His gun fired instantly. . . . They beat the
> drums to arms and the whole camp was up at once. A deploy was
> thrown out and soon a shout went up that the intruder was found. It
> was a big fat steer killed by the sentry. The animal was butchered and
> fires sprang up all over the camp.[7]

All picket guards kept an eye open for soldiers who might wander away
from where they were supposed to be. In the Continental army, a straggler
was not only a soldier who left his place in a battle formation or on a march
but also who distanced himself from the immediate vicinity of a camp.
Washington defined stragglers as "all Soldiers found beyond the nearest

Pickets in front and on the flanks; and beyond the extent of one mile estimated from the center of the Encampment in the Rear, without furloughs
in the usual form, or proper passes."[8] Straggling was a problem throughout the war. Washington frequently called attention to it and insisted that
special efforts be made to prevent it. Dr. Benjamin Rush, on the road to
Trenton from Philadelphia in late summer 1777, noticed soldiers of Washington's army "straggling from our lines in every quarter without an officer."[9]
An exasperated commander in chief, from the army's encampment in Passaic
County, New Jersey, in June 1777 complained that "the whole country is
overspread with straggling soldiers with the most frivolous pretences, under which they commit every specie of robbery and plunder." He had the
same grievance some five months later.[10]

Increasingly, small squads of picket men were stationed on roads leading to camp and on bridges to intercept stragglers.[11] Brigades were expected
to post pickets to "prevent their Soldiers Straggling." Such a brigade squad
typically consisted of one subaltern, one corporal, and eight privates. These
squads were also to detain any "countryman" or others who were heading
for camp without "permission from the nearest Brigadier or Field Officer."[12]
For army stragglers, field officers of the day were authorized "to inflict discretionary punishment" without any recourse to judicial proceedings, "not
to exceed fifty lashes."[13] Corporal punishment could be meted out for any
soldier for simply staying outside of camp at nighttime.[14]

Picket guards were expected to arrest deserters, and sometimes squads
were stationed at places, such as bridges, for the express purpose of capturing deserters.[15] For soldiers picked up while attempting to join the enemy,
summary justice could be administered. Division orders for troops of General John Sullivan stationed at Princeton in June 1777 declared that officers commanding "out parties" could have any of their men who attempted
to desert and were captured "hanged or Shot on the Spot." Furthermore,
whenever "out Guards Discover any Soldier attempting to Desert to the
Enemy," they should "Immedietly fire on them & kill them on the ground,"
and any soldier near the advanced lines without a pass should be considered a deserter and "punished as Such without further evidence; that no plea
of Ignorance of orders may be offered in excuse."[16]

Enlisted men sought relief and relaxation by going outside camp when
they could. The situation caused not only the problem of men being away
without leave but also their yielding to the temptation of stealing from local

citizens and venturing such a distance as to be in peril of running into enemy scouting parties. Measures had to be taken to keep a watch on even the legitimate activities of soldiers outside of camp. Thus, for example, general orders for Georgia Continental troops at Fort Howe on the Altamaha River in July 1778 required that any hunting or fishing parties allowed out of camp had to be accompanied by an officer "to prevent their straggling."[17]

Although troops were led to nearby streams to bathe about once a week, swimming was frowned upon because it was believed that spending prolonged time in the water was unhealthy. When the army was near settled communities, nude soldiers frolicked around intentionally to provoke the sensibilities of local women. General orders in August 1775 declared that the "guards and sentries" at the Cambridge, Massachusetts, bridge were "to put a stop" to the soldiers' "running about naked upon the Bridge, whilst Passengers, and even Ladies of the first fashion in the neighbourhood" were "passing over it, as if they meant to glory in their shame."[18] General Nathanael Greene, in May 1776, banned his troops from nude bathing at a millpond on Long Island, New York; the men had gone swimming "in the open view of the Women and they came out of the water and run up to the Houses Naked with a design to Insult and wound the modesty of Female Decency."[19] In a similar situation, Washington was of like mind. General orders from headquarters at Morristown in July 1777 stated, "It being injurious to the health of the soldiers on account of the foulness of the water, and utterly inconsistent with decency, for them to bathe in the Mill-pond, by Howel's mill, near the highway leading from Head Quarters, to the Court House; that practice is absolutely forbidden; and the guard and sentries posted near thereto are to take up and confine all offenders."[20]

While on an expedition against the Indians in the backcountry of New York in summer 1779, General John Sullivan, "determined to prevent a practice so dangerous to the health of the troops" as excessive bathing, ordered all officers to "see that twenty lashes be instantly inflicted upon any soldier" found engaged in unregulated swimming; furthermore, the brigadier generals were "to order a Centinel or two at the most suitable spots in order to detect delinquents of this kind."[21] General Alexander McDougall, commanding troops near Peekskill, New York, in August 1779, being concerned that soldiers stayed "continually in the Water" for long periods of time, instructed the brigadier generals to "put one or more Centinels at the Places usually resorted to."[22]

Picket guards had the responsibility of preventing moving about in the countryside without passes. At Valley Forge, the guards had instructions to prevent enlisted men and officers from leaving camp without a permit from the commanding officer of a regiment.[23] All military personnel could not go beyond the first outguard, normally one mile from camp, without having a pass from an officer commanding part of the troops on the lines or a brigadier general of the day.[24] A soldier having a pass from the commanding officer of his "corps" could not travel beyond the one-mile limit unless he was on assignment to purchase provisions.[25] The only other soldiers permitted to pass outguards were those who carried discharge papers.[26] General Anthony Wayne, in September 1780, introduced a standardized form for passes given by regimental commanders of his brigade: "A. B. Soldier in the . . . Regt of Pennsylvania Has permition to go . . . Miles to the Right, Left, or rear of the army & return this evening before roll call, he behaving as becometh a soldier."[27]

Civilians from time to time were allowed to visit the army, and Washington let it be known that "people who are innocently bringing refreshments to Camp are to be encouraged."[28] But all would-be visitors had to be checked out. Washington's orders in June 1777 at Middlebrook, New Jersey, stated the usual procedure: "Any parties of whatever kind, coming towards an out-guard, are to be stopped by the out sentries, and notice given to the guard, which is in most cases to be turned out, and the officer to send a proper person to examine such party, and give his orders accordingly."[29] Any person "on pretence of business" was to be detained until "the Letter or verbal Message" he or she was "Charged with" was "communicated at Head Quarters."[30] Anyone deemed "suspicious" was to be sent to an officer of the day, who upon further examination would either release or confine the person in question.[31] Sometimes, "inspection stations," manned by a squad of soldiers, were set up near camp for the sole purpose of screening civilian strangers; those who were allowed to pass received a "short ticket."[32]

During the military campaign near Philadelphia in 1777, there was fear of "an inundation of bad women from Philadelphia" and also the straggling of soldiers. A guard, therefore, was placed "on the road between the camp and the city." After the British occupied Philadelphia, those women who were allowed to pass "the first guards" were informed that "they cannot return again."[33] These restrictions were justified on the grounds that among the city women admitted to camp there might be spies and those who would entice soldiers to desert.

Pickets and outguards had the duty of detecting and apprehending army stragglers who plundered citizens in the neighborhood. Soldiers were expected to inform on comrades whom they knew had been engaged in marauding.[34] Outguards and patrols were authorized in January 1780 to inflict as many as five hundred lashes (far above the legal limit of one hundred) on any soldiers caught despoiling citizens of their property.[35] Soldier-plunderers often managed to evade guards and make their way back to camp, but frequent knapsack inspections and roll calls to some extent reduced marauding. Courts-martial sometimes ordered death sentences for soldiers convicted of this crime.[36] Heavy whipping and even running the gauntlet through the whole army were among other penalties incurred for plundering.[37] The crime of stealing from local inhabitants was not merely robbery; it alienated citizens from the American cause and reduced volunteer material support for the army.

Safeguards—troops stationed at various places to protect citizens and their property—though greatly needed, were sparingly used by the American and British armies during the Revolution. Scarcity of manpower was a factor, but most important was the danger that safeguards would be eliminated by enemy forces. The British army had long employed safeguards. Such troops formed a corps in which members wore blue coats with two "Flower-de-luces" embroidered on them, one in front and the other on the back, both under the inscription "The King's Safeguards": therefore, they were "generally known by all," and soldiers knew that to "disturb" safeguards during the performance of their duties could result in being put to death. The main role of the British safeguards, as it was for their American counterparts, was to "hinder the Stragling Souldiers who go a pillaging."[38] In the American Revolution, British and Continental army safeguards were individuals or small squads detailed from regular units. On rare occasions, however, company-size detachments, usually light infantry, acted as safeguards.[39] Picket guards and patrols, in a sense, served as safeguards with the responsibility "to restrain the Soldiers" from committing actions "oppressive to the Inhabitants."[40]

With provisions often so scarce throughout the army, Washington encouraged farmers to sell produce near camp. Usually, someone from the

Quartermaster Department was present at the marketplaces to make sure there was no price gouging.[41] The sale of farm products was generally conducted outside but near the perimeter of the camp. These marketplaces were kept close by because soldiers sometimes beat up and plundered vendors, and also many enlisted men were in the habit of "disposing of their Clothing to Country People for Vegitables & other Articles." To prevent abuses by soldiers, "proper guards" under an "officer or officers" were appointed "to superintend" markets and "preserve good order." Typically, orders provided that at a marketplace a "Subaltern Officer with a small Guard" be stationed to "see that no Violence is offered to the Country People." Soldiers causing trouble at a market were sent to the guardhouse.[42]

Preventing troops from stealing from farmers or damaging their property remained a disciplinary priority during the war. When the American army moved to New York and vicinity in spring 1776, one of the first orders required "Officers commanding the Guards, in and near the encampment," to be "particularly attentive to prevent any waste, or depradation, being committed upon the Fields, Fences, Trees, or Buildings about the camp."[43] For trampling on pastures and crops by soldiers and especially by horses of the wagoners, "immediate punishment" was ordered to be "inflicted in the most Exemplary Manner." A June 1779 directive compelled "the Brigades near the Meadows & fields of Grain" to "furnish the Necessary Guards for their Preservation."[44]

Safeguards were needed in the attempt to deter soldiers during daytime from filching chickens, eggs, ears of corn and other vegetables, fruit, and even watermelons, sometimes at a distance as far as three miles.[45] Orders for the artillery corps at West Point in July 1780 declared that "the plucking of green apples from the orchards of the Inhabitants is absolutely forbidden." It seems that the main concern was that the apples otherwise were to be made into cider for use of the army. To prevent the theft of the apples, a guard consisting of a "careful Sergeant," two corporals, and sixteen privates was stationed "over the orchards in the vicinity of Headquarters."[46]

Like other sentries, safeguards could shoot to kill if a soldier ignored a warning to halt. One incident, which raised the question of justifiable homicide, came before a court of inquiry held in General Benjamin Lincoln's division on August 22, 1781, as the army, on the lower Hudson River, readied itself for the Yorktown campaign. The panel examined the case of Matthew Adams, an infantryman, who had been killed by John Lewis, while acting as a safeguard on the evening of August 20. Several witnesses appeared before the court of inquiry. The sergeant of the guard of which Lewis was a member testified that Lewis had called out that the corporal of the guard be sent to him in order to take into custody Adams, whom Lewis had stopped. The sergeant of the guard further said that he soon heard a musket fire and "went down himself to the Sentinel, & saw a man's Coat by the side of a fence with a quantity of green corn in it & a man lying near it." Asked why the sentinel had fired, the sergeant of the guard answered that Adams had tried to run away, fearing he would be confined.

> Question of the Court
>
> What orders had you given the Corporal to deliver to the Sentinel?
> Answer: To stop every person he might perceive in the Cornfield & detain them until he had called the Serjeant of the Guard.

Corporal William Thomas then informed the court that he had been corporal of the guard at the time of the incident, and that he had posted John Lewis as a sentinel in a cornfield, with orders to stop any soldier in the cornfield and hold them until he called out to the sergeant of the guard. Corporal Thomas heard Lewis "hail twice" and call the sergeant of the guard, who advised Thomas to go to the sentinel. As he was on his way, Thomas heard Lewis order a man to stop and then fire at him. When Thomas arrived at the scene, he discovered a coat filled with corn on the ground, and a man "lying about two rods from the Sentinel." The man (Adams), who was still alive, "said the Sentry had shott him for getting a little corn, & that he had left his coat with him."

Henry Turner informed the court,

> That he was carrying the Corporal some provisions & as he came up to the Sentry, John Lewis, he heard him tell a person he should not go till the serjeant of the guard came.
>
> That the Prisoner [the man shot] said he had not eat anything for two or three days & had only taken a few ears of Corn. That the Sentinel told him it was his orders & that he should not go.
>
> That at this time another person came up & the man who had the corn steped behind him & attempted to escape. That the Sentry told the other to stand out of the way & ordered him to stop but he not doing it. The Sentry fired & the man fell.

John Lewis, in his own defense, said that he had acted under orders and was to detain anyone, "except those who came to bring provisions to their Mess Mates." In recalling the tragic event, Lewis said,

> That he had heard somebody breaking corn & walked towards them, that the man immediately run & he after him, in which he dropped his coat & Corn & jumped over the fence into the road—that he ordered him to stand, which he did at first, said he was a brother Soldier & was hungry & offered him his [———?] if he would let him go & not call the Serjeant of the guard—That he told him he would keep him untill the Serjeant came for it was his orders—On this two men came up, & the man steped behind one of them, walked across the road & began to run—That he call'd to him to Stop, which he would not do—on which he fired at him.

The court of inquiry exonerated Lewis, who "acted as a good Soldier, & was within the line of duty in firing on, & killing" Adams.[47]

Safeguards were used mostly when there was considerable distance between fighting forces, and therefore the main concern was protecting citizens from depredations by soldiers of one's own army. In some instances, safeguards were liable to assault by the enemy if no agreement existed between belligerent forces to protect them. In the northern theater of the war, where troops were relatively stationary, it was easier to maintain safeguards than in the south, where freewheeling partisan warfare persisted. Despite the recognition of both sides of the need to establish "neutral" safeguards, nothing much was accomplished.

The single safeguard at "the widow Ravenel's plantation" in South Carolina "for the purpose of protecting her house" was accosted by American troops who took away his sword. The deputy adjutant general of the southern British army complained that "such improper behavior will be the means of preventing the General's protecting the peaceable, helpless families as he would wish to do without respect to party."[48] The British army was more inclined than the Americans to offer protection to the property of civilians, regardless of their loyalties. A good example of this is General Alexander Leslie's stationing a safeguard at a rice plantation along Goose Creek, South Carolina, belonging to John Parker, a staunch patriot. When American troops overran the area, General Nathanael Greene, glad that Parker could "derive any security from the humanity of the enemy," ordered the guard to continue. Greene, however, through his aide Ichabod Burnet, let it be known that "it is out of our power" to afford "extensive protection to the good people of this country."[49]

Army hospitals were supposed to be protected by both sides. Normally, a small guard was posted at a hospital. Washington preferred, when he could, to employ partially disabled members of the Corps of Invalids for this duty.[50] After the British evacuated Camden, South Carolina, on May 9, 1781, General Greene did not interfere with the keep of sixty-one incapacitated British soldiers who were left behind, even though a small British guard of "internal police" remained at the hospital.[51]

Friction developed between the commanders of the two southern armies over whether patients in an army hospital could be made prisoners of war. The British command expressed disgust that Colonel Hezekiah Maham and his South Carolina cavalry troops burned the British army hospital at Fair Lawn, South Carolina, meanwhile "dragging away a number of dying People, to expire in swamps." This was "inhumane conduct" and "a species of barbarity hitherto unbeknown in civilized nations—especially when that hospital has been left without a guard for its defense." The persons at the hospital should have been sent to British lines "to prevent their perishing for want of necessaries and medicines."[52] Maham defended his actions by noting that the hospital was only a half mile from a British garrison of fifty men, that at Fair Lawn abatis had been constructed, and that the site was used as a staging area for British troops going to and from Charleston.[53] Greene reserved judgment on Maham's treatment of the convalescents at Fair Lawn. He did, however, inform Colonel Alexander Stewart, who at the time commanded the British army in South Carolina, "That making those in hospitals prisoners is opposed to the practice of all civilized nations is not admitted where no agreement to the contrary exists between the belligerent powers or the commanding Officers." Although Greene also pointed out that making agreements to protect hospital patients was not in the "interest of a country invaded," he believed that humane treatment should be followed.[54] Safeguards could not really be effective unless underpinned by written agreements between commanders of the opposing forces. Even then, there was still the problem of regular and irregular troops not feeling they were bound by such constraints.

9

Temporary Police Patrols

Patrols in the Continental army often, in their primary or secondary missions, acted as military police. Generally, there were two kinds of patrols: "Information or reconnaissance patrols, whose mission is to gain information of the enemy, terrain, etc."; and "Security patrols, whose mission is to provide protection in camp, on the march, or line of battle." Security patrols not only checked the duty alert of guards but also searched for delinquent soldiers.[1]

In relation to policing the Continental army, temporary patrols—those constantly being replaced in the regular guard service, or those created for a specific objective to be quickly accomplished—could be distinguished from permanent police units, namely the provost guard and the Maréchaussée Corps (see chapters 12 and 13). Field officers of the day, periodically during nighttime, sent out patrols to visit pickets and outguards. Normally, "old and new" field officers of the day and commanding officers of patrols met together every morning at 10:00 A.M.; those officers going off duty made reports of the occurrences during their watch. The oncoming field officers selected the routes for the new patrols and gave the officers commanding them their instructions.[2]

The patrols connected to the guard system were selected from the main or camp guards and were sent out every hour between tattoo and reveille.[3] The patrols "issued orders, delivered food, checked security arrangements, and took prisoners to jail, but their major duty was to keep the guards alert."[4] General orders of June 12, 1777, stated that "visiting rounds should be going all night, to see that the sentries are at their posts—alert, and acquainted with every particular of their duty."[5]

In addition to being visited by patrols making the rounds, the guard units outside of camp themselves sent out squads to investigate activity in their immediate vicinity. Sergeant Ebenezer Wild, stationed at Warwick, Rhode

Island, in February 1779, recounted one night's patrolling by members selected from his guard unit. After roll call at sundown,

> I mounted guard with sixteen men under my command. I marched
> with my men about 2 miles towards the Point, where I left my guard.
> I sent a corporal and four men down to the Point, at 11 o'clk I sent a
> corporal and four men out as a patrolling party, which went down to
> the Point and all round the shore. They discovered nothing remark-
> able. Came in again about 1 o'clk, at which time I sent out another
> party, which went the rounds as before and came in about three o'clk;
> at which time I sent another party, which went the rounds as usual
> and came in between 4 & 5 o'clk, and then I sent another party, which
> patrolled till daylight and then came in with the other corporal and
> four men from the Point. I went to the commissary's and got a gill of
> rum pr man. After I gave it to them, I dismissed them.[6]

Like MPs (Military Police) of a later time, special patrols searched out
misbehaving soldiers. General Alexander McDougall thought it was incumbent upon himself to press members of his division toward greater spirituality. In October 1778, with no military action pending, the New York general ordered his troops to attend morning and afternoon prayer sessions. To
better achieve this goal, McDougall further ordered that "a *sober* sergeant's
Party . . . patrol the camp of their respective Brigades and take prisoners"
all enlisted men "as shall be found straggling about or making any noise or
disorder to the dishonor of God and the Division."[7]

Patrols were used to shut down unlicensed "tippling houses" in "the
Neighbourhood of the Army." General orders of May 26, 1778, at Valley
Forge required that a patrol, consisting of a subaltern, a sergeant, a corporal, eight privates, and a commissary from each brigade, should "be sent
immediately into the vicinity of their respective brigades to seize the liquors
they may find in the unlicensed tippling-houses." The commissaries were
to provide receipts for the confiscated liquors.[8] Legitimate "Houses of Entertainment," which accommodated "Travellers & Strangers" who "must
necessarily be in the vicinity of the Camp," were, however, protected.[9]

When opportunity beckoned, some soldiers liked to slip out of camp at
night to engage in a binge at some secluded spot. The revelry, however, often
attracted attention. Captain Joseph Bloomfield, deputy judge advocate

general with the northern (New York) army, on September 1, 1776, reported from Fort Dayton that "haveing notice that some of my Company were Drunk" across the Mohawk River and "had been absent all Night from Garrison," he ordered a corporal and four privates to cross the river and bring back the revelers. The patrol confronted five of the drunken men, who insisted they would not submit until their "frolic was over." In an ensuing scuffle, the corporal of the patrol knocked down one of the resistors, whereupon his companions, thinking him dead, finally submitted to arrest.[10]

Fortunately, the Continental army usually avoided being stationed in urban areas and hence did not have much of a problem with soldiers being "out on the town." When American troops did stay in or near a city or town, commanders, as did their British counterparts,[11] sent out nightly patrols to round up drunken servicemen from taverns and collar others on the streets or at houses of ill repute who were out past strict curfew. The situation in New York City was especially hazardous. The British had the worst of it, occupying the city from September 1776 to the end of the war. The great fire of September 1776 left many buildings burnt-out shells, which sheltered a variety of derelicts and homeless persons; loyalist refugees crowded into the city. At least five hundred prostitutes plied their trade among soldiers. Even during the brief American occupation of New York City during summer 1776, it was difficult to prevent soldiers from getting into trouble. When two soldiers were brutally murdered at the site of a house of ill repute, a military detachment had to be employed to restrain revengeful comrades from pulling down the building.[12]

Tight restrictions on soldiers' liberty were effective in fending off potential misbehavior by troops in settled areas. Enlisted men had to remain in quarters after tattoo (sometimes as early as 8:00 P.M.), and whenever they went out into a town, they had to have passes. Patrols were expected to "visit all the Taverns."[13] Despite restrictions, troops managed to carouse in a town. General Sullivan's orders for his army stationed near Providence, Rhode Island, September 19, 1778, expressed "grief and astonishment" caused by soldiers "strolling about the Streets in town and Country the whole night Dancing and revelling in Houses, Plundering the Inhabitants." The adjutant general was ordered to increase the main guard so that three patrols could be sent out "from tatoo beating till Day Break." Each patrol, covering different sections of the town and vicinity, were to "examine every House where there is Dancing and revelling and seize all Soldiers that may be found there after nine o'Clock in the Evening and Deliver them over to the Officer of the Day," who would then order each culprit to receive "39 Lashes on the Spot." A reward of $5 was offered to any citizen or soldier who would either apprehend or "even give information of any Soldier found out Contrary to these orders."[14]

General Benjamin Lincoln, with his army in Charleston, South Carolina, under siege in April 1780, faced the same situation that confronted Sullivan in Providence. Lincoln ordered his brigadier generals to send out patrols into different parts of the city. Each patrol, consisting of one subaltern, two noncommissioned officers, and ten privates, were to seize every soldier without a pass from his regimental commander. The officer commanding the patrol was required to have a delinquent "punished instantly with 30 lashes on his bare back."[15]

Army patrols searched for escaped military prisoners[16] and outlaws who committed depredations within the vicinity of an encampment. Troops put some of the bandits in the New York Highlands out of action during summer 1779.[17] From headquarters at New Windsor in May 1781, Washington ordered a patrol under Major Samuel Logan and several other officers and fifteen to twenty "picked men" to seek out "a gang of Villains in this neighborhood." The patrol was provided with provisions for three days.[18] Straggling continued to be a major problem for the army. Men away from camp or garrison were prone to become absent without leave, or worse—deserters or plunderers. The patrols selected from the camp guards or picket guards regularly conducted searches in the neighborhood of a camp for army personnel who had gone beyond the camp's perimeter without passes. The officers commanding the patrols detained stragglers and either had them whipped on the spot or delivered to their respective regiments for punishment.[19]

Special patrols to round up stragglers were sent out directly from the brigades. Normally, the "patrollers" were dispatched by the brigade major after tattoo. When Washington's army paused briefly at Pompton, New Jersey, in mid-November 1779, three brigades each supplied a patrol, consisting of two subalterns and thirty enlisted men, to secure several roads in order to prevent straggling. The patrol from General George Clinton's brigade, from 7:00 P.M. to dawn, covered every night the roads leading to the Ringwood Iron Works and Morristown. The men from General Enoch Poor's brigade patrolled the "streets" toward Smith's Clove. Similarly, the troops from General Edward Hand's brigade took to "the Streets Near the

Iron Works down below the Tavern on the road leading to Newwork [New-ark]." For this triple assignment, the officers commanding the patrols were to have all houses searched for soldiers and "to order such as May be found out" to be confined in the provost jail to await punishment.[20]

General Horatio Gates, commanding the right wing of Washington's army at New Windsor, in November 1782 ordered that each of his two bri-gades provide a patrol, consisting of one captain, one subaltern, two ser-geants, and twenty-four "Rank and file." One patrol moved to the right from the encampment, and the other to the left.

> All Prisoners they have apprehended are to be examined, and if found delinquent, punished immediately on the spot with any number of lashes not exceeding one hundred to each delinquent—Such as are detected with the goods of the Inhabitants in their possession are to be reserved to be tried for their lives by a General Court martial. The officers commanding these patroles are as soon as relieved to report to the field Officers of the day.[21]

It turned out that these patrols "in some instances" were "guilty of irregu-larities in the houses where they rendezvous"; it was therefore ordered that officers commanding patrols should not "halt at houses or suffer any of their party to go into them except Merely to search for Soldiers that may be con-cealed there, and such search may be always under the direction of a Com-missioned or Non Commissioned Officer."[22] Patrols were warned not to molest or steal from local inhabitants.[23] Just after his southern army entered Charleston in December 1779, General Benjamin Lincoln served notice that no patrol could enter the house of a citizen unless permitted to do so by a civil magistrate in order to "quell a disturbance of the public peace" or help put out a fire.[24]

Soldiers were not allowed to carry "arms or Accoutrements" out of camp, unless on duty. The discharge of a weapon outside camp brought a quick police response. Regimental commanders sent out patrols under noncom-missioned officers to seize such culprits.[25] At other times, the general of-ficer of the day dispatched patrols to detect and apprehend all stragglers with firearms, and "every soldier so detected" was to receive thirty lashes "at the head of the corps he belongs to without trial."[26] When Washington's army was in New York City during the summer of 1776, each brigade was "to furnish a Patrole every two hours in the daytime," consisting of a sergeant and six enlisted men, who were to range "at least two miles at the North-ward of their respective Camps to take up all soldiers whom they can find with fire arms out of Camp and endeavour to prevent their Committing any disorder whatever."[27]

Stragglers abounded after a military defeat. Troops became separated from their fast-retreating comrades. It was therefore important for the army to reclaim the stragglers as quickly as possible before they deserted or were captured by the enemy. An army in victory had little problem with strag-gling, as the winning troops were more likely to maintain unit cohesion while occupying the battleground. In the immediate aftermath of two bat-tles (Brandywine, September 11, and Germantown, October 4, 1777), the degree of straggling posed a very serious problem. One member of the Chester County, Pennsylvania, militia recalled that just after the battle of Brandywine, he and his comrades seized about 150 American stragglers, "who had fled from their colors and were making for home."[28] To stem the tide of fleeing soldiers who became separated from their units after that battle, Washington immediately ordered the brigade commanders to have officers go out on the roads connected to the site of the battle "and on any other roads where stragglers may be found" and "bring them back to the army"; a search should also be made in Wilmington, Delaware. On this mission, the officers would proceed as close to the enemy as possible "and examine every house.[29]

The commander in chief was also concerned that straggling soldiers were showing up in Philadelphia. He called upon the Pennsylvania government to take measures to return such absentees to the army. Citizens, he insisted, should be required to deliver up stragglers to patrols, which "will pass thro' the town," and if the stragglers refused to cooperate, then notice of their whereabouts were to be given to the patrols.[30] The Supreme Executive Council of Pennsylvania appealed to "the Inhabitants of the City & Sub-urbs" for cooperation, warning that anyone harboring army fugitives would be "prosecuted with the utmost severity according to Law."[31]

Even before the battle of Brandywine, patrols from Colonel Stephen Moylan's Fourth Regiment of Continental Dragoons were used to search for "straggling soldiers" on roads leading to Philadelphia.[32] After the battle of Germantown, "small parties of Horse" were ordered "up the different Roads above the Present encampment of the Army [Perkiomen, Pennsyl-vania] as much as 10 Miles" to "stop all Soldiers and turn them back to the

Army."[33] Few questions were asked of the postbattle stragglers, and they were not punished unless deemed to be attempting to abscond from the army.

Desertion was almost a daily occurrence in the Continental army. Nearly one-fourth of the Continental soldiers deserted during the war.[34] Washington frequently vented his exasperation. In January 1777, he wrote John Hancock, president of Congress, to pressure state assemblies to pass a law providing for "a severe and heavy penalty upon those who harbor deserters." Unless citizens could be forced to inform on deserters when they returned home, "we shall be obliged to detach one half of the Army to bring back the other."[35] Officers and men were regularly detailed to pursue and capture deserters. General Benjamin Lincoln, as a division commander, made a strong effort at recovery. He wrote the commander in chief in May 1777, when the army was readying to start a campaign: "In order to prevent in some measure the too frequent desertions, and to promote the safety of this camp I have detached a few companies of good faithful men on whom we can depend as well for their attachment to the cause as for their bravery and activity, to act as scouts by day and patrols by night, they being always in front will render desertion, at least, more difficult & hazardous."[36] Several months later, with the incidence of desertion unabating, Washington ordered "that the Inst a Soldier is missing," the commanding officer of the "Corps to which he belongs" should report the matter to his brigadier general, who would then "direct an immediate pursuit."[37]

While some deserters quickly made their way home or escaped to hideouts in remote places (such as the backcountry), others taking their leave from the army lingered in the neighborhood of a camp, being "secreted" by Loyalists. Colonel William Malcolm wrote Washington from his station in the New York Highlands that "the Number of Deserters which lurk among the disaffected hereabouts oblige me to employ a Number of men pursuing them."[38] Since deserters usually fled individually or in small groups, squads of three to twelve men were considered adequate to search for the fugitives and apprehend them.[39]

Regimental commanders sent out patrols to seek out deserters from their troops. For example, on January 22, 1777, Colonel William Thompson, commander of the Third South Carolina Continental Regiment, then encamped at Nelson's Ferry on the Santee River in South Carolina, appointed a patrol consisting of Captain Richard Brown, Lieutenant William Goodwin, one sergeant, and eight privates. The patrol, which was given a list of sixty-two soldiers who had deserted the regiment, was "well mounted & accoutred." The searchers, who were ordered to return to their regiment on February 4, 1777, were to go "to such places as you think most likely to apprehend" any of the deserters from the regiment and "if necessary apply to a Magistrate & procure his warrant to search suspected haunts, break open & Enter houses." For every deserter seized, the state offered a $50 reward.[40]

Sergeant Joseph Plumb Martin recounted his experience in summer 1782 of attempting to track down deserters. Martin's Connecticut regiment had paused briefly at the Hudson River near King's Ferry, opposite Peekskill, New York. Three of his comrades, all "Old Countrymen," deserted and were expected to be heading for the British army in New York City. Martin and nine men were sent to overtake the fugitives before they reached their destination. The patrol especially was expected to search carefully the English Neighborhood, a wooded stretch of land forty-five miles to the south, between the Hackensack and Hudson Rivers, an area "infested" by Loyalists. The patrol "traveled so Hard" that six of the nine men had to drop out. Martin failed in his mission and, upon his return, was again sent out with twelve men to search for the same deserters. The fugitives managed to stay a short distance ahead of the patrol before finding refuge on Haverstraw Mountain, north of the English Neighborhood. Thus, Martin "had another useless and fatiguing expedition for nothing."[41]

Arresting deserters was a dangerous assignment. If captured, the culprits faced corporal punishment and possibly execution. Still, it is surprising to find so few reported violent confrontations. Most captives quietly submitted. One who did not was a Private Clefford, who deserted from the Second Rhode Island Continental Regiment in October 1779. Colonel Israel Angell sent Sergeant Noah Chaffee and Private John Gould to arrest Clefford; a local boy went with the two searchers to point out the house where Clefford was known to be hiding. Upon breaking into the house, Gould chased Clefford up the stairs. Clefford shot Gould in the head with a pistol, and the "boy that was with them ran off Screaming." Fortunately, the pistol ball did not "break" into Gould's skull. The intended prisoner, however, escaped.[42]

Scouting parties were expected to apprehend any deserters they ran across.[43] If a soldier deserted from a scouting party and was retaken, the officer in command was to cause the offender "to be hanged or Shot on the Spot."[44] The army constantly sent recruiters back to their home area, where they had the extra duty of seizing deserters. In spring 1779, Lieutenant William

Reynolds and four enlisted men went to York County, Pennsylvania, in search of recruits and deserters. At Hanover, the patrol entered a tavern where they seized as a deserter Daniel May, who had refused to enlist. The army group tied up May. A local magistrate, Daniel Messerly, who had been summoned by the tavern keeper, arrived and declared he was going to bring May to York, where the issue would be settled. Messerly, too, was bound by the soldiers. Reynolds and his cohorts were finally overpowered by other York County men and were thrown in jail.[45]

Patrols also on occasion pursued troops deserting en masse.[46] Of course, if the defection was large, the situation, in effect, became mutiny, and a sizable force was necessary to crush the rebellion. On May 22, 1780, thirty-one soldiers deserted from Fort Schuyler (near Rome, New York). The garrison's commander secured the services of forty Iroquois Indians to go after the deserters. Lieutenant Abraham Hardenbergh of the First New York Regiment accompanied the Indian search party. On May 24, the pursuers came upon sixteen of the deserters as they prepared to cross the Grand River; the other fifteen had already made it to the other side. The Indians exchanged arms fire with the fugitives on both sides of the river, killing thirteen deserters and capturing three. The deserters on the other side of the river refused to surrender. The next day, several Indians crossed the river and found that the deserters had scattered in different directions, leaving their food and packs behind.[47]

The nonpermanent police patrols of the Continental army were like a revolving door. Members were drawn in rotation from regular units. The short service for patrollers did not provide much policing experience or instill any special esprit de corps. For missions lasting several days or longer, the patrollers were entered on muster rolls as "On Command"—temporary duty, separate from their military units. The short-term patrollers, in their out-of-camp duty, acted as modern MPs in ferreting out their comrades who were disorderly or away without leave. An important function during the Revolutionary War was apprehending stragglers.

George Washington after the Battle of Princeton, January 3, 1777.
Painting by Charles Willson Peale, 1779–89. Oil on canvas.
Princeton University Art Gallery. Photo by Bruce M. White.

American Infantrymen in Different Uniforms. Sketch by Baron von Closen.
Library of Congress.

Baron von Steuben at Valley Forge, 1777. Painting by Augustus G. Heaton.
Courtesy National Archives, photo no. III-SC-83897.

The Initial Camp at Valley Forge. From Edmund S. Ellis, *The Youth's History of the United States* (New York: Cassell Publishing, 1887).

Washington's Headquarters at Valley Forge.
Photo courtesy Valley Forge National Historical Park.

Huts at Valley Forge.
Photo courtesy Valley Forge National Historical Park.

Horatio Gates. Mezzotint published by John Morris, London, 1778.
Courtesy National Archives, photo no. 148-GW-472.

Nathanael Greene. Mezzotint by V. Green from painting by Charles Willson Peale.
Courtesy National Archives, photo no. 148-GW-474.

Benjamin Lincoln. Painting by Henry Sargent, 1805.
Courtesy Massachusetts Historical Society.

Banner of Washington's Life Guard. From Benson J. Lossing, *The Pictorial Field-Book of the Revolution* (1851; reprint, Freeport, N.Y.: Books for Libraries, 1969).

Captain Bezaleel Howe. From Carlos E. Godfrey, *The Commander-in-Chief's Guard* (Washington, D.C.: Stevenson-Smith, 1904).

Provost   Officer

The Provost Company of Light Dragoons, 1778–1783 (Maréchaussée). Painting by
Frederick T. Chapman. The prisoner is a deserter from the light infantry legion
of Colonel Charles Armand. From Col. John R. Elting, *Military Uniforms in
America: The Era of the Revolution, 1755–1795* (San Rafael, Calif.: Company of
Military Historians, 1974).

Plundering Soldiers. Illustration by Felix O. C. Darley. From Benson J. Lossing, *Our Country: A Household History for All Readers* (New York: Johnson & Miles, 1877).

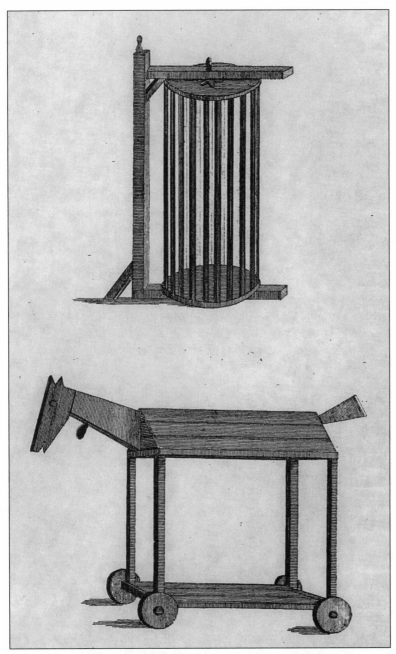

Military Punishments (British Army): Whirligig (Cage) and Wooden Horse.
Drawing by James Sparrow, 1788. From Francis Grose, *Military Antiquities
Respecting a History of the English Army*, vol. 2 (London: S. Hooper, 1788).

Typical Punishments in the Continental Army. From Randy Steffen, *The Horse Soldier, 1776–1943: The United States Cavalryman, His Uniform, Arms, Accoutrements, and Equipments,* vol. 1 (Norman: University of Oklahoma Press, 1977). Copyright University of Oklahoma Press.

Private and Drummer of Captain John Copp's Company, 1778. From T. W. Egley Jr., *History of the First New York Regiment, 1775–1783* (Hampton, N.H.: Peter E. Randall, 1981).

10

On the March

"Soldiers, keep by your officers. For God's sake, keep by your officers!" entreated General Washington as he viewed the march of his army along the bank of the Delaware River just before the battle of Trenton.[1] Armies on the move had a degree of vulnerability, and great care was needed to keep the line of march intact and in good order. General Steuben's *Regulations* stipulated that "the greatest attention on the part of the officers is necessary at all times, but more particularly on a march: The soldiers being then permitted to march at their ease, with the ranks and files open, without the greatest care, these get confounded one with another; and if suddenly attacked, instead of being able to form immediately in order of battle, the whole line is thrown into the utmost confusion."[2]

On a short trek while anticipating battle, there was little problem in maintaining good marching order. On long marches, however, measures had to be taken not only to prevent confusion in the ranks but also to prevent soldiers from drifting away on their own, becoming stragglers, or worse, plunderers. The easiest time to escape the army was during movement over long distances. A "standing model" for a march consisted of "general rules and regulations" applicable to a force of any size: the whole army, division, brigade, or corps. Normally, the army marched by platoons, but on a narrow roadway, troops marched three to four abreast. Ahead of the procession were the scouting parties and the pioneers, who made sure that forward passage was cleared of any obstacles. The infantry marched by infantry brigades, intermixed with artillery and cavalry units. Some baggage wagons followed their respective marching units or found their place at the end of the whole moving army. Advance and rear guards and flanking parties provided security against surprise attack and also a buffer against defecting soldiers. The size of the protective forces varied considerably, depending on the number of troops in the line of march and the proximity of the enemy.[3]

For a typical march of the army during summertime, troops were awakened around 4:00 A.M. After breakfast, as John W. Wright describes, the men were

> grouped by sizes around a kettle, some making "fire cakes" from their flour. When the "general" is sounded on the drums at five the men make their packs and strike tents, which are loaded into the wagons. The wagons immediately clear the field and report to the assembly point of the train. When the "assembly" sounds at six o'clock the regiments form, move into brigade formation, and brigades march to the color line where order of battle is formed. With the sounding of the "March" the advance guard cavalry trots ahead, and the columns follow the advance guard.[4]

If there was a chance of encountering the enemy, the army left behind at the old camp its tents, nonessential baggage, and the women. For the security of the old camp until it could be abandoned, each division provided a field officer; each brigade, a captain: and each regiment, a subaltern, a sergeant, a corporal, and twelve men. However, these guards were "to consist of men most unfit for duty, and who have the worst arms."[5] Eventually, the field officer left behind was to lead the "men well enough to march" and any stragglers collected to join the army on the march.[6] A single soldier might be detached from a march to pick up a comrade who had been left at camp for whatever reason. One corporal with Pennsylvania troops joining forces with Continentals in Virginia was given just such an assignment; but "some dispute arose six miles from the [Potomac River] ferry when the Soldier Shot the Corporal, & made his escape."[7]

A major general of the day had the responsibility of conducting the march of the whole army. Normally, in the line of march, a field officer or a captain selected by the adjutant general from each brigade was "to supervise the order of the march and correct all abuses on the spot."[8] One field officer commanded the advance guard and one commanded the rear guard. The advance guard, consisting of members drafted from the regiments, marched fifty to two hundred paces in front of the main body of troops. For further security, the advance guard staggered several small detachments even further ahead to make sure the way was clear. The same arrangement applied to the rear guard.[9] The advance guard also sent out flanking guards to a distance of about one hundred paces from the left and the right of the marching army.[10] Once a place was selected for halting the army, regimental and brigade quartermasters, assisted by artificers, pioneers, and "camp colour-men" (see chapter 11), labored to lay out the camp and render it "Commodious."[11] The advance guard was expected to serve as the "guards of the new camp."[12] Men from the advance and rear guards formed "a chain of sentinels, to prevent the soldiers from straggling."[13]

Although considerable amounts of military supplies and equipment were left at depots away from the line of march, many cargo wagons accompanied the army, some of these vehicles following the individual brigades and divisions, and others being relegated to the rear of the march. All the portable supplies and equipment of the army were considered baggage. There were four categories of baggage: military stores; commissary stores, including provisions; the "flying hospital"; and articles belonging to officers.[14] On a march that was expected to engage the enemy, the officer baggage was kept to an absolute minimum, and the men carried with them, besides their weapons, a knapsack, a haversack, a canteen, a blanket, ammunition, and one camp kettle for each five to six men.[15] One colonel noted in September 1779 that men of his regiment, "without shoes and barefooted," marched in a "separate column."[16] Guards, one or two per baggage wagon, were drawn from the rank and file, serving in squads commanded by a captain or a subaltern.[17] Usually accompanying the baggage at the rear of a march was a special guard, consisting of a captain or a subaltern and about forty to fifty men, including a drummer and a fifer.[18] It was the practice that soldiers least suited for battle, by reason of health or other factors, pulled baggage guard duty.[19]

For the army's march from the Middlebrook encampment in June 1777, general orders stipulated:

> The regimental Waggons to have a guard of a serjt and six privates, those to be least fit for duty. . . . The Quarter Mas. General, commanding military stores, and Commissary General each to be furnished, with a subaltern officer, a serjeant & 20 men to guard the stores in their several departments from the line. The Hospital department, to be furnished with a serjt and 10 Privates as a guard from the line. The Waggons in the Quarter Mas. department to march next to the Baggage, the military stores next, then the Provision, and the flying hospital in the rear of it marches in the same collumn with the Baggage.[20]

There was a tendency for soldiers to break ranks on a march and walk leisurely alongside the wagons. As the army prepared to march through Philadelphia, where it would be critically viewed by local citizens, Washington "strongly and earnestly enjoined" commanding officers to make sure "all their men who are able to bear arms (except the necessary guards) march in the ranks"; it was "really shocking" to see the lack of discipline in a large number of "strollers (for they cannot be called guards) with the wagons."[21] During a march, however, a man was assigned to walk on each side of a wagon, "as far back as the tail," so that if anything spilled out, "they may discover, and pick it up."[22] The wagonmaster for each brigade was required to provide space on wagons on a march for soldiers who became disabled or sick.[23]

The army had a Wagonmaster Department, and it was the duty of wagonmasters to supervise wagoners, to make sure that they adhered to the "rules and regulations of the Army" and, in the line of march, that wagons followed close to each other. A wagoner could not stop his vehicle to water his horses unless "the commanding officer of the collumn gives orders for a halt."[24] Wagonmasters were horse-mounted and were expected "to be constantly with their wagons, and to ride backwards and forwards frequently, to see that they move in good order."[25] Orders for the march through Philadelphia required the wagonmaster general, his deputies, and the various quartermasters to assist the field officers "in preventing any men who are allotted to attend the waggons from slipping into the city."[26]

It was Washington's policy to restrict access to baggage wagons. He allowed women to ride in wagons on a march only if they had permission from a general officer, and periodically he forbade the practice altogether.[27] The commander in chief did his best to discourage women from entering a line of march. In August 1777, he lamented that "in the present marching state of the army, every incumbrance proves greatly prejudicial to the service; the multitude of women in particular, especially those who are pregnant, or have children, are a clog upon every movement."[28]

Officers of the day or "police" on a march were authorized to take women off wagons and inflict "instant Punishment" on those women not permitted to ride on the wagons.[29] Even drummers were forbidden to put drums on a wagon unless they had special permission. Those who violated this rule were to be "immediately flogged" by order of any commanding officer in the baggage guard.[30] Women who were allowed to accompany a moving army were expected "to follow the Baggage" on foot.[31] Sarah Osborne was

one of the camp followers who occasionally was favored by being permitted to ride horseback or on a wagon, although she did her share of tramp-
ing behind the army. Sarah was married to a soldier in Washington's army
and had the reputation of keeping busy washing, mending, and cooking
for the soldiers.[32]

Sergeant Joseph Plumb Martin, returning to the marching army from
an assignment near Tappan, New York, in 1780 to pick up some of his comrades who had veered away from the line of march, had "an opportunity
to see the baggage of the army pass." When the baggage of the "middle
states" went by,

> it was truly amusing to see the number and habiliments of those at-
> tending it; of all the specimens of human beings, this group capped
> the whole. A caravan of wild beasts could bear no comparison with
> it. There was "Tag, Rag and Bobtail"; "some in rags and some in jags,"
> but none "in velvet gowns." Some with two eyes, some with one, and
> some, I believe, with none at all. They "beggared all description" their
> dialect, too was as confused as their bodily appearance was odd and
> disgusting. There was the Irish and Scotch brogue, murdered English,
> flat insipid Dutch and some lingoes which would puzzle a philoso-
> pher to tell whether they belonged to this world or some "undiscov-
> ered country."[33]

Unlike the French army, which had a special detachment of provost/
military police to gather up stragglers from a march,[34] American forces
detailed men from the ranks for this function. Normally, a rear guard for
marching Continental troops was established from each of the brigades. For
a march in July 1777, each brigade contributed one captain, two subalterns,
two sergeants, two corporals, and twenty privates as a rear guard.[35] The field
officer who commanded the rear guard was often called upon to employ a
detachment of a subaltern and about thirty men "to follow in the rear of
the baggage; to pick up all stragglers who escape from the rear guard."[36] A
regimental commander also was expected to order a squad of about six men
to the rear to apprehend stragglers.[37]

Extra arrangements were sometimes made for a rear guard. In June 1777,
one-fourth of General Maxwell's brigade served in this capacity; these troops
followed a half mile behind the army expressly for the purpose of picking
up stragglers.[38] Cavalrymen were occasionally assigned as part of the rear

guard.[39] The rear guard had the responsibility of delivering stragglers to a deputy quartermaster, who then returned the men to their units, where they might or might not be punished.[40] In instances where there was no resistance, commanding officers in a rear guard were not supposed to administer any severe punishment themselves. General Nathanael Greene's orders to the southern army in November 1781, however, stated that the rear guard of a march should punish apprehended stragglers who did not have "satisfactory" excuses for being away from their units.[41] Orders for the New Jersey Brigade in August 1780 declared that officers commanding platoons were "answerable for the mens straggling."[42]

One incident from the march of Sullivan's division in east-central New Jersey brought attention to the extent to which officers commanding in a rear guard in the line of march could discipline a soldier picked up for straggling. Edward Rock, an enlisted man, was the victim of "inhumane abuse" upon orders of a Lieutenant Sewell, who commanded the rear guard. A court of inquiry, considering that other officers were also involved in the beating of Rock, could not put full blame on Sewell. He therefore did not have to face a court-martial. Division orders made it clear that "officers who bring up the Rear of any Corps, on the March may with Propriety" strike a soldier for straggling, but in no instance should there be "wanton cruelty" as had been exhibited upon Edward Rock. Only if the soldier had insulted the arresting officer or officers "by word or Action" and continued to do so would there have been justification for summary harsh punishment.[43] Of course, distancing oneself from the line of march was considered a serious offense. As in an encampment, field officers of the day could exert "discretionary punishment" on any straggler, "not to exceed fifty lashes."[44] Stragglers thought to be intending to desert could receive up to one hundred lashes.[45]

A march was organized in such a way that it could swiftly be converted into battle formation. Harsh punishment awaited any soldier who during battle fled from his position. Brigadier generals and regimental commanders were ordered to put "some good officers in the rear" to stop any soldier who was not wounded from attempting "to run away" or retreat before orders were given to that effect and to "instantly put him to death."[46] Applying this rule, common to all armies, was Major William Boyce of the Virginia militia, who had teamed up with Continental troops commanded by General Steuben. At the battle of Petersburg, Virginia, on April 25, 1781,

Boyce was "riding along in the rear giving orders" when he spotted a young soldier who, claiming to be very sick, was "rolling" on the ground "in the rear of his platoon." When confronted by Boyce, the supposedly affected trooper tried to run away. The major "rode after him saying he would cut off his head as he was a coward." Needless to say, the lad was soon in the ranks, along with his comrades, firing at the enemy.[47]

Straggling from the line of march continued as a major problem. One solution, having the drummers slow the cadence beat in order to reduce the pace of the march so that the men were less likely to fall behind and "get lost," did not help much.[48] Another preventive measure was to insist that officers know "precisely the Number of Men in their Divisions or platoons" and "take a list of their names previous to their marching"; officers were to check frequently on the march to see if anyone was missing.[49]

Often compounding the problem of absenteeism from the line of a march were stragglers plundering property of the country people. The delinquent soldiers, aiming to supplement their insufficient rations, robbed orchards and stole corn and potatoes from gardens.[50] Sometimes, officers were derelict in encouraging soldiers to seize farm products. One regimental adjutant during a march "jumpt over into a mans garden to steal fruits &c, the men followed him like Sheep"; the colonel commanding the regiment "found it out and put sd officer under an Arrest" and did not blame "the men that followed him."[51]

The commander in chief was "mortified with repeated Complaints of the most licentious Excesses committed by particular Corps" during marches.[52] In July 1777, he was especially irked by the many depredations committed by men of General John Sullivan's division during a march. Washington received "Complaints from the People living contiguous to the Road of great abuses." Damages caused by Sullivan's troops amounted to more than by the "whole Army." Particularly, Sullivan's men had seized "a great number of Horses" and destroyed many fences. It seemed that most of the violations occurred when the army paused to camp. Washington ordered officers, "if no other means are sufficient," to "post Sentries round their encampments" and take prisoner any soldier trying to leave. Two soldiers of Sullivan's division were condemned to death for "plundering the habitants," and one of them was executed.[53]

Soldiers were warned about going "into the Houses or Barns to take straw or any other thing belonging to Inhabitants."[54] Occasionally, guards were stationed along the route of the army to prevent "horses of the Army breaking into the fields of Grain."[55] During the Philadelphia campaign of 1777, brigade commanders sent two or three mounted officers into the line of march of the previous day "to examine all houses, barns and huts on the way" in order to "collect and bring in all stragglers from the army."[56]

Camp followers and unattached militia tagging along at the rear of a marching army caused trouble. Washington complained that "the followers of the Army and Volunteers [militia] not under the orders of any officer have taken advantage of the Position and movement of the Army" to "seize the Property of the inhabitants for their own use." In August 1781, he required that all "Volunteers" be "formed into Companies," commanded by officers appointed by "the Authority of their State or the Election of the Company." Such officers had to report to the adjutant general. The trailing militiamen who refused to submit to the military authority as prescribed were to be arrested and jailed.[57]

II

Officer of Police

An unwelcome intruder proved a ceaseless annoyance to the enlisted men. The regimental officer of police had the duty of inspecting living quarters of the troops and the grounds of his regiment to make sure that soldiers conformed to regulations regarding cleanliness and sanitation. He and the noncommissioned officers and drummer who accompanied him were known as the camp (or garrison) police, and sometimes, as the internal police. No other officer had a more intimate contact with the rank and file. The officer of police himself normally did not order punishment, but his reports on infractions did lead to severe penalties.

The primitive living conditions in the Continental army enhanced the importance of camp police. The policing of a military area had a much more pervasive meaning to the ragtag soldiers of the Revolutionary army than it does for modern GIs. In the American army of the twenty-first century, *police call* "refers to the cleaning of an area, typically in and around barracks, housing, and work stations. A police call is an informal formation, normally under the supervision of a noncommissioned officer (NCO), in which soldiers are placed on line and move through the area picking up trash and debris. On most Army posts, police calls are held daily, in the mornings."[1] Police call in the Continental army involved a more structured system of control and attention to a wider variety of camp conditions.

The officer of police, who might also be regarded as a "regimental officer of the day,"[2] was a subaltern, usually a lieutenant, although in garrisons sometimes a captain was employed.[3] Regimental adjutants daily appointed an officer of police.[4] Having a noncommissioned officer serve as officer of police was strictly forbidden. Major James Randolph Reid faced a court-martial for appointing a sergeant "to do the duty of officers of Police"; he was reprimanded in general orders for this "unwarrantable departure" from regulations."[5]

The officer of police had its counterpart in the British army.[6] In the American practice, in accordance with Steuben's *Regulations*, the officer of police was assisted by four noncommissioned officers and a drummer.[7] The "drummer of the police" was required to visit "constantly" the regimental adjutant's office, "to be ready at all times to communicate the necessary signals."[8] With the ideal number of subalterns per regiment being sixteen (from four companies), although the count varied greatly from only a few to over twenty, on average, a subaltern pulled a tour as officer of police about every two weeks.[9]

The duty performance of the officer of police was freely monitored. The general officer of the day, the commander of a brigade to which the regiment belonged, and a field officer of the day were expected to "superintend the police of the camp."[10] Brigade inspectors and subinspectors were to "inspect the Police of the Camp."[11] A captain of the day, also referred to as "Police Captain," was appointed at the brigade level, "who is generally to superintend the Police of their respective Brigades" and to give "such directions to the Regimental Officers of Police as shall be Necessary for the Cleanliness of Camp."[12]

The commander of the regiment had the responsibility of drawing up "all General regulations for the internal Police of the Regiment" consistent with the overall standards for procedure of the army.[13] All officers of a regiment were expected to afford the "Strictest attention" in support of the officer of police in doing his duty.[14] In attending to the cleanliness of the camp and "internal regulations" in general, both the officer of police and the regimental commanding officer were "answerable" for "any neglect or irregularity."[15] The officer of police was "bound to see that there be no neglect in the Quarter Masters, or Camp-colour-men," in reference to sanitation details.[16] Any problem regarding "filthiness" was to be referred to a brigadier general, who would "afford a Remedy to it."[17]

Besides overseeing camp or garrison sanitation, the officer of police had other duties. He was to make sure that "the Public property" was "not left exposed to Loss or Damage" and that fatigue parties were "employed Steadily on the Business" on which they were ordered.[18] He was "to be present at all distributions in the regiment" and "to form and send off all detachments for necessaries," such as water, wood, or straw.[19]

The foul odors arising from offal, human and animal, rotten food, and dead animal carcasses made camp living almost intolerable. General William

Moultrie, coming to the vicinity of General Nathanael Greene's camp near Charleston, South Carolina, found that "the air was so infected with the stench of camp that we could scarcely bear the smell." Greene was expecting the British evacuation of Charleston and therefore had kept his army "on the same ground."[20] The commander of the southern army blamed the "disagreeable Stench" on neglect in tending to the latrines.[21] Army physician Dr. James Tilton recalled after the war that the American camp at Kingsbridge, New York, in October 1776 was so "excessively filthy" that "excrementitious matter" was scattered everywhere, resulting in a "disagreeable smell" throughout the encampment.[22] Except for the winter cantonments, Washington moved his army frequently in order to escape a buildup of unsanitary conditions.

Of the duties of camp police, none was more important and far-reaching than the prevention of disease. Physical disability reaped a heavy toll on Washington's army. Military hospitals were overcrowded, and the sick too often remained in camp. While etiology was still in its infancy, and the recognition of germ causation of disease was all but unknown, the belief in the connection between unsanitary conditions and disease had already been accepted.

The incidence of Washington's troops who were unable to serve because of illness and wounds averaged 18 percent for the period of the whole war. During the early years, smallpox reached epidemic proportions and decimated the expeditionary force sent into Canada. Even with the near eradication of smallpox through inoculation of the troops, the rate of sickness continued at a high level. At Valley Force in April 1778, the sick (absent and present) amounted to 6,109 men out of a total force of 25,802; in December 1782, 1,119 out of a total of 12,224. Ninety percent of deaths in the Continental army were owing to disease.[23] Dr. James Tilton reported that "more Surgeons died in the American service than Officers of the Line; a strong evidence that infection is more dangerous than the Weapons of War."[24]

Dr. Benjamin Rush, upon entering his brief stint as surgeon general for the Middle Department in April 1777, penned "To the Officers in the Army of the United American States: Directions for Preserving the Health of Soldiers" (subsequently published in a newspaper and then as a pamphlet). Rush advocated close attention to proper diet, food preparation, cleanliness of body, bedding, and clothes, avoidance of overcrowding in living quarters, and, in general, a sanitary environment.[25]

Indeed, diseases attributed to poor hygiene plagued the army. American army physicians subscribed to the theory held by the British army physician Sir John Pringle that putrefaction was the leading cause of disease. According to Pringle, the major sources for putrefaction were tainted marsh water; exposed human excrement; rotting straw used for bedding in tents; and overcrowded military hospitals. The infectious diseases most feared were putrid fever (typhus and typhoid fever—the two were indistinguishable at the time), dysentery, and, chiefly in southern climes, malaria. Typhus was caused by rickettsia protozoa from the feces of body lice; typhoid fever by food contaminated with bacteria usually borne by flies; malaria by protozoan parasites borne by mosquitoes; and dysentery by protozoan parasites or bacteria usually transmitted by flies. Poor body hygiene particularly made for the spread of typhus. The bloodsucking lice embedded themselves in clothing next to the skin; without blood, lice starve to death.[26]

Although soldiers were repeatedly instructed to practice cleanliness and neatness, the greater emphasis in camp hygiene was placed on reducing putrilage that emitted noxious odors. Soldiers were often "exposed to the putrid Steams of dead Horses, of the Privies, and of other corrupted Animal or Vegetable substances."[27] George Washington observed in March 1778 at Valley Forge that "much Filth and Nastinesss is spread among the Hutts, which will soon be reduc'd to a state of putrefaction and cause a Sickly Camp."[28] It was a main responsibility of the officer of police to ensure that regulations were followed regarding latrines,[29] which in the Continental army were called *vaults*. This duty was not easily accomplished because of the numerical size of the army, the distance of vaults from the troops, and the laxity of commanding officers in insisting upon the complete enforcement of the regulations.

Regimental quartermasters directed the digging of the vaults and saw to it that they were covered with fresh dirt daily.[30] Normally, vaults were placed in a single line, one hundred fifty yards in front of the camp for the men and one hundred yards in the rear for officers. When possible, vaults were located "upon the Brink of the Precipices or in such places as are least obnoxious."[31] To provide for a little privacy, tree and bush branches were "interwoven" along the vaults.[32] Heavy rains impeded the digging and use of the facilities.[33]

"Camp colour-men" from each regiment covered the vaults with earth daily, and every three days, dug new vaults, filling up entirely the old ones.[34] The "particular duty" of a camp colour-man was "to attend the Quarter

Master and Quarter Master serjeant, to sweep the Streets of their respective encampments, to fill up the old necessary Houses and dig new ones, to bury all Offal, Filth, and Nastiness, that may poison or infect the health of the Troops."[35] The term *camp colour-men* was carried over from the British army, where camp colour-men assisted the quartermasters in marking out new encampments for their regiments by staking out the borders with flags, or "colours"; the main task was to dig latrines and make sure the new area was clean. The American army also borrowed from the British the practice of having at least two camp colour-men per company.[36] Selected by either the commander or adjutant of a company and placed under the direction of quartermasters, camp colour-men served for a discretionary period of time. In the main army, service was for at least a week. At Fort Schuyler, men were selected to be "constantly" employed as camp colour-men.[37] It is not beyond the realm of possibility that some misfits drew permanent "latrine duty."

Camp colour-men are not to be confused with pioneers, who were employed as military laborers, chiefly for opening roads, digging trenches, building bridges and fortifications, and the like. In the southern theater of operations, many pioneers were blacks, either impressed into service or hired out by owners.[38]

Understandably, there were few if any enlisted men who volunteered to be camp colour-men. On occasion, men deficient in clothing or without bayonets found themselves appointed to the job. One sentry considered negligent when on duty was sentenced to be a camp colour-man for one week.[39] One soldier, convicted of drunkenness, while confined in the guardhouse was put out on work release as a camp colour-man.[40] Soldiers convicted by courts-martial of relatively minor infractions, such as gambling at cards, found themselves attending to the latrines and the like.[41] The officer of police was charged with seeing that there was "no neglect" among the quartermasters or camp colour-men.[42] Any camp colour-man who left a job unfinished, upon being reported to a quartermaster sergeant, faced a whipping of five lashes on the bare back.[43]

Enlisted men paid little heed to the frequent reading of orders that they use the latrines. They often relieved themselves not far from their tents or huts and even "in the Ditches and Fortifications." Some men went to the vaults of other regiments, "dirtying the seats" there.[44] Yet, for a soldier experiencing an urgent call of nature, there was good reason to hold back until reaching a vault. Swift punishment followed for anyone apprehended violating the latrine orders. Although some of the non-latrine-users were tried by regimental courts-martial,[45] normally, commanders of regiments used their discretionary authority to mete out summary punishment, as long as it came within the general rules and regulations of the army. Sentries from the quarter guards were "posted at proper places" with orders to take prisoner any soldier relieving himself anywhere other than the specified "necessaries." Five lashes was the usual punishment.[46] Ten lashes were recorded at Valley Forge.[47] Orders for Colonel Henry Jackson's Additional Continental Regiment stated that a latrine violator was "to be immediately tied up, and receive twenty lashes."[48]

There were threats of even harsher punishments. Orders for the Ninth Massachusetts Regiment declared that any noncommissioned officer or private "who shall be found easing himself within a half mile of the Camp, except in the sinks," would, if a noncommissioned officer, be reduced in rank to a "private centinel," and if a private, receive thirty lashes "without benefit of a court martial."[49] General George Weedon issued brigade orders, obviously not enforced, that guards "fire on any man who should be found easing himself other than in the vaults."[50] In some instances soldiers detected in noncompliance with the latrine orders, in addition to corporal punishment, could be fined one dollar, to be paid to an informer. Any women or children found in similar comprising positions were to be immediately expelled from camp.[51]

While officers of police kept a close eye on camp cleanliness, quartermasters (regimental and brigade) had responsibility for camp cleanups. Camp colour-men, and sometimes fatigue parties, regularly went about burying carcasses of dead horses and other animals within and near camp.[52] For the cleanliness of camp, "particular attention" was expected "to be paid to the Slaughter Pens, that no offensive smell may proceed from them."[53] Brigade and regimental quartermasters had charge of seeing that "offal and other offensive matter" were buried daily, and persons could be "arrested for the smallest inattention" to this duty.[54] Slaughterhouses had to be located outside of camp. General orders for General John Sullivan's army in the Indian expedition of 1779 required that "no Cattle" be slaughtered "within the Chain of Sentinels."[55] Steuben's *Regulations* recommended that killing cattle occur at least fifty yards "in the rear of the wagons." Frequently, slaughterhouses were located three hundred yards to a mile from camp.[56] Officers of police inspected all the environs of camp to ensure that there was nothing that would "occasion a bad smell." Soldiers had the habit of throwing scraps of meat and bones on the ground as discards from their messes. Camp colour-men, under direction of regimental quartermasters, gathered the miscellaneous garbage and hauled it "out of Camp at a proper Distance" and buried or burned it.[57]

A company officer shared responsibility with the officer of police for inspecting tents. The portable shelters for the common soldiers were placed in a row, two feet apart; six to eight occupants (generally referred to as a "mess") resided in the six-and-a-half-feet-square by five-feet-high space.[58] The tents were to be kept clean and every utensil "in proper order." No "bones or other filth" were to be near the tents, and in good weather, the tents were to be "struck about two hours at noon, and the straw and bedding aired." The soldiers were forbidden from eating in the tents.[59] In readying for a march, the officer of police superintended the loading of the regimental baggage, paying "particular Attention, that the Tents, and Tent-Poles are first put in the Wagons."[60]

Officers of police were expected to adhere strictly to Steuben's *Regulations* affecting camp life.[61] Not the least of the obligations was to ensure that the soldiers kept their huts clean.[62] The men, however, seldom showed any concern for personal hygiene and sanitation. Garbage stacked up in the corners of the huts. General Lafayette at Valley Forge complained that the soldiers lived in "little shanties which are scarcely gayer than dungeon cells."[63] The typical army hut, sheltering twelve noncommissioned officers and privates, measured fourteen by sixteen feet and was six and a half feet high. Clay or mud filled the gaps between logs as side walls; roofs were made of split slabs or were thatched; and fireplaces against a wall were constructed of stone or wood covered with clay.[64]

A checklist for inspection of huts included:

> roofs made waterproof
> poles set up outside for airing blankets
> "rubbish" between huts removed "to a suitable distance" and destroyed
> floors swept every day
> care exercised in use of candles and fire
> doors and windows opened daily during warm weather
> bedding, straw, and bunks frequently aired
> powder from musket cartridges or a little bit of tar burned daily, thought to purify the air[65]

With smoke escaping from the fireplace (green wood was often used) and the burning of powder or tar, no wonder Surgeon Albigence Waldo at Valley Forge observed that from the smoke and intense cold his eyes "started out from their Orbits like a Rabbit's eyes."[66]

The policing of barracks and garrisons resembled that for huts. Officers of police saw that "the quarters of their respective regiments" were kept clean and the bedding aired.[67] "All Nausious dust & filth" had to be removed.[68] Brigade orders at West Point in December 1780 read, "The Police Officers of Regiments are to see that no soldiers cut or split wood on the floors of the Barracks" and have "their Arms Placed or hang'd up in such a manner that they may find them in an Instant."[69]

Officers of police visited the men during "cooking hours" to make sure "Cooking is properly performed." Food had to be inspected "both as to the quality and the manner of dressing it, obliging the men to accustom themselves more to boiled meats and soups and less [to] the broiled and roasted." Company commanders also inspected the camp kitchens.[70] The daily meat ration for each enlisted man usually consisted of one pound of beef or fish, or three-fourths of a pound of pork;[71] with the meat preserved in brine or salt and sometimes on the verge of spoiling, boiling was the most thorough method of cooking available. Washington strongly recommended to the troops that they supplement their diet with salad greens. At the Middlebrook encampment in June 1777, he ordered the officers of police to send out a party every morning to gather "French sorrel," goosefoot, and watercress that grew plentifully about the camp and "have them distributed among the men."[72]

An uncovered kettle was issued for every mess; this utensil weighed two to three pounds and had a capacity of nine quarts. When troops were bivouacked in tents, it was absolutely mandatory that all cooking be done in camp kitchens, located at the edge of a company area; although the same applied in reference to huts, soldiers occasionally broiled meat in the coals of their fireplaces. Normally, six men formed a mess; sometimes, a whole company. The six men would generally cook their rations together; however, occasionally, women were employed to work the camp kitchens.[73]

The officers of police had stern instructions to prevent soldiers from using fence rails for fuel in their messes. All members of a mess were deemed equally culpable if no one informed on whoever had stolen the fences from the countryside. An officer of the police, on his own authority, could order twenty lashes for anyone determined to be a primary offender.[74]

It was essential to maintain the purity of the water supply. With not enough wells in camp, water had to be drawn from brooks and streams. Unfortunately, women and men, too, washed clothing in the runs from which the army obtained water for cooking and drinking.[75] Private Elijah Fisher observed at the Whitemarsh camp that "the Water we had to drink and to mix our flour with" came from "a brook that run along by the Camp, and so many a dippin' and washin' in it which made it very Dirty and muddy."[76] It became a practice to post sentries "on all the Springs in and near the Camp" to prevent the water from being polluted.[77]

For soldiers to fill their canteens, they had to apply to the officer of police, who several times a day ordered "the drummer of Police" to beat four flams (double strokes, the first being a grace note), which signaled the men who desired water to assemble at the center of the regimental parade ground with their canteens. The officer of police then formed these men into a platoon, and a noncommissioned officer led them to the water and brought them back.[78]

When troops drew rations from the commissary stores, officers of police attended to make sure there was an equitable distribution and that a representative of each mess showed up to receive the appropriate issue. For a while, until Congress and Washington intervened, officers frequently "picked out all the best bits for their own consumption." Whenever there was deficiency in the supply of a particular article, soldiers were expected to accept a substitute.[79] Importantly, men had to draw enough food so it could be cooked preparatory to a march and to "have provisions by them, ready for any emergency."[80] It was incumbent upon officers of police, and other officers as well, to persuade soldiers from "the vile practice of Swallowing the whole ration of Liquor at a Single Draught" and instead drink it at intervals, mixed with water.[81]

Along with other special duty personnel, officers of police kept a watchful eye on sutlers. General orders at Newburgh in March 1783 declared that officers of police should daily visit sutlers "to discover and report any disorderly practices" to their regimental commanders, who in turn reported to their brigade commanders.[82] Officers of police were to examine any person not belonging to the army who attempted to patronize sutlers in camp and send them to the general officer of the day for further examination.[83] Especially, sutlers could not indulge in excessive pricing and receive items belonging to the army as payment. Officers of police, along with other officers of the day, were to remind sutlers and keepers of "dram shops near the Army" to require that enlisted men have signed permission from an officer to make purchases; this, however, appears to be a temporary measure instituted when vendors proliferated in a camp vicinity. For violation of army regulations, a sutler upon conviction faced dismissal and even punishment of up to thirty-nine lashes.[84] Officers of police were also charged with preserving order at the army markets.[85]

The regimental officer of police was the linchpin in the implementation of rules and regulations affecting living conditions of the enlisted men. He was the main functionary in the camp police. Keeping a camp clean and safe presented a monumental task. The regiment formed the primary context for a soldier's duty, and it was at this level, therefore, that the fundamental supervision of camp conditions occurred. The burden of responsibility for neglect in maintaining camp cleanliness and order fell less to the officer of police, who served tours on a daily basis, than to the regimental and company commanders and ultimately the commanders of brigades. Washington constantly reproved his officers for not being as attentive as they should to the conduct and habits of the soldiers. The commander in chief, nevertheless, toward the end of the war, as the army paused at Verplanck's Point in October 1782 before going into winter cantonment, expressed satisfaction "with the internal police and order of the encampments."[86]

12

Provost Marshal

The provost marshal in a limited way served as the chief of police of the Continental army. Assisted by a provost guard, he primarily had custody of prisoners awaiting trial by general court-martial and, upon conviction, responsibility for executing the sentence; secondarily, he was expected to maintain order and apprehend delinquent soldiers.[1]

Although borrowing from British and European precedents, the provost marshal in the Continental army lacked the range of discretionary authority found in other armies. In the British experience by the seventeenth century, the provost marshal was "the principal gaoler of the Army" and in charge of "all manner of tortures." He could "arrest and detain any persons subject to military law" who committed an offense. Often, he was referred to as the hangman or executioner of the army. Typically, a provost marshal in the British army was a sergeant assisted by twelve men; when in charge of prisoners, the provost marshal was a subaltern, assisted by a provost guard consisting of a sergeant, a drummer, and thirty soldiers.[2] The French army in the early eighteenth century had a grand provost, who was served by lesser provosts. A regimental *prévôté* consisted of a provost, lieutenant provost, a clerk, an executioner, and five archers.[3]

In February 1780, Timothy Pickering, a member of the Board of War, received a response from General Steuben in answer to questions about the staff departments of the Prussian army. Steuben noted the duties of the grand provost in the Prussian army. "The function of that Officer," replied Steuben, was "to watch for the Police of the whole Army to hinder marauding and every other disorder that can be committed by the soldiers." The grand provost had the command of a "detachment of Light-Horse," from whom he sent out "different Patrols at different hours of the Day and even in the night" in camp and into the countryside to quell disturbances among soldiers and to search for deserters and "suspected persons." Prisoners were delivered to the provost guard. The grand provost "has the right to have hanged on the Spot all those he finds plundering and marauding," for which purpose "he has always a hangman that follows him wherever he goes."[4] The Continental army never adopted a provost department according to the French and Prussian models. The Maréchaussée Corps, established in 1778 (see chapter 13), however, did resemble in many aspects its European counterparts.

Only eighteen days after he assumed command of the army, George Washington applied to Congress for permission to appoint a provost marshal. The legislators complied on July 29, 1775. Washington took more than five months to fill the position, most likely because he wanted to be sure of a proper job description, and there was no rush of candidates. It was decided that the provost marshal should be a sergeant, although initially he should be addressed as "Captain of the Provost." In any event, the provost marshal was not to be a commissioned officer. At first, the provost marshal found himself answering to many bosses, receiving orders from "Headquarters, the General in Chief, the Adjutant and Quarter Master Generals." In time, however, though working closely with the adjutant general, the provost marshal's only direct line of responsibility was to the commander in chief.[5]

Because soldiers have a certain disdain for military police, it was difficult to find someone who would serve as provost marshal. Late in the war, Washington advertised for candidates. General orders for March 3, 1780, announced: "A man that can be well recommended for sobriety, integrity and industry is wanted to fill the Office of Provost Marshal."[6] For July 16, 1780: "A Trusty Serjeant who can write a good hand is wanted for a Provost Marshal."[7] For July 18, 1781: "An Active industrious Serjeant is much wanted to serve as Provost Marshal. Any officer who can recommend a suitable person is requested to send his name to the Orderly office."[8] Washington on January 10, 1776, appointed Sergeant William Marony as the first provost marshal. The official title was "Provost Marshal to the Army of the United Colonies."[9]

The provost marshal was expected to oversee executions. On June 27, 1776, general orders mentioned that Marony should proceed "immediately to make the arrangements" for the hanging of Sergeant Thomas Hickey, who had been convicted of treason, sedition, and mutiny (see chapter 5). On June 28, Marony received a warrant from the commander in chief for the execution of Hickey that day at 11:00 A.M. At quarter to eleven, Marony, a chaplain, and eighty soldiers brought the condemned man to the fated tree, located in a field between two army brigades. After the execution, Marony returned the warrant, with the notation that it was "fully executed."[10]

Marony found himself in trouble on several occasions. He was accused, though not tried, for keeping possessions of some of the men in his custody, including prisoners of war, during the move of the army from Boston to New York City.[11] Marony would miss the next hanging, scheduled for October 2, 1776. The condemned, James McCormick of the Sixteenth Continental Regiment, was to be transferred for execution from Kingsbridge a short distance to Washington's encampment at Harlem Heights. Somehow, at Kingsbridge on October 1, McCormick was accidentally released. For his being absent without leave, Washington "suspended" Marony on October 1.[12]

Sergeant Thomas Bryan of the Fourth Maryland Regiment immediately replaced Marony as provost marshal and served until the end of 1776.[13] A Sergeant Prentice acted as provost marshal from January 14 to February 15, 1777,[14] and was succeeded by Sergeant Henry Snagg, who continued in the post for nearly a year, February 15, 1777, to January 23, 1778.[15] A Sergeant Howe followed as provost marshal "Pro-Tempore," continuing until July 1778.[16] Sergeant John Weiss, formerly drum major of the First Rhode Island Regiment, served a stint as provost marshal "to part of the army then lying on the Hudson" (October 1, 1777, to July 1778), and when some of these troops made a junction with Washington's force, Weiss went with them and became provost marshal for the whole army, lasting from July 1778 to March 1780.[17] Sergeant Thomas O'Bryn (also Brien or Brian) served as provost marshal from March 9 through May 1780.[18] No one replaced O'Bryn for nearly a year. In the meantime, Sergeant William Hutton, appointed "assistant to the Provost Marshal" on January 6, 1780, acted in the capacity of provost marshal; on April 19, 1781, he was made officially provost marshal.[19]

Like Marony, Hutton found himself in serious trouble several times. A general court-martial tried him on July 12, 1780, for abetting the escape of a counterfeiter, Samuel Harris, from the provost jail. Hutton was acquitted.[20] On another occasion, Hutton received a warrant for the execution of two prisoners, but he refused to carry out the warrant, claiming that he had been appointed provost marshal only the day before and had been unable to secure an executioner. A court-martial's verdict of April 21, 1781, accepted Hutton's excuse that he had not had time to make preparations for the hangings. Hutton had attended the site where troops were drawn up to witness the executions, but he still refused to act. Washington was highly indignant over the acquittal and reversed the court's judgment. The commander in chief declared:

> To allow such a precedent as Mr. Hutton contends for to be established might upon future occasion operate seriously should a criminal of consequence require a hasty execution.
>
> In the Civil line a High Sheriff whose office is of a similar nature to that of Provost Marshal in the military is obliged to execute his Warrant himself if he cannot procure a common Executioner.
>
> Mr. Hutton is dismissed from his office.[21]

Sergeant Asa Andrus of the First Connecticut Regiment was appointed provost marshal on July 19, 1781,[22] and presumably served until November 1782. There is mention in an orderly book of April 24, 1782, "Provost Marshal tried & acquitted."[23] Andrus may also be the person referred to in orders of Adjutant General Edward Hand of January 19, 1782. A George Williams was charged with a "disturbance in the Provost Marshal's Quarters abusing his Wife in a Scandalous manner & for being drunk & absent from roll call." A court-martial found that the charge filed by the provost marshal "is not supported," but Williams was convicted of being drunk and absent from roll call and sentenced to fifty lashes.[24]

The idea of having a grand provost appealed to Washington. On November 14, 1782, general orders announced that "a Grand provost will be appointed by the General."[25] Such a position would coordinate the activities of the provost marshal and provost guard with the Maréchaussée Corps and offer some guidelines for the provosts of those troops under separate commands from the main army. With the war over and the army soon to disintegrate, however, a grand provost did not become a reality.

As the main functions of his office, the provost in Washington's army was expected:

1. to confine all prisoners charged with capital crimes
2. to detain temporarily other arrested persons who were to be turned over to the quarter guards for trial by regimental courts-martial

3. to "provide a suitable Person, when necessary to execute the Sentences of General Courts Martial"
4. to notify regiments of their soldiers confined in the provost jail
5. to report every morning to the adjutant general the number of prisoners, their crimes, and on whose order they were being held
6. to post sentries from the provost guard to provide security at a general court-martial
7. to patrol the "Avenues & Environs of the Camp" and arrest and confine "all disorderly and suspicious Persons"
8. to "suppress Riots & Disturbances"
9. to "inform the Quarter Master General of all Persons who keep unwarranted & destructive Dram Shops; and all other pernicious & Camp Nuisances"
10. to "take up Stragglers"
11. to "see that sutlers closed shop at tattoo and not sell any liquor after that time"
12. to maintain the provost jail
13. to cause anyone who fired a gun without permission to be "tied up" and receive twenty lashes[26]

Officers were often careless in sending soldiers arrested for noncapital crimes to the provost jail instead of to the custody of the regimental quarter guard. Officers who ordered soldiers to the provost jail were expected "to note at the bottom of the charge against them, the names of witnesses, their Rank and the Regiment to which they belong."[27] If any officer neglected to do this, he was to be cited in the daily report of the provost marshal, and the prisoner discharged after forty-eight hours.[28] Those prisoners detained in the provost jail who, upon conviction by a general court-martial, received less than a death sentence were to be remanded "without delay" to regimental commanders to implement punishment.[29] Although the provost marshal had the exclusive responsibility for inflicting capital punishment, on rare occasions he was called upon to supervise a whipping, generally at the grand parade.[30]

Military regulations required that a soldier upon arrest be tried within eight days.[31] The brigadier general of the day determined from among the prisoners detained by the provost marshal who should face a general or regimental court-martial.[32] At Valley Forge, the brigadier general and field officers of the day, upon being relieved from their tours of duty, were ordered to examine the charges against prisoners in the provost jail and to discharge those who "appear to be improperly confined or the length of whose imprisonment may be deemed a sufficient Punishment for their Crimes, or whose offences are so trifling as to make the Process of a General Court Martial unnecessary."[33] The brigadier general of the day was also expected to visit prisoners in the provost jail during his tour of duty and report on their treatment and the length of their confinement.[34]

A provost guardhouse was established in every encampment of the main army. The quartermaster general selected a house, barn, or other building or directed construction of a special edifice.[35] At Cambridge, Massachusetts, an "old School house" was converted for use of the provost marshalcy.[36] Serving the same function were "an old meeting house" at Kakiat, New York,[37] and the courthouse at White Plains, New York.[38] General William Heath, commanding troops east of the Hudson River in 1782, had a provost guardhouse erected on Pollopel's Island in the Hudson River at the northeast entrance into the Highlands.[39] At Valley Forge, an old stone barn was at first commandeered as a provost guardhouse, and later several huts were constructed for this purpose; subsequently, a special facility was built along the bank of the Schuylkill River, adjacent to the "new Bridge."[40] A provost guardhouse typically contained a "Guard-room" and room for confinement of prisoners; sometimes, there was space for living quarters for the provost marshal.[41]

When the army marched, large covered wagons transported provost prisoners under guard. In General Greene's southern army in November 1781, this mobile provost jail had fifteen prisoners.[42] Washington's army, in addition to the provost guardhouse, had other places of confinement at the regimental level and, for those receiving prison sentences, in correctional facilities at Albany, Baltimore, Hartford, Philadelphia, and Carlisle.

Inmates of the provost and other military jails endured poor living conditions, not the least being insufficient and contaminated food, extreme weather, and overcrowding. The most dangerous criminals were fettered with ball and chain and kept on half rations. Those placed in isolation received only bread and water.[43] The American garrison at West Point had one of the worst provost jails. As a Loyalist military leader who was incarcerated there recounted, it was a "dungeon" carved from rock, roofed in by ill-connecting planks, and water collected ankle-deep on the floor. The captive, handcuffed and in irons, was fed only "stinking beef, and rotten flour, made up into balls or dumplins," which were served in an unwashed wooden bowl that had "contracted a thick crust of dough, grease, and dirt."[44]

Initially, at Valley Forge, prisoners in the stone barn that served as a provost jail "suffered severely from the cold." Because of the "great numbers of Prisoners" under such distress, brigade courts-martial were ordered to be held every day until all the inmates were tried. A court-martial discharged John McClure, a civilian detained for illegal sutlery, because "his sufferings in the provost have sufficiently punished him for his crimes."[45]

The size of the provost guard remained relatively constant. In May 1776, the provost marshal (as "Captain of the Provost") had the assistance of one subaltern, two sergeants, two corporals, one drummer, and twenty-four privates;[46] in January 1777, one sergeant and twenty-five privates.[47] With troops of the main army and of the Highlands command in close proximity along the Hudson River in July 1777, the provost guard, stationed at Peekskill, doubled in size because of the arrest of many Loyalists and outlaws. In addition to the provost marshal, there were two subalterns, two sergeants, two corporals, two drummers and fifers, and fifty privates.[48] Just after the battle of Yorktown, the provost marshal with Washington's army in Virginia commanded a guard of one subaltern, two sergeants, two corporals, and twenty privates.[49] The provost guard each day was relieved in rotation by details from the line regiments of a different division.[50] On the march, only the provost and rear guards proceeded with fixed bayonets.[51]

A mélange of inmates occupied the provost jail. Two reports of the provost guard in 1776 indicate soldiers under arrest for stealing, desertion, aiding the enemy, sleeping on duty, leaving a guard, drunkenness, and disobedience of orders.[52] Officers under arrest, upon their honor, were expected to appear before a court-martial or, at the very worst, were confined to quarters. Only enlisted men and civilians were confined in the provost jail. Washington on occasion had to reprimand officers who sent members of staff departments and wagonmasters to the provost for imprisonment. In one particular case, involving a scaleman, whose job was to separate supplies for distribution, he said that "it is very difficult to get people of common honesty to undertake the lower duties of the Staff," and unless "they are guilty of something very criminal," they should be reported to their "superiors," who would have them discharged from employment.[53]

Besides convicted persons waiting in the provost jail for prison transfer, there were those who were sentenced to duty in the Continental navy.

Among these fortunates, who in most cases would otherwise have been hanged, were Alexander McDonald, John Rowley, and Michael Reynolds; they had to stay put until "further orders" placed them aboard certain "Continental Frigates."[54]

Although regulations limited a stay in the provost jail to serious offenders, there was often overcrowding. Washington expressed concern at Valley Forge that many prisoners "are improperly detained in the Provost."[55] Civilians facing court-martial for military crimes as well as occasionally those who had engaged in treasonable activity triable in state courts found themselves in the provost jail. All too often, civilians were subjected to needless imprisonment after charges against them had been dropped by a court-martial.[56] Persons in camp or its vicinity without proper passes and "who cannot give a good account of themselves" were apprehended and committed to the provost jail.[57]

Civilians arrested in a military zone for aiding the enemy went before a court-martial. Thomas Ryan and Thomas Butler violated regulations prohibiting citizens from trading with the enemy in Philadelphia. They tried to bring into the city eight quarters of mutton and a bull beef. Ryan was fined £50 and confined to the provost guardhouse until he paid this sum to the adjutant general "to be applied for the use of the sick in Camp."[58] Butler was also convicted of attempting to carry flour into Philadelphia, and his aggregate sentence was to receive 250 lashes.[59] Joseph Edwards was fined £100 for trying to drive cattle into British-held Philadelphia and was lodged in the provost jail until this sum was paid; moreover, he had to pay $20 to each of the "light horsemen" who arrested him. The main fine went for aid to the camp sick.[60]

In June 1777, about thirty "inhabitants" were confined in the provost guard at Morristown. Adjutant General Timothy Pickering complained to Governor William Livingston of New Jersey that these prisoners were really the responsibility of the state. These "dangerous persons, inimical to the interests of the United States" were a "burthen upon the army." They had been "confined a considerable time—and cannot be tried but by the civil authority."[61]

The provost and other army jails often were called upon to temporarily hold prisoners of war. These captives were ultimately paroled, exchanged, or wound up at detention camps or barracks. Militia or Continentals provided escort from place to place. Among the captives, Loyalists who had enlisted in refugee military units serving in an adjunct capacity with the British army proved the most dangerous and most likely to escape. In November 1780, the Chevalier de Chastellux, the *maréchal de camp* of the French army in America, visited Fishkill, New York, "a military town" serving as a garrison and supply depot. He found that the Americans had made "ample provision" for everything for a military installation, including "a provostry and a prison, surrounded by palisades and in front of this is placed a guardhouse." Peeking through the barred window of the guardhouse, Chastellux viewed about thirty "wretches," Loyalists who had enrolled in British military service.[62]

Tight security governed prisoners in the custody of the provost marshal. A squad of soldiers kept watch in and around the guardhouse, and those malefactors charged or convicted of a capital offense were usually shackled. Yet, the change in guardhouse buildings as the army moved to different locations posed a security risk. Some prisoners escaped. At Valley Forge, Captain Joshua Brown of the Fifteenth Massachusetts Regiment went before a court-martial for "Suffering two prisoners to escape from the Provost-Guard" but was acquitted.[63] When prisoners broke out of a provost jail at West Point, Washington advised General William Heath, commander of the troops in the Highlands area, that the person "who had the principal charge of the provost," if an officer, should be placed under arrest, and if a sergeant, should be "confined and tryed, for suffering the escape."[64] William Marney of the First Massachusetts Regiment was tried by a court-martial in January 1781 for letting three prisoners escape from the provost jail at West Point; the case ended in acquittal.[65]

While Benedict Arnold commanded at West Point, he had the reputation of neglecting the welfare of prisoners. Washington wrote him on August 13, 1780, that several escapees from the provost jail at West Point had turned themselves in at army headquarters. The reason they had fled was that as prisoners they had been denied water unless they paid "exorbitantly" for it. Washington told Arnold to discover the "inferior Officers" who must be guilty of this mistreatment and have them punished with "great severity."[66]

In September 1780, one of the most notorious figures of the Revolution found himself imprisoned by the provost guard of the main army. Ensign James Moody, a member of a Loyalist regiment, had been captured by troops under General Anthony Wayne. As a British operative behind American lines, Moody went on spy missions, kidnapped high-ranking civilians and rebel officers, fought in skirmishes with American troops, preyed on Continental army mails, and at the end of his career would attempt unsuccessfully the theft of the papers of the Continental Congress. After four weeks of excessively cruel treatment in the West Point jail, Moody was transferred to the custody of the provost guard under Washington's direct command. At an encampment near Steenrapie (present-day River Edge, in Bergen County, New Jersey), Moody was lodged in a "Dutchman's barn" in the center of the camp. He was kept in handcuffs and leg irons. Unless he could miraculously escape, Moody's fate was inevitable: he would be hanged either for being a spy or for murder. The former was difficult to prove because Moody traveled with his commission in his pocket and usually wore his military uniform. But Moody had killed two militia officers during two different skirmishes, and therefore he was to be tried for murder by court-martial. Governor William Livingston pressed Washington to hang Moody.

Colonel Alexander Scammell, the army's adjutant general, visited Moody, and finding that the prisoner's legs were terribly lacerated, ordered removal of the leg irons until the flesh healed. Still, escape would be most difficult. Moody remained in handcuffs, and a squad from the provost guard kept watch over the prisoners—one sentinel inside the cell, one outside the door, and four others posted nearby. The inside guard provided Moody with a "watch-coat" upon request. Moody then used this to conceal his efforts to rid himself of the handcuffs, which he managed to do by bending the bolt back and forth in a hole in a post while the guard was not looking. Freeing himself, Moody ran out of the cell, and knocking down the outside guard, grabbed his musket. Evading the other guards, he did not get very far before he heard cries through the camp of "Moody is escaped from the Provost!" Shouldering the musket, the escapee joined the ranks of the searchers, unrecognized because of the extreme darkness of the night. Crawling through a gap in the chain of sentinels that protected the camp, Moody found refuge in the woods, and by a circuitous route, eventually reached British-held New York City.[67]

At times, the commander in chief pardoned en masse prisoners detained by the provost guard, usually on the occasion of celebrating a major wartime event. On May 7, 1778, Washington, in recognition of "a season of Great Joy" because of news of the Franco-American Alliance (February 6, 1778), proclaimed "pardon and releasement to all prisoners now in confinement in the Provost, or any other place."[68] Just after the capitulation at

Yorktown, Washington set free soldiers confined in the provost jail, ordering them back to their "respective Corps."[69] With news of the signing of the preliminary Articles of Peace in Europe having arrived, and wanting to promote goodwill among the American troops soon to disband, Washington in 1783 used the occasion of the anniversary of the Franco-American Alliance to declare "a full and free pardon to all Military prisoners now in confinement," ordering those released to return to their military units.[70]

Throughout the war, the provost marshalcy attended almost exclusively to the incarceration of prisoners and the execution of capital sentences. The provost marshalcy lacked the manpower and resources, however, to implement its other designated function: to root out misconduct in camp and vicinity. It occurred to the commander in chief that a special mobile corps could fill the void as actual military police.

13

The Maréchaussée Corps

A mounted provost corps made sense. It could range in and out of camp, preserving order and taking up troublemakers, suspected persons, marauders, and stragglers. Collectively and individually, members of the corps could act in the capacity of modern military police. Soldiers of a mounted provost corps could be given any number of special assignments, such as serving as escorts, guards, couriers, and camp police. As fully equipped dragoons, the Maréchaussée Corps could be employed in scouting and as cavalry in combat.

European armies had a long tradition of using mounted provost units. The name Maréchaussée, which translates as "corps of mounted constabulary," was taken from the French army's *maréchaussée*, or provincial cavalry, which patrolled highways and acted as police on a march. The word itself comes down from the early Middle Ages: the *Privots de Marechaux*, the military force used to protect the highways. By the eighteenth century, the maréchaussée were considered as provost troops of the army per se, charged with keeping order among the soldiers and performing executions.[1]

Washington realized the need for a tighter disciplined and trained army. Foreign officers in the Continental army were suggesting the creation of a Maréchaussée Corps. The commander in chief asked Captain Bartholomew Von Heer, who had extensive European military service before coming to America, to draw up a plan for one. Von Heer turned to another veteran European officer, Colonel Henry Emanuel Lutterloh, to prepare "outlines," which Von Heer then drafted and sent to Washington.[2]

Lutterloh, a native of Brunswick, Germany, had served as a brigade major and aide-de-camp under Ferdinand, the Duke of Brunswick, during the Seven Years' War. Coming to America in 1777, in July he secured appointment as deputy quartermaster general. Lutterloh expected to become quartermaster general upon the resignation of Thomas Mifflin in March 1777, but he was denied the office because the congressional Committee at Camp, and the Congress generally, thought it was dangerous to have a foreigner in such a sensitive position and had doubts about Lutterloh's "Talents or Ability." Lutterloh thereupon resigned from the army; however, he returned to service in September 1780 as commissary general of forage. Leaving the Continental army at the end of 1782, he retired to a plantation near Wilmington, North Carolina.[3]

Bartholomew Von Heer, a native of Bayreuth, Germany, had been a cavalry lieutenant in Frederick the Great's army, also during the Seven Years' War, and had seen service in the French and Spanish armies. During his European army career, Von Heer claimed to have done the "Duty as a Marishosy [Maréchaussée]." Not long after his arrival in America, in November 1775, he joined Colonel James Livingston's Canadian regiment as lieutenant and adjutant, receiving his commission from General Richard Montgomery. Von Heer served six months with the American force that invaded Canada, being wounded twice, and was involved in the ill-fated siege of Quebec. When his regiment disbanded, Von Heer subsequently was brevetted major in the northern Continental army, then commanded by Major General Horatio Gates. Von Heer soon found, however, that by the army's "new Regulations," he was not included in any state quota and was therefore out of the army. Von Heer settled in Reading, Pennsylvania, where he caught the eye of a fellow Pennsylvanian, Joseph Reed, then serving as the army's adjutant general; Reed recommended Von Heer to Congress as one "who may render the public some service." Von Heer became adjutant to Major Nicholas Dietrich Baron de Ottendorff's Independent Company on March 19, 1777, but in less than a month, he transferred as a captain to Colonel Thomas Proctor's Fourth Continental Artillery.[4]

On February 5, 1778, the "Committee of Camp," a delegation of four congressmen sent to Valley Forge to assess the needs for army reorganization, submitted a report that included a proposal for establishment of a Maréchaussée Corps (see table). Congress accepted the report on May 20, and a week later, included it in the legislation for rearrangement of the army.[5]

Congress's expectation that men for the Maréchaussée Corps would be selected from various army units proved unrealistic. Washington disapproved of using men assigned to one army unit to fill those of another. Von Heer, throughout the war, on his own had to seek out fresh recruits. One

		Drs.	Per month	Rat. Per day	
1	Captain of Provosts at	50	Total – 50	3	Total - 3
4	Lieutenants	33⅓	133⅓	2	8
1	Clerk	33⅓	33⅓	2	2
1	Qtr. Master Serjt.	15	15	1	1
2	Trumpeters	10	20	1	2
2	Serjeants	15	30	1	2
5	Corporals	10	50	1	5
43	Provosts or Privates	8⅓	358⅓	1	43
4	Executioners	10	40	1	4
63			680		70

This Corps to be drafted from the several Brigades mounted on Horseback and armed and accoutred as light dragoons. Their Business is to watch over the Regularity and good order of the Army in Camp, Quarters or on a March, Quell Riots, prevent marauding, straggling and Desertion, detect Spies, regulate Sutlers and the like.

of Lutterloh's suggestions did not make it into the legislation for the Maréchaussée table of organization. He had recommended "4 Negroes to performe the Executions, as Whitemen would not do as well, nor perhaps be got so easy."[6]

Von Heer was appointed captain of the Maréchaussée on June 1, 1778. In anticipation of instructions to be issued to Von Heer, General Steuben presented to Washington a discourse on the role of mounted police in the Prussian army.[7] The commander in chief closely followed Steuben's direction when he set forth the duties of the Maréchaussée in "Instructions" to Von Heer and in general orders. Washington expressed his "hope that the Institution, by putting men on their Guard will operate more in preventing than punishing Crimes." The chief responsibilities of the new corps included:

> patrolling the camp and its vicinity "for the purpose of apprehend-
> ing Deserters, Marauders, Drunkards, Rioters, Stragglers, and
> all other Soldiers that may be found violating general orders;
> likewise all Countrymen or Strangers that may be found near
> the pickets or in camp, without passes";

taking charge of the regulation of sutlers on a march to secure all soldiers who "have loitered in Camp" as well as stragglers;

on the day of battle, posting "in the rear of the second line or reserve, and send[ing] patroles on the roads to the right and left, in order to rally and collect all fugitives" until a "superior officer arrives to take command of them";

ensuring that persons apprehended should "not be ill treated by words or actions, unless they attempt to escape, or make resistance," in which case troops nearby may be called upon for assistance;

submitting a written report on prisoners confined the previous day every morning to the adjutant general, under whose "immediate command" the captain of the Maréchaussée served;

(and for the executioners) "remain[ing] with the Provost Guard" until "a detachment of the Maréchaussée" can "attend the prisoner to the Place of Punishment."[8]

Ironically, the Maréchaussée Corps, which, Von Heer had advised when submitting his plan, should be filled only with "American born," would consist almost entirely of men of German extraction, some of whom were immigrants. Von Heer made the base for gathering recruits the town of his residence, Reading, along the Schuylkill River in Berks County, Pennsylvania. Reading had military significance in having a munitions depot, an army hospital, and a prisoner of war camp. The town's population was almost entirely German. Recruits came largely from the German sections of Berks and Lancaster Counties and from Philadelphia. Several recruits came from out of state; one was a Mohawk Indian, and the first lieutenant, Phillip Strubing, had emigrated from Geneva, Switzerland. Six of Von Heer's recruits were Hessian prisoners of war.[9]

Although he did not say so explicitly, the commander in chief had no objections to having a mobile police force consisting of Germans, who at best spoke only broken English. Undoubtedly, in the back of Washington's mind was a preference for an independent police corps, made up of foreigners, who would behave with complete detachment from the common soldiers. There were already two German units in the army: the Pennsylvania German Regiment, and the "Free and Independent Chasseurs" (Legion) commanded by Lieutenant Colonel Charles Armand, the Marquis de la

Rouerie. In 1778, Washington considered forming another German outfit to be commanded by two Hessian officers who had deserted. He told Congress such a unit would consist of "German inhabitants" and also "prisoners and deserters from the foreign troops." The "New Corps" did not materialize in part because on February 28, 1778, Congress prohibited the enlistment of prisoners of war in the American army.[10] Despite this policy, some Hessian deserters were enlisted—in the Maréchaussée, for example.

Captain Von Heer initially had difficulty in recruitment because enlistment in the Maréchaussée warranted only a Continental army bounty. States paid a bounty to their troops entering Continental service; the state award was often substantially higher than its Continental army counterpart. Von Heer petitioned Congress that his recruits should be entitled to a state bounty. Congress complied on July 29, 1778, voting that recruits for the Maréchaussée would receive bounties from the state where they enlisted. Most of this burden fell on Pennsylvania. Congress promised to credit the Maréchaussée to the quota of troops required from Pennsylvania in return for payment of the state bounty. The Pennsylvania Council, however, adamantly refused to follow Congress's direction, and it was not until July 1781 that Von Heer's troops were assigned to the Pennsylvania quota.[11] Meanwhile, throughout the war, members of the Maréchaussée never received a bounty from Pennsylvania.

With the lure of both receiving a bounty and becoming a dashing cavalryman in an elite corps, men quickly signed up for duty with the Maréchaussée, pledging to serve three years or for the duration of the war. Washington ordered the Quartermaster Department to provide the Maréchaussée with sixty-three of the army's best horses, along with "proper Saddles and bridles."[12] By the end of July 1778, Von Heer had enlisted all the men that he needed, and then some: sixty recruited in Pennsylvania, and eleven at the army's encampment at Fredericksburg, New York.[13] During the course of the war, an average of forty-five to fifty men were present and fit for duty of the total allotted number of sixty-three.[14]

Von Heer brought Baron de Wolfen into the Maréchaussée as a lieutenant without Wolfen having received a commission. General Steuben discovered Wolfen at camp and found him to be a person "totally unqualified for any Business which depended on Discretion." Steuben turned Wolfen over to Von Heer. Richard Peters of the Board of War wrote Washington that Wolfen did not lack bravery, "but he has killed more Horses than he has slain Enemies." Steuben recommended to Congress that a small sum be given Wolfen so that he could return to Europe. Meanwhile, Wolfen quickly drew $200 on Congress's account with a Dutch banking firm. Congress, not wanting to alienate its Dutch moneylenders, honored the payment, and Wolfen left the country.[15]

The wearing of flashy attire enhanced the esprit de corps of Von Heer's troopers. As the Maréchaussée wintered at Reading in early January 1780, a Hessian officer on parole there observed that "their uniform was a blue coat with yellow flaps, collar, and facings, and vest, with leather trousers," and a casquet (a metal frame worn over a hat as protection against saber blows). The trumpeters sported a yellow coat with blue facing or, in common with many army musicians, a captured British uniform.[16] Von Heer tried unsuccessfully to have the Quartermaster Department supply his men with bearskin robes.[17]

Clothing for the Maréchaussée was almost always in short supply or delayed in arriving. A small part of the problem may have been because Von Heer's paperwork was deemed "not very intelligible." In December 1780, he had to go before the Board of War to explain one of his returns.[18] Also, the Board of War seemingly placed the needs of the Maréchaussée at the lowest priority and gave it no access to the military stores of the states. Once, Washington informed Von Heer that the "articles" requested were unavailable at the time: "there are neither stockings, nor shirts in Store, and what shoes we have on hand are for a particular occasion." The commander in chief added, "I do not know of any use overalls can be to horsemen."[19]

The Maréchaussée was always in need of good horses. Occasionally, a detachment from the Maréchaussée was sent into the countryside as an impressment party, and presumably some fine mounts were obtained in this way.[20]

Despite the persistence of the commander in chief and Von Heer to have the Maréchaussée included in Pennsylvania's quota of Continental soldiers, thereby providing to Von Heer's troops a state bounty and some regularity of pay, the Maréchaussée, as "independent Foreign Troops," found themselves in a kind of limbo. Congress insisted that Pennsylvania consider the Maréchaussée as part of the state's Continentals, but this came to no avail until summer 1781, and even then there were no benefits. In June 1781, Washington assured Von Heer that the Maréchaussée troopers were "entitled to the same pay, depreciation of pay, and all other emoluments, which have been granted to the other Troops" raised in Pennsylvania and said that he hoped Congress would again push for measures giving relief to the Maréchaussée.[21] The Pennsylvania government continued to drag its feet, using the same dodge as before, that men for Von Heer's unit should be drafted from existing Pennsylvania regiments—an idea that Washington again vetoed.[22]

Not only did the Maréchaussée troopers frequently have to do without necessary equipment and supplies but they went for long periods without pay. In July 1781, Von Heer's men had not been paid for sixteen months.[23] In 1782, Robert Morris, the superintendent of finance, came to the rescue of the Maréchaussée. Although recognizing that men were attracted to join the Maréchaussée "owing to Circumstances of Personal acquaintances and Influence," Morris, despite the "narrowness" of funds, drew money from the national treasury to bear "the heavy Expence of Cloathing, Horses, Accoutrements, &c" required by the Maréchaussée and also gave Von Heer's troopers £12 per man as a bounty (Pennsylvania at the time offered £15 to each of its recruits). The expenditures were charged to Pennsylvania, with the superintendent of finance only hoping for reimbursement.[24]

Various factors impeded the success of a separate police corps in Washington's army. Von Heer brought his troopers to join Washington's army at the end of July 1778.[25] For only the remainder of that year, and very rarely thereafter, did the Maréchaussée exercise its intended mission of policing the army at large. With slight misstatement, Von Heer complained in 1780 that his light dragoons "never acted in the Duty of Maréchaussée; but always performed the Services in Camp & on the Lines."[26]

To some American soldiers, Germans in the army were of the same breed as the hated Hessian mercenaries employed by the British. Hessian troops were considered brutish by nature, and they were accused of atrocities. Many soldiers in the Continental army hailed from areas where xenophobia ran high. Of all the ethnic groups in America, the Germans were the least assimilable, and their Old Country ways courted ridicule. It was a miscalculation that a detached company of Germans could effectively perform as the military police of the army. For the common soldier, it was bad enough to be arrested, but it was more of an insult to be apprehended by "uncouth" German military police.

A nasty rivalry between the Maréchaussée and the commander in chief's Life Guard developed at camp. The arrest of guardsmen for marauding by

Von Heer's troops sparked attempts by the guardsmen to seek revenge, which led to more arrests (see chapter 5). That many of the culprits from the Life Guard were acquitted may indicate a general disrespect of the Maréchaussée. With the troops of the Maréchaussée being considered too abrasive, its role became increasingly supplementary to the regular camp police. Von Heer's troopers would also receive line assignments and spend long periods of time at Reading.

It was not as if members of the Maréchaussée were not culpable for misdeeds. At a court-martial in March 1779, three of Von Heer's dragoons were tried for planning to desert to the enemy and to take with them two horses belonging to Von Heer. Two of the accused, Heinrich Lily and Heinrich Winkler, were acquitted, while the third, trumpeter Ludwig Wolfe, was sentenced to one hundred lashes.[27] Baron de Wolfen, Von Heer's ersatz lieutenant, was tried for "disobedience of orders, cursing and damning the service," for striking a soldier with a sword, "and confining him afterwards and for offering to have him punished again without a trial," all of which occurred when Wolfen was drunk.[28]

Von Heer himself faced a court-martial for extorting bribes in the licensing of sutlers. He was severely reprimanded, with Washington stating that he expected Von Heer to behave in the future.[29] Once, following an argument, the Maréchaussée captain had David Parks, a wagoner, whipped. A court-martial investigated and ordered that Von Heer be reprimanded. Washington approved the sentence, commenting that an officer should "avoid putting himself in a situation that exposes him to intrusion and insults; which often proceed from an ignorance of the rules of decorum and which lead to such disagreeable disputes and violence."[30] Von Heer was court-martialed in May 1782, and again he was reprimanded for "immoderately beating" a soldier "without sufficient cause.[31]

During the brief period when the Maréchaussée acted as a military police corps, Captain Von Heer took his duty of regulating sutlers all too seriously. Unlicensed civilians entered camp to sell liquor to soldiers, in return often receiving as payment military clothing, provisions, or accoutrements. Although this was a punishable offense by the army, the civilians were generally gone before the transactions were detected. Von Heer decided to go after the civilian violators. As the army encamped at Middlebrook, New Jersey, Elisha Ayers of Basking Ridge, Somerset County, swore out an affidavit "proving sundry personal abuses upon himself & family, & the destruction of his property by a company of light horse" commanded by Von Heer. When the governor of New Jersey, William Livingston, informed Washington of the complaint, the commander in chief pledged that Von Heer should be speedily tried either by a court-martial or by a civilian court, preferably the latter. Washington urged Livingston to help bring a civil suit against Von Heer and to use his influence with the New Jersey legislature to pass a law preventing citizens from engaging in commerce prohibited by army regulations "between the people and the Soldiery."[32] There is no evidence that Von Heer was ever held to account. Civil versus military jurisdiction was always a delicate matter with Washington.

Starting in early 1779, the Maréchaussée was used for a variety of purposes: patrols for intelligence gathering; couriers in charge of "public Money"; and frequent assignments on the line as light dragoons. At different times during 1779, Von Heer's troopers served as cavalry attached to the commands of Generals William Maxwell, Anthony Wayne, and Lafayette.[33] Frustrated by the distractions from the stated mission of the Maréchaussée as a mounted provost corps and insufficient material and financial support, Von Heer asked General Steuben in December 1779 to use his influence to obtain for him command of a light infantry company per se.[34] A few months later, Von Heer asked Washington that his corps be organized as "an independent Troop of Light Horse" and remove the name Maréchaussée,[35] but the commander in chief was cool to the idea.

Washington vetoed a suggestion that the Maréchaussée be annexed to the legion commanded by Lieutenant Colonel Armand. Armand's legion consisted largely of German deserters. To Washington, the Maréchaussée should not be converted "to any other purpose than that for which it was raised."[36] Congress voted for an army reorganization on October 21, 1779, with the law taking effect on January 1, 1780. While many units were reduced or disbanded, the Maréchaussée was not mentioned, implying its status remained unchanged. Washington eventually got around to asking Congress to state specifically that no changes were meant to affect the Maréchaussée. "Its continuance," said Washington, "appears to me necessary for a variety of useful purposes."[37] Congress, in December 1780, resolved that the Maréchaussée should continue "upon their former Establishment."[38]

Still disillusioned that his precious Maréchaussée had been diverted from its basic function, Captain Von Heer was not enthusiastic about bringing his troopers out of the 1779–80 winter quarters at Reading to rejoin the main army. Washington on March 30, 1780, ordered Von Heer and the Maré-chaussée to proceed to Burlington, New Jersey, to serve in the line as a replacement for Henry Lee's legion, which had been scheduled to link up with General Nathanael Greene's southern army.[39] Washington became annoyed that he did not have immediate compliance from Von Heer. The Maré-chaussée captain claimed that he did not receive Washington's order until April 21, and besides, Lee had not yet left Burlington.[40] On May 11, Washington again directed the Maréchaussée to join the main army, this time at headquarters in Morristown, and by the end of the month, Von Heer and his men had arrived.[41]

The Maréchaussée again found themselves employed as a combat unit. Washington confided to General Robert Howe, commandant at West Point, on June 20, 1780, that "the scarcity of Cavalry has obliged me to divert the Maréchaussée Corps of Horse from their proper occupation and put them upon ordinary field duty."[42] Yet, amazingly, despite their acquired role as regular cavalry, the Maréchaussée never saw combat, either in skirmishes or in battle, at any time during the war.

The closest the Maréchaussée came to encountering battle was near Springfield, New Jersey, on June 23, 1780. Von Heer and his men were undoubtedly with Washington as the commander in chief brought troops from Morristown to Pompton, New Jersey, sixteen miles above Springfield. From Pompton, Washington had striking capability against an expected British move through the Highlands to attack West Point; or he could help General Nathanael Greene, with fifteen hundred Continentals and some militia, to turn back an oncoming six-thousand-man British force under General Wilhelm Knyphausen. As fighting broke out between Greene's troops and the invaders, Washington started to lead reinforcements to aid him, but the battle ended with the enemy withdrawing back to Elizabethtown. Washington returned to Pompton and then on to encampment at New Windsor on the Hudson. All of Washington's Life Guard, commanded by Major Caleb Gibbs, fought at Springfield, becoming fully engaged with the enemy.[43] It is highly probably that Washington, who occasionally used men from the Maréchaussée for special duty, relied on Von Heer's corps briefly as a substitute for his Life Guard.

The Maréchaussée, posted with Washington's army, for the remainder of 1780 went on scouting missions and provided patrols to search for stragglers; sometimes, it simply performed "the duties of the Camp." For a while, the Maréchaussée was joined with the Fourth Regiment of Continental Dragoons, commanded by Colonel Stephen Moylan.[44] For order of battle, the Maréchaussée were directed to connect with Captain Henry Bedkin's Independent Troop of Horse near the light infantry and receive orders from General Lafayette.[45]

During 1781, it seems that Von Heer's corps remained at Reading, except for a few troopers attached to Washington's Life Guard. The army strength reports do not include the Maréchaussée. For most of the Maréchaussée, their three-year enlistments expired that summer.[46] Because of lack of pay and insufficient material support, Von Heer had great difficulty in obtaining reenlistments and new recruits.[47] Washington alerted the Board of War that the Maréchaussée was on the verge of disbandment.[48] Although Pennsylvania had finally decided to include the Maréchaussée in the state's military quota, no benefits were received from the state. With pleas from Washington, some back pay was allowed by Congress, however, which helped to restart recruiting.[49] The commander in chief assured Von Heer that he considered "your Troop of essential utility to the Army; having had ample experience of their fidelity and promptness in executing their duty on every occasion."[50]

Washington wrote Congressman Joseph Jones in July 1781 that the Maréchaussée Corps consisted of about forty men and half that number of horses, "12 of which are with me, and from the smallness of the number are continually on duty, carrying orders to one part and another of the Camp."[51] A small detachment of the Maréchaussée, commanded by Lieutenant Mytinger, accompanied Washington to the Head of Elk, as the army journeyed southward for the siege of Yorktown. Two of the Maréchaussée remained with Washington at the Head of Elk. Mytinger and the others were sent to Baltimore to await further orders. There is no indication that any of the Maréchaussée were with the American army at Yorktown.[52] Von Heer himself was still busy in Pennsylvania, lining up new recruits and trying to secure additional forces, arms, and equipment.[53]

With some additional financial help from Congress, the Maréchaussée was again fully operative by mid-1782. During the fall of 1782, fifty-three men (including three officers) were engaged for duty. Of these, thirteen were on command (detached assignments), and the others mounted every day with guards "for the purpose of scouring the environs of the camp."[54] Some of Von Heer's men served with Washington's Life Guard but were not brought into it.[55] Most likely, the Maréchaussée again wintered (1782–83) at Reading and rejoined the army along the Hudson in spring 1783.

While the Maréchaussée Corps stayed a fixture in the main army, the southern command experimented with the employment of mounted provost units on a makeshift basis. General Benjamin Lincoln in summer 1779 unsuccessfully tried to prevail upon Governor John Rutledge of South Carolina to send to the army a troop of horse militia "to attend the Provost of the Army" in order to pursue deserters and to patrol "the vicinity of the Camp as executioners of Military law." Lincoln felt that the creation of such a group would have a "salutary" effect by fostering terror in "the minds of the men."[56] The South Carolina governor would not comply and generally did not encourage militiamen to join up with Continental forces.

General Greene, whenever he could, established a mounted provost unit from local militia. His primary objectives were to use the unit to curtail marauding and straggling. Briefly during the summer 1781, Captain John R. McClarry, as "Captain of Marshalsea," commanded a group of mounted militia.[57] During part of 1782, Colonel Morton Wilkinson, a wealthy South Carolina planter, and his militia regiment also performed duties as mounted provosts.[58]

On May 26, 1783, Congress granted furloughs to soldiers who had enlisted for the duration of the war, on condition that they would be fully discharged upon the formal signing of a peace treaty. The members of the Maréchaussée came under this sweeping provision. Troops were dismissed from service either on October 18 or November 3–4.[59] Von Heer received a promotion to brevet major on September 30, 1783, and was officially released on November 4. The certificate of discharge, in the handwriting of Benjamin Walker and signed by Washington, read, "In the several services in which Major Von Heer has been employed under my observation he has conducted himself as a zealous, active and good officer."[60]

At war's end, Von Heer and his officers received compensation in the form of loan office certificates issued for depreciation of pay, commutation of five years' pay in lieu of a pension, and $500, the same as that given to foreign officers who had commanded independent corps.[61] The former Maréchaussée captain and his family lived at Reading until 1785, and then they moved to the falls of the Schuylkill River. A warrant for three hundred acres of bounty land in Coshocton County, Ohio, was issued to Von Heer on July 30, 1789.[62]

Until he returned home to Mount Vernon, Washington required the service of a small detachment of horsemen. A sergeant, a corporal, and eight privates from the Maréchaussée were persuaded to stay in service two extra months. These men, Washington noted, were "extremely faithful and serviceable." For them, Washington secured a total of $166.60 as pay for this extra duty.[63] Members of the special detail carried dispatches for Washington and were presumably with him during his triumphal entry into New York City on November 25, 1783. The remnant Maréchaussée accompanied Washington on the first leg of his homeward journey from West Point, arriving at Philadelphia on December 8. The faithful dragoons were then discharged, and the now former commander in chief traveled the rest of the way with two aides and several servants.[64]

One may wonder why George Washington placed such a high value on the Maréchaussée, repeatedly defending it before Congress and helping to prevent it from being removed from the army organization. The commander in chief respected the experience of European armies, which fielded mounted provost corps. The Maréchaussée in the American army, as a free-ranging force to cover a whole encampment and its surrounding area, provided a flexibility that enabled quick apprehension of deserters, marauders, stragglers, and any misbehaving soldiers. The Maréchaussée could also be drawn upon for special duty, such as patrolling and scouting, and could even serve as a backup and relief for the Life Guard. As an independent company, the Maréchaussée could easily be employed in any way Washington saw fit, without disrupting personnel within the commands of the divisions, brigades, or regiments. In a crunch, Von Heer's troopers could function as combat-ready cavalry.

Washington was impressed by the soldierly quality of the Maréchaussée. Its members always presented a sharp appearance and were willing to perform any duty. Although several of the Maréchaussée deserted to the enemy (a factor Washington dismissed as not reflecting on the honor of the Maréchaussée as a whole), the commander in chief's trust in the loyalty of the mounted provost corps never diminished. Since the Maréchaussée spent long periods away from the main army during wintertime, there was little opportunity for Von Heer's troopers to grate on the commander in chief's nerves.

The Maréchaussée never had a chance to prove its mission from the start. The creation of a German military-type constabulary in the American army was unrealistic. If the Maréchaussée had been allowed to persist as a mounted provost corps, army morale would have suffered. The exercise of a limited authority to administer summary and instant punishment would surely have caused resentment. One can only imagine, if a hangman, as in European armies, had ridden with the Maréchaussée (the four executioners were detached to the provost marshal), what repercussions might have ensued.

A major reason for the failure of the Maréchaussée to fulfill its intended role was that it only supplemented and even duplicated other police personnel already in place in camp, particularly the quarter and other guards and duty officers. As a matter of fact, the Maréchaussée troops were instructed not to interfere with the jurisdiction of the quarter guards. Yet, in spite of all the drawbacks, the Maréchaussée, as an independent mounted police corps, was an unusual experiment in the Continental army.

14

Corporal Punishment

"The worst men are the best soldiers" was an argument successfully used in debate in the British Parliament to prevent the removal of flogging from the army's code of military justice.[1] George Washington probably would not have agreed, but in any event, the Continental army wound up with its fill of the dregs of society. The fear of being subjected to enormous pain inflicted even for the least of infractions constantly hung over the brow of a soldier, although it became quite evident that physical correction did not prove much of a deterrent.

A latter-day criminologist and advocate for corporal punishment states what well might have been on the minds of early Americans: "Pain is not only the primary ingredient of punishment but it is also a necessary condition of justice. For without it there can be no punishment. And there can be no justice without punishment."[2] Not only did corporal punishment in the eighteenth century serve as retributive justice, it also provided swift and cost-effective punishment. In the army, it prevented the loss of service by a culprit.

Discipline must be maintained. It "is the very Life-Blood of an army which is Diseased or Healthy as Lanquor or Activity governs its Circulation," so noted orders from General Robert Howe from his Highlands command at West Point.[3] To George Washington, "an Army without Order, Regularity & Discipline, is not better than a Commission'd Mob"; it is "Subordination & Discipline (the Life and Soul of an Army) which next under providence . . . make us formidable to our enemies."[4] The commander in chief advised a Virginia neighbor, Colonel William Woodford, to "reward and punish every man according to his merit without partiality or prejudice."[5]

Almost no one questioned the necessity of harsh punishment to keep soldiers in line. The public was inclined to view the common soldier with disdain, and seldom could men in the ranks expect civilian advocacy on their behalf. Persons enlisting in the Continental army realized that in doing so they accepted the status of second-class citizens. They forfeited civil liberties and subjected themselves to the law of "military necessity."[6] Especially in wartime, discipline was harsh because infractions jeopardized the fighting capabilities of the army. While corporal punishment might be mitigated in peacetime, in an army facing an enemy, swift and certain punishment was required.

In the eighteenth century, corporal punishment existed in civilian life. It was exacted primarily on the "lower sort" of society; gentlemen escaped the lash or other physical correction. The Revolutionary military leaders, like their civilian counterparts, feared the potentiality of any kind of resistance from the underclass. In many ways, Revolutionary War soldiers found themselves in a status not much different from slavery. Like African bondsmen, they were allowed no participation in governance, trial by their peers, or freedom of mobility. Like slaves, soldiers were expected to follow strictly the orders of their masters. Consequences of disobedience and other errant behavior were the lash or other punishment causing physical harm, even death—penalties not reserved for similar offenses committed by either upper-class civilians or members of the army's officer corps.

It was not easy for a well-intentioned and dutiful Continental soldier to avoid confronting military justice. Typically in an army, as one writer has observed, many soldiers "are drawn irresistibly towards whatever will do themselves the most harm."[7] Punishment in the Continental army was uneven and hit-or-miss. Offenders received disparate sentences, and some avoided detection. As one historian notes, "like players in a deadly game of roulette," Continental army soldiers "found themselves at the mercy of capricious justice."[8]

Corporal punishment was mandated by a court-martial or determined simply by a decision of specially assigned officers, such as a regimental commander or certain duty personnel. Physical correction could be applied to all offenses, ranging from personal misconduct, such as intoxication, to grave crimes, such as desertion, mutiny, or treason. A variety of odd punishments were carried into the American army from long-standing British military practice. Most of these fell into disuse during the early part of the war or were made illegal under the Articles of War; flogging became the preponderant method of punishing the enlisted men.

Lesser penalties were often levied in conjunction with being whipped. Thus, one culprit who received one hundred lashes and another who had to run a gauntlet both had the front of their heads shaved without using soap, and tar and feathers were substituted for the lost hair.[9] Some delinquents were ordered to wear a halter around their necks for several weeks or sit for a period of time on a gallows with a rope around their necks.[10] Such light correction had the purpose not only to cause humiliation but also to provide a reminder of the ultimate penalty. "Extraordinary fatigue" duty was sometimes prescribed.[11] An old civilian standby, the pillory, was used, whereby one sat with neck and arms in holes clamped down in vertical planking.[12] One might also be required to carry a barrel on his shoulders, with his head protruding through a hole.[13]

A severe penalty that was sparingly used in the British army and by American colonists never surfaced in the Continental army: tying neck and heels together, with the back arched; victims were constantly in a state of semi-strangulation.[14] Among Georgia militiamen, however, a version of this punishment appeared: a musket was placed under the thighs of a seated victim and another over his head, with both weapons being brought together as close as possible and tied fast—the ordeal lasting for ten minutes.[15]

For delinquency of "a trifling nature," officers at the regimental and company levels and also the men themselves imposed correction designed to ridicule the victim and produce laughter. None of these punishments came up for review in the chain of command. One such sport was the "Buffalo Daddy." According to the recollections of a veteran army musician, a "large face and hollow head," with a pair of horns attached, was placed over the head of the victim. This contraption was lined inside with a sheepskin, with the woolen side, covered with grease and lampblack, pressing against the face. A large buffalo skin was clapped around the body of the victim, girted by a rope, one end of which was tied to a foot or a leg, and the other end, about twelve feet long, was used as a tether. The unfortunate wearer was moved about to make him sweat. After an hour or so,

> the Buffalo Daddy was taken off. The lamp-black and grease having by that time fastened themselves completely to his sweaty face, they caused him to look like a teaze-major [one who stokes fire at a glass manufactory] to a congregation of black-smith's shops. The moment his mask was pulled off, tremendous loud laughing and huzzaing were

raised by the soldiers, who would assemble to witness this humorous sort of camp fandango. His appearance, as a matter of course, would have justified a priest of Bramin in laughing heartily. After this, our duty was to play him several times down and up the parade ground, in order to show him off to the best advantage to the officers and soldiers occupying the barracks.[16]

For drunkenness or disorderly conduct, soldiers were often sentenced to "wear the clog [or log]" for several days or a week; more serious offenses extended the time up to several months. The culprit was shackled to a piece of wood, weighing twenty to thirty pounds, which he dragged with him wherever he went, including attendance at parade and fatigue duty. Soldiers enduring this punishment usually had to turn their coats inside out. A variation was to wear a three-pound "clog" around one's neck or a board on the back while on fatigue duty.[17]

A punishment for minor offenses, such as "getting drunk and neglecting duty," was to be placed in "the Cage," a wooden structure in which a person had to remain standing, while being fed only bread and water. This ordeal could last for a maximum of thirty-six hours.[18] Although not mentioned as such, the cage was probably similar to the whirligig in the British army, in which a person stood and was whirled around. At other times, a soldier could be confined in the "dungeon," a dark cell of some type, where he, too, would be kept on bread and water; this penalty could last from a week to a month.[19]

One of the most injurious punishments, carried over from British practice in the French and Indian War, was riding the wooden horse (or mare, or timbermare). Two boards nailed together to form an inverted V were supported by four legs; pieces of wood represented a horse's head at one end of the device and a tail at the other. The victim was straddled over the sharp ridge, with his hands tied behind him; the unfortunate man also had muskets or other weights attached to his ankles. Soldiers moved the wooden horse along, with vibrations intensifying the pain and causing ruptures. Some victims were emasculated. The punishment normally was limited to fifteen minutes, and never more than a half hour. Because of the extent of bodily injury it caused, its use appears to have been discontinued after the early phase of the war.[20]

Picketing, reserved for cavalry and artillery units, like most of the odd punishments, usually accompanied a flogging. The prisoner, hoisted along an upright pole, had his wrist tied to a hook at the top; a heel rested on a peg driven into the ground. The sufferer had to shift his weight toward either his wrist or his heel. The ordeal became especially excruciating when the heel rammed into a sharpened peg, which in some instances drove through the foot. Because of the likelihood of permanent bodily damage, picketing was rarely used in the American army.[21]

The gauntlet (or gantelope) accounted for about 2 percent of the punishments in Washington's army. It could be implemented in two ways: running the gauntlet, in which a soldier passed between two lines of his comrades striking him with switches; or having a group of soldiers, one by one, lash a prisoner tied to a wagon wheel. Running the gauntlet was the preferred method in the Continental army. Running the gauntlet was practiced to the extreme in European armies as punishment for desertion, often resulting in death. A maximum sentence in the British army typically had the culprit make thirty-six runs between lines of one hundred fifty or more men—six runs up and six down, for three days.[22]

With many troops participating in running the gauntlet, the punishment served as a collective retribution and brought close to the common soldier a lesson of deterrence. With punishment generally inflicted on the grand parade ground, a gauntlet victim rarely might be sent through a group of camp guards, but most likely the men of a full brigade. A brigade gauntlet could stretch a half mile. In General Greene's southern army, a soldier once was sent "through the whole army."[23] Running the gauntlet was a means by which the number of lashes could exceed the limit of one hundred set by Congress.

Although running the gauntlet was most often reserved for deserters, the punishment was applied to a variety of offenses, especially those committed against one's fellow troopers. For example, a Maryland soldier, found "guilty of an attempt to commit Sodomy," had to "run the Gauntlope three times through the Brigade."[24] By contrast, a lieutenant convicted "for attempt[ing] to commit Sodomy" with a soldier was simply dismissed from the service "with infamy."[25] During General John Sullivan's Indian campaign of summer 1779, two soldiers charged with "painting themselves" as Indians and threatening the lives of two officers ran the gauntlet through three regiments.[26]

A soldier running the gauntlet was stripped to the waist. Because "the delinquent runs so rapidly and the soldiers are so apt to favor a comrade," it became necessary "to impede his steps" by having a sergeant go on ahead, moving backward and pointing a bayonet at the culprit's breast to slow his motion. This made the back of the victim an easy target, and officers could better watch to make sure each soldier delivered a heavy blow. Hickory sticks were generally used for this punishment.[27]

A Revolutionary War veteran recalled viewing an occasion when a soldier was forced to run the gauntlet. The victim was sent down two lines of one hundred men each, with six feet in between. The troops were ordered not to spare the victim, and anyone doing so would undergo the same treatment. The prisoner was soon "in one general gore of blood," and after this torture, was remanded to prison.[28]

Another veteran tells of a soldier running a gauntlet for having stolen a shirt. Five hundred men lined up in two rows, a "narrow lane" in between, with soldiers facing each other. The victim "ran down, up and down again, which was three times through. Each time, each man struck him once or more on his bared back as he passed. . . . Supposing 500 men to give three cuts each, [it] would equal 1500 lashes. They cut the poor fellow so severely, that splinters an inch long were pulled out of his back with pincers. After the splinters were pulled out, his back was washed with salt and water."[29]

Washington eventually vetoed court-martial sentences of running the gauntlet. In September 1777, he upheld a running of the gauntlet on condition that no more than the legal limit of one hundred lashes were administered.[30] As late as January 1780, Washington was approving sentences of men to run gauntlets through their brigades.[31] Although having allowed the penalty on occasions, commanders of the southern army, Generals Lincoln and Greene, overturned court-martial decisions providing for the gauntlet.[32] Washington came to the conclusion that running the gauntlet was "unconstitutional and inadmissible."[33] In reference to two men being sentenced to the gauntlet for desertion in March 1781, Washington's orders stated his disapproval on grounds that the punishment "being an indeterminate mode" of correction was "not authorized by any Article of war and repugnant to the Spirit if not the letter of the 3d Article 18th Section of the Articles of war."[34]

Flogging was the preferred correction for any misbehavior, for trivial as well as serious offenses. It frequently substituted for the death penalty. Whipping had been a mainstay of civilian and military justice during the colonial period and for discipline in European armies. In the Continental army, the ultimate penalty was a choice between death and one hundred lashes. While a hundred lashes was also harsh by modern standards, in eighteenth-century military systems it was considered just retribution, and most American commanders desired a substantial increase above that number. In the British army, one thousand lashes was the maximum, and there were occasions when that amount was greatly exceeded.

Desertion was regarded as a most heinous crime deserving death. So many deserters were apprehended, however, that it was impractical to execute all of them. A great number of executions would cast the American army as grossly inhumane, thereby undermining the morality of the rebel cause; furthermore, it would undoubtedly produce rebelliousness among the troops. As it was, Washington and other commanders felt impelled to remit death sentences, often in the moments just before execution. Culprits were then returned to their units with impunity.

The congressional limitation in the 1775 Articles of War of thirty-nine lashes, raised to one hundred lashes in 1776, was considered too lenient for the most serious crimes. Washington rued the situation where there was no intermediate penalty between one hundred lashes and death. He tried unsuccessfully to have Congress raise the limit in flogging to five hundred stripes. At Valley Forge, the commander in chief informed the Committee of Congress, then investigating the army, that

> to inflict capital punishment upon every deserter or other heinous offender, would incur the imputation of cruelty, and by the familiarity of the example, destroy its efficacy; on the other hand to give only a hundred lashes to such criminals is a burlesque on their crimes rather than a serious correction, and affords encouragement to obstinacy and imitation. The Courts are often in a manner compelled by the enormity of the facts, to pass sentences of death, which I am as often obliged to remit, on account of the number in the same circumstances, and let the offenders pass wholly unpunished. This would be avoided, if there were other punishments short of the destruction of life, in some degree adequate to the crime; and which might be with propriety substituted.[35]

A council of general officers, acting upon a recommendation from Washington, in August 1778 proposed hard labor, with the detainee kept on bread and water, as an alternative to the death penalty. Congress refused to act on this recommendation.[36]

Washington generally adhered to the congressional restriction by disapproving sentences in excess of one hundred lashes, even if sentences were based on a conviction of multiple charges against a single culprit.[37] Yet, courts-martial continued occasionally to mete out excessive lashes, especially when related to plundering,[38] a few of which instances Washington let pass. Punishments of more than one hundred lashes were approved by generals commanding wings of the army, who usually had the last say in the review of court-martial sentences other than death. General Thomas Conway approved five hundred lashes in March 1778.[39] Both generals Heath and Sullivan approved up to five hundred lashes for single individuals who owed a "back allowance."[40] A regimental court-martial sentenced a Delaware soldier in October 1777 to five hundred lashes for stealing $5 from a comrade; the commanding officer, Colonel David Hall, however, remitted three hundred stripes.[41] One soldier who deserted repeatedly had received one hundred lashes each time he was caught; General Robert Howe finally gave up on him and prohibited further punishment. Of course, the general thereby had to release other deserters in custody at the time.[42]

As a sample of some of the cases under Washington's jurisdiction in which more than the legal penalty was allowed, a theft of two horses led to a soldier being whipped two hundred times, one hundred for each crime, and a New Jersey trooper received one hundred and fifty lashes for "quitting his post and riding General Maxwell's horse."[43] One hundred lashes became the standard penalty (short of death) for desertion and even for being absent without leave. One lad in General Lincoln's southern army received one hundred stripes for trying to go home to "fetch clothes and a Blanket," considering that the army had reneged on the promise to furnish him with adequate clothing.[44] Enlisting twice in different units for bounty merited the same penalty.[45]

Although there was always a discrepancy in meting out punishments, varying from lenity to severity for the same crimes, certain patterns emerged. Theft of a shirt from another soldier resulted in fifty lashes; shirt and overalls, one hundred; and stealing clothes from a military store, one hundred.[46] One soldier who stole stockings and also threatened an officer endured one hundred lashes and was chained to "a Log block" weighting fourteen pounds for four weeks while doing duty as a camp colour-man.[47] Stealing a "piece of linen" from a house brought fifty stripes.[48]

Robbing citizens of any of a variety of articles resulted in penalties of one hundred lashes, and for being an accessory, fifty.[49] At the Middlebrook encampment, court-martial penalties occasionally exceeded the hundred lashes for plundering. Three privates who robbed two houses each received one hundred stripes for each robbery.[50] A further sampling shows one hundred lashes issued for sleeping while on sentry duty,[51] stealing a musket and selling it to an artificer,[52] drawing a sword on an officer and threatening to kill him,[53] and making a false alarm on the lines.[54] For repeatedly being drunk, a soldier could expect twenty sobering lashes.[55] Still worse, if he was caught inebriated at the "time of Inspection," he was liable for fifty stripes,[56] and if caught drunk on guard duty, one hundred to one hundred and fifty lashes.[57] Minor mishaps in camp duty brought on whippings: for example, for not cleaning arms, twenty-five lashes;[58] "for repeated unsoldier like appearance on Parade—being overmuch dirty," thirty-nine lashes;[59] and for firing a musket without authorization, twenty stripes.[60]

Civilians seized for trading with, or in other ways aiding, the enemy were whipped at camp.[61] Normally, transgressions by women camp followers were punished by ducking and/or drumming out of the army.[62] At least two women are known to have been flogged. In January 1778, Mary Johnson, who instigated a plot involving her husband, Private William Johnson, and other soldiers planning to desert, received one hundred lashes.[63] In March 1783, a regimental court-martial sentenced a woman camp follower to thirty-nine lashes each on four different days for stealing a pocketbook from a private containing $3 in cash and a $26⅔ order on the paymaster.[64]

Summary whippings without conviction by a court-martial were common. Especially, robbery by armed soldiers of homes of civilians received swift and harsh punishment. Washington permitted his officers to mete out on the spot one hundred to one hundred and fifty lashes for plundering of civilians.[65] Any soldier carrying plunder was to be turned over immediately to a brigadier general or regimental commander for instant whipping.[66] Stragglers could be flogged on the spot if they could not give a good account of themselves. "Catchrolls" (special roll calls) were held, and men absent upon their return were punished "at troop beating."[67]

Flogging was almost a daily occurrence in the military camps. It was not unusual to have ten whippings in one day.[68] Most of the punishments took place on the regimental level at the time of morning or evening roll calls; sometimes, there were whippings at the time of guard mounting on the parade ground.[69] The victim, stripped to the waist (only rarely also with "naked Buttocks"), was tied to a tree or post, called the "Adjutant's Daughter,"

at the head of which troops lined up in a hollow square or parallel formation. The ordeal was sometimes referred to as "putting on a new shirt." The
punishment was under the direction of either the provost marshal or, most
likely, the regimental adjutant. Regimental drummers and fifers did the
whipping. In cavalry units, the trumpeter had this unenviable task.[70] Before the punishment began, normally the chaplain denounced the prisoner
for "his base Conduct" and warned the assembled soldiers "against bringing themselves to such a shameful Punishment."[71]

A cat-o'-nine-tails served as the preferred instrument for flogging. Consisting of nine knotted cords attached to a handle, it cut deeply into the
flesh with each firmly delivered blow. Before fifty lashes were completed,
the back of the victim "would be all cut and like jelly." When a cat-o'-nine-
tails became soaked with blood, a dry one was substituted in order to maintain maximum effect.[72] Frequently, punishment was stretched over several
days, before the wounds healed, "in which case the wounds are in a state
of inflammation and the terror of the punishment is greatly aggravated."[73]
Victims had varying tolerance for pain; some cried out pitifully, while others bore their suffering without a whimper. Usually, the victim was given a
lead bullet to chew on, which was soon reduced to a flattened and jagged
state.[74] Sometimes, regimental surgeons were ordered to stand by to "see
that the Criminals do not receive more lashes than their strength will bear."[75]

A British general commented on the horrors of flogging:

> When the skin is thoroughly cut up, or flayed off, the great pain sub-
> sides. Men are frequently convulsed and screaming, during the time
> they receive from one lash to three hundred lashes, and then they bear
> the remainder, even to eight hundred, or a thousand lashes, without
> a groan; they will often lie as if without life, and the drummers ap-
> pear to be flogging a lump of dead, raw flesh.[76]

Washington's orders required that, upon completion of a whipping, the
victim's back "be well washed with Salt and water."[77] A former drummer
in the American army recalled an incident in which a soldier underwent
seven hundred lashes:

> When this prisoner was thus whipped, he was found to be still liv-
> ing. He was then untied and laid down with his face to the ground,
> and then pack salt strewed over his back. They then took a small

paddle-board and "*patted*" it down, beating it thus into the gashes, and then laid him by for awhile until he recovered a little. The salt was put upon it thus, after all, in mercy to him (to cleanse his wounds and enable them to heal) cruel as it would seem.[78]

Corporal punishment in the American Revolutionary army may be viewed as counterproductive. Despite the severity, it did not contribute to lowering the incidence of misbehavior. The army saw no reduction of its desertion rate; camp brutality undoubtedly was one of many factors that caused men to abscond. Desertion throughout the war amounted to nearly 25 percent of the troops.[79] Few deserters were returned to the army; once gaining distance, they were protected by friends and kin, and when necessary, found refuge in frontier regions or in Vermont. Several times during the war, Washington proclaimed amnesty to all deserters who would return to the army within a specified time period, and on occasion, remitted sentences because of a culprit's youth or other extenuating circumstances. Yet, soldiers who stayed with the army lived in constant fear of military brutality. The stories that discharged soldiers brought home of inhumanity in the army discouraged enlistments. Lieutenant Colonel David Cobb of a Massachusetts regiment saw clearly the problem. Because "the Continental officers are so cruel and severe," he declared, "men can never be got to serve under 'em."[80]

In the army, no protest was mounted against the use of corporal punishment. Officers were reluctant to challenge the long-standing military practice, and, of course, enlisted men could not do so. Civilians did not relate to the plight of the common soldier. Regimental surgeon Dr. James Thacher in 1780, however, did note that corporal punishment in the army "has become a subject of animadversion, and both the policy and propriety of the measure have been called in question." He pointed out objections to military corporal punishment: it "is disreputable to an army; it will never reclaim the unprincipled villain, and it has a tendency to repress the spirit of ambition and enterprise in the young soldier; and the individual thus ignominiously treated, can never, in case of promotion for meritorious services, be received with complacency as a companion for other officers."[81]

Dr. Benjamin Rush, the one-time physician general of the Middle Department of the Continental army, several years after the war, in an essay attacked the use of corporal punishment. He argued that the practice "increased propensities to crimes"; furthermore, "a man who has lost his character at a whipping post, had nothing valuable left to lose in society." Victims harbor a "spirit of revenge against the whole community." Rush recommended, as a substitute, prison sentences during which culprits would undergo rehabilitation through useful work.[82] This view did not fit with that of the military, which then considered exemplary justice as a deterrent to have priority over recovery.

A half century after Rush's remarks, Major General Charles J. Napier published in London a lengthy discourse on the horrors and shortcomings of corporal punishment in the British army, calling for abolition of the practice. He condemned corporal punishment as torture. For many reasons, the use of flogging brought unequal suffering to victims, and it branded a man "like a felon for life." Flogging had a deleterious effect upon soldiers witnessing the punishment: "seeing a man tortured, of seeing his blood spring, his convulsions and writhings, of agony, and hearing his horrible shrieks is . . . mischievous to the human heart and hardens it against the noble feelings." As substitutes for corporal punishment, Napier recommended imprisonment, transportation out of the country, forfeiture of pay and pension, and modified bodily punishment not causing permanent injury. Of the latter, he favored blistering, whereby hot plaster would be patted onto the skin between the shoulders, causing blistering and pain almost equal to that inflicted by a cat-o'-nine-tails. Blistering, however, left no disfiguration.[83]

Not until near the end of the Revolutionary War did George Washington even indirectly question the feasibility of corporal punishment. He seems never to have been concerned, however, with the terrible suffering endured by soldiers being punished, although he condemned, from time to time, punishment that did not fit the crime. It is entirely possible, during his long military career, that Washington never witnessed any military corporal punishment, although it seems likely that he must have chanced upon such an occurrence. His headquarters were always located a distance from the scenes of punishment. The commander in chief made his camp inspection rides during the morning.[84] Even during the French and Indian War, Washington, as commander of the Virginia Regiment, separated himself from his men, preferring to stay at his headquarters in Alexandria, Virginia, trusting to his subordinates at Forts Cumberland, Loudoun, and the like to discipline and train the troops. His detachment from the common soldiers was also evident during his participation in the western military campaigns of 1755 and 1758.

One might contrast George Washington with Brigadier General Daniel Morgan. The hero of the battles of Saratoga and Cowpens never wearied of telling the story of how he had been whipped 399 times for knocking down a British officer while serving as a teamster to the British-American forces in western Pennsylvania during 1755 or 1756. Morgan's vigorous physical constitution saw him through the ordeal, but he never forgot the awful punishment he suffered. Throughout his career as a military commander, he never subjected his troops to the lash.[85]

In general orders of November 12, 1782, Washington suggested that to "reclaim" soldiers "who are not lost to all sense of virtue and military pride," different "modes of punishment may be introduced which by awakening the feelings of honor will have a better influence than corporal."[86] Washington, however, never made recommendations for reform of the military code of justice that would lessen the distress of enlisted men under the constant fear of corporal punishment.

15

Drummers and Fifers

The beginning of the Revolutionary War and its impending end were signaled by the roll of a drum. Early on the morning of April 19, 1775, sixteen-year-old William Diamond beat an "assembly" on his drum calling minutemen to arms on Lexington Green.[1] About 10:00 A.M., October 17, 1781, a drummer boy appeared on a British parapet at Yorktown and beat a "parley," prefacing the surrender of Cornwallis's army. Throughout the war, drumbeats accompanied by tunes played by fifers communicated commands governing the motion and movements of troops. The military field music could be heard at a great distance, and during battle, the drums sounded from beneath the roar of the weaponry, and the high-pitched fifes from above.

Drummers and fifers had a dual role in promoting army discipline. Their music indicated the various duties and activities of camp life and regulated the movements of troops on the march and in battle. The sounds of the drums and fifes elevated the martial spirit and morale. Conversely, as in British military practice, all flogging in the Continental army was administered by the drummers, and musicians overall participated in the rituals affecting other punishments.

Many (but not the majority) of drummers and fifers were mere boys, usually in their early teens, but sometimes as young as ten or eleven years old. Some were the children of soldiers and their wives who resided at camp. A few blacks served as field musicians. Frequently, the boy drummers and fifers were orphans or sons of officers.[2] From the British perspective, "such boys, from being bred in the Regiment from their infancy, have a natural affection and attachment to it, and are seldom induced to desert, having no other place to take shelter at."[3] The field musicians kept to a busy schedule, with the daily issuance of calls and practice. They had two masters, a drum major and a fife major, who directed performance and training and often supervised floggings. The common musicians bivouacked among other soldiers. Although exempted from camp duties, such as standing guard, they answered immediately to company commanders.[4]

The field musicians did not carry arms. In many ways, they were non-combatants, enjoying a kind of quasi-independence among the other troops.[5] Because of their conspicuous presence in battle, they experienced high casualties. An attempt by the Board of War to have Congress require drummers and fifers to engage in camp duty came to naught because the musicians insisted that their enlistment agreements precluded such service.[6]

Similar to English and Hessian military practice, the American army initially had one or two drummers and fifers each per company. By 1778, in some instances companies had as many as four drummers.[7] Normally, nine or ten companies formed a regiment. In May 1778, Congress fixed the size of an infantry regiment at 585 men, including all personnel, of whom there were ten drummers and ten fifers; in October 1780, the number of troops in a regiment was increased to 728, with the same number of musicians as before.[8] On average, seven to eight drummers and as many fifers were allocated to a regiment.[9] Whenever drummers and fifers of the various regiments joined together, such as playing at brigade or divisional parades, they were referred to as a "corps" of musicians.[10]

Congress in 1776 set the pay for drummers and fifers at $7⅔ per month (the same pay as a corporal), and $8⅔ for drum and fife majors; the regular musicians in artillery regiments also drew $8⅔.[11] Drummers were expected to keep their instruments in repair from their own pay.[12] The field musicians wore distinctive uniforms. Most often they sported their regimental uniforms in reverse colors. Thus, if the regular uniform called for a blue coat with yellow facing, the drummers and fifers had yellow coats with blue facing. Otherwise, the wearing of a scarlet coat marked the musician.[13]

Between playing calls that summoned troops to duty and practicing daily, the field musicians had little time to themselves. They sounded routine and irregular calls. For major signals, an orderly drummer at the guardhouse gave out a preliminary beat to alert camp musicians of the impending call so that all could play in unison.[14] The field musician's duties began at dawn with the playing of "reveille." This call, unlike that in modern times, was a drawn-out affair employing several tunes and lasting as long as twenty minutes.[15] The "troop," or "assembly," played anytime between 8:00 and 9:30 A.M., indicated morning roll call and was also used one half hour before guard mounting.[16] The "pioneer's march" sent men off on work details. For drawing provisions or gathering for dinner (at 12:00 noon), the musicians sounded the "roast beef." The "retreat" was played for the evening roll call at sunset, and "tattoo" came forth at bedtime, about 9:00 P.M., when troops were to remain in their quarters until the next reveille; no musicians or soldiers were to be out at night.[17]

Irregular calls that were sounded, not part of the regular routine, included the "general," a signal to strike tents and prepare to move out; and the "march," indicating the beginning of a march, which proceeded ordinarily at 75 steps per minute, or for a long march, 96 paces per minute. Sometimes, the troops were ordered to move along at quickstep (120 steps) or double time (140). Drummers were expected to play all the while, except in rare instances when a part of the march was uncadenced.[18] On a march, drummers were prohibited from putting their instruments on a wagon or cart, unless they were sick or lame, in which event consent was required from "the Senior Officer" of a regiment; anyone violating this rule was "to be immediately punished."[19]

Soldiers on a march were treated to lively melodies played by the fifers, with accompaniment from the drummers. The musicians particularly rendered the popular march tune "Over the Hills and Far Away." This piece had long been part of theatrical fare in colonial America. It was sung repeatedly in George Farquhar's *The Recruiting Officer* and appeared in various ballad operas, such as John Gay's *The Beggar's Opera*. Some soldiers may have joined in by singing lyrics of the song, of which the first two of many verses are:

> Our prentice Tom may now refuse
> To wipe his scoundrel Master's Shoes,
> For Now he's free to sing and play
> Over the Hills and far away
>
> We all shall lead more happy lives
> By getting rid of brats and wives
> That scold and brawl both night and day—
> Over the Hills and far away.[20]

George Washington very much wanted his troops to make a good impression on the residents of Philadelphia as they paraded through the city's streets on the way to meet up with an advancing British army. He ordered that "The drums and fifes of each brigade are to be collected in the center of it and a tune for the quick step played, but with such moderation, that the men may step to it with ease, and without *dancing* along, or totally disregarding the music, as too often has been the case."[21] The ragtag soldiery did not quite measure up to the commander in chief's expectations. Congressman John Adams viewed the procession and commented that "our soldiers have not quite the air of soldiers. They don't step exactly in time. They don't hold up their heads quite erect, nor turn their toes so exactly as they might."[22]

Among their irregular duties, drummers and fifers all too frequently were called upon to perform for funerals of officers and sometimes for common soldiers. As a procession wound its way to the place of interment, drummers beat a slow roll, with their instruments muffled, and fifers played a dirge, the one most often used being "Roslin Castle," a Scottish Jacobite melody. After the body was placed in the ground and as the participants were leaving, the musicians struck up a lively tune.[23] The playing of the "dead march" sometimes had a despondent effect on the troops. In the southern army, in August 1782, because the playing of it had such a "tendency to depress the Spirits of the Sick in camp," General Nathanael Greene decreed that "this practice be discontinued."[24]

"To arms" signaled danger from the enemy. The drumbeat started at the main guard and was taken up by all drummers in the camp; troops scurried to their alarm posts.[25] The sounding of an alarm was the gravest command in the army. Chaplain Philip Vickers Fithian commented, "There is something forceably grand in the Sound of Drums & Fifes, when they are calling such an Army as ours to contend with another of perhaps equal Force! Whenever they come together the Death of many must be the Consequence."[26] Although "to arms" at times probably involved fife tunes, essentially, it was the "long roll," which is defined as "a continuous series of paired strokes rapidly executed on the drum."[27]

Indeed, the foremost rudimentary skill the young drummer had to learn was the long roll. Some drummers, it may be presumed, never achieved much beyond this stage, although a good drummer needed to have the mastery of various types of strokes. The long roll, however, made for effective accompaniment for any fife tune.[28] A drummer's manual (1815) explained how to practice the long roll:

In learning the Long Roll which is the foundation of Drum-beating;—The Boy must strike the drum twice with each stick beginning with the left Hand first, throwing his arms up between each as in the first position and gradually lowering them according to the closing of the Roll.—Be sure he keeps the Buttons of the Sticks as far as possible from the Drum head between each time he Strikes and both sticks should strike as even as near the same Weight on the Drum as possible. Pay attention to his Arms so that the Elbows and wrists move in Good form And not touch the Sides and the Drum to be struck as near the centre as possible.—In so doing the Boy will never fail having a Good even Roll.[29]

The military drummers used snare drums, which produced greater volume than those of today. These instruments were greater in diameter and three times deeper than snare drums presently used, and the gut snares were also thicker. The drums had vellum heads, and the sides were made of wood. Leather rims held together the head and the base of the drum. A drummer carried his instrument, supported by a shoulder belt, in front, against his left leg. The fifes, with six finger holes, were much the same as those used today, except a little thicker.[30]

With the great demand for drummers and fifers, the army had difficulty in maintaining the desired level of skill among the musicians. Washington, from his Middlebrook headquarters in June 1777, lamenting that "the music of the army being in general very bad," threatened drum and fife majors with reduction in rank and pay unless they "exert themselves to improve" the quality of the field music. The commander in chief insisted that the musicians keep to a schedule of practice.[31] Captain Robert Gamble, from Fort Montgomery, complained that "the Drums & Fifes in Stead of Improving . . . have Grone a Great Deal worse."[32]

A major problem at the beginning of the war was that drummers frequently beat on their instruments individually, which confused soldiers as to the actual military signals. A Rhode Island sergeant, encamped with part of his division near Pompton, New Jersey, in December 1776, noted that a drummer "made a Misteak & Beat at Midnight," causing the soldiers to strike their tents, eat breakfast, and prepare to march.[33] The cacophony arising from the indiscriminate music in camp became intolerable. Washington finally had all he could take of the noise; in October 1776, he declared that "the constant beating of Drums on all occasions is very improper" and ordered no drum beating except "on the parade, and Main Guard—All fatigue parties to march with the Fife, and no Drum to beat, on any account, after Retreat-Beating, but by special order."[34]

To provide uniformity and quality in the playing of martial music, daily practice sessions were required, usually two hours in the morning (most likely 9:00–11:00 A.M.) and two in the afternoon (3:00–5:00 or 4:00–6:00 P.M.). Rarely were practices limited to only one hour.[35] Drummers and fifers who absented themselves from either the morning or afternoon practices faced being assigned duty "in the ranks."[36] Washington decreed in May 1778 that "any Drummer that shall be found practicing at any other than the time" specified "shall be severely punished."[37] The musicians, of course, had to practice a fair distance from camp. Drummers and fifers at West Point "frequently went down the declivity on the East side of the Plain" to Colonel Thaddeus Kosciuszko's garden to "practice in Martial Music because it was out of the sight and hearing of the camp."[38]

Regimental commanders appointed a drum major and a fife major for each of their units. Extra pay for the men holding this position initially came from deducting four shillings from the monthly wages of the field musicians. This was the custom in the British army, but Washington thought that reducing the pay of the musicians was counterproductive. He proposed that, instead, a dollar be added to the monthly pay of each drum and fife major. Congress voted for the measure on July 26, 1776.[39]

The drum and fife majors conducted the daily practice sessions. Adult musicians did not have to attend these gatherings, but some did anyway to offer their assistance.[40] The drum and fife majors saw to it that instruments were "kept neat and clean" and that their charges powdered their hair daily and shaved at least three times a week.[41] As with the regular musicians, drum and fife majors often lent assistance to soldiers during military engagements. During the battle of Rhode Island, a regimental drum major was "blown up" while delivering ammunition to an artillery battery.[42]

Occasionally, a drum or fife major found himself director of a regimental band. Such ensembles, which included woodwinds and horns, numbering about eight to ten men, were underwritten by contributions from officers. Seven military bands became permanent fixtures in the Continental army, those belonging to the regiments headed by Colonels Thomas Proctor, John Crane, Samuel B. Webb, Christian Febiger, Henry Jackson, and Philip

Van Cortlandt and Lieutenant Colonel Henry Lee's Partisan Corps. Some-times, the bandsmen joined with the regular field musicians in such mili-tary functions as marches, parades, and executions. The bands played for officers' dinners and dances and other festive events.[43] On parade or on a march, a favorite rendition of the Continental army bands was the march from *Le Huron* (The Huron), an opera by Ándre Grétry (1768).[44]

Like their charges, drum and fife majors could get into trouble. Will-iam Loudon, a drum major in an artillery regiment, quarreled with Rich-ard Savage, an artilleryman. In an ensuing struggle, Loudon fatally stabbed Savage. For some reason, Loudon was turned over to a civilian court for trial, in which he was convicted of manslaughter. Being allowed to plead benefit of clergy (exemption from the death penalty by demonstrating the ability to read), he was merely branded on the hand and released back to his regiment.[45] Lieutenant James Verrier, adjutant to the Third North Caro-lina Regiment, faced court-martial for "cruelly and unnecessarily beating the Fife Major" while in "the execution of his duty." Verrier was convicted of beating the fife major, but "not cruelly," and received a reprimand. An-other such assault was deemed more serious. A private of the Third New York Regiment, in January 1780, was convicted of sneaking into the tent of Fife Major Andrew Garner and attempting to kill him; Garner was knocked unconscious. A brigade court-martial sentenced the aggressor to be shot.[46]

Drum and fife majors were not immune from being whipped. In fall 1776, the drum major of Colonel Paul Dudley Sargent's Massachusetts Regiment underwent fifteen lashes for theft, and several days later, suffered another twenty strokes for being drunk and neglecting his duty.[47] Patrick Ivory, drum major of the First Maryland Regiment, in August 1777 was sentenced to one hundred lashes and reduction in rank to that of a "pri-vate Drum[mer]" for stealing.[48]

On August 19, 1778, the commander in chief appointed John Hiwell, a fife major and director of Colonel John Crane's regimental band, as inspec-tor and superintendent of music in the army. Hiwell served in this capac-ity until the end of the war at the rank of lieutenant and with the pay of a captain of artillery. His major responsibilities included providing instruc-tion to the drum and fife majors, obtaining musical instruments, and at-tending parades to oversee the performance of the musicians.[49] Washing-ton ordered the "Inspector of Music" to make sure that "exact uniformity in the different beats prevail throughout the army."[50] Hiwell conducted inspections of every regiment and corps "to examine into the state of the Music; and the number of Instruments in each," making his report directly to Washington.[51]

About the only time all the musicians of a camp assembled and played together was for a drumming-out ceremony. It was not unusual to have more than one hundred musicians participating. A Massachusetts private writing during the siege of Boston noted about one such occasion that "if the infernal regions had ben opened and cain and Judas and Sam Haws [the writer] had been present their could not have ben a biger uproar."[52] For a drumming out, whether for a soldier, an officer, or a camp follower, the musicians constantly played the "rogues march." The prisoner appeared with his coat turned inside out, a halter around his neck, and usually a paper attached to his back with the offense printed on it. A drummer, holding the end of the halter, led the prisoner up and down the lines of the assembled troops and finally out of the camp, whereupon the youngest drummer kicked him in the backside.[53]

Some enlisted men were expelled after a flogging. A soldier of General McDougall's brigade, in April 1777, found guilty of attempting to go to the enemy and using threatening language toward an officer, received one hundred lashes and was stripped of his clothing and drummed out of the army.[54] Timothy Downing, a deserter, received thirty-nine stripes in January 1776, and since he was deemed "worthless and incorrigible," he was drummed out of the army.[55] In a similar situation, a ne'er-do-well soldier after being expelled was delivered to the Quartermaster Department, where it was considered "he may make an useful laborer tho' not qualified as a soldier."[56] At Valley Forge, a soldier convicted of theft was "mounted on a horse back foremost, without a Saddle, his Coat turned wrong side out, his hands tied behind him," and "drummed out of the Army (never more to return) by all the drums of the division to which he belongs."[57] Probably the last drumming-out ceremony in Washington's army occurred just as the troops were readying to return home permanently. The culprit, a "principal in a Mutiny," received one hundred lashes and was drummed out with "a Label on his back, with the word *Mutiny* on it."[58]

Women camp followers sometimes were ceremoniously expelled. The wife of a New Jersey soldier was drummed out "with a paper pind to her back," inscribed with "A THIEF"; she "went off with Musick."[59] The aforementioned Mary Johnson, upon receiving one hundred lashes, was escorted out of camp to the sounds of "all the Drums and Fifes of the Division."[60] On the regimental level, drummers and fifers played the "whores march" as accompaniment to the ouster of prostitutes from the army.[61]

Lieutenant William Barton of the First New Jersey Regiment, detached to Newark, New Jersey, in November 1778, gives an account of the misfortune of one teenage girl. Barton ran across a "young Lad" in Newark and immediately enlisted him in the army. The next day, while Barton dined, the enlistee was called in and asked to bring a tankard to the table, whereupon the recruit made a curtsy in doing so. This and several other circumstances led the lieutenant to suspect the new enlistee to be a woman. A doctor was called in, and he "soon made the Discovery by Pulling out the Teats of A Plump Young Girl, which caused Great diversion." The young woman explained her conduct by saying that she had run away from home because her father would not let her marry a young man of her choice. The next morning, Barton ordered "the Drums to beat her Threw the Town with the whores march, they did so which was Curious seeing her dress'd in mens Clothes and the whores march Beating."[62]

The army drummed out a few officers for offenses of criminal intent, such as perjury, fraud, sodomy, and desertion.[63] For an officer to be cashiered, normally, he would simply be ordered to "depart" the army and not return, the best-known cases being the dismissions of Major General Adam Stephen for excessive drinking and negligence and of Colonel Mordicai Buckner for cowardice.[64] Notices of cashiering an officer were submitted to newspapers for publication. Being tossed out of the army was the ultimate dishonor for an officer as a gentleman.

A captain who was drummed out for forging a furlough pass for himself received more than the full treatment:

> The sentence of the Court Martial was that the Culprit should be dressed in Women's Cloths, and having a wooden Sword by his Side, and a wooden Musket in his Hand, be placed on the Back of an old Horse to be carried thro the Camp in this ridiculous Manner, and sent from Guard to Guard until he should get Home. This Sentence was executed, with the addition of throwing Cow-Dung and almost every Kind of Excrement at the Rider.[65]

Soldiers discovered that the unauthorized playing of the "rogues march" could reinforce protest demands. Once, after subsisting for a long while on hard biscuit and herring, which produced scurvy, troops at Carlisle Barracks kept some of the herring for several days. They then put the fish on poles, which they shouldered, and marched up and down the parade ground to the music of the "rogues march." Upon concluding this *fish drill*," the men left the herring on the parade ground for "an official inspection" and then withdrew "quietly and orderly" to their quarters.[66]

Drummers and fifers performed a ceremonial role for executions. The musicians joined with troops in escorting the condemned to the gallows or the firing squad. Chaplain Oliver Hart, witnessing an American execution in New York City, observed that the whole army assembled and then marched slowly: "the drums muffled beat the dead march and the fifes playing answerable thereto."[67] For one occasion of capital punishment at Morristown, Washington ordered the Artillery Corps band and two drummers and two fifers from the Pennsylvania division "to attend the Criminals to the place of execution."[68] There were variances in the number and placement of musicians in the march to the death scene. A military treatise, published during the Civil War, offered a guideline for a procession for execution by firing squad. The order of march should be as follows:

1. Provost-marshal
2. Band of the prisoner's regiment, playing a funeral march
3. Firing party
4. Coffin, borne by four men
5. Prisoner and Chaplain
6. Escort[69]

When running a gauntlet was scheduled, the field musicians were ordered into the woods to collect hickory sticks, three to five feet long. The soon-to-be-switches were bundled like sheaves of wheat and brought to camp. As the lines of soldiers formed for the punishment, each man drew a stick out of the bundles.[70]

Floggings were under the direction of the adjutant. It was his duty to see that the drum or fife major was on the scene to ensure that the lashes the drummers administered were "well laid on." Drummers were required to flog with both hands. A drum or fife major attending the punishment held at the ready a rattan with which to smack a negligent flogger, and if necessary, he could order the punisher to be whipped himself. At the rear of the drum or fife major, the adjutant carried a cane, which he might use to edge on the drum or fife major in his duty. Often, a regimental captain served in the place of the adjutant at whippings.[71] Despite the supervision to guarantee that floggings would be as harsh as possible, drummers wielding the cat-o'-nine-tails succeeded occasionally in mitigating the severity of the punishment, depending largely on the degree of popularity of the culprit.[72]

General Alexander McDougall in October 1777 was so disgusted that his soldiers "spread Destruction & Desolation wherever we encamp," especially the burning of fence rails, he ordered a captain from each regiment to serve as a special inspector to prevent such misbehavior. Each had the authority to inflict five lashes on any fence-stealing culprit; "for this purpose," the drum major was to accompany the captain-inspector "in his Visit to be ready to do his duty."[73]

After tying a prisoner to the whipping post, a drummer administered a set number of lashes (as little as five and seldom more than twenty-five), and successive drummers took over this duty at the same ratio.[74] By rotating floggers, a consistency in the maximum strength behind the blows could be maintained. In implementing the sentence of a general court-martial, normally the drummers from each regiment of the brigade to which the culprit belonged spelled each other at the whipping post.[75] Even the youngest boy drummers participated in the flogging. The twelve-year-old son of Major Ezra Putnam of a Massachusetts regiment, who served as a drummer, could not escape this duty.[76]

The boy musicians had to have the stamina of adults. Although enlisting for short periods of time, their being in the Continental army was no summer camp experience. A youngster served for a year or less and then went home, only to return again for another stint or two. Of course, some of the boy musicians had no home to go to, and presumably they were the ones who most likely graduated into the regular soldiery. Many of the boy fifers and drummers came from poor families and had been bound out in servitude, and it was not much of a step to exchange masters by going into military service. There was not much latitude allowed for childhood. A boy musician had responsibilities similar to that of adults, adhered to a strict schedule of training and performance, endured the horrid deprivations of the army, and engaged in the inhumane punishment of comrades. In short, a boy musician learned how to survive. There is an amusing anecdote, probably more propagandistic than truthful, that attests to the toughness of the young musicians in the American army. The *New-Jersey Gazette* of January 21, 1778, printed the following:

> When Colonel Webb with some others were taken in a late expedition to Long-Island, a little fifer of the smallest size belonging to the State of Connecticut was made prisoner with them, and carried to Rhode-Island. The Colonel being called before the British General, the little fifer followed close at his heels, as anxious to know his fate. Says the General to him, Who are you? I am, answered the boy, one of King Hancock's men. The General asks, Can you fight? The boy replies, yes sir, I can. Upon this the General calls in one of his fifers, and asks our stripling whether he dare fight him. He answers, yes sir! The General orders his fifer to strip, and give him battle. The boy stripped as fast, and fell on with such fury, that in a few moments the British fifer was so beaten, that it was thought our little hero would soon have finished him, had he not been rescued. The British General, with a generosity natural to great minds, but seldom displayed by modern Brittons ordered him to be set at liberty for his valour, and he is since returned home.[77]

As might be expected, soldiers held grudges against certain drummers for being too eager to whip as hard as they could. An incident in the Delaware Regiment reveals that animosity. Thomas Clark, a drummer, went into a mess tent, and a messmate, Andrew Meers, sought to keep Clark from eating breakfast because Clark "did not Deserve any for whiping A man so hard." An argument ensued. Meers told Clark that he "did not know how to whip or else he would not have abus'd the man so that he whipp'd yesterday." Drummer Clark replied that "he was oblig'd to do his Duty," and "perhaps some day or other" Meers "might fall into his hands & then he would know whether he understood whipping or Not." Meers gave Clark "a stroake in the Side which almost Deprived him of his breath." Since it was allowed in a regimental court-martial that drummer Clark had used "provoking Language," Meers, the defendant, got off with only a sentence that he apologize to Clark in the presence of their commanding officer.[78]

The young field musicians were under the same code of military justice as the regular soldiers, and then some. Drummers were warned that they could "depend on being punished, if their Drums are injured, or destroyed for want of Care."[79] A young drummer in Colonel John Lamb's artillery regiment was sentenced to death for trying to desert to the enemy, but because of his extreme youth, Washington commuted his punishment to fifty lashes.[80] Drum and fife majors had the power to arrest and bind over for trial by court-martial any of their musicians for misdemeanors. Thus, a drum major at Fort Schuyler had a drummer confined for breaking down a door and threatening assault.[81]

At a regimental court-martial, an army musician for "disposing of his fife" was sentenced to receive thirty lashes and stoppage of pay until the fife was paid for.[82] One time, the commander of a regiment confined nine drummers and fifers "for not attending their Duty," releasing them when they promised to do better in the future.[83]

Since the field musicians practiced a good distance from camp, there was the temptation to steal fowl, fruits, and vegetables, which could be hidden in the drum cases.[84] At West Point, musicians "under pretence of getting wood" went upriver by boat and raided orchards of farmers along the banks.[85] Colonel Charles Armand, a cavalry commander, reported to Washington widespread theft in the countryside as American troops marched to meet the British at the battle of Brandywine. "I stop'd today three Drummers at a mile and a half from their Camp," he complained, who "had been at the distance of three miles—they were returning with a Hen and Eggs," which they said their drum major had asked them to fetch.[86]

The strict penalties for being out of camp without a pass, especially between tattoo and reveille, applied to musicians as well as regular soldiers. Regimental commanders ordered up to fifty lashes for such breach of conduct, and there could be more if decreed by a general court-martial. But the young musicians took the risk. On summer nights, they liked to escape the stench and vermin of camp or garrison and find a cool spot in the countryside to sleep. At West Point, a flat rock along the Hudson River beckoned. Somehow, they managed to crawl past sentinels to return at the crack of dawn.[87]

The young musicians not only were dispensers of brutality but were also its victims. Samuel Dewees, a young fifer in the Continental army, many years after the war left an astoundingly perceptive narrative of his experiences. His precise account rivals Joseph Plumb Martin's famous narrative, *Private Yankee Doodle*, and even surpasses that volume in its description of the oppressive nature of army life. Dewees came from a poor family, and at a tender age, was bound out as a farm hand. At age sixteen, he tagged along with his father, who was a recruiting sergeant, and then again resumed servitude. He enlisted in the army at age eighteen as a waiter to one Pennsylvania officer and then to another. Subsequently, Dewees signed up as a fifer, stationed mostly at Carlisle Barracks.[88]

"Sammy" had a mischievous streak. He created his own entertainment, such as shooting rats with a bow and arrow; and visiting cellars, getting his body blackened with a coat of fleas, and then running outside to shake them off.[89]

"Myself and three other musicians (Drummers and Fifers) received at one time 12 lashes each upon our bared buttocks," Dewees writes. This misfortune resulted when Dewees and his companions went to a creek to wash their clothes, which "were very full of lice." A soldier came up,

> and began to abuse one of our Fifers. We ran to the support of our comrade, and gave the fellow a kind of a "rough-and-tumble" flogging and tumbled him down into a ditch which was near by, and put one of his knees out of joint. Apart from this we did him no great injury otherwise. We daubed his face over with soap or white clay, and rolled him about a little. It was rough treatment it is true, but we did not meditate to injure him materially.
>
> [The next day] as we were outside the camp, practicising in playing the Fife and beating the Drum, we beheld our Fife Major and the Adjutant of the regiment coming towards us. Noticing that the Fife Major had something under his coat, I began to "*smell a rat,*" as did also others of our company. It was not long until I found that my apprehensions were (feelingly) correct. We were all called up and our sentence read to us, which was, that we were to whip one another and I was the first ordered to strip and prepare to ride a sort of jockey race. A large Drummer was ordered to take my two hands and arms over his shoulder and hoist me upon his back. He did so, and the cat-o'-nine-tails handed to another, who was ordered to give me twelve lashes. I thought when I had theory as my guide, the receipt of twelve lashes would be nothing—the veriest trifle, but when theory was reduced to practice, and I the object by which it was to be tested, I found out that it was a serious matter. When I was made to take the first lesson or rather to receive the first cut, I thought it could not be less than the receipt of boiling lead would have been upon the part affected,

and I began to kick and sprawl like a cat, and to bawl out lustily. I threw the big Drummer off his feet and "broke for the mountains," running for life. The officers called out aloud "come back," "come back." I yielded and came back, but it was because I could not do otherwise. I returned begging for quarters all the way, but begging was in vain. The big fellow shouldered me again, but if he did, I threw him a second time, and broke away again. They caught me and mounted me upon my stumbling charger a third time, and gave me my allowance of twelve lashes and three in addition to make the count good and for my kicking against my judges, executioners and the cat-o'-nine-tails. Another was then hoisted, (it was the one that whipped me) and as I had received more than I wanted, I had no idea of receiving the Major's rattan upon my back for remissness in duty, I am fully persuaded that I gave him 12 lashes as hard as he gave to me. The two others had to lash each other as my comrade and myself had done.[90]

As the war drew to a close, it was decided to do something about the special status of the field musicians. By the terms of their enlistment, they had continued to avoid various camp duties. A breach in the no-arms-for-musicians policy came in January 1782; garrison orders for West Point and its ancillary forts declared that "full grown" drummers and fifers were to be given arms and ammunition.[91] Because of their quasi-independent status in the army, the musicians came up on the short end of clothing issues. General William Heath, commander of the northern wing of the army, complained that many of the musicians were "very naked."[92]

In December 1781, the secretary at war, Benjamin Lincoln, wrote Congress that drummers and fifers should be detailed from the ranks. Lincoln argued:

The method hitherto practiced in the Army of enlisting men to serve as fifers and drummers and paying them additional pay is attended with manifest injury to the service for nothing is more common than to see men employed in that duty who are in every respect fit for soldiers, whilst boys hardly able to bear arms are put in the ranks, and the Commanding officers of Corps have not the power of remedying this evil without violating the engagement of the men enlisted as *drummers or fifers*.

The secretary at war therefore recommended that Congress should order "that for the future no recruit should be *engaged* as drummer or fifer; but that the commanding officers of Corps should be authorized to employ such of their men on that duty from time to time."[93] Congress responded by enacting a resolution: "That in future no recruit shall be inlisted to serve as a drummer or fifer. When such are wanted, they shall be taken from the soldiers of the corps, in such numbers and of such description as the commander in chief or the commanding officer of a separate army shall direct, and be returned back and others drawn out as often as the good of the service shall make necessary."[94]

This new policy came too late in the war to be fully tested. Probably the only result was that the musicians lost their extra pay. New musicians, like those already serving as drummers and fifers, would be on special assignment. At least there was one consolation for the army musicians at the end of the war: like common soldiers who were allowed to keep their weapons, they left the army in possession of their instruments.[95]

16

The Executioners

Witnessing executions left common soldiers with feelings of horror and revulsion. As if the mutilating strokes of the lash were not enough, capital punishment was deemed an ultimate necessity in establishing a well-ordered and disciplined army. The ritualized carrying out of death sentences embedded in the minds of the soldiery ghastly scenes as the consequence of transgressions against military authority.

Capital punishment in the Continental army reinforced the notions of early Americans that executions should be a communal experience, involving as many spectators as possible as well as the participation of the clergy. In the army, there was great difficulty obtaining hangmen because an executioner most likely would be known to his comrades; thus, outsiders were sometimes brought in as executioners. Actual executioners remained under a cloud of anonymity, often with faces blackened or other disguise.

Provosts in the army, like county sheriffs, had responsibility for hangings, and if an executioner could not be found, they were expected to perform the task themselves; the provost marshal and other provosts, however, seem to have successfully weaseled out of having to act as executioners. There is no evidence that any of the four executioners assigned to the Maréchaussée Corps acted as hangmen, although it can be presumed that on occasion they did. Except for some condemned Tories, there is no indication that the American army ever indulged in the civilian practice of the time to reprieve a condemned criminal on condition that he serve as the executioner of another.[1] Death by firing squad was also staged as a communal experience, and with one or more members of the firing party shooting blanks, the anonymity of the actual executioners was preserved.

The two kinds of capital punishment in the Continental army were hanging and shooting. Among northern troops, hanging was the more prevalent mode. In Nathanael Greene's southern army, but not so with other

Continental troops in the south, executions were most likely by firing squad; death warrants were sometimes left blank as to the form of execution, in case a hangman could not immediately be found.[2]

ashington was a strong proponent of the military death penalty. "Examples must be made," or "we may as well disband the Army at once," he said.[3] He held two criteria governing army executions: they should be conducted for the most exemplary effect, and they should be infrequent. The commander in chief informed General George Clinton that executions should be reserved only for "the most notorious, and such, whose punishment would strike terror into their accomplices and adherents who are not yet apprehended. By making Executions too common, they lose their intended force and rather bear the appearance of cruelty than justice."[4]

Although the Articles of War made capital penalties equally applicable for both officers and enlisted men,[5] only soldiers from the rank and file were executed in the Continental army. Soldiers met death for offenses as slight as forging a discharge, selling "regimental clothes," or assault. Most executions related to desertion and plundering.[6] One former Continental officer was executed; Thomas Shanks, who as an ensign was cashiered for theft and subsequently captured as a British spy, was hanged at Valley Forge on June 4, 1778.[7] Two Pennsylvania navy lieutenants, Samuel Lyons and Samuel Ford, convicted of desertion from Fort Mercer, went before a firing squad in Philadelphia on September 2, 1778.[8]

The commander in chief had to be careful that there were not too many executions in a short period of time. To put all those condemned to death would certainly cause unrest in the ranks and lead to erosion of public support for the army. Washington, as did the commanders of armies other than the main force under him, frequently resorted to granting pardons, usually at the very last moment before a prisoner was to be executed. Those who gained mercy were men who had officers, influential family members or other citizens, or members of the convicting court-martial asking for clemency. Youth and reputation of a good character could be mitigating circumstances. In a few instances, pardons were issued on the basis that the culprit had been sick at the time of the offense or had been "subject to turns of delirium or insanity."[9] General Greene, commanding the southern army, had the same view as Washington about avoiding an excessive number of executions; Greene advised one of his officers to refrain from executing one of two condemned soldiers who had been of better character, because "one will serve for an example as well as both."[10]

On occasion, Washington issued pardons to condemned criminals en mass.[11] At least six times, he discharged all military prisoners in his army, including those under a death sentence: June 10, 1777, just after the execution of a deserter; May 7, 1778, in recognition of the new Franco-American Alliance; July 4, 1779, commemorating independence; May 30, 1780, at Morristown, although condemned Connecticut mutineers were excluded; February 6, 1783, on the anniversary of the signing of the Franco-American Alliance; and June 2, 1783, after the cessation of hostilities.[12]

Although he insisted on reviewing capital sentences, Washington gave leeway to his generals to order executions. By congressional determination, the commanders of separate armies (e.g., Sullivan, in charge of the Canadian invasion army in 1776 and the Indian expeditionary force in 1779; Schuyler and Gates, commanding the northern army; and the commanders of the southern army) did not have to seek permission from the commander in chief to execute offenders. Often, blank execution warrants were sent from headquarters, leaving commanders to fill in the names, with the understanding that one or more of those under sentence of death would receive clemency.[13] At times, however, Washington had to rebuke generals whom he considered to be in command of detachments, for conducting executions without seeking clearance from the commander in chief. Thus, Washington reprimanded General Preudhomme de Borre for having hanged a Tory whose case, Washington felt, came under the jurisdiction of civil authority.[14] Overall, generals showed proper deference to Washington's authority regarding executing capital sentences. Even General Benedict Arnold, from his new command post at West Point, barely a month before his own treason was revealed, wrote Washington for permission to hang two spies.[15]

Congress granted military courts-martial the authority to try and sentence to death any person deemed a "traitor, assassin, and spy, if the offence be committed within seventy miles of the headquarters of the grand or other armies of the states."[16] Most civilians executed as spies were caught attempting to convince American soldiers to desert.[17] Any civilian known to be associated with Loyalist refugee military units ran the risk of being considered a spy. In some instances, persons under suspicion for being at the wrong place at the wrong time were fair game, such as the three young Loyalists who were hanged after being caught hiding in a barn near the Morristown encampment.[18] Stealing army cattle also merited the death penalty.[19] Of course, there were advantages to executing spies rather than soldiers. The deterrent value doubled: a lesson to both civilians and soldiers. Putting spies to death did not run the risk of adversely affecting soldier morale. Civilian authorities and vigilante and militia groups (especially in the Deep South) did their full share in putting to death alleged spies and traitors.

Executions in Washington's army did not proceed at a high rate, in large measure owing to the liberal clemency policy. One estimate finds that of 693 courts-martial "authorized" by Washington, 84 resulted in sentences of death. Allen Bowman states that of 225 individual death sentences, about 40 were carried out. Another source estimates 45 to 75 executions.[20] These figures do not account for executions in the southern army or other separate commands that did not require Washington's approval of court-martial sentences. Drumhead courts-martial (with no trial records), particularly by militia groups, that ordered capital punishment were not taken into account. Still, it seems the number of executions for all the Continental army could not have much exceeded 100.

Washington insisted that executions be conducted in the "most public manner possible," preferably "at some convenient Place near the Grand Parade."[21] Hanging sites were generally on a rise of ground, so as to enhance the view by spectators.[22] Executions by firing squad had no fixed place but generally were held in a field not far from the grand parade ground.[23] In establishing an encampment site, one of the duties of the Quartermaster Department was to erect a gallows, which was left standing even when the troops moved out. At Valley Forge, the gallows was erected on the property of David Stephens, just north of the Gulph Road.[24] At the Middlebrook encampment of 1778–79, the hanging site was a little more distant from the main body of troops than usual, being located at the "artillery park," about five miles from the center of camp.[25] Forts and garrisons had their own gallows. Deserters were hanged at the "Flag Bastion" at Stony Point.[26] In urban areas, such as Boston, New York City, and Philadelphia, military offenders were dispatched on the commons or nearby; thus, for example, a firing squad did its work near the Centre Tavern at Centre Square in Philadelphia.[27] When the army was on the move, "the crutch of the road" served as a makeshift execution site.[28]

The selective enforcement of the death penalty served as both an expiation of sins for many of the soldiery and a frightful warning against temptation to commit major transgressions of the military code. Hence, the widest possible audience was desired for witnessing executions. Sometimes, the whole army, except for men on detached duty, was drawn up for the spectacle. At a bare minimum, forty to fifty troops from each brigade attended.[29] At garrisons, as many troops as could be gathered from the vicinity assembled for an execution, with the minimum size of the group equaling that of a regiment.[30] Executions drew civilians from a wide area. Twenty thousand persons witnessed the execution of Sergeant Thomas Hickey in New York City in June 1776. Four thousand troops and civilians attended the hanging of two soldiers from General John Sullivan's expeditionary force at Easton, Pennsylvania, on June 12, 1779; a sergeant commented, "I never saw so many spectators in my life."[31] Army Surgeon James Thacher noted that for one execution "a girl walked seven miles in a torrent of rain to see a man hanged, and returned in tears, because the criminal was reprieved."[32]

The provost marshal or other army provost normally had the responsibility of conducting an execution by hanging; a commanding officer had responsibility for selection of a firing squad.[33] When the army was lacking a provost marshal, Washington, in sending out signed death warrants to a commanding officer, simply mentioned that the "blanks are left for the name of the person acting as provost marshal and for the time of execution."[34]

The adjutant general's department had oversight for executions. One time, Washington ordered that an execution should be conducted "at such place as the Deputy Adjutant General shall decide."[35] The commander in chief expressly designated Adjutant General Alexander Scammell to take charge of the execution of the British spy Major John André.[36] For detached corps or wings of the army, an adjutant or occasionally a brigade major supervised a hanging.[37] At garrisons such as West Point, the commanding officer was expected to "direct the necessary preparations" for an execution.[38]

Ritual played an important role in bringing a soldier to his mandated death. Washington, in sending a signed death warrant to General Horatio Gates in February 1777, said that Gates should "direct the Ceremony as you please."[39] Typically, soldiers as witnesses to the spectacle were brought onto the parade ground and marched off to the site of the execution, where they formed a circle or three sides of a square. The field officer of the day had responsibility for assembling and parading the troops. A procession consisting of the condemned person or persons, an escort guard, a chaplain, and musicians set out from the provost jail or other guardhouse.[40] The slow "dead march" sounded until reaching the place of execution.

Sometimes, a "detachment of the Maréchaussée" was deemed sufficient to "attend the prisoner to the place of Punishment."[41] Otherwise, the escort guard was quite large. For the Thomas Hickey execution in New York City in June 1776, brigade majors were required to furnish the provost marshal with twenty men from each brigade, "with good arms and bayonets, as a guard on the prisoner to and at the place of execution."[42] In February 1780, for the execution of two soldiers for robbery, the Pennsylvania division supplied a death escort of a captain, a subaltern, four sergeants, four corporals, fifty privates, two drummers, and two fifers; in addition, the "corps of Artillery" sent "a band of Music to attend the Criminals to the place of execution."[43] For the hanging of the most prominent victim of army justice, Major John André, a guard of sixteen commissioned officers, twenty-five sergeants, one hundred and eighty rank and file, and twelve drummers and fifers accompanied the prisoner to the gallows.[44]

The ritual of army executions resembled those in the civilian sector. One or more clergymen met with the condemned prisoner in his cell during his final days, accompanied him in the death procession, and at the site of execution were expected to offer a prayer and a brief address. Chaplains in the army were few; only 218 chaplains served in the Continental army during the war. They were not commissioned officers and were contracted for six- or twelve-month tours of duty.[45] While initially it was planned to have one chaplain per regiment, Congress in May 1777 limited the number of chaplains to one for each brigade.[46] Washington ordered that the condemned "criminals" be "attended with such Chaplains, as they choose."[47] Some chaplains tried to avoid any role in executions and had to be ordered to participate. The adjutant general made the assignments.[48]

Chaplains attempted to impress upon the doomed men the need to become penitent and ask for God's mercy in hopes of achieving a state of grace. Some of the condemned men sought salvation; others, however, remained hardened and indifferent. The Reverend Ammi R. Robbins visited a soldier under sentence of death twice in one day and found that the prisoner "appeared much affected but dreadfully ignorant."[49] Chaplains Samuel Kirkland (Congregationalist) and William Rogers (Baptist) visited two condemned prisoners with the message of "their awful condition by nature and practice, their amazing guilt in the sight of an Holy God; the spirituality of the divine law; the necessity of an interest in Jesus Christ; their own inability to obtain salvation, and the great importance of a due preparation for another world."[50] On one occasion, in accordance with a New England custom, two soldiers condemned by a court-martial of the Connecticut line, a day before their scheduled execution, were sent under guard to hear a sermon at the Redding Meeting House.[51] George Washington, always a pragmatist, saw an opportunity in having chaplains interview condemned spies. He urged the reverends to obtain as "ample confession from them as possible," especially with an eye for gaining intelligence of the enemy.[52]

At the execution site, usually a chaplain (or chaplains) offered a prayer and gave a "solemn address" for the benefit of the condemned person and the assembled soldiery, always alluding to the awful consequences of breaking military rules. The prisoner was then allowed his last words.[53] A prisoner did not always exhibit remorse and Christian sentiments, indicating a failure of assisting chaplains to effect a reformation in the character of the condemned. Lieutenant Ebenezer Elmer, of the Second New Jersey Regiment, commented on one execution, "the poor wretch who was executed appeared to leave the world with that careless stupidity which had before marked his life."[54]

In contrast to Lieutenant Elmer's observation, a Philadelphia newspaper reported on March 8, 1777:

> This day, between the hours of twelve and one o'clock, Brint Debadee, a soldier belonging to the tenth Pennsylvania regiment, was shot upon the commons in Philadelphia, pursuant to the sentence of a general court-martial. This unhappy man was in his twenty-fourth year, in the vigor of life, and it is hoped his untimely and dreadful end will be a warning to others, who, when they desert, not only defraud their officer and abuse their country, but are also guilty of the dreadful and heinous crime of perjury. Of his past misconduct he appeared very sensible, and behaved in his last moments with great resignation and calmness, declaring that he sincerely forgave all his enemies, and hoped that his example would be serviceable to some of his thoughtless brother soldiers. He was attended by the Rev. Coombe, and the Rev. Mr. Rogers. The last gentleman, being a chaplain in the service,

delivered to the soldiers present a pathetic address, suitable to the melancholy occasion.[55]

While most clergymen welcomed the opportunity to sermonize at the launching of a condemned man into eternity, the experience was but one of the unpleasant duties of a chaplain. The Reverend Abiel Leonard, who performed many functions of the chaplaincy, suffered from bad health and became despondent and had "fits of lunacy"; he committed suicide by slitting his throat with a razor in summer 1777.[56]

Just as the condemned prisoner arrived at the execution site, before the ministrations of a chaplain, the field officer of the day or someone from the adjutant general's department read the death warrant.[57] For the hanging of Major John André, Colonel Alexander Scammell read the order for execution.[58] It was the usual practice in a military hanging for the prisoner to mount a baggage wagon, which was brought under a gibbet or a tree limb;[59] the platform gallows was not much in use at the time. The prisoner was compelled to stand on top of his coffin on the wagon, which added to the length of the drop. At the moment of execution, a signal was given to lead forward the horse pulling the wagon, whereupon the victim's body was jerked off the wagon, as much swinging as dropping. All too often, it seems that even with sufficient drop distance and the noose properly adjusted, death resulted from strangulation rather than from a broken neck. On one occasion, reportedly it took several hours for a hanged soldier to die, even though several comrades were called in to pull down on his legs and feet.[60]

Except for the executioners in the Maréchaussée Corps, there were no designated hangmen. The Maréchaussée, however, were assigned only to the main army and were often absent from camp. In any case, it was the duty of the provost marshal or other provost to conduct a hanging or find someone to do it for him. As previously noted, Provost Marshal William Hutton refused to carry out a pair of hangings and therefore was court-martialed. At that time, General William Heath, under whose command the condemned men were held, informed Washington that the deputy adjutant general could have furnished Hutton with a hangman "if to be found."[61]

Understandably, soldiers did not volunteer as hangmen. Increasingly, the army had to appoint someone from the ranks to serve in this capacity. For the few hangings in General Greene's southern army, the dubious honor was meted out to an army sergeant; for example, in 1781 to Sergeants Robert McConkle and Isaac Middleton.[62] At the execution of Major John André, a Tory by the name of Strickland, who was under arrest, acted as the hangman in return for his freedom; the reluctant executioner "disguised himself by smearing his face with stuff like shoe-blacking, producing a hideous effect."[63] In June 1780, as Washington's army moved about in northeast New Jersey, several captured "refugee negroes" were impressed into the role of hangmen.[64]

At a scheduled military execution in Carlisle, Pennsylvania, a convicted deserter was brought out to the gallows. No hangman had been found, and Lieutenant Richard Butler, the adjutant, stepped up to an old soldier named O'Connor, handed him the rope, and ordered him to fasten it around the condemned prisoner's neck. O'Connor adamantly refused. Butler then called upon the major to go back into the barracks and fetch a cat-o'-nine-tails. The old soldier was tied to the foot of the gallows, stripped to the waist, and given one hundred lashes. After the ordeal, O'Connor walked up to Lieutenant Butler and thanked him. Butler then, with the rope in one hand and a pistol in the other, approached another soldier and ordered him to perform the hanging; if he refused, Butler declared, he would "blow his brains out." The designated hangman took the rope and went to the gallows. As he placed the noose around the neck of the condemned prisoner, an officer on horseback rode up and announced a reprieve. As the ritual of death had now been interrupted, the intended hangman was "knocked and kicked about like a dog while Mr. O'Connor was applauded by every soldier in the garrison, and treated with all imaginable respect for his manly conduct."[65]

Executing a person with whom other soldiers were sympathetic ran the risk of causing riot or mutiny. On one occasion, troops protested against the pending execution of a soldier wrongly accused. The incident occurred at the end of the Rhode Island campaign of 1778–79 when troops petitioned General John Sullivan to seek redress for long-overdue pay. The petition was handed to a colonel to pass on to Sullivan, but the colonel refused to forward the document and arrested the messenger, who was tried by court-martial and sentenced to be hanged for mutiny. Soldiers marched on the quarters of Sullivan and secured the release of the falsely accused prisoner.[66]

After hangings, which were usually scheduled in the forenoon, corpses were left suspended until sunset.[67] A hole was dug under the gallows, and when the rope was cut, the corpse fell into it and was covered over.[68] It was the prerogative of the hangman to strip the body of an executed person for clothes that he could use himself. One soldier recalled such a situation at an execution at Peekskill, New York, on November 12, 1779. A brigade major, who was in charge of the execution,

> procured a ragamuffin fellow for an executioner, to preserve his own immaculate reputation from defilement. After the culprit had hung the time prescribed by law, or custom, the hangman began stripping the corpse, the clothes being his perquisite. He began by trying to pull off his boots, but for want of a bootjack he could not readily accomplish his aim. He kept pulling and hauling at them, like a dog at a root, until the spectators, who were very numerous, the guard having gone off, growing disgusted, began to make use of the stones, by tossing several at his pretty carcass. The brigade major interfering in behalf of his aide-de-camp, shared the same usage; they were both quickly obliged "to quit the field." As they retreated the stones flew merrily. They were obliged to keep at a proper distance until the soldiers took their own time to disperse, when they returned and completed their business.[69]

Soldiers normally displayed little emotion over the execution of comrades. A bit of gallows humor sometimes eased the tension. In September 1780, troops advancing toward Paulus Hook "were ordered to march by the Soldier who was taken from the ranks & executed" for marauding. The passing soldiers, who themselves had been on short rations for about a month, had sympathy for their unlucky comrade. The body had been left hanging for some time. As the troops passed by the corpse, one of them slapped the body on the thigh, saying, "well Jack you are the best off of any of us—it won't come to your turn to be hanged again this ten years."[70]

While the practice of dissecting corpses of executed criminals, mainly for the purpose of medical instruction, was catching on in civilian life, such surgical "anatomizing" did not become part of the military execution schedule, largely because the army in the field was at a distance from any medical training center. One military dissection, however, is reported. On the night of the Easton, Pennsylvania, hangings of June 12, 1779, a physician dug up one of the corpses, "cut his arm and Leg and Examined him and the next night then buried him again."[71]

The same ritual of execution was employed for those going before a firing squad as those who wound up on the gallows. It appears, however, that the sermonizing by chaplains, an essential part of the gallows ritual, was less evident at firing squads, probably because the event was conducted at ground level, thereby limiting visibility and audibility. A chaplain or chaplains did attend the condemned and offered prayers. A procession of a large guard, musicians, and clergy accompanied condemned soldiers from the provost guardhouse to the site of execution. A large body of troops were drawn up to form a hollow square, with the open side being the execution place; by this arrangement, the witnessing troops not only had a clear view of the event but could also measure the reactions of comrades in the line opposite them.[72]

As with hangings, the adjutant general's department had general responsibility to see that death by firing squad was carried out. A brigade commander was charged with ordering the selection of firing squads, usually from the prisoner's own regiment. The regimental adjutant had immediate oversight of the execution.[73] In General Greene's southern army, as was done in hangings, a sergeant was named to be responsible for the execution of a warrant for death by shooting.[74]

Firing squads varied from four to twenty soldiers but usually consisted of a noncommissioned officer and ten to twelve privates.[75] Members of a firing squad were drawn by lot. At least one of the muskets used in the shooting was loaded with a cartridge without shot; thereby, no one in the firing party knew whether or not he fired a fatal volley.[76] At the execution site, an embankment was thrown up to prevent shots at the prisoner from "doing other damage." The condemned man was blindfolded, and his hands were tied behind him. He was then forced to kneel down next to a coffin, which sat at the edge of a freshly dug grave. The firing squad approached to within about sixteen to eighteen feet (rarely, as close as ten feet) of the victim. An officer, with the wave of his hand, signaled three commands: ready, aim, and fire.[77] If the round of firing did not instantly kill, then the person commanding the firing squad or a soldier stepped up to shoot a musket or pistol ball into the head at close range. The ritual of death concluded with troops filing by for a close view of the corpse.[78]

Death by firing squad was a grisly affair. Veterans after the war who had viewed one such event recalled that "it was the most revolting spectacle they had ever witnessed during the Revolutionary War." On this particular occasion, a multiple execution of four culprits in June 1781, the head of one victim was "literally blown in fragments from off his body"; for the victims in general, handkerchiefs covering the eyes caught fire, and "the fence and even the heads of rye for some distance within the field were covered with blood and brains."[79] A drummer boy recalled a similar horror:

> There was four Men selected to shoot him [a condemned deserter] under the Direction of an Officer, and they fired by the word of command as they were advancing on a quick step, the Criminal was blind folded and caused to kneel down, two balls went through his head and one through his Body, they must have been very near to him when they fired, for the Powder from the muzzels of their Guns blacked his face. . . . The whole of his Head was blown off except the bare face, two Men were digging a grave to bury the Corps, and when they had got it barely deep enough to cover the Body, they took it up to lay it in and the wind quackeled in the throat of the Corps, and one of the Men said "dam you hold your tongue now 'tis too late for you to say a Word."[80]

Although the vivid scenes of the horrors of military executions left deep impressions upon the minds of the common soldiers, such events were taken in stride. When General Greene, upon assuming the command of the southern army, made good his promise to have the first deserter who was caught shot, he sent officers throughout the camp during the night after the execution "to listen to the talk of the soldiers." Greene was "happy to find that the measure had taken its desired effect, and that the language of the men was only—'We must not do as we have been used to: it is new lords new laws.'"[81] Still, soldiers had a hard time accepting the execution of soldiers as mutineers merely because they had protested the want of pay and breach of contract as to length of service. Samuel Dewees recalled that after a multiple execution for mutiny, soldiers "were afraid to say or to do any thing, for so trivial appeared the offences of these men that were shot, that they knew not what in the future was to be made to constitute crime." Dewees commented that thereafter he avoided coming into contact with officers, "lest they might construe my conduct in some way or other into an offence."[82]

Officers seemed little affected by executions. On June 24, 1779, the day that a deserter from a New York regiment went before a firing squad, an officer in the Sullivan Indian expedition commented, "we had an elegant dinner at which was present thirty-five gentlemen of the different Regiments."[83] General Greene's sympathy for his men, however, contrasted with the brazen disregard of Sullivan's officers. On August 6, 1781, after a sergeant had been "Shot to Death," Greene ordered that his troops "immediately" receive "good dry straw to Sleep on."[84]

Executions in the Continental army did not always result from the full legal process of a court-martial. Summary justice sometimes occurred whereby conviction was hastily decided upon by a commanding officer. There were also drumhead courts-martial, which may be defined as impromptu trials "conducted at the whim of a commander, or as the result of emergencies or special situation"; *drumhead* denotes the informality of the proceedings, which were usually held on a march when a drum served as a judicial bench.[85]

Although executions stemming from summary and drumhead justice were common in the partisan warfare in the south, a few similar situations occurred in Washington's main army. The commander in chief authorized the instant execution of marauders, deserters, and spies, although he preferred adhering to the military justice system. Extraordinary circumstances, such as during military operations, demanded swift and exemplary punishment. In October 1776, Washington ordered his generals to station officers at the rear of regiments, when the army was in motion, "to shoot any officer, or Soldier who shall presume to quit his Ranks, or retreat, unless the Retreat is ordered by proper Authority."[86] The commander in chief advised a New Jersey magistrate that "the most effectual way" of curtailing the "traitorous practices" of Tories was by "shooting some of the most notorious offenders wherever they can be found *in flagrante delicto*."[87] At the siege of Yorktown in 1781, Washington ordered that any American deserter "found within the Enemies lines" should be "instantly Hanged."[88]

Troops of General de Borre's brigade on July 31, 1777, ran across a civilian, Richard Evans, who had been trying to persuade soldiers to desert. A drumhead court-martial was immediately held; Evans was convicted and hanged two hours later (5:00 P.M.).[89] A Pennsylvania soldier caught while attempting to desert to the enemy on June 24, 1781, was sentenced on the same day at 3:00 P.M. and shot at the time of evening roll call.[90] Upon quelling a rebellion of the New Jersey line in January 1781, General Robert Howe chose one man from each of the three regiments, using a list supplied by officers; two of those selected immediately went before a firing squad made up of fellow mutineers.[91] Sometimes, swift retribution startled troops. A Maryland officer with Washington's army on a march in August 1777 was surprised to view the body of a Tory hanging from the "Limb of a Sycamore

Bush, close on the side of the road," done in by persons unknown—the army, local militia, or vigilantes.[92] Sometimes, the execution of a deserter happened so quickly that most troops were unaware of it. On a march in June 1780, soldiers were surprised to discover the corpse of a deserter hanging from a limb over the road.[93]

On the night of July 8, 1779, while Major Henry Lee's cavalry patrolled in the vicinity of Stony Point, on the Hudson River, a detachment from the unit, led by Captain Philip Reed, intercepted three deserters from the Maryland line attempting to go to the enemy. Reed immediately had the prisoners cast lots for who would be shot. The selection being made and the deed done, Reed had the executed culprit's head cut off, and the next morning sent the gruesome trophy to the Virginia camp at Smith's Clove, where it was placed on a pole at the gallows. When Washington received Lee's report of the incident, he only disapproved of the beheading, not the summary execution. Lee wanted to have more beheadings, but Washington ordered that there be no "diversifying the punishment" beyond regulations.[94]

Although Washington at times acknowledged that capital punishment accomplished retribution and encouraged reformation, he considered that the overriding goal in execution of the death penalty was to provide deterrence. He further recognized that to set awful examples was effective to warn soldiers away from behavior detrimental to, and destructive of, the army—chiefly desertion, marauding, and mutiny.[95] In reference to the widespread problem of desertion, Washington declared that he preferred "clemency to severity," yet "forbearance is folly and mercy degenerates into cruelty." Thus, he was "determined to convince every man, that crimes of so atrocious a nature shall not be committed with impunity."[96]

Unfortunately, the death penalty in the Continental army was often administered unfairly, involving a selection of persons to be put to death over those who were equally or more culpable. Deterrence generally prevailed over justice, and too often decent men, with exemplary service records, were put to death. In many instances, victims were condemned for committing acts in protest against military authority, mostly brought on by hunger and other deprivations, not being paid, or having their enlistment contracts illegally extended.

One such unfortunate was Sergeant Samuel Glover, who had a sterling service record and had fought heroically at the battles of Brandywine, Germantown, and Stony Point. Enlisting in 1775 as a private, he rose by merit to the rank of sergeant. When the war turned southward, Glover's Second North Carolina Regiment was ordered from the New York Highlands to join General Benjamin Lincoln's army in South Carolina. The march began on November 23, 1779, but by mid-February 1780 had proceeded no further than Wilmington, North Carolina. The North Carolina soldiers, led by Glover, refused to march further until pay arrears of some fifteen months were given them. Glover was convicted of mutiny and shot.[97]

Sergeant Glover left a wife and two small children. The widow, Ann Glover, petitioned the North Carolina General Assembly for an annual subsistence allowance. Her husband, she pointed out, had been considered by every officer of his regiment a good soldier, and he "never was accused of being intentionally Guilty of a breach of the Laws, Martial or Civil." Sergeant Glover had simply joined in the protest carried on by his "brother soldiers," who, like Glover himself, had performed honorable and loyal service; and because the men had not been paid, their families were in abject poverty.[98]

Capital punishment in America's Revolutionary army underscored the low regard in which enlisted men were held by their officers and indeed by their countrymen. Common soldiers had to endure the harshest of penalties, including death, for crimes that went unpunished when committed by officers. A disaffected lieutenant colonel anonymously published in the New-Jersey Gazette in December 1777 an opinion piece on military affairs. The author complained that "we now see boys of yesterday's growth raised to the command of veterans"; the officers had an "ignorance of military affairs, and a clownish diffidence of their own importance." Officers charged with crimes such as "stealing and pillaging" were "acquitted with honor." For enlisted men, such deeds could bring a death sentence.[99]

At war's end, common soldiers wondered whether their service had been worthwhile. An orderly sergeant under General Horatio Gates's command, in January 1783 jotted down in his orderly book a quote from the writings of Tom Brown, an English author: "What signifies a Soldier in time of peace?—Posh! A Soldier naked! Is that such a Wonder? What are they good for else but hanging or starving, when we have no occasion for them."[100]

NOTES
INDEX

Notes

Abbreviations

AWP W. W. Abbot et al., eds., *The Papers of George Washington, Revolutionary War Series*, 14 vols. to date (Charlottesville: University Press of Virginia, 1983–2004); Colonial Series (10 vols., 1983–95) and Confederation Series (5 vols., 1992–97) noted separately

BL Frederick S. Allis Jr., ed., *The Benjamin Lincoln Papers*, microfilm edition (Boston: Massachusetts Historical Society, 1967)

EAOB *Early American Orderly Books, 1748–1817*, from the holdings of the New-York Historical Society, microfilm edition (Woodbridge, Conn.: Research Publications, 1977)

FWW John C. Fitzpatrick, ed. *The Writings of George Washington from the Original Manuscripts, 1745–1799*. 39 vols. (Washington, D.C.: U.S. Government Printing Office, 1931–44)

GO General Orders

GP *The Horatio Gates Papers, 1726–1828*, microfilm edition (Stanford, N.C.: Microfilming Corporation of America, 1978; original depositories indicated per item in microfilm edition)

JCC Worthington C. Ford, ed., *Journals of the Continental Congress, 1774–1789*, 34 vols. (Washington, D.C.: U.S. Government Printing Office, 1904–37)

LC Library of Congress, Washington, D.C.

LD Paul H. Smith, ed., *Letters of Delegates of Congress, 1774–1789*, 26 vols. (Washington, D.C.: Library of Congress, 1976–2000)

MHSP *Proceedings of the Massachusetts Historical Society*

NG Richard K. Showman et al., eds., *The Papers of Nathanael Greene*, 12 vols. to date (Chapel Hill: University of North Carolina Press, 1976–2001)

NYHS New-York Historical Society

NYPL New York Public Library

OB   Orderly (Order) Book

PCC   Papers of the Continental Congress, National Archives and Records
         Service, Washington, D.C.

PMHB   *Pennsylvania Magazine of History and Biography*

PNJHS *Proceedings of the New Jersey Historical Society*

RWR   Revolutionary War Records, microfilm collection, National Archives
         and Records Service, Washington, D.C.

SCHGM South Carolina Historical and Genealogical Magazine

SCHM   *South Carolina Historical Magazine* (succeeds *SCHGM*)

Steuben *The Papers of General Friedrich Wilhelm Steuben, 1774–1790*, edited
Papers   by Edith von Zemenszky, microfilm edition (Millwood, N.Y.: Kraus
         International Microfilming, 1982; original depositories indicated per
         item in microfilm edition)

VHS   Virginia Historical Society, Richmond

WMQ   *William and Mary Quarterly*

WP   George Washington Papers, Library of Congress

1. Preconditions

1. Washington to John Campbell, Earl of Loudoun, Jan. 10, 1757, *AWP*, Colonial Series, 4:84.

2. Douglas E. Leach, *Arms for Empire: A Military History of the British Colonies in North America, 1607–1763* (New York: Macmillan, 1973), 370; John Shy, *Toward Lexington: The Role of the British Army in the Coming of the American Revolution* (Princeton: Princeton University Press, 1965), 143; David T. Zabecki, "Robert Rogers," in Richard L. Blanco, ed., *The American Revolution, 1775–1783: An Encyclopedia*, 2 vols. (New York: Garland, 1993), 2:1429–31.

3. James Titus, *The Old Dominion at War: Society, Politics and Warfare in Late Colonial Virginia* (Columbia: University of South Carolina Press, 1991), 45; John Shy, "A New Look at Colonial Militia," *WMQ*, 3d ser., 20 (1963): 184; Alan Rogers, "Provincial Troops," in Alan Gallay, ed., *Colonial Wars of North America, 1512–1763* (New York: Garland, 1996), 592–93.

4. J. Clarence Webster, ed., *The Journal of Jeffery Amherst . . . 1758 to 1763* (Chicago: University of Chicago Press, 1931), 328–32; Arthur G. Doughty, ed., *An Historical Journal of the Campaigns in North America for the Years 1757, 1758, 1759, and 1760*, by Captain John Knox, 3 vols. (1769; reprint, Freeport, N.Y.: Books for Libraries, 1970), 1:166; Fred Anderson, *A People's Army: Massachusetts Soldiers and Society in the Seven Years' War* (Chapel Hill: University of North Carolina Press, 1984), 60; Herbert L. Osgood, *The American Colonies in the Eighteenth Century*, vol. 4 (1925; reprint, Gloucester, Mass.: Peter Smith, 1958), chaps. 15–17; George Geib, "Forbes Campaign of 1758," in Gallay, *Colonial Wars*, 212.

5. F. Anderson, *People's Army*, 53; Alan Rogers, *Empire and Liberty: American Resistance to British Authority, 1753–1763* (Berkeley: University of California Press, 1974), 153n, 154n.

6. Washington to Dinwiddie, Mar. 9, 1754, *AWP*, Colonial Series, 1:73.

7. Titus, *Old Dominion at War*, 43.

8. Peter Wraxall to Henry Fox, Sept. 27, 1755, in Stanley Pargellis, ed., *Military Affairs in North America, 1748–1765* (New York: D. Appleton-Century, 1936), 141.

9. Gen. John Forbes to William Pitt, Sept. 6, 1758, in Gertrude Kimball, ed., *The Correspondence of William Pitt with Colonial Governors*, vol. 1 (New York: Macmillan, 1906), 342.

10. James Wolfe to Lord George Sackville, July 30, 1755, quoted in A. Rogers, *Empire and Liberty*, 63.

11. Arthur Griffiths, *The English Army, Its Past History, Present Condition, and Future Prospects* (London: Cassell, Pelter & Galpin, 1879), 266–71, quote on 269; J. A. Houlding, *Fit for Service: The Training of the British Army, 1715–1795* (Oxford: Clarendon, 1981), 116–19, 345–46; A. J. Barker, *Redcoats: The British Soldier in America* (London: J. M. Dent & Sons, 1976), 31–39; Eric Robson, "The Armed Forces and the Art of War," in J. o. Lindsay, ed., *The New Cambridge Modern History*, vol. 7 (Cambridge, Eng.: Cambridge University Press, 1957), 183–84.

12. "Sketch of an Order about the Rank &c of the Provincial Troops in North America," in Pargellis, *Military Affairs*, 44, 44n.

13. F. Anderson, *People's Army*, 124–25.

14. An Act . . . for Making Provision Against Invasions and Insurrections (Oct. 1755), and An Act for Preventing Mutiny and Desertion (June 1757), in W. W. Hening, comp., *The Statutes at Large . . . , Virginia (1619–1792)*, 13 vols. (Richmond, Va., 1819–23), 6:560, 7:87–92; Washington to Dinwiddie, Oct. 8 and 11, 1755, John Robinson to Washington, June 21, 1757, *AWP*, Colonial Series, 2:84, 102, 173n, 174n, 4:249; Titus, *Old Dominion at War*, 44, 67.

15. Washington to Adam Stephen, Nov. 18, 1755, *AWP*, Colonial Series, 2:172.

16. Washington to William Cocks, Dec. 28, 1755, *AWP*, Colonial Series, 2:241.

17. Dinwiddie to Washington, May 8, 1756, *AWP*, Colonial Series, 3:103, 4:106n; "Minutes of a Court-Martial Held at Winchester," May 2, 1756, in R. A. Brock, ed., *The Official Records of Robert Dinwiddie* (Richmond: Virginia Historical Society, 1884), 2:399–401.

18. Washington to John Stanwix, July 15, 1757, *AWP*, Colonial Series, 4:306.

19. Washington to Dinwiddie, Aug. 3, 1757, *AWP*, Colonial Series, 4:360, 321n; Titus, *Old Dominion at War*, 105.

20. Titus, *Old Dominion at War*, 68 (quote), 104–5.

21. F. Anderson, *People's Army*, 135.

22. F. Anderson, *People's Army*, 120–23; A. Rogers, *Empire and Liberty*, 59–60. See Orderly Books, Aug.–Oct. 1760, *GP* (NYPL), for members of Pennsylvania and Virginia regiments tried by regular army courts-martial.

23. See, for example, Sept. 1757 entry in E. C. Davies, ed., *Journal of Gen. Rufus Putnam . . . 1757–1760* (Albany: J. Munsell's Sons, 1886), 45; May 1758 entry in Brigette Burkett, ed., *The Journal of Johann Michael Lindenmuth* (Rockport, Maine: Picton, 2000), 47; and June 1760 entry in *Journal of the Hon. William Hervey . . . 1755 to 1814, with Order Books at Montreal, 1760–63* (Bury St. Edmunds, Eng.: Paul & Mathew, 1906), 70.

24. F. Anderson, *People's Army*, 136.

25. William H. Hill, *Old Fort Edward* (Fort Edward, N.Y.: privately printed, 1929), 179.

26. July 22, 1760, entry in *Diary and Journal (1755–1807) of Seth Metcalf* (Boston: Historical Record Survey, 1939), 7.

27. F. M., *Luke Gridley's Diary of 1757 . . .* (n.p.: Acorn Club, 1907), 30–31.

28. "Journal of Phineas Lyman," Oct. 9, 1757, quoted in Hill, *Old Fort Edward*, 148.

29. "Diaries Kept by Lemuel Wood, July 20, 1759," *Essex Institute Historical Collections* 19 (1882): 144.

30. Roger Morris to Washington, Nov. 3, 1755, *AWP*, Colonial Series, 2:155; Don Higginbotham, *George Washington and the American Military Tradition* (Athens: University of Georgia Press, 1985), 14–15; Fred Anderson, *Crucible of War: The Seven Years' War and the Fate of Empire in British North America* (New York: Alfred A. Knopf, 2000), 290.

31. "Invoice of Sundery Goods," Dec. 6, 1755, and "Address," Jan. 8, 1756, *AWP*, Colonial Series, 2:208–9, 257–258n; Oliver L. Spaulding Jr., "The Military Studies of George Washington," *American Historical Review* 29 (1924): 675–80; Houlding, *Fit for Service*, 326–63; Higginbotham, *George Washington and Military Tradition*, 15.

32. Spaulding, "Military Studies of Washington," 679.

33. F. Anderson, *Crucible of War*, 290.

34. F. Anderson, *People's Army*, 79–80.

35. Quotes from Francis Markham, *Epistles of Warre* (1622/1662) in Claver Scott, *Under the Lash: A History of Corporal Punishment in the British Armed Forces* (London: Torchstream Books, 1954), 8; and Vaughan Lovell-Knight, *The History of the Office of the Provost Marshal and the Corps of Military Police* (Aldershot, Eng.: Gale and Polden, 1943), 18–19.

36. Doughty, *Historical Journal*, 1:408.

37. Doughty, *Historical Journal*, 2:137.

38. Doughty, *Historical Journal*, 1:236.

39. Order by General Amherst, issued at Oswego, July 29, 1760, in Barker, *Redcoats*, 24; July 30, 1760, entry in Webster, *Journal of Amherst*, 222–23.

40. Alan J. Guy, *Oeconomy and Discipline: Officership and Administration in the British Army, 1714–1763* (Manchester, Eng.: Manchester University Press, 1985), 14.

41. GO, Fort Edward, June 10, 1759, *Expedition of the British and Provincial Army under General Jeffery Amherst Against Ticonderoga and Crown Point (Commissary Wilson's Orderly Book)* (Albany: J. Munsell, 1857), 16.

42. "A Narrative of the Massacres in Lancaster County," in Leonard W. Labaree, ed., *The Papers of Benjamin Franklin*, vol. 11 (New Haven: Yale University Press, 1967), 69.

43. Labaree, *Papers of Franklin*, 69n.

44. Howard H. Peckham, *Pontiac and the Indian Uprising* (Chicago: University of Chicago Press, 1947), 211; Harry M. Ward, *Major General Adam Stephen and the Cause of American Liberty* (Charlottesville: University Press of Virginia, 1989), 86–90.

45. Gen. Thomas Gage to Gen. Henry Conway, June 24, 1766, in Clarence W. Alvord and Clarence E. Carter, eds., *The New Regime, 1765–1767* (Springfield: Illinois State Historical Library, 1916), 324; Lawrence D. Cress, "The Standing Army, the Militia and the New Republic: Changing Attitudes Toward the Military in American Society, 1768 to 1820" (Ph.D. diss., University of Virginia, 1976), 82–83.

46. "Disposition of His Majesty's Forces in North America," Aug. 1763, in Clarence W. Alvord and Clarence E. Carter, eds., *The Critical Period, 1763–1765* (Springfield: Illinois State Historical Library, 1915), 14-16; Bernhard Knollenberg, *Origin of the American Revolution* (New York: Macmillan, 1960), 88.

47. Gage to Conway, June 15, 1766, and "General Distribution of His Majesty's Forces in North America," Feb. 22, 1767, in Alvord and Carter, *New Regime*, 339–40, 512–13; Lawrence H. Gipson, *The British Empire Before the American Revolution*, vol. 11, *The Triumphal Empire . . . 1766–70* (New York: Alfred A. Knopf, 1965), 128–29.

48. Gage to Maj. Gen. Alexander Mackay, May 15, 1769, quoted in Shy, *Toward Lexington*, 361.

49. Shy, *Toward Lexington*, 363.

50. Edward Countryman, *A People in Revolution: The American Revolution and Political Society in New York, 1760–1790* (New York: W. W. Norton, 1981), 39–43.

51. Oliver N. Dickerson, ed., *Boston under Military Rule, 1768–1769: A Journal of the Times* (Boston: Chapman & Grimes, 1936), viii–x; Merrill Jensen, *The Founding of a Nation: A History of the American Revolution, 1763–1776* (New York: Oxford University Press, 1968), 346, 349.

52. Oct. 6, 1768, entry in Dickerson, *Boston under Military Rule*, 3.

53. Oct. 31, 1768, entry in Dickerson, *Boston under Military Rule*, 17.

54. "Resolution of the Massachusetts House of Representatives, June 21, 1769," quoted in John P. Reid, *In Defense of the Law: The Standing Army Controversy . . .* (Chapel Hill: University of North Carolina Press, 1981), 162.

55. Shy, *Toward Lexington*, 325–27, 329; Cress, "Standing Army," 95, 108; Adam N. Lynde, "The British Army in North America, 1755–1783: Defeat as a Consequence of the British Constitution" (Ph.D. diss., Temple University, 1992), 449–50; Clarence E. Carter, "The Office of the Commander in Chief: A Phase of Imperial Unity on the Eve of the Revolution," in Richard B. Morris, ed., *The Era of the American Revolution* (1939; reprint, New York: Harper & Row, 1965), 205–7.

56. Randolph Downes, *Council Fires on the Upper Ohio* (Pittsburgh; University of Pittsburgh Press, 1940), 132.

57. John R. Alden, *General Gage in America* (Baton Rouge: Louisiana State University Press, 1948), 221.

2. The Common Soldier

1. Wayne E. Lee, *Crowds and Soldiers in Revolutionary North Carolina: The Culture of Violence in Riot and War* (Gainesville: University Press of Florida, 2001), 218.

2. GO, Aug. 7 and 11, 1782, RWR, M853, roll 10, vols. 63 and 66; John W. Wright, "Some Notes on the Continental Army," *WMQ*, 2d ser., 11 (1931): 198–99; Robert K. Wright, "Not Is Their Standing Army to be Despised: The Emergence of the Continental Army as a Military Institution," in Ronald Hoffman and Peter J. Albert, eds., *Arms and Independence: The Military Character of the American Revolution* (Charlottesville: University Press of Virginia, 1984), 72; John C. Fitzpatrick, "The Story of the Purple Heart . . . ," *Daughters of the American Revolution Magazine* 56, no. 2 (1922): 70; "Badge of Military Merit," *Historical Magazine* 3 (1859): 1–3. One example of an enlisted man becoming an officer was Richard Pollard, who in turn was made sergeant, sergeant major, lieutenant, and captain; Francis B. Heitman, comp., *Historical Register of Officers of the Continental Army* (1914; reprint, Baltimore: Genealogical Publishing, 1973), 445.

3. John Adams to William Heath, Oct. 5, 1775, in Robert Taylor et al., eds., *The Papers of John Adams*, 10 vols. (Cambridge: Harvard University Press, 1977–96), 3:183.

4. Capt. Persifer Frazer, quoted in John W. Krueger, "Troop Life at the Champlain Valley Forts During the American Revolution" (Ph.D. diss., State University of New York at Albany, 1984), 174.

5. James K. Martin, "A 'Most Undisciplined Profligate Crew': Protest and Defiance in the Continental Ranks, 1776–1783," in Hoffman and Albert, *Arms and Independence*, 124 (quote); James K. Martin and Mark E. Lender, *A Respectable Army: The Military Origin of the Republic, 1763–1789* (Arlington Heights, Ill.: Harlan Davidson, 1982), 90; John Shy, *A People Numerous and Armed: Reflections on the Military Struggle for American Independence* (New York: Oxford University Press, 1976), 173; Edward C. Papenfuse and Gregory A. Stiverson, "General Smallwood's Recruits: The Peacetime Career of the Revolutionary War Private," *WMQ*, 3d ser., 30 (1970): 117–32; John R. Sellers, "The Common Soldier in the American Revolution," in Stanley J. Underdal, ed., *Military History of the American Revolution . . . 6th History Symposium . . . Air Force Academy* (Oct. 10–11, 1974), (Washington, D.C.: Office of Air Force History, USAF, 1976)), 151–61; Mark E. Lender, "The Social Structure of the New Jersey Brigade: The Continental Line as an American Standing Army," in Peter Karsten, ed., *The Military in America: From the Colonial Era to the Present* (New York: Free Press, 1986), 65–78.

6. Shy, *People Numerous and Armed*, 171–73; John Resch, *Suffering Soldiers: Revolutionary War Veterans, Moral Sentiment, and Political Culture in the Early Republic* (Amherst: University of Massachusetts Press, 1999), 8–10, 22–46.

7. Charles P. Neimeyer, *America Goes to War: A Social History of the Continental Army* (New York: New York University Press, 1996), 16.

8. Neimeyer, *America Goes to War*, 20; Howard L. Applegate, "Constitutions like Iron: The Life of the American Revolutionary War Soldiers in the Middle Department, 1775–1783" (Ph.D. diss., Syracuse University, 1966), 436.

9. Lender, "Social Structure of the New Jersey Brigade," 69; Mark E. Lender, "The Enlisted Line: The Continental Soldiers of New Jersey" (Ph.D. diss., Rutgers University, 1975), 122.

10. Neimeyer, *America Goes to War*, 21–23.

11. Sellers, "Common Soldier in the American Revolution," 158; Papenfuse and Stiverson, "General Smallwood's Recruits," 126–27.

12. Lee, *Crowds and Soldiers*, 217; Walter J. Fraser Jr., "Reflections of 'Democracy' in Revolutionary South Carolina: The Composition of Military Organization and the Attitudes and Relationships of the Officers and Men, 1775–1780," *SCHM* 78 (1977): 202–12 (quote, 211).

13. Walter F. Wallace, "'Oh, Liberty! Oh Virtue! Oh, My Country!' An Exploration of the Minds of New England Soldiers During the American Revolution" (M.A. thesis, Northern Illinois University, 1974), 155–56.

14. Lender, "Social Structure of the New Jersey Brigade," 68.

15. Applegate, "Constitutions like Iron," 434; Neimeyer, *America Goes to War*, 20.

16. Papenfuse and Stiverson, "General Smallwood's Recruits," 121.

17. Sellers, "Common Soldier in the American Revolution," 155.

18. Sellers, "Common Soldier in the American Revolution," 155; Kenneth A. Lockridge, *Literacy in Colonial New England . . .* (New York: W. W. Norton, 1974), 77–78, 88; Harold E. Selesky, *A Democratic Survey of the Continental Army That Wintered at Valley Forge, 1777–1778* (New Haven, Conn., 1987), 33–34.

19. Richard H. Kohn, "The Social History of the American Soldier: A Review and Prospectus for Research," *American Historical Review* 86 (1981): 557.

20. E. Alfred Jones, "English Convicts in the American Army in the War for Independence," *PNJHS* 7 (1922): 286–91; Martin and Lender, *Respectable Army*, 92.

21. John B. Trussell, *The Pennsylvania Line: Organization and Operations, 1776–1783* (Harrisburg: Pennsylvania Historical and Museum Commission, 1977), 249–51; Papenfuse and Stiverson, "General Smallwood's Recruits," 120–21; Selesky, *Democratic Survey of the Continental Army*, 26–28, 146–47, 151–52, 156–60, 163–66.

22. Michael J. O'Brien, *A Hidden Phase of American History: Ireland's Part in America's Struggle for Liberty* (New York: Dodd, Mead, 1919), 135–36.

23. Applegate, "Constitutions like Iron," 57–58.

24. Lender, "Social Structure of the New Jersey Brigade," 73; William Livingston to Washington, Dec. 1, 1777, in Carl E. Prince et al., eds., *The Papers of William Livingston*, 5 vols. (Trenton: New Jersey Historical Commission, 1979–88), 2:115-18n, 128–29.

25. Philip S. Foner, *Blacks in the American Revolution* (Westport, Conn.: Greenwood, 1975), 57–59; Trussell, *Pennsylvania Line*, 248.

26. David O. White, *Connecticut's Black Soldiers, 1775–1783* (Chester, Conn.: Pequot, 1973), 18–24, 27–29, 31–33, 35.

27. Neimeyer, *America Goes to War*, 76–77.

28. Horatio Gates to Jeremiah Powell, July 2, 1779, *GP* (NYHS).

29. L. P. Jackson, "Virginia Negro Soldiers and Seamen in the American Revolution," *Journal of Negro History* 27 (1942): 251–54, 257.

30. May 21, 1780, entry in Harriette Forbes, ed., *The Diary of Rev. Ebenezer Parkman* (Worcester, Mass.: Westborough Historical Society, 1899), 246–47; Richard R. Forry, "Edward Hand: His Role in the American Revolution" (Ph.D. diss., Duke University, 1976), 59–60; Arthur J. Alexander, "How Maryland Tried to Raise Her Continental Quotas," *Maryland Historical Magazine* 42 (1947): 188; Paul V. Lutz, "A State's Concern for the Soldiers' Welfare: How North Carolina Provided for Her Troops During the Revolution," *North Carolina Historical Review* 42 (1965): 315; Paul V. Lutz, "Land Grants for Service in the Revolution," *New York Historical Society Quarterly* 48 (1964): 223–24, 231–32; Jesse H. Vivian, "Military Land Bounties During the Revolutionary and Confederation Periods," *Maryland Historical Magazine* 61 (1966): 232–33, 235–37; Charles K. Bolton, *The Private Soldier under Washington* (1902; reprint, Port Washington, N.Y.: Kennikat, 1964), 48.

31. C. Bolton, *Private Soldier*, 55.

32. See, for example, John Clapsy pension application, in John C. Dann, ed., *The Revolution Remembered: Eyewitness Accounts of the War of Independence* (Chicago: University of Chicago Press, 1980), 365–66.

33. Recruiting instructions for Capt. Samuel Walker, RWR, M859, #111, 31557.

34. Mordecai Gist to Gov. Thomas Sim Lee, Nov. 14, 1780, *Steuben Papers* (NYHS).

35. Alexander Graydon, *Memoirs of His Own Time with Reminiscences of the Men and Events of the Revolution*, ed. John S. Littel (Philadelphia: Lindsay and Blackstone, 1846), 133–36.

36. John Paterson to William Heath, Mar. 31, 1780, in *The Heath Papers, Collections of the Massachusetts Historical Society*, 7th ser., 5 (1905): 44; Applegate, "Constitutions like Iron," 40, Jean F. Hankins, "Conscription for the Continental Army," in Blanco, *American Revolution*, 1:365.

37. George J. Svejda, *Quartering, Disciplining, and Supplying the Army at Morristown, 1779–1780* (Washington, D.C.: National Park Service, 1970), 62–63.

38. Kohn, "Social History of the American Soldier," 557.

39. Charles H. Lesser, *The Sinews of Independence: Monthly Strength Reports of the Continental Army* (Chicago: University of Chicago Press, 1976), 24–27, 53.

40. James E. Gibson, *Dr. Bodo Otto and the Medical Background of the American Revolution* (Springfield, Ill.: Charles E. Thomas, 1937), 98, 120; Richard L. Blanco, "Continental Hospitals and American Society, 1775–1781," in Maarten Ultee, ed., *Adapting to Conditions: War and Society in the Eighteenth Century* (University: University of Alabama Press, 1986), 160; Mark M. Boatner III, *Encyclopedia of the American Revolution* (New York: David McKay, 1966), 698.

41. Quoted in Friedrich Kapp, *The Life of John Kalb* (New York: Henry Holt, 1884), 139; Charles Royster, *A Revolutionary People at War: The Continental Army and American Character* (New York: W. W. Norton, 1979), 60.

42. Horatio Gates to Washington, May 7, 1779, *GP* (NYHS); Jonathan Smith, "How Massachusetts Raised Her Troops in the Revolution," *MHSP* 55 (1923): 368.

43. Lender, "Enlisted Line," 258–60.

44. Alexander Scammell to Col. Timothy Pickering, Feb. 6, 1778, in Octavius Pickering, *The Life of Timothy Pickering*, vol. 1 (Boston: Little, Brown, 1867), 204; Neimeyer, *America Goes to War*, 119, 124–25.

45. William Malcolm to Gates, July 26, 1778, *GP* (NYHS); Alexander McDougall to Gen. Heath, Nov. 29, 1781, Alexander McDougall Papers, NYHS.

46. Washington to George Clinton, Feb. 16, 1778, *AWP*, 13:552.

47. Ebenzer Huntington to Andrew Huntington, July 7, 1780, in "Letters of Ebenezer Huntington, 1774–1782," *American Historical Review* 5 (1900): 725.

48. S. Sidney Bradford, "Hunger Menaces the Revolution, December 1779– January 1780," *Maryland Historical Magazine* 61 (1966): 1–23.

49. George F. Scheer, ed., *Private Yankee Doodle: Being a Narrative of Some of the Adventures and Sufferings of a Revolutionary Soldier*, by Joseph Plumb Martin (Little, Brown, 1962), 172.

50. See, for example, "Memorial from the Brigadier Generals and Field Officers of the Brigades Encamped at Hartford" to Gen. Gates, Nov. 1, 1778, *GP* (NYHS).

51. Washington to James Mease, July 18, 1777, *AWP*, 10:322.

52. Quoted in Howard C. Rice and Anne S. K. Brown, eds., *The American Campaign of Rochambeau's Army*, vol. 1 (Princeton: Princeton University Press, 1972), 33.

53. Quoted in Allen Bowman, *The Morale of the American Revolutionary Army* (1943; reprint, Port Washington, N.Y.: Kennikat, 1964), 19.

54. Washington to John Hancock, Oct. 24, 1777, *AWP*, 11:576.

55. Dec. 17, 1780, entry in William Seymour, *A Journal of the Southern Expedition, 1780–1783* (Wilmington: Historical Society of Delaware, 1896), 11.

56. Scheer, *Private Yankee Doodle*, 101.

57. Jacob Weiss to Col. John Mitchell, Mar. 6, 1780, in Melville J. Boyer, ed., *The Letter Book of Jacob Weiss, DQG of the Revolution* (Allentown, Pa.: H. Ray Haas, 1956), 91.

58. John Adams to Nathanael Greene, May 9, 1777, in Taylor et al., *Papers of John Adams*, 5:185.

59. Aug. 31, 1776, entry in Mark E. Lender and James K. Martin, eds., *Citizen Soldier: The Revolutionary War Journal of Joseph Bloomfield* (Newark: New Jersey Historical Society, 1982), 103.

60. Gen. Edward Hand to Washington, n.d., RWR, M859, #III 31546.

61. Brigade Orders, June 12, 1778, in *EAOB*, roll 5, no. 59; "Orderly Book of Captain Robert Gamble, 1779," *Collections of the Virginia Historical Society* II (1892): 257.

62. Martin and Lender, *Respectable Army*, 129.

63. "Diary of Lieutenant James McMichael of the Pennsylvania Line, 1776–1778," *PMHB* 16 (1892): 139.

64. Scheer, *Private Yankee Doodle*, 145–46.

65. GO, May 8, 1777, and Jan. 8, 1778, *AWP*, 9:368, 13:171; Bonnie S. Stadelman, "The Amusements of the American Solders During the Revolution" (Ph.D. diss., Tulane University, 1969), 81–110, 195–96 (concerning the northern army); GO, July 20, 1776, in Ebenezer Elmer, "Journal of an Expedition to Canada," *PNJHS*, 1st ser., 2 (1846): 165.

66. GO, May 31, 1777, *AWP*, 9:567–68.

67. Oct. 6, 1776, entry in Frederick R. Kirkland, ed., *Journal of Dr. Lewis Beebe: A Physician on the Expedition Against Canada, 1776* (Philadelphia: Historical Society of Pennsylvania, 1935), 28.

68. GO, Feb. 4, 1778, RWR, M853, roll 3, vol. 21; Garrison Orders, May 6, 1781, RWR, M853, roll 8, vol. 5; Corps of Artillery Orders, July 2, 1780, in *EAOB*, roll 11, no. 12; Artillery Orders, June 29, 1780, in *EAOB*, roll 11, no. 12; Garrison Orders, Aug. 16, 1782, and Regimental Orders, Aug. 26, 1782, in *EAOB*, roll 16, no. 162; June 27 and Aug. 19, 1782, entries in Almon W. Lauber, ed., *Order Books of the 4th New York Regiment . . . 2d New York Regiment* (Albany: State University of New York Press, 1932), 384, 610; Applegate, "Constitutions like Iron," 307; Holly A. Mayer, *Belonging to the Army: Camp Followers and Community During the American Revolution* (Columbia: University of South Carolina Press, 1996), 110–12.

69. Martin and Lender, *Respectable Army*, 131–32.

70. Washington to Col. David Mason, Sept. 2, 1777, *AWP*, 11:127.

71. Gates to Richard Peters, Oct. 23, 1780, *GP* (LC).

72. James H. Edmonson, "Desertion in the American Army During the Revolutionary War" (Ph.D. diss., Louisiana State University, 1971), 260–61.

73. Edmonson, "Desertion," chap. 5; Bowman, *Morale of American Revolutionary Army*, 73–76; Arthur Alexander, "Desertion and Its Punishment in Revolutionary Virginia," *WMQ*, 3d ser., 3 (1946): 389–90; Arthur Alexander, "A Footnote on Deserters from the Virginia Forces During the American Revolution," *Virginia Magazine of History and Biography* 55 (1947): 139.

74. Ricardo Herrera, "Self-Government and the American Citizen as Soldier," *Journal of Military History* 65 (2001): 49; Martin, "'Most Undisciplined Profligate Crew,'" 134; C. Bolton, *Private Soldier*, 137.

75. Committee on the Pennsylvania Mutiny to Samuel Huntington, Jan. 7, 1781, Jesse Root to Jonathan Trumbull Sr., Jan. 8, 1781, Committee on the Pennsylvania Mutiny to Joseph Reed, Jan. 8, 1781, and James Madison to Thomas Jefferson, Jan. 9, 1781, *LD*, 16:554, 572–73, 559–61, 581.

76. Letter of Anthony Wayne, May 20, 1781, in Charles J. Stillé, *Major-General Anthony Wayne and the Pennsylvania Line in the Continental Army* (1893; reprint, Port Washington, N.Y.: Kennikat, 1968), 265–66; C. Bolton, *Private Soldier*, 141.

77. Henry Knox to William Knox, Feb. 4, 1781, *Henry Knox Papers*, microfilm edition (Boston: Massachusetts Historical Society, 1960), 5:131; Lender, "Enlisted Line," 240–42; James Thacher, *Military Journal During the American Revolutionary War, 1775 to 1783* (Hartford, Conn.: Silas Andrus & Son, 1854), 251–53; Herrera, "Self-Government and the American Citizen," 49.

78. Andrew A. Zellers-Frederick, "Mutiny in Philadelphia, Pennsylvania (June 1783)," in Blanco, *American Revolution*, 2:1147–51; Charles H. Bennett and Donald R. Lennon, *A Quest for Glory: Major General Robert Howe and the American Revolution* (Chapel Hill: University of North Carolina Press, 1991), 146–47; Harry M. Ward, *The Department of War, 1781–1795* (Pittsburgh: University of Pittsburgh Press, 1962), 28–30.

79. Committee on the Pennsylvania Mutiny to Washington, Jan. 15, 1781, *LD*, 16:600.

80. Howard H. Peckham, ed., *Memoirs of the Life of John Adlum in the Revolutionary War* (Chicago: Caxton Club, 1968), 56.

81. Letter of Henry Knox, Sept. 1776, quoted in Stuart L. Bernath, "George Washington and the Genesis of American Military Discipline," *Mid-America* 49 (1967): 84; Nathanael Greene to William Ellery, Oct. 4, 1776, *NG*, 1:307.

82. Jacob Francis pension application, in Dann, *Revolution Remembered*, 392–93.

83. Articles of War, June 30, 1775, and Sept. 20, 1776, *JCC*, 2:114, 5:796.

84. Col. Anthony Wayne to Gen. Schuyler, Feb. 12, 1777, in Stillé, *Major-General Anthony Wayne*, 55–56.

85. Royster, *Revolutionary People*, 79.

86. Royster, *Revolutionary People*, 93.

87. John S. Hanna, comp., *History of the Life and Service of Captain Samuel Dewees* (Baltimore: R. Neilson, 1844), 239.

88. Fraser, "Reflections of 'Democracy,'" 203.

89. Caroline Cox, *A Proper Sense of Honor: Service and Sacrifice in George Washington's Army* (Chapel Hill: University of North Carolina Press, 2004), 81, 105 (quote), 270n81.

3. Military Justice

1. Samuel Adams to James Warren, Jan. 7, 1775, in Harry A. Cushing, ed., *The Writings of Samuel Adams*, vol. 3 (1907; reprint, New York: Octagon Books, 1968), 250.

2. Joseph W. Bishop Jr., *Justice under Fire: A Study of Military Law* (New York: Charterhouse, 1974), 8; Sisson C. Pratt, *Military Law: Its Procedure and Practice*, 19th ed. (London: Keegan Paul, Trench, Turner, 1920), 3–5.

3. William Winthrop, *Military Law and Precedents*, 2d ed. (Washington, D.C.: GPO, 1920), 12n; Robert K. Wright Jr., *The Continental Army* (Washington, D.C.: Center of Military History, 1983), 39.

4. "Rules and Regulations for the Massachusetts Army," in Peter Force, comp., *American Archives*, 4th ser., 1 (Washington, D.C.: M. St. Clair Clarke and Peter

Force, 1837), 1350–55; "Rules and Orders of the Army of Observation of the Colony of Rhode Island," in John R. Bartlett, ed., *Records of the Colony of Rhode Island . . .* (Providence: J. Crawford Greene, 1862), 7:340–46; Robert H. Berlin, "The Administration of Military Justice in the Continental Army During the American Revolution, 1775–1783" (Ph.D. diss., University of California at Santa Barbara, 1976), 5–15.

5. An Ordinance for the Better Government of the Forces to be Raised . . . , in Hening, *Statutes at Large, Virginia,* 9:35–48.

6. George Mason to Washington, Oct. 14, 1775, *AWP,* 2:165, 166n.

7. "Rules and Regulations of the Military Association of Pennsylvania," in Force, *American Archives,* 4th ser., 5 (1844), 705–14.

8. June 14–15, 1775, entry in *JCC,* 2:89–90; Berlin, "Administration of Military Justice," 22.

9. June 30, 1775, entry in *JCC,* 2:111–22; Bradley Chapin, *The American Law of Treason: Revolutionary and Early National Origins* (Seattle: University of Washington Press, 1964), 29; Cox, *Proper Sense,* 94–95; John T. White, "Standing Armies in Time of War: Republican Theory and Military Practice During the American Revolution" (Ph.D. diss., George Washington University, 1978), 120.

10. Roger Sherman to Joseph Trumbull, July 6, 1775, *LD,* 1:599; *AWP,* 1:46n.

11. Richard Henry Lee to Washington, June 29, 1775, *AWP,* 1:45.

12. Washington to John Hancock, Oct. 5, 1775, *AWP,* 2:100, 103n.

13. GO, Jan. 3, 1776, *AWP,* 3:13; Nov, 7, 1775, entry in *JCC,* 3:331–34; "Minutes of Conference," Oct. 18–24, 1775, in William B. Wilcox, ed., *The Papers of Benjamin Franklin,* vol. 22 (New Haven: Yale University Press, 1982), 230–33; Chapin, *American Law of Treason,* 32–33.

14. Washington to John Hancock, Sept. 21, 1775, and GO, Jan. 3, 1776, *AWP,* 2:24–25, 3:13; see also 1:279n; June 30, 1775, entry in *JCC,* 2:112; Berlin, "Administration of Military Justice," 42–43, 55.

15. Col. Joseph Reed to President of Congress, July 25, 1776, in Force, *American Archives,* 5th ser., 1 (1848), 576.

16. Washington to President of Congress, Sept. 2 [5], 1776, *AWP,* 6:398–99.

17. William Tudor to John Adams, Sept. 6, 1776, in Taylor et al., *Papers of John Adams,* 5:13.

18. William Tudor to John Adams, July 7 and Sept. 23, 1776, in Taylor et al., *Papers of John Adams,* 4:367, 5:36.

19. John Adams to James Warren, Sept. 25, 1776, in Taylor et al., *Papers of John Adams,* 5:38, 39n; see also 476n; Aug. 13, 19–20, and Sept. 19–20, 1776, entries in L. H. Butterfield, ed., *The Diary and Autobiography of John Adams,* vol. 3 (Cambridge, Mass.: Harvard University Press, 1961), 407, 409–10, 410n, 433–34; June 14, 1776, entry in *JCC,* 5:442; Edward Rutledge to Robert R. Livingston, Aug. 19, 1776, *LD,* 5:26.

20. Articles of War, Sept. 20, 1776, in *JCC,* 5:788–807.

21. Articles of War, Apr. 14, 1777, and Mar. 30, 1786, in *JCC,* 7:264–66, 30:145–46; Washington to Brig. Gen. Samuel Holden Parsons, Apr. 19, 1777, *AWP,* 9:212.

22. James Wilkinson, *Memoirs of My Own Time*, vol. 1 (1846; reprint, New York: AMS, 1973), 77; S. Sidney Ulmer, *Military Justice and the Right to Counsel* (Lexington: University Press of Kentucky, 1970), 24–26.

23. Court-Martial, Jan. 8, 1779, in *BL*.

24. GO, June 30, 1775, "Orderly Book of Capt. William Coit's Company at the Siege of Boston, 1775," *Collections of the Connecticut Historical Society* 7 (1899): 28–29.

25. Section 18, Article 1, Sept. 20, 1776, in *JCC*, 5:806.

26. Washington to Gen. Lord Stirling, Mar. 5, 1780, in *FWW*, 18:71–72.

27. Court-Martial, July 13, 1779, in *BL*.

28. Officers to Nathanael Greene, Mar. 28, 1782, and Greene's answer, Mar. 29, 1782, in "Journal of Lieut. William McDowell of the First Pennsylvania Regiment in the Southern Campaign," William H. Egle, ed., *Pennsylvania Archives*, 2d ser., vol. 15 (Harrisburg: E. K. Meyers, 1893), 316–17.

29. Commission, June 19, 1775, and instructions, June 22, 1775, from the Continental Congress, in *AWP*, 1:7, 21.

30. S. V. Benét, *A Treatise on Military Law and the Practice of Courts-Martial* (New York: D. Van Nostrand, 1862), 9, 140–41. On military law supplemental to the Articles of War, see Mayer, *Belonging to the Army*, 241–48, 261–62. On custom of war and the execution of John André, see Alexander Hamilton to Col. John Laurens, Oct. 11, 1780, in Harold C. Syrett, ed., *The Papers of Alexander Hamilton*, 27 vols. (New York: Columbia University Press, 1961–87), 2:468.

31. Benét, *Treatise on Military Law*, 8.

32. Sept. 20, 1776, and Apr. 14, 1777, entries in *JCC*, 5:802, 7:265; William T. Generous Jr., *Swords and Scales: The Development of the Uniform Code of Military Justice* (Port Washington, N.Y.: Kennikat, 1973), 11–12.

33. Extract of GO, 1st Connecticut Line, July 4, 1779, in *EAOB*, roll 7, no. 83; Richard L. Blanco, "Military Justice in the Continental Army," in Blanco, *American Revolution*, 1:853.

34. General Court-Martial, Highlands headquarters, Feb. 10, 1782, in *EAOB*, roll 15, no, 156; H. Ward, *Major General Adam Stephen*, 197–99.

35. "Remarks on the Rules and Articles for the Government of the Continental Troops [Memorial to Congress, Oct. 1775]," in Force, *American Archives*, 4th ser., 3 (1837), 1164.

36. Fraser, "Reflections of 'Democracy,'" 208; T. W. Egly Jr., *History of the First New York Regiment, 1775–1783* (Hampton, N.H.: Peter E. Randall, 1981), 257.

37. Harry M. Ward, *William Maxwell and the New Jersey Continentals* (Westport, Conn.: Greenwood, 1997), 107.

38. Articles of War, Section 14, Article 3, Sept. 20, 1776, in *JCC*, 5:801.

39. July 29, 1775, and Aug. 10, 1776, entries in *JCC*, 2:221, 5:645; Washington to Secretary at War, Mar. 25 and Sept. 11, 1782, and GO, Oct. 7, 1782, in *FWW*, 24:301, 301n, 25:148, 239, 239n; Heitman, *Historical Register*, 313, 342, 550.

40. William Tudor to John Adams, July 31, 1775, in Taylor et al., *Papers of John Adams*, 3:107; William Tudor to Washington, Aug. 23, 1775, in *AWP*, 1:354–55.

41. Muster Roll, Mar. 15, 1778, and "Acknowledgment," Mar. 24, 1778, in Herbert A. Johnson, ed., *The Papers of John Marshall* (Chapel Hill: University of North Carolina Press, 1974), 1:15–16, 16n; Leonard Baker, *John Marshall: A Life in Law* (New York: Macmillan, 1974), 51; Heitman, *Historical Register*, 381; Berlin, "Administration of Military Justice," 162.

42. GO, Oct. 19, 1777, in *AWP*, 11:553; Division Orders, Sept. 21, 1776, "Elisha Williams' Diary, 1776," *PMHB* 48 (1924): 345.

43. Quoted in Ulmer, *Military Justice*, 27.

44. William Tudor to John Adams, c. Aug. 15, 1775, in Taylor et al., *Papers of John Adams*, 3:128; Blanco, "Military Justice," 851.

45. Lafayette to Washington, Jan. 13, 1778, in Stanley J. Idzerda, ed., *Lafayette in the Age of the American Revolution*, 5 vols. (Ithaca: Cornell University Press, 1977–83), 1:234–35.

46. "Sentiments on a Peace Establishment," enclosed in a letter to Alexander Hamilton, Mar. 2, 1783, in *FWW*, 26:385–86.

47. Washington to the Board of Officers, Feb. 12, 1783, in *FWW*, 26:124–2"5.

48. "Thoughts on Courts Martial and the Duty of Judge Advocate," Mar. 4, 1783, in *Henry Knox Papers*, 3:12–13.

49. Mar. 30, May 19 and 31, 1786, enties in *JCC*, 30:145–46, 290, 316–22; GO, June 23, 1776, and July 6, 1777, in *AWP*, 3:169, 10:205; *Black's Law Dictionary*, 4th ed. (St. Paul, Minn.: West, 1968), 431.

50. Seymour Wurfel, "Military Due Process: What Is It?" *Vanderbilt Law Review* 6 (1953): 275, 277; "Uniform Code of Military Justice," in Frederick B. Wiener, *The Uniform Code of Military Justice* (Washington, D.C.: Combat Forces, 1950), 25–248.

51. Benét, *Treatise on Military Law*, 39.

52. Wurfel, "Military Due Process," 279; Bishop, *Justice under Fire*, 114; Generous, *Swords and Scales*, 198; Gordon D. Henderson, "Courts-Martial and the Constitution: The Original Understanding," *Harvard Law Review* 71 (1957): 296–97, 323; Wiener, *Uniform Code of Military Justice*, 7.

53. Edward T. Pound, "Unequal Justice," *U.S. News & World Report*, Dec. 16, 2002, 20; Ulmer, *Military Justice*, 54; Bishop, *Justice under Fire*, 39; Daniel Walker and C. George Niebank, "The Court of Military Appeals: Its History, Organization and Operation," *Vanderbilt Law Review* 6 (1953): 230–31.

54. Lafayette to Washington, Jan. 13, 1778, in Idzerda, *Lafayette in the Age of Revolution*, 1:235.

4. The Supervisors

1. Max B. Garber, *A Modern Military Dictionary* (Washington, D.C.: privately printed, 1936), 216; Trevor N. Dupuy et al., comps., *Dictionary of Military Terms* (New York: H. W. Wilson, 1986), 162 (quotes).

2. GO, July 29, 1778, in *BL*; GO, Sept. 19, Oct. 28–29, 1780, July 25, Oct. 4 and 31, 1781, in *FWW*, 20:72, 261, 22:418, 23:171, 304; GO, Dec. 3, 1777, in "A

Whitemarsh Orderly Book, 1777," *PMHB* 45 (1921): 219; GO, Sept. 21–23, 1780, in Lauber, *Order Books of New York Regiments*, 506, 902.

3. Quoted in Kapp, *Life of Kalb*, 136–37.

4. GO, June 5, 1777, in *AWP*, 9:607–8.

5. GO, Nov. 5, 1777, and June 11, 1778, in *FWW*, 10:13–14, 12:47.

6. GO, July 2, 1781, in *EAOB*, roll 14, no. 140.

7. GO, June 5, 1777, in *AWP*, 9:608.

8. GO, May 21, 1776, in *AWP*, 4:349; GO, July 28, 1781, in *EAOB*, roll 14, no. 143; Aug. 25, 1776, entry in "Capt. Jedehiah Swan's Orderly Book," *PNJHS*, n.s., 2 (1917): 185.

9. GO, Jan. 31, 1780, in *FWW*, 17:472–73.

10. GO (McDougall), Aug. 8, 1779, in *EAOB*, roll 7, no. 87.

11. GO, June 5, 1777, in *AWP*, 9:608.

12. GO, May 21, 1776, in *AWP*, 4:349; Mar. 28, 1780, entry in "Order Book of John Faucheraud Grimké," *SCHGM* 19 (1918): 184.

13. GO, June 15, 1777, in *AWP*, 10:42.

14. GO, Dec. 25, 1782, in *FWW*, 25:464; Orders, Sept. 18, 1777, in Worthington C. Ford, ed., *Correspondence and Journals of Samuel Blackley Webb*, 3 vols. (New York: Wickersham, 1893–94), 1:292.

15. OB, Nov. 23, 1782, in *GP* (NYPL); A. S. Salley, ed., *An Orderly Book of the Third Regiment, South Carolina Line* (Columbia: Historical Commission of South Carolina, 1942), 17.

16. GO, Aug. 2, 1781, *FWW*, 22:454.

17. GO, Sept, 3, 1780, *FWW*, 19:497.

18. Orders, Feb. 16–20, 1777, in Salley, *Orderly Book of Third Regiment*, 16–17.

19. GO, June 5, 1777, *AWP*, 9:609.

20. GO, May 7 and 21, 1776, *AWP*, 4:225, 349.

21. GO, June 3, 1777, *AWP*, 9:598 (quote); Nov. 7, 1777, entry in *Valley Forge Orderly Book of General George Weedon* (1902; reprint, New York: Arno, 1971), 120; Marvin Kitman, *George Washington's Expense Account* (New York: Simon and Schuster, 1970), 229–30; Nov. 23–24, 1780, entries in Howard C. Rice, ed., *Travels in North America in the Years, 1780, 1781, and 1782*, by the Marquis de Chastellux, 2 vols. (Chapel Hill: University of North Carolina Press, 1963), 1:105–6, 109; Gerald E. Kahler, "Gentlemen of the Family: General George Washington's Aides-de-Camp and Military Secretaries" (M.A. thesis, University of Richmond, 1997), 95; John W. Jackson, *Valley Forge: Pinnacle of Courage* (Gettysburg, Pa.: Thomas, 1992), 41–42; Noel F. Busch, *Winter Quarters* (New York: Liveright, 1974), 96–97; John B. Trussell, *Birthplace of an Army: A Study of the Valley Forge Encampment* (Harrisburg: Pennsylvania Historical and Museum Commission, 1976), 95, 97.

22. GO, July 29, 1781, and Mar. 12, 1783, in *FWW*, 22:477, 26:209; Division Orders, Aug. 17, 1780, and Brigade Orders, Aug. 18, 1780, in *Orderly Book of the New Jersey Brigade . . . 1781* (Hackensack: Bergen County Historical Society, 1922), 20–21.

23. GO, Sept. 7, 1782, and Mar. 12, 1789, in *FWW*, 25:135, 26:209.

24. June 15, 16, and 17, 1775, entries in *JCC*, 2:91, 94, 97.

25. GO, Jan. 13, 1777, in *AWP*, 8:55, 55n; James B. Fry, "The Adjutant-General's Department," in T. F. Rodenbough and William L. Haskins, eds., *The Army of the United States* (New York: Argonaut, 1966), 23; Heitman, *Historical Register*, 68, 244, 272, 461, 484.

26. May 27, 1778, and Aug. 1, 1782, entries in *JCC*, 11:453, 22:425.

27. May 17, 1779, entry in *JCC*, 14:600–601; OB, Dec. 22, 1782, in *GP* (NYPL).

28. Aug. 1, 1782, entry in *JCC*, 22:425–27.

29. Sept. 14, 1775, and June 2, 1778, entries in *JCC*, 2:349, 11:560; Heitman, *Historical Register*, 229, 377.

30. Nov. 17, 1778, entry in *JCC*, 12:1137–38; Orders, Aug. 1782, in *NG*, 11:499–500; see also 9:162n, 10:320n, and 11:576; Maj. Ichabod Burnet to Maj. John Habersham, Aug. 26, 1782 (abstract), in *NG*, 11:576; Heitman, *Historical Register*, 313.

31. Thomas Simes, *The Military Guide for Young Officers*, vol. 1 (Philadelphia: R. Bell and R. Aitken, 1776), 11.

32. GO, Dec. 18, 1775, Jan. 2 and 29, 1776, Sept. 25 and 29, 1777, in *AWP*, 2:572, 3:10–11 (quote), 210, 11:318, 343.

33. GO, Jan. 15 and Oct. 14, 1777, in *AWP*, 8:72, 11:502; George Smith, *An Universal Military Dictionary* (1779; fascimile, Ottawa, Ont.: Museum Restoration Service, 1969), 2 (quote).

34. GO, Oct. 8, 1775, Apr. 15 and 17, 1776, in *AWP*, 4:65, 6:320; Washington to Nicholas Fish, Mar. 23, 1780, in *FWW*, 18:146.

35. June 22, 1779, entry in *JCC*, 14:758.

36. Alexander Scammell to Washington, Nov. 16, 1780, WP; Heitman, *Historical Register*, 484.

37. Sept. 19, 1776, *JCC*, 5:787.

38. Joseph R. Riling, *Baron Von Steuben and His Regulations* (includes fascimile of *The Regulations for the Order and Discipline of the Troops of the United States*) (Philadelphia: Ray Riling Arms Books, 1966), 134–35.

39. GO, Nov. 9, 1777, in *AWP*, 12:177. For similar instances, see GO, May 21, July 17, 1776, and Feb. 12, 1777, in *AWP*, 4:348–49, 5:353, 8:343; and Feb. 27, 1776, entry in *The Orderly Books of Colonel William Henshaw* (Worcester, Mass.: American Antiquarian Society, 1948), 94–95.

40. GO, Oct. 8, 1775, in *AWP*, 2:122–23; GO, July 1, 1775, in "Orderly Book of Capt. Coit's Company," 34.

41. Court-martial proceeding, Fort Schuyler, "Some Unpublished Revolutionary Manuscripts," *PNJHS*, 2d ser., 13 (1894–95): 17–18.

42. Regimental Orders, Jan. 17, 1776, in "Diaries of Lieut. Jonathan Burton, of Wilton, N.H.," in Isaac W. Hammond, ed. *State Papers of New Hampshire*, vol. 14 (Concord, N.H., 1885), 685; GO, June 17, 1777, in Worthington C. Ford, ed., *General Orders of Major-General William Heath . . .* (Brooklyn, N.Y.: Historical Printing, 1890), 22; Regimental Orders, Nov. 1, 1777, RWR, M853, roll 3, vol. 17

(quote); Garrison Orders, Aug. 25. 1780, in *EAOB*, roll 12, no. 123; Lender and Martin, *Citizen Soldier*, July 8, 1776, 68.

43. Lawyn C. Edwards, "Sergeant Major," in Jerold E. Brown, *Historical Dictionary of the U.S. Army* (Westport, Conn.: Greenwood, 2001), 424.

44. Riling, *Baron Von Steuben*, 144; Jan. 15, 1776, entry in Doyen Salsig, ed., *Parole, Quebec—Countersign, Ticonderoga: Second New Jersey Regimental Orderly Book, 1776* (Rutherford, N.J.: Fairleigh Dickinson University Press, 1980), 46–47; Arnold G. Fisch and Robert K. Wright, *The Story of the Noncommissioned Officer Corps: The Backbone of the Army* (Washington, D.C.: Center of Military History, 1989), 162; Richard B. Begg, "Sergeant Major," *Army* 16, no. 2. (Jan. 1966): 27–28 (quote).

45. Steuben to Alexander Hamilton, May 6, 1779, abstract, *Steuben Papers* (NA); John Hancock to Washington, July 24, 1775, in *AWP*, 1:165; Washington to Michael Ryan, Apr. 10, 1778, and Congressional Resolution of Aug. 1, 1782, in GO, Dec. 26, 1782, in *FWW*, 11:234, 25:475–76; May 27, 1778, entry in *JCC*, 11:542; Fry, "Adjutant-General's Department," 1–2.

46. Aug. 1, 1782, entry in *JCC*, 22:425–27.

47. *NG*, 11:194n.

48. GO, June 20, 1779, in *FWW*, 15:290.

49. GO, Oct. 4 and 24, 1776, in *AWP*, 6:462, 7:21; Sept. 5 and 18, 1776, entries in "Elisha Williams' Diary" (1924), 339, 343.

50. GO, Sept. 24, 1776, and Oct. 8, 1777, in *AWP*, 6:213, 11:428; July 14, 1776, entry in Peter Kinnan, *Order Book . . . 1776* (Princeton: Princeton University Press, 1931), 11.

51. GO, Apr. 15 and June 25, 1776, in *AWP*, 4:65, 5:95; GO, July 26, 1770, in *FWW*, 15:490.

52. GO, Feb. 27, 1776, in *AWP*, 3:380.

53. GO, Aug. 17, 1775, in *AWP*, 1:317; GO, Apr. 8, 1778, in *FWW*, 11:228–29; GO, June 19, 1779, OB Gen. Hand, in *EAOB*, roll 7, no. 84.

54. GO, Aug. 17, 1775, Feb. 27, Apr. 15, May 1, 21, and 25, June 23, and Oct. 25, 1776, and Feb. 7, 1778, in *AWP*, 1:317, 3:380, 4:65, 181, 349, 384, 5:77, 7:27, 13:465.

55. GO, Sept. 23, 1776, in *AWP*, 6:375.

56. Steuben to Washington, July 18, 1778, in *Steuben Papers* (WP).

57. GO, May 13 and Nov. 5, 1779, in *FWW*, 15:66, 17:78; Gov. Alexander Martin to Nathanael Greene, Aug. 29, 1782, in *NG*, 11:599.

58. Feb. 18, 1779, entry in *JCC*, 13:198; GO, Apr. 27 and June 20, 1779, in *FWW*, 14:445–46, 15:228.

59. Col. Arendt to Washington, Aug. 7, 1777, in *AWP*, 9:48n.

60. J. P. Sanger, "The Inspector General's Department," in Rodenbough and Haskins, *Army of the United States*, 12; David A. Clary and W. A. Whitehorne, *The Inspectors General of the United States, 1777–1903* (Washington, D.C.: Center of Military History, 1987), 18, 21.

61. Dec. 13, 1777, entry in *JCC*, 9:1026; Clary and Whitehorne, *Inspectors General*, 21–29; J. D. Hittle, *The Military Staff: Its History and Development* (Harrisburg, Pa.: Stackpole, 1961), 172–73.

62. Dec. 13, 1777, entry in *JCC*, 9:1023–26.

63. Sanger, "Inspector General's Department," 14–15; Heitman, *Historical Register*, 518.

64. GO, June 15, 1778, in *FWW*, 12:66–67; David R. Chesnutt and C. James Taylor, eds., *The Papers of Henry Laurens*, vol. 13 (Columbia: University of South Carolina Press, 1992), 458n.

65. Aug. 28, 1778, and Feb. 18, 1779, entries in *JCC*, 11:820–23, 13:196–97.

66. John Laurens to Henry Laurens, Mar. 25, 1778, in Chesnutt and Taylor, *Papers of Laurens*, 36; Friedrich Kapp, *The Life of Frederick William von Steuben* (New York: Mason Brothers, 1859), 126.

67. James R. Jacobs, *The Beginning of the U.S. Army, 1783–1812* (Princeton: Princeton University Press, 1947), 9; John M. Palmer, *General Von Steuben* (1937; reprint, Port Washington, N.Y.: Kennikat, 1966), 210.

68. Riling, *Baron Von Steuben*, 10–11; Rudolf Cronau, *The Army of the American Revolution and Its Organizer* (New York: privately printed, 1923), 40, 46.

69. Washington to Henry Laurens, Apr. 30, 1778, in Chesnutt and Taylor, *Papers of Laurens*, 223.

70. Aug. 20, 1778, and Sept. 25, 1780, entries in *JCC*, 11:819–23, 17:855–61.

71. Dec. 4, 1780, entry in *JCC*, 18:1118.

72. Washington to Maj. Gen. Benedict Arnold, Aug. 8, 21, and Sept. 7, 1780, in *FWW*, 19:342, 417, 20:10.

73. GO, Aug. 11, Dec. 17, 1779, July 6, and Aug. 29, 1780, in *FWW* 16:77, 17:281, 19:126, 466.

74. Washington to Maj. Gen. Benjamin Lincoln, Oct. 26, 1779, in *FWW* 17:30; Bennett and Lennon, *Quest for Glory*, 94, 169n13; Heitman, *Historical Register*, 536.

75. *AWP*, 1:169n.

76. See, for example, GO, Aug. 6, 1777, in *AWP*, 10:576.

77. *AWP*, 1:134n; Adrian C. Leiby, *The Revolutionary War in the Hackensack Valley: The Jersey Dutch and the Neutral Ground* (1962; reprint, New Brunswick: Rutgers University Press, 1980), 188–91; Harry M. Ward, *Between the Lines: Banditti of the American Revolution* (Westport, Conn.: Praeger, 2002), 77–78; Heitman, *Historical Register*, 568.

78. Council of General Officers, July 26, 1779, in *NG*, 4:263, 264n; Washington to Henry Laurens, Joseph Spencer, and Nathaniel Scudder, Aug. 20, 1779, in *FWW*, 16:35–36; Jan. 12, 1780, entry in *JCC*, 16:47.

79. Steuben to Washington, n.d., in Kapp, *Life of Steuben*, 484–85.

80. Jan. 10, 1782, entry in *JCC*, 22:30–33.

81. Resolution of Congress, Aug. 1, 1782, in GO, Dec. 26, 1782, Washington to Secretary at War, Aug. 16, 1782, and GO, Nov. 22, 1782, *FWW*, 25:475–76, 25–26, 367; Clary and Whitehorne, *Inspectors General*, 57.

82. Washington to Walter Stewart, Feb. 8, 1782, GO, Feb. 11, 1782, and Washington to Brig. Gen. Elias Dayton, May 7, 1782, in *FWW*, 23:490, 495, 24:230; *NG*, 10:490n.

83. Steuben to Greene, abstract, Feb. 17, 1782, Greene to Gen. Anthony Wayne, abstract, Apr. 10, 1782, Greene to Robert R. Livingston, Apr. 12, 1782, and John Baptiste Ternant to Greene, abstract, Sept. 27, 1782, in *NG*, 10:377, 11:28, 35, 700, 701n; Washington to Count Rochambeau, Jan. 14, 1781, in *FWW*, 23:446.

84. Washington to Steuben, July 9, 1782, in *FWW*, 24:412.

85. Apr. 15, 1784, entry in *JCC*, 26:230; Kapp, *Life of Steuben*, 527; Heitman, *Historical Register*, 416.

5. Washington's Life Guard

1. Duke of York to Cornwallis, July 26, 1788, in Charles Ross, ed., *Correspondence of Charles, First Marquis Cornwallis*, vol. 1 (London: John Murray, 1859), 409; *The Oxford English Dictionary*, 2d ed. (Oxford: Clarendon, 1989), 8:915; J. W. Fortesque, *A History of the British Army*, vol. 1 (London: Macmillan, 1910), 293, 324; S. Fischer-Fabian, *Prussia's Glory: The Rise of a Military State* (New York: Macmillan, 1981), 88; Pierre Gaxotte, *Frederick the Great*, trans. R. A. Bell (New Haven: Yale University Press, 1942), 13, 80, 177; Lynde, "British Army in North America," 102–13, 469.

2. Edward H. Curtis, *The Organization of the British Army in the American Revolution* (New Haven: Yale University Press, 1926), 3.

3. GO, Mar. 11, 1776, in *AWP*, 3:448–49.

4. Washington to the President of Congress, June 18, 1778, in *FWW*, 12:82; Howard W. Wehman, "To Major Gibbs with Much Esteem," *Prologue: The Journal of the National Archives* 4 (Winter 1972): 227. For brief backgrounds on Gibbs and Lewis, see Arthur S. Lefkowitz, *George Washington's Indispensable Men: The 32 Aides-de-Camp Who Helped Win American Independence* (Mechanicsburg, Pa.: Stackpole Books, 2003), 46–48.

5. Henry Laurens to Washington, Dec. 8, 1778, PCC, r23, i13, 2:207; July 29, 1780, entry in *JCC*, 11:750; Carlos E. Godfrey, *The Commander-in-Chief's Guard* (1904; reprint, Baltimore: Genealogical Publishing, 1995), 90, 140, 175, 177, 185, 205, 207, 233.

6. Washington to Gibbs, May 1, 1777, in *AWP*, 9:320–21, 322n, 323n; Kahler, "Gentlemen of the Family," 138; Washington to Gibbs, Dec. 1, 1783, WP.

7. Gibbs to John Chaloner, Feb. 18, 1780, in "The Commander-in-Chief's Guard," *PMHB* 38 (1914): 86.

8. Entry of May 20, 1780, in James R. Nichols, ed., "The Doughboy of 1780: Pages from a Revolutionary Diary," *Atlantic Monthly* 134 (1924): 463.

9. Martha Daingerfield Bland to Frances Bland Randolph, May 12, 1777, quoted in *AWP*, 9:321n, 322n.

10. Washington to Gibbs, June 18, 1780, quoted in Wehman, "To Major Gibbs with Much Esteem," 229–30.

11. Nov. 26, 1780, entry in Rice, *Travels in North America*, 1:114.

12. Svejda, *Quartering, Disciplining*, 39, 54; Lefkowitz, *George Washington's Indispensable Men*, 48. One civilian noted that Washington, with his army as it moved

through New Jersey, was escorted by fifty of the Life Guard with drawn swords; entry of Jan. 26, 1778, in Albert C. Meyers, *Sally Wister's Journal* (Philadelphia: Ferris Leach, 1902), 184.

13. George W. P. Custis, *Recollections and Private Memoirs of Washington* (Philadelphia: William Flint, 1859), 257; Svejda, *Quartering, Disciplining*, 40; Godfrey, *Commander-in-Chief's Guard*, 68–69.

14. Godfrey, *Commander-in-Chief's Guard*, 21.

15. "Examining James Mason," June 20, 1776, in Force, *American Archives*, 4th ser., 6 (1843), 1155–56; June 23, 1776, entry in Edward Bangs, ed., *Journal of Lieutenant Isaac Bangs . . . 1776* (Cambridge, Mass.: J. Wilson and Son, 1890), 48; Louis H. Schmidt, "George Washington's Bodyguards Were Wisely Selected and Loyal," *Picket Post*, no. 12 (Jan. 1946): 19; Douglas S. Freeman, *George Washington*, 7 vols. (New York: Charles Scribner's Sons, 1949–57), 4:118–21; Philip Ranlet, *The New York Loyalists* (Knoxville: University of Tennessee Press, 1986), 156–57.

16. Washington's Warrant to the Provost Marshal, June 28, 1776, in Godfrey, *Commander-in-Chief's Guard*, 31; Benson J. Lossing, "Washington's Life Guard," *Historical Magazine* 2 (1858): 131.

17. William Eustis to Dr. David Townshend, June 28, 1776, in Edward F. Slafter, ed., "Letter of Governor Eustis—with Notes," *New England Historical and Genealogical Register* 23 (1869): 208; Boatner, *Encyclopedia of the American Revolution*, 752.

18. Chapin, *American Law of Treason*, 35.

19. Ranlet, *New York Loyalists*, 156.

20. GO, Sept. 11, 1776, in *AWP*, 6:277; Sept. 11, 1776, entry in *Orderly Books of Henshaw*, 231.

21. GO, Sept. 13, 1776, in *AWP*, 6:29.

22. Washington to Cols. Alexander Spotswood, Alexander McClanachan, Abraham Bowman, Charles Lewis, and Edward Stevens and Lt. Col. Christian Febiger, Apr. 30, 1777, in *AWP*, 9:315, 315n.

23. Washington to Gibbs, Apr. 22, 1777, in *AWP*, 9:236.

24. H. P. Livingston to the Commissary, Aug. 16, 1777, in "Commander-in-Chief's Guard," 84.

25. Godfrey, *Commander-in-Chief's Guard*, 39–41, 205–6, 253.

26. Fred A. Berg, *Encyclopedia of Continental Army Units* (Harrisburg, Pa.: Stackpole Books, 1972), 135.

27. "Journal of . . . Crévecouer," July 1, 1781, in Rice and Brown, *American Campaigns of Rochambeau's Army*, 31–32; Evelyn M. Acomb, ed., *The Revolutionary Journal of Baron Ludwig von Closen, 1780–1783* (Chapel Hill: University of North Carolina Press, 1958), 92.

28. GO, OB of First Virginia Regiment, Mar. 17, 1781, VHS; Washington to Henry Laurens, July 22, 1778, PCC, r168, i152, 6:186; GO, Mar. 17, 1778, and Washington to the President of Congress, June 18, 1778, in *FWW*, 11:98, 12:82.

29. John B. Linn and William H. Egle, eds., *Pennsylvania Archives*, 2d ser., vol. 11 (Harrisburg: Clarence N. Bush, 1896), 127; Godfrey, *Commander-in-Chief's*

Guard, 54–55; J. Jackson, *Valley Forge*, 231; Berg, *Encyclopedia of Continental Army Units*, 135.

30. Mar. 30, 1778, entry in *Elijah Fisher's Journal While in the War for Independence* (1880; reprint, New York: William Abbatt, 1909), 19.

31. Letter of Steuben, n.d., in Godfrey, *Commander-in-Chief's Guard*, 56.

32. Clary and Whitehorne, *Inspectors General*, 38.

33. Mar. 18, 1778, entry in *Elijah Fisher's Journal*, 19; Washington to Lafayette, May 18, 1778, in Idzerda, *Lafayette in the Age of Revolution*, 2:53–54; Paul J. Sanborn, "Barren Hill, Pennsylvania, Engagement," in Blanco, *American Revolution*, 1:95–99.

34. June 23, 1778, entry in *Elijah Fisher's Journal*, 23.

35. Nathanael Greene to Joseph Reed, Oct. 26, 1778, in *NG*, 3:19, 19n; Samuel Hazard, ed., "Part of a Diary of Major Gibbs, 1778," *Pennsylvania Archives*, 1st ser., vol. 6 (Philadelphia: Joseph Severns and Co., 1853): 134–36.

36. GO, Oct. 23, 1778, in *FWW*, 13:135–39; Oct. 6–28, 1778, entries in *Elijah Fisher's Journal*, 25–28; Godfrey, *Commander-in-Chief's Guard*, 66, 68, 128–29, 186, 191, 266; James Neagles, *Summer Soldiers: A Survey and Index of Revolutionary War Courts-Martial* (Salt Lake City: Ancestry, 1986), 90.

37. GO, Oct. 23, 1778, in *FWW*, 13:136–37; Godfrey, *Commander-in-Chief's Guard*, 64–65; V. W. Richter, "General Washington's Body Guards," *Concord Society Historical Bulletin*, no. 3 (Detroit, 1924): 14.

38. Aug. 6 and Oct. 15, 1779, entries in *Elijah Fisher's Journal*, 31–32; Appendix: Records of the Officers and Men, in Godfrey, *Commander-in-Chief's Guard*, 113–273.

39. Washington to Lt. William Colfax, Oct. 2, 1779, in *FWW*, 16:393.

40. Sept. 16, 1779, entry in *Elijah Fisher's Journal*, 32.

41. Jan. 7, 1780, entry in *Elijah Fisher's Journal*, 33; Lossing, "Washington's Life Guard," 132.

42. GO, Apr. 12 and 15, 1780, in *FWW*, 18:250, 263; GO, July 17 and 20, 1780, RWR, M853, roll 6, vols. 38, 40.

43. Boatner, *Encyclopedia of the American Revolution*, 633; Lossing, "Washington's Life Guard," 132.

44. GO, Apr. 5 and June 25, 1780, in *FWW*, 18:221, 19:63. At Morristown were divisions of Stirling, St. Clair, and George Clinton.

45. Caleb Gibbs to William Maxwell, June 8, 1780, WP; GO June 9, 1780, in *FWW*, 18:492, 486n; Godfrey, *Commander-in-Chief's Guard*, 73; Thomas Fleming, *The Forgotten Victory: The Battle for New Jersey—1780* (New York: Reader's Digest, 1973), 168–70.

46. Quoted in H. Ward, *William Maxwell*, 152.

47. H. Ward, *William Maxwell*, 152–53; Fleming, *Forgotten Victory*, 215.

48. GO, Sept. 7, 1780, in *FWW*, 20:11.

49. Washington to Maj. Gen. William Heath, Apr. 8, 1781, in *FWW*, 21:432.

50. *FWW*, 12:82n; extract of GO, Apr. 23, 1781, RWR, M853, roll 8, vol. 50; "Return of Troops . . . West Point," Jan. 4, 1784, PCC, r45, i38, 383.

51. *FWW*, 23:62n; William Nelson, "Biographical Sketch of William Colfax, Captain in Washington's Body Guard," *PNJHS*, 2d ser., 4 (1875–77): 46–50; quotation in Andrew P. Mellick, *The Story of an Old Farm* (Somerville, N.J.: Union Gazette, 1889), 477–78.

52. Washington to Lt. William Colfax, Aug. 4, 1782, in *FWW*, 24:462; see also 24:88n; Godfrey, *Commander-in-Chief's Guard*, 140–41; Kitman, *George Washington's Expense Account*, 254.

53. David B. Mattern, *Benjamin Lincoln and the American Revolution* (Columbia: University of South Carolina Press, 1995), 116; Howard H. Peckham, ed., *The Toll of Independence: Engagements and Battle Casualties of the American Revolution* (Chicago: University of Chicago Press, 1974), 87; Henry B. Carrington, *Battles of the American Revolution, 1775–1781* (1877; reprint, New York: Promontory, n.d.), 619–20; Godfrey, *Commander-in-Chief's Guard*, 77–78, 140.

54. Asa B. Gardner, "The Last Cantonment of the Main Continental Army of the Revolution," *Magazine of American History* 10 (1883): 357; Godfrey, *Commander-in-Chief's Guard*, 80–81, 83, 86.

55. GO, May 1, 1782, in *EAOB*, roll 16, no. 159; Lossing, "Washington's Life Guard," 133.

56. GO, June 2, 1783, in *FWW*, 26:463–64; R. Wright, *Continental Army*, 179.

57. Berg, *Encyclopedia of Continental Army Units*, 22; Godfrey, *Commander-in-Chief's Guard*, 99, 140, 185–86, 189; and for list of members of the Life Guard who were engaged to serve during the war, see 95–97. For forty-seven names and enlistment records of Pennsylvanians who served in the Life Guard, see Linn and Egle, *Pennsylvania Archives*, 2d ser., vol. 11 (1896), 128–29. For a list of Virginians who served in the Life Guard, see May 28, 1785, entry in "Return of Men Considered as Part of the Quota of the State of Virginia and Consequently Settled for Depreciation," in *Muster and Pay Rolls: War of the Revolution, 1775–1783, Collections of the New-York Historical Society*, vols. 47–48 (New York: NYHS, 1916), 48:634.

58. GO, June 6 and 7, 1783, in *FWW*, 26:472, 477; H. Charles McBarron Jr. and Frederick P. Todd, "Commander-in-Chief's Guard, 1777–1783," in John R. Elting, *Military Uniforms in America: The Era of the American Revolution, 1755–1795* (San Rafael, Calif.: Company of Military Historians, 1974), 11.

59. Berg, *Encyclopedia of Continental Army Units*, 135; Godfrey, *Commander-in-Chief's Guard*, 98.

60. GO, Mar. 3, 1783, *FWW*, 27:181; Godfrey, *Commander-in-Chief's Guard*, 98–99.

61. Godfrey, *Commander-in-Chief's Guard*, 99–103.

62. Godfrey, *Commander-in-Chief's Guard*, 189; Oct. 6, 1783, entry in *JCC*, 25:646–47.

63. Instructions to Bezaleel Howe, Nov. 9, 1783, in *FWW*, 27:237–39; Godfrey, *Commander-in-Chief's Guard*, 102–3.

6. Generals' Guards

1. Humphrey Bland, *A Treatise of Military Discipline*, 4th ed. (London: Samuel Buckley, 1741), 201.

2. F. Anderson, *People's Army*, 80.

3. Mar. 27, June 24–26, July 4 and 6, 1755, entries in Charles Hamilton, ed., *Braddock's Defeat: The Journal of Captain Robert Cholmley's Batman . . . Halkett's Orderly Book* (Norman: University of Oklahoma Press, 1959), 66, 78, 112, 118, 119; GO, Fort Edward, June 8, 1759, in *Expedition of the British and Provincial Army*, 14.

4. "A Report of the Guards near Bound Brook," May 14, 1777, in "Some Unpublished Revolutionary Manuscripts," 151; Riling, *Baron Von Steuben*, 94–97; John W. Wright, "Some Notes on the Continental Army," *WMQ*, 2d ser., 12 (1932): 88.

5. Letter quoted in Kapp, *Life of Kalb*, 140.

6. Muster Roll . . . Sullivan's Life Guard commanded by Aaron Man, Captain, Jan. 20, 1779, RWR, M246, #133.

7. Alpheus Parkhurst pension application, in Dann, *Revolution Remembered*, 57.

8. "A Weekly Return," Dec. 13, 1777, and "Detail of Camp and Advanced Guards," July 4, 1778, *GP* (NYHS); OB, Dec. 29, 1782, *GP* (NYPL); Garrison Orders (Lancaster, Pa.), Jan. 11, 1778, and Division Orders, Jan. 24, 1781, RWR, M853, roll 3, vol. 17, roll 8, vol. 51; OB, Oct. 31, 1780, and May 1, 1782, in *EAOB*, roll 15, no. 126, roll 16, no. 159; Division Orders, OB of Capt. Thomas Hamilton, Sept. 18, 1779, VHS misc. ms.; Report . . . Guards . . . Bound Brook, May 5, 9, 11, 13–14, 17, and 19, 1777, in *BL*; Steuben to Baron de Frank, June 4, 1779, in William L. Stone, trans. and ed., *Letters of Brunswick and Hessian Officers During the American Revolution* (1891; reprint, New York: Da Capo, 1970), 244, 246; GO, June 12, 1782, in *FWW*, 22:199; *AWP*, 4:341n.

9. GO, Aug. 4, 1781, in *EAOB*, roll 14, no. 143; GO, Apr. 20 and June 6, 1781, in *FWW*, 21:483, 22:167; Peter Angelakos, "The Army at Middlebrook," *PNJHS* 70 (1952): 113.

10. Brigade Orders, May 26, 1777, in "Orderly Book of Major William Heth of the Third Virginia Regiment," *Collections of the Virginia Historical Society* 11 (1892): 341.

11. Quoted in "Revolutionary Army Orders for the Main Army under Washington," *Virginia Magazine of History and Biography* 22 (1932): 12–13.

12. Mayer, *Belonging to the Army*, 175–76.

13. Otho Williams to Gates, Oct. 28, 1780, in *GP* (NYHS).

14. Benjamin Rush to John Adams, Oct. 21, 1777, in Taylor et al., *Papers of John Adams*, 5:317.

15. Remarks on the Continental Brigade, 1779, RWR, M859, #111-31475.

16. Robert McCready's journal quoted in Mayer, *Belonging to the Army*, 173.

17. GO, Sept. 20, 1777, in *AWP*, 11:275.

18. GO, OB of Maj. Gen. Gates, Nov. 23, 1782, *GP* (NYPL); Mayer, *Belonging to the Army*, 175.

19. Extract of Go, Jan. 19, 1782, in *EAOB*, roll 15, no. 156. After 1777, officers could not take aides with them on leave; Lender, "Enlisted Line," 192.

20. GO, May 17, 1778, in *FWW*, 11:397.

21. GO, Jan. 18–19, 1782, in *FWW*, 23:450–51; Mayer, *Belonging to the Army*, 173–74.

22. *NG*, 5:343n.

23. Kapp, *Life of Kalb*, 141.

24. William Maxwell to Nathanael Greene, Dec. 24, 1779, in *NG*, 5:206–7.

25. Henry Woodman, *The History of Valley Forge* (Oaks, Pa.: John Francis Jr., 1922), 49–52, 66–67; Edward Pinkowski, *Washington's Officers Slept Here: Historic Homes of Valley Forge and Its Neighborhood* (Philadelphia: Sunshine, 1953), 26–37.

26. *Memoirs of Capt. Lemuel Roberts* (1809; reprint, New York: New York Times, Arno, 1969), 39–40; Lender, "Enlisted Line," 194–95.

27. Garrison Orders (Lancaster, Pa.), Jan. 8, 1778, RWR, M853, roll 3, vol. 17; *AWP*, 12:447n.

28. Nathanael Greene to Walter Stewart, Sept. 23, 1779, and Stewart to Greene, Sept. 22, 1779, in *NG*, 4:405, 405n.

29. Nathanael Greene to Walter Stewart, Sept. 23, 1779 (2 letters), and Stewart to Greene (abstract of letters), Sept. 22–23, 1779, in *NG*, 4:405–6, 405–7nn.

30. Maj. Gen. Stirling to Washington (Aug.–Sept. 1777), in *AWP*, 11:105.

31. Paul D. Nelson, *William Alexander, Lord Stirling* (University: University of Alabama Press, 1987), 110.

32. Brig. Gen. Thomas Conway to Washington, Sept. 1, 1777, in *AWP*, 11:106–7.

33. Brigade Orders, Nov. 2, 1778, RWR, M853, roll 2, vol. 197.

34. Edward Hand to Col. Walter Stewart, July 16, 1782, RWR, M853, roll 17, vol. 162.

35. Washington to Charles Lee, Mar. 14, 1776, in *AWP*, 3:468.

36. Washington to Maj. Gen. Henry Knox, Nov. 13, 1782, in *FWW*, 25:338–39; Roger S. Champagne, *Alexander McDougall and the American Revolution in New York* (Schenectady, N.Y.: Union College Press, 1975), 179, 184–5, 189.

37. Washington to Major Generals and Officers commanding brigades, Jan. 22, 1780, in *FWW*, 17:430; Allan S. Everest, *Moses Hazen and the Canadian Refugees in the American Revolution* (Syracuse: Syracuse University Press, 1976), 85–89; Berg, *Encyclopedia of Continental Army Units*, 16.

38. Harry E. Wildes, *Anthony Wayne: Trouble Shooter of the American Revolution* (New York: Harcourt, Brace, 1941), 63–65; Wilkinson, *Memoirs*, 51; H. Ward, *William Maxwell*, 35–36.

39. Joseph Trumbull to Gov. Trumbull, Dec. 17, 1776, in Force, *American Archives*, 5th ser., 3 (1853), 1265; Franklin Dexter, ed., *The Literary Diary of Ezra Stiles*, vol. 1 (New York: Charles Scribner's Sons, 1901), 106; Wilkinson, *Memoirs*, 105–7; Edward W. Harcourt, ed., *The Harcourt Papers*, vol. 11 (Oxford, Eng.: James Parker, 1880), 185–89; John R. Alden, *General Charles Lee: Traitor or Patriot?* (Baton Rouge: Louisiana State University Press, 1951), 153–58.

40. H. Ward, *Between the Lines*, 77–78; Leiby, *Revolutionary War in the Hackensack Valley*, 188–91 (includes Thomas Ward's memorandum in the Henry Clinton Papers, Clements Library, University of Michigan, Ann Arbor).

7. Camp and Quarter Guards

1. Riling, *Baron Von Steuben*, 94.

2. Division Orders, Jan. 2, 1777, in *BL*; GO, Feb. 18, 1777, in *EAOB*, roll 4, no. 42; Nathanael Greene's Plan for 1780—Quartermaster General Department, RWR, M859, #111-31519; GO, Sept. 1, 1775, in *AWP*, 1:395; Greene's After Orders, June 7, 1777, Otho Williams to Greene, Feb. 3, 1780, and Greene's Orders, Nov. 19, 1781, in *NG*, 2:105, 5:343, 9:591; Scheer, *Private Yankee Doodle*, 31, 119, 161, 273.

3. Garber, *Modern Military Dictionary*, 191.

4. A Report of Guards Mounted in the Vicinity of Bound Brook Belonging to the Division of Maj. Gen. Lincoln, May 13, 1777, in *BL*; Report of the Field Officer of the Day at West Point, Aug. 14, 1780, and Morning Report of the Main Guard at West Point, Aug. 6, 1780, RWR, M246, roll 135; GO, Providence, R.I., July 25, 1777, RWR, M853, roll 5, vol. 32; Regimental Orders, 2d regiment Cont. artillery, Jan. 29 and May 6, 1780, in *EAOB*, roll 10, no. 102, roll 11, no. 127; GO, Dec. 7, 1779, Apr. 7 and 29, 1780, in *FWW*, 17:233, 18:232, 314; Dec. 27, 1779 (Book #4) and May 6, 1780 (Book #6), in Lauber, *Order Books of New York Regiments*, 210, 341; Lord Stirling's Brigade Orders, Aug. 16, 1776, in "Orders of Mercer, Sullivan, and Stirling, 1776," *American Historical Review* 3 (1897–98): 309; Svejda, *Quartering, Disciplining*, 52.

5. May 25, 1776, entry in *Orderly Books of Henshaw*, 139; GO, Feb. 12, 1777, in *AWP*, 8:313; GO, Apr. 8, 1778, and Apr. 16, 1783, in *FWW*, 11:228, 26:327; J. Wright, "Some Notes on the Continental Army" (1931), 185; Dupuy et al., *Dictionary of Military Terms*, 107.

6. Svejda, *Quartering, Disciplining*, 56.

7. Svejda, *Quartering, Disciplining*, 56; Harold Peterson, *The Book of the Continental Soldier* (Harrisburg, Pa.: Stackpole, 1968), 98; M. M. Quaife, ed., "A Boy Soldier under Washington: The Memoir of Daniel Granger," *Mississippi Valley Historical Review* 16 (1929–30): 558.

8. De Kalb to Comte de Broglie, Dec. 25, 1777, in Kapp, *Life of Kalb*, 142.

9. GO (McDougall), May 29 and Aug. 1, 1777, in *EAOB*, roll 14, nos. 42, 43; GO, July 24, 1775, in *AWP*, 1:164; GO, Mar. 12, 1783, in *FWW*, 26:210.

10. Quoted in Quaife, "Boy Soldier," 540–41.

11. GO, Nov. 9, 1777, in *AWP*, 12:1777; GO, Apr. 8 and Aug. 1, 1778, in *FWW*, 11:229, 12:258; GO, Aug. 19, 1780, RWR, M853, roll 7, vol. 43; Aug. 16, 1777, entry in "Orderly Book of the Pennsylvania State Regiment of Foot," *PMHB* 22 (1898): 476–77.

12. Riling, *Baron Von Steuben*, 96; H. L. Scott, *Military Dictionary* (New York: D. Van Nostrand, 1864), 135 (quote).

13. GO, June 27, 1781, in *FWW*, 22:269.

14. GO, Feb. 8, 1780, and Oct. 25, 1782, in *FWW*, 17:506–7, 25:298–99; Brigade Orders, Jan. 6, 1782, RWR, M853, roll 9, vol. 57; Brigade Orders, Feb. 11, 1780, and Wing Orders, Sept. 9, 1780, in Lauber, *Order Books of New York Regiments*, 249, 893; "Orderly Book of Pennsylvania State Regiment," 318.

15. Brigade Orders, Aug. 14, 1782, RWR, M853, roll 10, vol. 65; July 30, 1780, entry in *Orderly Book of New Jersey Brigade*, 3; GO, Sept. 3, 1792, RWR, M853, roll 10, vol. 64.

16. GO, Sept. 8, 1780, in *FWW*, 20:13.

17. Steuben to Washington, Dec. 28, 1780, in *Steuben Papers* (WP); J. Wright, "Some Notes on the Continental Army" (1931), 186; Frederic Kidder, *History of the First New Hampshire Regiment in the War of the Revolution* (Albany: J. Munsell, 1868), 40.

18. Aug. 16, 1780, and Sept. 3, 1781, entries in Lauber, *Order Books of New York Regiments*, 881, 889; Division Orders, Aug. 17, 1780, in *Orderly Book of New Jersey Brigade*, 20.

19. GO, June 5 and 15, 1777, in *AWP*, 9:608, 10:42; also 4:225n (quotes); Jan. 27, 1779, entry in "Order Book of John Faucheraud Grimké," *SCHGM* 14 (1913): 108–9; Bland, *Treatise of Military Discipline*, 163–64; May 19, 1778, entry in "Orderly Book of the 2d Pennsylvania Line," *PMHB* 36 (1912): 323.

20. General After Orders, Mar. 28, 1780, in Lee Wallace, ed., *The Orderly Book of Capt. Benjamin Taliaferro* (Richmond: Virginia State Library, 1980), 110; Lender and Martin, *Citizen Soldier*, 100.

21. Henry R. Bellas, ed., *Personal Recollections of Captain Enoch Anderson . . .* , Papers of the Historical Society of Delaware 16 (Wilmington, 1896), 15.

22. Scheer, *Private Yankee Doodle*, 48.

23. Scheer, *Private Yankee Doodle*, 64–65.

24. OB, Oliver Spencer's Additional Regiment, July 18, 1780, and General Court-Martial, Aug. 18, 1781, in *EAOB*, roll 11, no. 113, roll 14, no. 140; Morning Orders, Light Camp, Aug. 14, 1781, RWR, M853, roll 8, vol. 52; July 27, 1776, entry in *Orderly Books of Henshaw*, 195; GO, Jan. 6, May 5, 1778, and Feb. 4, 1780, in *FWW*, 10:273, 11:353, 17:485.

25. GO, Sept. 6, 1777, in Joseph B. Turner, ed., *The Journal and Order Book of Captain Robert Kirkwood of the Delaware Regiment of the Continental Line*, Papers of the Historical Society of Delaware 56 (Wilmington, 1910), 162.

26. GO, May 16, 1779, in *EAOB*, roll 7, no. 79.

27. Detachment Orders, June 13, 1781, RWR, M853, roll 8, vol. 52.

28. GO, May 8, 1779, in *FWW*, 15:27–28.

29. Riling, *Baron Von Steuben*, 102–5.

30. May 25, 1776, entry in *Orderly Books of Henshaw*, 139; GO, June 27, 1781, in *FWW*, 22:269.

31. Aug. 4, 1776, entry in *Orderly Books of Henshaw*, 204–5.

32. Regimental Orders, 2d Continental Artillery, Apr. 10, 1780, in *EAOB*, roll 11, no. 103.

33. Orders, Aug. 29, 1781, RWR, M853, roll 9, vol. 55.

34. OB, GO of Gates, June 3, 1778, in *GP* (NYPL).

35. OB, GO of Gates, Nov. 19, 1782, in *GP* (NYPL).

36. Bland, *Treatise of Military Discipline*, 209.

37. Orders, July 11–19, 1776, in "Journal of Bayze Wells, of Farmington, in the Canada Expedition, 1775–1777," *Collections of the Connecticut Historical Society* 7 (1899): 254–56; GO, Ft. Schuyler, Sept. 4, 1777, and Regimental Orders, June 29,

1782, in *EAOB*, roll 4, no. 42, roll 16, no. 158; Brigade Orders, May 26, 1777, in "Orderly Book of Heth," 341; Scheer, *Private Yankee Doodle*, 174; Riling, *Baron Von Steuben*, 94–95; Bland, *Treatise of Military Discipline*, 206.

38. Bland, *Treatise of Military Discipline*, 209.

39. Lord Stirling's Brigade Orders, Aug. 16, 1776, in "Orders of Mercer, Sullivan, and Stirling," 309; Sept. 18, 1776, entry in Salsig, *Parole, Quebec*, 241; Quaife, "Boy Soldier," 541.

40. GO, Aug. 5, 1775, in "Orderly Book of Coit," 85; Garrison Orders, Jan. 11, 1778 (Lancaster), RWR, M853, roll 3, vol. 17; Bland, *Treatise of Military Discipline*, 210.

41. Brigade Orders, Sept. 29, 1780, in Lauber, *Order Books of New York Regiments*, 513.

42. Nov. 4 and 7, 1775, entries in "Journal of Simeon Lyman," *Collections of the Connecticut Historical Society* 7 (1899): 124–25.

43. Scheer, *Private Yankee Doodle*, 217–18.

44. *NG*, 1:304n, 305n; Royster, *Revolutionary People*, 226; Peckham, *Memoirs of John Adlum*, 24–37.

8. Picket Men and Safeguards

1. Applegate, "Constitutions like Iron," 132.

2. H. Scott, *Military Dictionary*, 135; Garber, *Modern Military Dictionary*, 221; Angelakos, "Army at Middlebrook," 76.

3. GO, Sept. 10 and 15, 1777, in *AWP*, 11:181, 232; Proceedings of a Council of General Officers, Sept. 23, 1777, in *NG*, 2:164.

4. GO, May 7, 1776, in *AWP*, 4:221; GO, Feb. 5, 1780, in *FWW*, 17:494; July 18, 1777, entry in Turner, *Journal and Order Book of Kirkwood*, 118; Jan. 29, 1780, entry in Robert C. Bray and Paul E. Bushnell, eds., *Diary of a Common Soldier in the American Revolution, 1775–1783: The Military Journal of Jeremiah Greenman* (DeKalb: Northern Illinois University Press, 1978), 168; Bland, *Treatise of Military Discipline*, 206. On one occasion, a reserve picket was ordered for each brigade, consisting of one captain, one subaltern, two drum and fife, four sergeants, and fifty privates; GO, Feb. 5, 1780, in *FWW*, 17:494.

5. J. Jackson, *Valley Forge*, 140.

6. Riling, *Baron Von Steuben*, 108–110.

7. An account by Isaac Loftus, quoted in J. Jackson, *Valley Forge*, 140.

8. Washington to Bartholomew Von Heer, Oct. 11, 1778, in *FWW*, 13:70.

9. Benjamin Rush to John Adams, Oct. 1, 1777, in L. H. Butterfield, ed., *The Letters of Benjamin Rush*, vol. 1 (Princeton: Princeton University Press, 1951), 155.

10. GO, June 11 and Nov. 6, 1780, in *FWW*, 18:503, 20:303.

11. GO, Aug. 31, 1782, in *FWW*, 25:98; GO, June 28, 1781, in *EAOB*, roll 14, no. 140.

12. GO, May 31, 1777, in *AWP*, 9:369; GO, June 25, 1780, in *FWW*, 19:63.

13. GO, June 11 and Aug. 6, 1780, in *FWW*, 18:503, 19:337 (quote); Oct. 24, 1776, entry in "Elisha Williams' Diary, 1776," *PMHB* 49 (1925): 55; Regimental Orders,

Oct. 26, 1780, in "Orderly Book of Captain Daniel Livermore's Company, Continental Army, 1780," *Collections of the New Hampshire Historical Society* 9 (1889): 236.

14. Oct. 5, 1780, entry in "Orderly Book of Livermore's Company," 204; Jan. 1780 entry in Bray and Bushnell, *Diary of Greenman*, 168.

15. Edmonson, "Desertion," 274–75.

16. June 5, 1777, entry in Turner, *Journal and Order Book of Kirkwood*, 78.

17. "Order Book of Samuel Elbert, Colonel and Brigadier General in the Continental Army," *Collections of the Georgia Historical Society* 5, pt. 2 (1902): 148.

18. GO, Aug. 22, 1775, in *AWP*, 1:346.

19. GO, May 18, 1776, in *NG*, 1:215.

20. GO, July 7, 1777, in *AWP*, 10:213.

21. July 6, 1779, entry in William A. Ellis, ed., "The Order Book of Lieut. Colonel Francis Barber . . . 1779," *PNJHS* 65 (1947): 146.

22. GO, OB of McDougall, Aug. 17, 1779, in *EAOB*, roll 7, no. 87; *NG*, 4:169n.

23. Mar. 3, 1778, entry in *Valley Forge Orderly Book*, 248.

24. GO, Aug. 4, 1775, and Sept. 22, 1776, in *AWP*, 1:219, 6:365; GO, Aug. 20, 1778, in *FWW*, 12:338.

25. OB of Gates, July 18, 1778, in *GP* (NYPL).

26. GO, Jan. 17, 1777, in *AWP*, 8:88.

27. Sept. 24, 1780, entry in "Orderly Book of the First Pennsylvania Regiment . . . 1780," *Pennsylvania Archives*, 2d ser., vol. 11 (1896), 625.

28. GO, Aug. 5, 1781, in *EAOB*, roll 14, no. 140.

29. GO, June 12, 1777, in *AWP*, 10:7–8.

30. GO, July 9, 1781, in *FWW*, 22:342.

31. GO, Apr. 10, 1780, in *FWW*, 18:241; GO, Apr. 10, 1780, in Lauber, *Order Books of New York Regiments*, 313.

32. GO, Aug. 5, 1781, RWR, M853, roll 8, vol. 53; Sept. 6, 1777, entry in Turner, *Journal and Order Book of Kirkwood*, 164.

33. GO, Aug. 24, 1777, in *AWP*, 11:55; Nov. 21, 1777, entry in "Whitemarsh Orderly Book," 208.

34. Brigade Orders, Aug. 19, 1777, in Turner, *Journal and Order Book of Kirkwood*, 151.

35. GO, Jan. 28, 1780, and Nov. 23, 1783, in *FWW*, 17:459–60, 25:368; Jan. 18–20, 1780, entries in Bray and Bushnell, *Diary of Greenman*, 168; S. Sydney Bradford, "Discipline in the Morristown Winter Encampments," *PNJHS* 80 (1962): 16–17.

36. See, for example, July 22, 1781, entry in William Feltman, *The Journal of Lieut. William Feltman of the First Pennsylvania Regiment, 1781–1782* (Philadelphia: Henry Cary Baird, 1853), 8; GO, July 25, 1777, and Mar. 13, 1780, in *FWW*, 8:453, 18:109–10; Evening Orders, July 22, 1777, in Turner, *Journal and Order Book of Kirkwood*, 123; Feb. 28, 1781, entry in "Extracts from the Journal of Lieutenant John Bell Tilden," *PMHB* 19 (1895): 222; and H. Ward, *Between the Lines*, 13–15.

37. GO (Greene), Dec. 11, 1781, in *NG*, 10:25n, 34.

38. Lovell-Knight, *History of Provost Marshal and Military Police*, 24.

39. Abraham Davenport to Washington, Aug. 10, 1781, in Charles S. Hall, ed., *Life and Letters of Samuel Holden Parsons* (1905; reprint, New York: James Pugliese, 1968), 391; May 10, 1779, entry in "Journal of Capt. Samuel Page in the Campaign of 1779," *Historical Collections of the Essex Institute* 4 (1862): 248.

40. Orders, Nov. 14, 1782, in *EAOB*, roll 16, no. 162.

41. Wayne K. Bodle and Jacqueline Thibaut, *Valley Forge Research Report*, 3 vols. (Valley Forge National Historical Park, May 1980), 1:252–53, 3:64; Reginald P. Bolton, *Relics of the Revolution: The Story of the Discovery of the Buried Remains of Military Life in Forts and Camps on Manhattan Island* (New York: privately printed, 1916), 34–37.

42. OB, Jan. 24, 1783, in *GP* (NYPL); GO, July 5, 1782, RWR, M853, roll 10, vol. 64; GO, Aug. 6, 1776, in *AWP*, 6:34; *NG*, 1:253n.

43. GO, May 5, 1776, in *AWP*, 4:204.

44. OB (Hand), June 30, 1779, in *EAOB*, roll 7, no. 84.

45. Col. Armand to Washington, c. Sept. 2, 1777, and GO, Sept. 7, 1777, in *AWP*, 11:121, 161; GO, Aug. 2, 1781, in *FWW*, 22:454; Gen. Greene's Orders, July 28, 1776, in *NG*, 1:268.

46. OB, Corps of Artillery, West Point, July 9, 1780, in *EAOB*, roll 11, no. 112.

47. At a Court of Inquiry, Aug. 22, 1781, in *BL*.

48. Maj. John Doyle to Gen. Francis Marion, Nov. 9, 1781, in Robert W. Gibbes, *Documentary History of the American Revolution . . . South Carolina*, 3 vols. (1855; reprint, New York: Arno, 1971), 3:208–9.

49. John Parker to Greene, Sept. 20, 1782, and Maj. Ichabod Burnet to John Parker, Sept. 1, 1782, in *NG*, 11:681, 684.

50. Washington to Board of War, May 18, 1778, in *FWW*, 11:417.

51. Greene to Samuel Huntington, May 14, 1781, *NG*, 6:250; see also 236n; Maj. John Doyle to Gen. Marion, Nov. 20, 1781, in Gibbes, *Documentary History*, 3:213.

52. Francis Marion to Greene, Nov. 18, 1781, Col. Alexander Stewart to Greene, Nov. 20, 1781, Greene to Thomas McKean, Nov. 21, 1781, and Greene to Marion, Nov. 24, 1781, in *NG*, 9:589–90, 594–95, 598, 618; Maj. John Doyle to Gen. Marion, Nov. 20, 1781, in Gibbes, *Documentary History*, 3:213.

53. Greene to Marion, Nov. 24, 1781, and Col. Hezekiah Maham to Greene, Nov. 27, 1781, in *NG*, 9:618, 630–31.

54. Greene to Col. Alexander Stewart, Nov. 23, 1781, in *NG*, 9:612–13.

9. Temporary Police Patrols

1. Garber, *Modern Military Dictionary*, 226 (quotes); G. Smith, *An Universal Military Dictionary*, 199; *Oxford English Dictionary*, 11:351–52.

2. OB of Gates, Dec. 25, 1782, in *GP* (NYPL); GO, Dec. 25, 1782, in *FWW*, 25:464.

3. Brigade Orders, Apr. 4, 1782, RWR, M853, roll 9, vol. 59; Orders, Apr. 5, 1781, West Point, in *EAOB*, roll 13, no. 133.

4. Applegate, "Constitutions like Iron," 133.

5. GO, June 12, 1777, in *AWP*, 10:7.

6. Feb. 23, 1779, entry in "Journal of Ebenezer Wild," *MHSP* 6 (1890–91): 121.

7. Oct. 26, 1778, entry in "Extracts from the Fredericksburg Orderly Book—1778," *Historical Magazine* 5 (1861): 57.

8. GO, May 26, 1778, in "Orderly Book, May 18–June 11, 1778," *MHSP* 7 (1864): 134; GO, Nov. 24, 1777, in *AWP*, 12:371; Nov. 24, 1777, entry in "Whitemarsh Orderly Book," 211–12; GO, OB of Gates, June 8, 1778, in *GP* (NYPL).

9. GO, Apr. 6, 1778, RWR, M853, roll 3, vol. 16.

10. Sept. 1 and 2, 1776, entries in Lender and Martin, *Citizen Soldier*, 103–4.

11. Sylvia R. Frey, *The British Soldier in America: A Social History of Military Life in the Revolutionary Period* (Austin: University of Texas Press, 1981), 65; Hugh C. Rogers, *The British Army of the Eighteenth Century* (New York: Hippocrene Books, 1977), 51; Bland, *Treatise of Military Discipline*, 173.

12. Jedediah Huntington to Joshua Huntington, Apr. 20, 1776, in Albert C. Bates, ed., *Huntington Papers: Correspondence of Joshua and Jedediah Huntington During the Period of the American Revolution, Collections of the Connecticut Historical Society* 20 (1923): 281; Bruce Bliven Jr., *Under the Guns: New York, 1775–1776* (New York: Harper & Row, 1972), 222–24.

13. Garrison Orders (Lancaster, Pa.), Jan. 6, 1777, and Regimental Orders (Cambridge, Mass.), Sept. 13, 1777, RWR, M853, roll 3, vols. 17, 18.

14. Orders, Sept. 19, 1778, RWR, M853, roll 3, vol. 16.

15. General After Orders, Apr. 15, 1780, in L. Wallace, *Orderly Book of Benjamin Taliaferro*, 135–35.

16. For example, in 1780, see Bray and Bushnell, *Diary of Greenman*, 188.

17. H. Ward, *Between the Lines*, 79–80.

18. Washington to Lt. Col. Ebenezer Stevens, May 2, 1781, *FWW*, 22:23–24.

19. Orders, June 28, 1780, and Nov. 14, 1782, RWR, M853, roll 5, vol. 3, roll 10, vol. 64; OB of Capt. Thomas Hamilton, Oct. 15, 1779, VHS; Nov. 14, 1782, entry in Lauber, *Order Books of New York Regiments*, 702.

20. OB of Capt. Thomas Hamilton, Brigade Orders, Nov. 10, 1779, VHS; GO, Sept. 18, 1776, Orders, June 20, 1778, and Garrison Orders (West Point), Apr. 7, 1781, RWR, M853, roll 2, vol. 15, roll 4, vol. 24, roll 8, vol. 50; Division Orders, July 20, 1781, in *EAOB*, roll 14, no. 139; GO, Nov. 15, 1779, in Lauber, *Order Books of New York Regiments*, 116; Albert H. Heusser, *George Washington's Map Maker: A Biography of Robert Erskine* (New Brunswick: Rutgers University Press, 1966), 196, 198, 202.

21. OB of Gates, Nov. 19, 1782, in *GP* (NYPL).

22. GO, Dec. 2, 1782, in *FWW*, 25:386.

23. GO (OB of McDougall), July 17, 1777, in *EAOB*, roll 4, no. 43; July 17, 1777, entry in Ford, *Correspondence of Webb*, 1:246.

24. Instructions to the Officers of the Main Guard, Dec. 13, 1779, in *BL*.

25. GO, Apr. 10 and 11, 1778, RWR, M853, roll 3, vol. 19.

26. GO, Oct. 31, 1781, RWR, M853, roll 8, vol. 53.

27. June 1776 entry in "Orderly Book of Capt. Abraham Dodge," *Essex Institute Historical Collections* 80 (1944): 218–19.

28. William Hutchinson pension application (1836), in Dann, *Revolution Remembered*, 149.

29. GO, Sept. 12, 1777, in *AWP*, 11:204; "Orderly Book of Gen. John Peter Gabriel Muhlenberg," *PMHB* 34 (1910): 464; Sept. 12, 1777, entry in Turner, *Journal and Order Book of Kirkwood*, 168.

30. Washington to Thomas Wharton Jr., Sept. 13, 1777, in *AWP*, 11:221, 221n; see also 7:202n.

31. Washington to Wharton, Sept. 13, 1777, quotes from letters of Supreme Executive Council to Col. Lewis Nicola, and Thomas Wharton Jr. to Washington, in *AWP*, 11:221–22, 222n.

32. GO, Aug. 8, 1777, in *AWP*, 10:551–52.

33. "Orderly Book of Muhlenberg," Oct. 5, 1777, quoted in *AWP*, 11:392n.

34. Edmonson, "Desertion," 14, 20, 252.

35. Washington to John Hancock, Jan. 31, 1777, in *AWP*, 8:202.

36. Benjamin Lincoln to Washington, May 22, 1777, in *BL*.

37. GO, Aug. 11, 1777, in *AWP*, 10:582.

38. Col. William Malcolm to Washington, Sept. 14, 1777, and Gen. John Sullivan to Washington, Dec. 4, 1777, in *AWP*, 11:229, 12:557.

39. Brigade Orders, Trenton, Feb. 8, 1777, in George H. Ryden, ed., *Letters to and from Caesar Rodney* (Philadelphia: University of Pennsylvania Press, 1953), 165; Nov. 12, 1779, entry in Edward Field, ed., *The Diary of Colonel Israel Angell, 1778–1781* (Providence, R.I.: Preston and Rounds, 1899), 91; Regimental Orders, July 23, 1780, in Lauber, *Order Books of New York Regiments*, 227; Egly, *History of First New York Regiment*, 84; Edmonson, "Desertion," 285.

40. OB, Jan 21–22, 1777, in Salley, *Orderly Book of Third Regiment*, 8–11.

41. Scheer, *Private Yankee Doodle*, 260–62.

42. Oct. 13–14, 1779, entry in Field, *Diary of Angell*, 80–81.

43. See, for example, Maj. Gen. John Sullivan to Washington, May 23, 1777, in *AWP*, 9:509.

44. June 5, 1777, entry in Turner, *Journal and Order Book of Kirkwood*, 78.

45. Paul E. Doutrich, "York County," in John B. Frantz and William Pencak, eds., *Beyond Philadelphia: The American Revolution in the Pennsylvania Hinterland* (University Park: Pennsylvania State University Press, 1998), 104.

46. See, for example, Bray and Bushnell, *Diary of Greenman*, 138; Ebenezer Huntington to Andrew Huntington, Dec. 1, 1775, in Ford, *Correspondence of Webb*, 1:123; and Edmonson, "Desertion," 166, 284–85.

47. Heitman, *Historical Register*, 273; Edmonson, "Desertion," 282–84.

10. On the March

1. From "Memoirs" of Elisha Bostwick, in Henry S. Commager and Richard B. Morris, eds., *The Spirit of 'Seventy-Six*, vol. 1 (Indianapolis: Bobbs-Merrill, 1958), 512.

2. Riling, *Baron Von Steuben*, 67.

3. GO, Aug. 16, 1777, in *AWP*, 10:633; GO, June 1, 1778, in *FWW*, 12:5; Order of March, June 1, 1778, in W. T. Saffell, *Records of the Revolutionary War*, 3d ed. (1891; reprint, Baltimore: Genealogical Publishing, 1969), 364–67; John W. Jordan, ed., "Order of March of the Pennsylvania Line from Valley Forge, June 18, 1777," *PMHB* 39 (1915): 221–22; "Journal of Lieut. Col. Adam Hubley," in Frederick Cook, ed., *Journals of the Military Expedition of Major-General John Sullivan Against the Six Nations in 1779* (1887; reprint, Freeport, N.Y.: Books for Libraries, 1972), 154; J. Wright, "Some Notes on the Continental Army" (1931), 100–103.

4. J. Wright, "Some Notes on the Continental Army" (1931), 100.

5. GO, June 22, 1777, in *AWP*, 10:104.

6. GO, Dec. 10, 1777, in *AWP*, 12:586; GO, After Orders, Aug. 22, 1780, in *FWW*, 19:426; June 16, 1779, entry in Ellis, "Order Book of Barber," 72; Edmonson, "Desertion," 271–72.

7. May 31, 1781, entry in E. Lee Shepard, ed., *Marching to Victory: Capt. Benjamin Bartholomew's Diary of the Yorktown Campaign* (Richmond: VHS, 2002), 1, 8.

8. Division Orders, Nov. 18, 1778, in Hall, *Life and Letters of Parsons*, 202.

9. GO, June 1, 1778, in *FWW*, 12:5–6; J. Wright, "Some Notes on the Continental Army" (1931), 100, 103.

10. GO, Dec. 25, 1776, and Order of March, June 14, 1777, in *AWP*, 7:436, 10:34; GO, June 1, 1778, in *FWW*, 12:6; Greene's Orders, Nov. 29, 1779, in *NG*, 9:637; Gen. Sullivan's Instructions to Col. Hall, May 22, 1777, in Otis G. Hammond, ed., *Letters and Papers of Major-General John Sullivan*, vol. 1 (Concord: New Hampshire Historical Society, 1930), 340–41; Order of March, May 24, 1779, in "Journal of Hubley," 146; July 24, 1779, entry in "Journal of William Rogers," in Cook, *Journals of Military Expedition*, 253.

11. GO (addenda), in "Orderly Book of Muhlenberg," Aug. 16, 1777, quoted in *AWP*, 10:633n; J. Wright, "Some Notes on the Continental Army" (1931), 101.

12. Riling, *Baron Von Steuben*, 67.

13. Riling, *Baron Von Steuben*, 69–71.

14. Greene's Orders, Aug. 27, 1781, in *NG*, 9:222.

15. Greene's Orders (abstracts), Dec. 29, 1781, Feb. 18 and Mar. 5, 1782, in *NG*, 10:131, 377, 443; GO, Sept. 7, 1777, in *AWP*, 11:168; July 1777 entry in "The Diary of Captain John Chilton," *Tyler's Quarterly and Genealogical Magazine* 12 (1931): 286.

16. John W. Wright, "Some Notes on the Continental Army," *WMQ*, 2d ser., 13 (1933): 89.

17. Order of March, June 14, 1777, and GO, July 4, 1777, in *AWP*, 10:35–36, 180; Orders, Nov. 18, 1778, in Hall, *Life and Letters of Parsons*, 202.

18. GO, After Orders, June 30 and July 29, 1780, in *FWW*, 19:100, 278.

19. Order of March, June 14, 1777, and GO, Sept. 4 and Dec. 15, 1777, in *AWP*, 10:35, 11:143, 12:610; Greene's Orders, July 31, 1777, in *NG*, 2:130.

20. Order of March, June 14, 1777, in *AWP*, 10:35–36.

21. GO, Aug. 23, 1777, in *AWP*, 11:49.

22. GO, July 4, 1777, in *AWP*, 10:180.

23. GO, July 4, 1777, in *AWP*, 10:179.

24. GO, June 14, July 15, and Aug. 9, 1777, in *AWP*, 10:36, 284, 561; Erna Risch, *Supplying Washington's Army* (Washington, D.C.: Center of Military History, 1981), 70–74.

25. GO, July 29, 1777, in *AWP*, 10:453.

26. GO, Aug. 23, 1777, in *AWP*, 11:50.

27. GO, July 4 and Aug. 23, 1777, in *AWP*, 10:180, 11:50; GO, May 31, 1778, in *FWW*, 11:498; Aug. 28, 1777, entry in *Valley Forge Orderly Book*, 25.

28. GO, Aug. 4, 1777, in *AWP*, 10:496.

29. OB of John Lamb, June 19, 1781, in Mayer, *Belonging to the Army*, 48.

30. GO, July 4, 1777, in *AWP*, 10:180.

31. GO, July 10, Aug. 27, and Sept. 13, 1777, in *AWP*, 10:236, 11:73, 212; Greene's Orders, abstract, Mar. 21, 1782, in *NG*, 10:529.

32. Deposition of Sarah Osborne (1831), in Dann, *Revolution Remembered*, 243–44.

33. Scheer, *Private Yankee Doodle*, 197–98.

34. Lee Kennett, *The French Armies in the Seven Years' War: A Study in Military Organization and Administration* (Durham: Duke University Press, 1967), 85.

35. July 5, 1777, entry in Turner, *Journal and Order Book of Kirkwood*, 98.

36. GO, Aug. 22, 1777, in *AWP*, 11:341.

37. Riling, *Baron Von Steuben*, 131.

38. Order of March, June 14, 1777, in *AWP*, 10:34.

39. Nov. 19, 1781, entry in Feltman, *Journal*, 27.

40. GO, Aug. 20, 1781, in *EAOB*, roll 14, no. 140.

41. Greene's Orders, abstract, Nov. 28, 1781, in *NG*, 9:633n.

42. Orders, Aug. 1, 1780, in *Orderly Book of New Jersey Brigade*, 4.

43. Division Orders, Aug. 8, 1777, in Turner, *Journal and Order Book of Kirkwood*, 134–35; Christopher L. Ward, *The Delaware Continentals, 1776–83* (Wilmington: Historical Society of Delaware, 1941), 179–80.

44. Aug. 6, 1780, entry in *FWW*, 19:337; After Orders, Aug. 6, 1780, in *Orderly Book of New Jersey Brigade*, 9.

45. Edmonson, "Desertion," 175.

46. GO, Oct. 1, 1776, and Sept. 15, 1777, in *AWP*, 6:445, 11:231; Sept. 6 and 15, 1777, entries in *Valley Forge Orderly Book*, 36, 52; Oct. 1, 1776, entry in "Elisha Williams' Diary, 1776," *PMHB* 49 (1925): 45.

47. "Journal of Daniel Trabue," in Lille D. Harper, *Colonial Men and Times* (Philadelphia: Innes and Sons, 1916), 92.

48. Edmonson, "Desertion," 365.

49. After Orders, Sept. 20, 1777, in "Orderly Book of Muhlenberg," 470.

50. Sept. 2, 1778, entry in "Orderly Book of Capt. Simion Brown . . . Rhode Island Campaign," *Essex Institute Historical Collections* 58 (1922): 254; Sept. 18, 1778, entry in Rebecca D. Symmes, ed., *A Citizen-Soldier in the American Revolution:*

The Diary of Benjamin Gilbert . . . (Cooperstown: New York State Historical Association, 1980), 37.

51. "A Narrative of Henry Hollowell of Lynn, 1775–1780," in Harold K. Sanderson, ed., *Lynn in the Revolution*, vol. 1 (Boston: W. B. Clarke, 1909), 169.

52. GO, Aug. 9, 1780, in *FWW*, 19:348.

53. Washington to Sullivan, July 25, 1777, and GO, July 25, 1777, in *AWP*, 10:420, 402.

54. Evening Orders, July 28, 1777, in Turner, *Journal and Order Book of Kirkwood*, 126.

55. GO, Aug. 9, 1780, in *FWW*, 19:348.

56. GO, Sept. 17, 1777, in *AWP*, 11:251–52.

57. GO, Aug. 1, 1781, in *FWW*, 22:443–44.

11. Officer of Police

1. Krewasky A. Salter, "Police Call," in J. Brown, *Historical Dictionary of the U.S. Army*, 371.

2. GO, June 7, 1777, in *AWP*, 9:589.

3. Garrison Orders, Corps of Artillery (West Point), Sept. 19, 20, and 23, 1780, in *EAOB*, roll, no. 112; Regimental Orders, July 21, 1780, and Garrison Orders (West Point), Jan. 30, 1781, RWR, M853, roll 6, vol. 40, roll 8, vol. 49.

4. Regimental Orders, Aug. 27, 1780, in Lauber, *Order Books of New York Regiments*, 46.

5. GO, Feb. 18, 1781, in *FWW*, 21:240.

6. H. Rogers, *British Army in the Eighteenth Century*, 51–52.

7. OB, John Lamb's 2d Art. Regiment, Jan. 31, 1780, in *EAOB*, roll 10, no. 100; Garrison Orders (Burlington Barracks), Dec. 12 and 13, 1781, and Regimental Orders, Dec. 24–25, 28, 1781, and Jan. 3 and 8, 1782, in *EAOB*, roll 15, no. 152; Regimental Orders, Sept. 23, 1782, and Garrison Orders (West Point), Oct. 3, 1782, in *EAOB*, roll 16, no. 162, vol. 2.

8. Riling, *Baron Von Steuben*, 84.

9. Gen. Weedon to Gen. Lee, June 6, 1781, in Thomas Balch, ed., *Papers of the Maryland Line During the Revolution* (Philadelphia: Seventy-Six Society, 1857), 149; Jan. 12, Feb. 1 and 13, 1782, entries in Bray and Bushnell, *Diary of Greenman*, 242–45; Lesser, *Sinews of Independence*, 120–21, 140–41, 156–57, 181, 208, 232, 252; Peterson, *Book of the Continental Soldier*, 254–57.

10. GO, Aug. 1, 1779, and Jan. 13, 1780, in *FWW*, 16:34, 17:472; GO, June 28, 1779, and Regimental Orders, Jan. 13, 1780, in *EAOB*, roll 7, no. 84, roll 10, no. 102; Orders, Feb. 12, 1780, and June 27, 1781, RWR, M853, roll 5, vol. 33, roll 8, vol. 53; James D. Scudieri, "The Continentals: A Comparative Study of a Late Eighteenth-Century Standing Army, 1775–1783" (Ph.D. diss., City University of New York, 1993), 141.

11. Congressional Resolution, "Inspector General's Dept.," July 1, 1779, in *Steuben Papers* (NYHS); "Report of the Board of War, Inspector's Dept.," Aug. 23,

1780, in *Steuben Papers* (NYHS); Orders, Valley Forge, June 15, 1778, RWR, M853, roll 4, vol. 24.

12. Brigade Orders, Feb. 3, 5, 6, 8, 21, and Mar. 9, 1780, in Lauber, *Order Books of New York Regiments*, 238, 241, 243, 245, 270, 280; GO, Mar. 12, 1783, in *FWW*, 26:209.

13. Regimental Orders, June 21, 1781, in *EAOB*, roll 13, no. 132; Orders, Aug. 17, 1782, RWR, M853, roll 10, vol. 65.

14. Regimental Orders, Feb. 7, 1781, in Ford, *Correspondence of Webb*, 2:320.

15. GO (McDougall), May 17, 1777, and Brigade Orders, Feb. 1, 1780, in *EAOB*, roll 4, no. 43, roll 10, no. 101; June 11, 1779, entry in "Journal of Capt. Samuel Page in the Campaign of 1779," *Historical Collections of the Essex Institute* 5 (1863): 4.

16. GO, June 2, 1777, in *AWP*, 9:589.

17. Feb. 5, 1781, entry in "The Department of Police in the Camp," *Steuben Papers* (NYHS).

18. Oct. 26, 1780, entry in "Orderly Book of Livermore's Company," 231.

19. Inspector's Orders, May 2, 1778, in "Orderly Book of the Second Pennsylvania Continental Line," *PMHB* 36 (1912): 53; Riling, *Baron Von Steuben*, 84.

20. William Moultrie, *Memoirs of the American Revolution*, vol. 2 (1802; reprint, New York: Arno, 1968), 356.

21. Greene's Orders, Sept. 28, 1782, in *NG*, 11:701.

22. James Tilton, *Economical Observations on Military Hospitals and the Prevention and Cause of Diseases Incident to the Army* (Wilmington, Del.: Wilcox, 1813), pt. 2, 32–33.

23. Richard L. Blanco, *Physician of the American Revolution: Jonathan Potts* (New York: Garland STPM, 1979), 205–6; Mary C. Gillett, *The Army Medical Department, 1775–1818* (Washington, D.C.: Center of Military History, 1981), 3; Lesser, *Sinews of Independence*, 64–65, 240.

24. Dr. James Tilton quoted in James E. Gibson, "The Role of Disease in the 70,000 Casualties in the American Revolutionary Army," *Transactions and Studies of the College of Physicians of Philadelphia* 17 (1949): 127.

25. "To the Officers in the Army of the United American States: Directions for Preserving the Health of Soldiers," in Butterfield, *Letters of Benjamin Rush*, 140–47.

26. Howard N. Simpson, *Invisible Armies: The Impact of Disease on American History* (Indianapolis: Bobbs-Merrill, 1980), 116–17; George C. Dunham, *Military Preventive Medicine* (Carlisle Barracks, Pa.: Medical Field Service School, 1931), 771, 858–61; John Duffy, *Epidemics in Colonial America* (Baton Rouge: Louisiana State University Press, 1958), 229–32; Stanhope Bayne-Jones, *The Evolution of Preventative Medicine in the United States Army, 1607–1939* (Washington, D.C.: Army Office of the Surgeon General, 1968), 11–12; Gillett, *Army Medical Department*, 3; Blanco, *Physician of the American Revolution*, 46–47, 76.

27. British surgeon Donald Monro, *An Account of the Diseases . . . British Military Hospitals* (1764), quoted in Gillett, *American Medical Department*, 4–5.

28. Mar. 13, 1778, entry in *Valley Forge Orderly Book*, 254.

29. GO, Aug. 7, 1781, in *FWW*, 22:471.

30. GO, July 29, 1778, and July 5, 1781, in *FWW*, 12:246, 22:329; Brigade Orders (Artillery), July 29, 1778, in *EAOB*, roll 5, no. 62; Apr. 14, 1778, entry in *Valley Forge Orderly Book*, 288.

31. Brigade Orders, Jan. 28, 1782, in *EAOB*, roll 15, no. 157.

32. GO, Sept. 2, 1782, in *FWW*, 25:105.

33. OB, 2d New York Continental Regiment, Feb. 8, 1780, in *EAOB*, roll 10, no. 101.

34. July 28, 1776, entry in *Orderly Books of Henshaw*, 107; GO, Aug. 12, 1777, in *AWP*, 10:590; GO, Apr. 11, 1779, in *FWW*, 14:367.

35. GO, Aug. 1, 1775, in *AWP*, 1:206.

36. GO, Aug. 1, 1775, and Oct. 24, 1776, in *AWP*, 1:206, 7:24; GO, OB of Sir William Howe, Nov. 7, 1776, in *EAOB*, roll 14, no. 40; July 24, 1777, entry in Turner, *Journal and Order Book of Kirkwood*, 122; Regimental Orders, June 30, 1778, in "Orderly Book of Adjutant Silvanus Reed," *Collections of the New Hampshire Historical Society* 9 (1889): 387–88; *NG*, 1:108n; Bland, *Treatise of Military Discipline*, 248; *Oxford English Dictionary*, 2:810; Lesser, *Sinews of Independence*, 135.

37. GO, June 2, 1777, in *BL*; OB of Marinus Willet, Aug. 11, 1777, and GO (Fort Schuyler), Mar. 13, 1778, in *EAOB*, roll 4, no. 42; OB of Heth, May 22, 1777, VHS; Orders, Oct. 10, 1781, in *EAOB*, roll 25, no. 149; Brigade Orders, Aug. 13, 1777, in Turner, *Journal and Order Book of Kirkwood*, 142; Brigade Orders, Sept. 2 and 28, 1776, in "Elisha Williams' Diary" (1924), 326, 350.

38. Benjamin Quarles, *The Negro in the American Revolution* (Chapel Hill: University of North Carolina Press, 1961), 102–5; Joseph T. Wilson, *The Black Phalanx: A History of Negro Soldiers of the United States* (1890; reprint, New York: Arno, 1968), 41–42, 67–68; Mattern, *Benjamin Lincoln*, 91–92, 96–97; Mark M. Boatner III, "The Negro in the American Revolution," *American History Illustrated* 4 (Aug. 1969): 39.

39. Garrison Orders (West Point), Jan. 15, 1781, RWR, M853, roll 8, vol. 49; Light Infantry Orders, Oct. 15, 1782, in "Revolutionary Army Orders for the Main Army under Washington," *Virginia Magazine of History and Biography* 19 (1911): 278; Regimental Orders, July 20, 1782 (Burlington Barracks), in *EAOB*, roll 16, no. 158.

40. Mar. 19, 1782, entry in Bray and Bushnell, *Diary of Greenman*, 245.

41. Neagles, *Summer Soldiers*, 265, 273.

42. GO, June 22, 1777, in *AWP*, 5:589.

43. Regimental Orders, Apr. 15, 1778, in "Revolutionary Army Orders for the Main Army under Washington," *Virginia Magazine of History and Biography* 15 (1908): 423.

44. Orders, Aug. 17, 1780, RWR, M853, roll 6, vol. 42; GO, Apr. 14, 1778, in *FWW*, 11:260–61; July 28, 1776, entry in *Orderly Books of Henshaw*, 197.

45. Jan. 1776 entry in "Diaries of Jonathan Burton," 678.

46. GO, Apr. 14 and Aug. 26, 1778, in *FWW*, 12:359, 14:367; Apr. 14, 1778, entry in "Orderly Book of 2d Pennsylvania Line," 493; Greene's Orders, July 14, 1782, in *NG*, 11:443.

47. Brigade Orders, Sept. 6, 1777, in *Valley Forge Orderly Book*, 38.

48. Regimental Orders, Feb. 17, 1780, RWR, M853, roll 5, vol. 34.

49. Regimental Orders, June 24, 1781, RWR, M853, roll 8, vol. 51.

50. Quoted in Blanco, *Physician of the American Revolution*, 179; Mayer, *Belonging to the Army*, 261.

51. Feb. 12, 1779, entry in "Orderly Book of the Seventh Pennsylvania Regiment," *Pennsylvania Archives*, 2d ser., vol. 11 (1896), 423.

52. Division Orders, May 22, 1777, OB of 11th Virginia. Regiment, in *EAOB*, roll 4, no. 45; GO, Oct. 27, 1781, RWR, M853, roll 8, vol. 53; GO, Jan. 7, Mar. 13, and July 3, 1778, Feb. 20, 1780, and Oct. 29, 1781, in *FWW*, 10:273, 11:74–75, 12:154, 18:34, 23:287.

53. OB, Brigade of Artillery, July 29, 1778, in *EAOB*, roll 5, no. 62.

54. Orders, Apr. 14, 1778, RWR, M853, roll 3, vol. 16; Apr. 14, 1778, entry in *Valley Forge Orderly Book*, 289; GO, Apr. 21, 1777, in *AWP*, 9:224; GO, July 3, 1778, and Oct. 5, 1781, in *FWW*, 12:154, 23:177.

55. Aug. 16, 1779, entry in Lauber, *Order Books of New York Regiments*, 139.

56. Orders, Aug. 7, 1780, in *EAOB*, roll 14, no. 140; GO, Sept. 6, 1777, in *AWP*, 11:158; Riling, *Baron Von Steuben*, 86; J. Wright, "Some Notes on the Continental Army" (1932), 9.

57. OB of Heth, May 27, 1778, VHS; Orders, July 29, 1778, in *BL*; Orders, Mar. 13, 1778, RWR, M853, roll 3, vol. 21; GO, May 4, 1776, in *AWP*, 4:198; Division Orders, in Turner, *Journal and Order Book of Kirkwood*, 122; Regimental Orders, July 29 and Oct. 5, 1778, "Orderly Book of the First Pennsylvania Regiment," 303–4, 373; "Diaries of Jonathan Burton," 678; Regimental Orders, Mar. 18, 1782, in *EAOB*, roll 10, no. 102.

58. GO, Sept. 13, 1777, in *AWP*, 11:212; Riling, *Baron Von Steuben*, 77–78; C. Keith Wilbur, *Picture Book of the Continental Soldier* (Harrisburg, Pa.: Stackpole Books, 1969), 68.

59. Riling, *Baron Von Steuben*, 83.

60. Regimental Orders, Aug. 24, 1781, in *EAOB*, roll 14, no. 143.

61. Regimental Orders, June 2, 1781, in *EAOB*, roll 14, no. 138.

62. GO, Jan. 29, 1778, in *FWW*, 10:403–4; Riling, *Baron Von Steuben*, 83.

63. Quoted in Louis Gottschalk, *Lafayette Joins the American Army* (Chicago: University of Chicago Press, 1937), 104.

64. GO, Dec. 18, 1777, *FWW*, 10:171; Thacher, *Military Journal*, 153; Bodle and Thibaut, *Valley Forge Research Report*, 3:35; Trussell, *Birthplace of an Army*, 20–21.

65. Regimental Orders, Mar. 8 and 22, in *EAOB*, roll 10, no. 101, roll 41, no. 106; Orders, May 27, 1778, and Sept. 8, 1782, RWR, M853, roll 4, vol. 24, roll 10, vol. 64; GO, Jan. 29, 1778, and Feb. 10, 1783, in *FWW*, 10:40, 26:111; Trussell, *Birthplace of an Army*, 24–25.

66. Dec. 22, 1777, entry in "Diary of Surgeon Albigence Waldo," *PMHB* 21 (1897): 309.

67. Regimental Orders, June 1, 1777, and Garrison Orders (West Point), Dec.

21, 1780, RWR, M853, roll 3, vol. 17, roll 7, vol. 47; Orders (Fort Schuyler), Mar, 24, 1782, in *EAOB*, roll 4, no. 42.

68. Garrison Orders, May 5, 1781, M853, roll 8, vol. 51.

69. Brigade Orders, Dec. 17, 1780, RWR, M853, roll 7, vol. 47.

70. Sept. 21, 1780, entry in Lauber, *Order Books of New York Regiments*, 505; GO, Sept. 21, 1780, *Orderly Book of New Jersey Brigade*, 53; Brigade Orders, Oct. 10, 1780, "Orderly Book of Livermore's Company," 210; June 11, 1779, entry in "Journal of Samuel Page" (1863), 4; Apr. 29, 1778, entry in "The Military Journal of Colonel Icabod Godwin," *Collections and Proceedings of the Maine Historical Society*, 2d ser., 5 (1894): 40; GO, July 14, 1776, in *AWP*, 1:114.

71. Oie W. Stephenson, "The Supplies of the American Revolutionary Army" (Ph.D. diss. University of Michigan, 1919), 204–5.

72. GO, June 9, 1777, in *AWP*, 9:652.

73. Regimental Orders, Oct. 5, 1778, in "Orderly Book of the First Pennsylvania Regiment," 378; Riling, *Baron Von Steuben*, 79; Aug. 29, 1780, entry in Lauber, *Order Books of New York Regiments*, 469; Risch, *Supplying Washington's Army*, 193–94; Mayer, *Belonging to the Army*, 63; Peterson, *Book of the Continental Soldier*, 147, 149.

74. Brigade Orders, July 7, 1780, RWR, M853, roll 6, vol. 40; Orders, Sept. 21, 1780, in *EAOB*, roll 13, no. 125; Brigade Orders, Sept. 6, 1777, in Saffell, *Records of the Revolutionary War*, 339; GO, Aug. 23, 1780, in *FWW*, 19:430.

75. Brigade Orders, Oct. 24, 1778, *Pennsylvania Archives*, 2d ser., vol. 11 (1896), 392.

76. Quoted from the diary of Elijah Fisher, in Risch, *Supplying Washington's Army*, 194; Ray Thompson, *Washington at Whitemarsh: Prelude to Valley Forge*, 2d ed. (Fort Washington, Pa.: Bicentennial, 1974), 88.

77. GO (McDougall), June 10, 1779, in *EAOB*, roll 7, no. 87.

78. Inspector's Orders, May 2, 1778, in "Orderly Book of the Second Pennsylvania," 53; June 15, 1779, entry in "Journal of Samuel Page" (1863), 6; Riling, *Baron Von Steuben*, 85.

79. Inspector's Orders, May 2, 1778, in "Orderly Book of the Second Pennsylvania," 53; Washington to Richard Peters, Sept. 16, 1777, in *AWP*, 11:184–85; Memorial of Board of General Officers, Aug. 7, 1777, in *NG*, 2:133; Aug. 11, Sept. 4 and 11, 1777, entries in *JCC*, 8:629, 710–11, 732–33.

80. GO, Oct. 10 and 22, 1777, in *AWP*, 11:471, 572.

81. GO, May 16, 1782, RWR, M853, roll 9, vol. 20.

82. OB of Gates, Mar. 1, 1783, in *GP* (NYPL).

83. Orders, July 7, 1781, in *EAOB*, roll 14, no. 140.

84. Garrison Orders (West Point), June 28, 1780, and Orders, Aug. 31, 1781, in *EAOB*, roll 12, no. 118, roll 14, no. 140; Garrison Orders, Feb. 8, 1781, RWR, M853, roll 8, vol. 49.

85. Garrison Orders (West Point), Feb 22, 1781, and Oct. 3, 1782, RWR, M853, roll 8, vol. 50, roll 10, vol. 64; Orders, Sept. 16, 1781, in *EAOB*, roll 14, no. 140.

86. GO, Oct. 24, 1782, quoted in *Pennsylvania Gazette and Weekly Advertiser*, Nov. 6, 1782.

12. Provost Marshal

1. For definitions in historical perspective, see Dupuy et al., *Dictionary of Military Terms*, 177; John R. Elting, Dan Cragg, and Ernest L. Deal, *A Dictionary of Soldier Talk* (New York: Charles Scribner's Sons, 1984), 242; John P. Wissler and H. C. Gauss, *Military and Naval Dictionary* (New York: L. R. Hamersly, 1905), 124; and *Oxford English Dictionary*, 12:723–24.

2. Bland, *Treatise of Military Discipline*, 207; Lovell-Knight, *History of Provost Marshal and Military Police*, 19–20; Pratt, *Military Law*, 17; *History of the Corps of Military Police* (Fort Gordon, Ga.: Military Police School, 1948), 1; Francis Grose, *Military Antiquities Respecting a History of the English Army*, 2 vols. (London: S. Hooper, 1786–88), 1:249–54; S. F. Crozier, *The History of the Corps of Royal Military Police* (Aldershot, Eng.: Gale and Polden, 1951), 3–9.

3. John A. Lynn, *Giant of the Grand Siècle: The French Army, 1610–1715* (Cambridge, Eng.: Cambridge University Press, 1997), 402.

4. Timothy Pickering to Steuben, with questions on Prussian staff departments and Steuben's response, Feb. 5, 1780, in *Steuben Papers* (NYHS).

5. Washington to the President of Congress, July 21, 1775, PCC, r166, i152, 1:37; July 29, 1775, entry in *JCC*, 2:221; GO, Jan. 19, 1776, in *AWP*, 3:144–45; see also 3:59n.

6. GO, Mar. 3, 1780, in *FWW*, 18:70.

7. GO, July 16, 1780, in *FWW*, 19:189.

8. GO, July 18, 1781, in *FWW*, 22:394.

9. Washington to William Marony, Jan. 10, 1776, WP (omitted in *AWP*); GO, Jan. 10, 1776, in *AWP*, 3:59.

10. GO, June 27, 1776, in *AWP*, 5:112; Washington to Provost Marshal of the Army, June 28, 1776, WP; William Marony to Washington, June 28, 1776, in Godfrey, *Commander-in-Chief's Guard*, 32–33.

11. GO, Mar. 22, 1776, in *AWP*, 3:511; Freeman, *George Washington*, 4:208.

12. Maj. Gen. Heath to Washington, Sept. 29, 1776, GO, Oct. 1, 1776, and Heath to Washington, Oct. 3, 1776, in *AWP*, 6:429, 429n, 444, 459, 460n; see also 6:446n and 527n.

13. GO, Oct. 1, 1776, in *AWP*, 644–45; Virgil D. White, transcriber, *Index to Revolutionary War Service Records*, vol. 1 (Waynesboro, Tenn.: National Historical Publishing, 1995), 344.

14. GO, Jan. 14, 1777, in *AWP*, 8:63.

15. GO, Feb. 15, 1777, in *AWP*, 8:341; Virgil D. White, abstractor, *Genealogical Abstracts of Revolutionary War Pension Files*, vol. 3 (Waynesboro, Tenn.: National Historical Publishing, 1991–92), 3237.

16. GO, Jan. 23, 1778, in *AWP*, 13:319; Jan. 23, 1778, entry in *Valley Forge Orderly Book*, 205.

17. Apr. 20 and 22, 1784, entries in *JCC*, 26:253, 271–72; *FWW*, 18:70n; Dorothy M. Muir, *General Washington's Headquarters* (Troy, Ala.: Troy State University Press, 1977), 71.

18. GO, Mar. 9 and May 30, 1780, in *FWW*, 18:96, 451.

19. GO, Jan. 6, 1780, Apr. 20 and 22, 1781, in *FWW*, 17:359, 21:482, 497.

20. GO, July 18, 1780, in *FWW*, 19:209.

21. After Orders, Apr. 20, 1781, Washington to Heath, Apr. 20, 1781, and GO, Apr. 22, 1781, in *FWW*, 21:482, 482n, 483, 485, 497; Neagles, *Summer Soldiers*, 55, 168.

22. GO, July 19, 1781, in *FWW*, 22:397.

23. Orders, Apr. 24, 1782, in *EAOB*, roll 16, no. 152.

24. Extracts from GO of Edward Hand, Adjutant General, Jan. 19, 1782, in *EAOB*, roll 16, no. 156.

25. GO, Nov. 14, 1782, in *FWW*, 25:344.

26. GO, Aug. 22, 1780, RWR, M853, roll 7, vol. 43; Jan. 2, 1782, entry in *EAOB*, roll 15, no. 157; GO, Instructions to William Marony, Jan. 12, 1776, and GO, Feb. 14, May 31, 1776, Jan. 28, and June 1, 1777, in *AWP*, 3:305–6, 4:407–8, 8:168, 9:578; GO, Oct. 20, 1780, in *FWW*, 20:222; Brigade Orders, May 31, June 1, 1776, in *Orderly Book of Henshaw*, 144; R. Wright, *Continental Army*, 39.

27. GO, July 17, 1781, in *EAOB*, roll 14, no. 140.

28. GO, Aug. 22, 1780, RWR, M853, roll 7, vol. 42.

29. GO, Feb. 19, 1778, RWR, M853, roll 3, vol. 20; GO, June 3, 1781, WP; Garrison Orders (West Point), June 3, 1781, in *EAOB*, roll 14, no. 144; GO, Apr. 22, 1776, and Oct. 6, 1777, in *AWP*, 4:103, 11:404.

30. See, for example, GO, Sept. 11, 1776, in *AWP*, 6:277.

31. Maurer Maurer, "Military Justice under General Washington," in *Military Analysis of the Revolutionary War: An Anthology by the Editors of Military Affairs* (Millwood, N.Y.: KTO, 1977), 58.

32. GO, Aug. 22, 1780, in *FWW*, 19:424; *Orderly Book of New Jersey Brigade*, 25; Berlin, "Administration of Military Justice," 127.

33. GO, June 9, 1778, in *FWW*, 12:39–40.

34. GO, Apr. 4, 1778, in *FWW*, 11:220.

35. Orders, June 23, 1776, and Oct. 31, 1781, RWR, M853, roll 8, vol. 53.

36. GO, Jan. 19, 1776, in *AWP*, 3:144.

37. GO, July 30, 1780, in *FWW*, 19:278.

38. Report of the Prisoners in the Court House at White Plains, Oct. 27, 1776, RWR, M246, #135.

39. *FWW*, 21:461n; Gardner, "Last Cantonment of the Main Army," 357.

40. Orders, Jan. 10, 1778, RWR, M853, roll 3, vol. 20; Jan. 15 and Mar. 3, 1778, entries in *Valley Forge Orderly Book*, 193, 248.

41. GO, Apr. 25, 1777, in *AWP*, 9:264; GO, Mar. 12, 1783, in *FWW*, 26:210; Dec. 4, 1782, entry in Lauber, *Order Books of New York Regiments*, 711.

42. Nov. 7, 1781, entry in Feltman, *Journal*, 4.

43. GO, Aug. 31, 1776, in *AWP*, 4:406; May 29, 1776, entry in *Orderly Books of Henshaw*, 141; Apr. 16, 1776, entry in "Orderly Book of Capt. Enoch Putnam," *Essex Institute Historical Collections* 67 (1931): 372; Applegate, "Constitutions like Iron," 144.

44. James Moody, *Lieut. James Moody's Narrative of the Exertions and Sufferings in the Cause of Government since the Year 1776* (1783; reprint, New York: Arno, 1968), 28–29.

45. Orders, Jan. 3 and Apr. 4, 1778, RWR, M853, roll 3, vols. 20 and 18; Orders, Dec. 30, 1777, in *EAOB*, roll 5, no. 48; Dec. 30, 1777, and Jan. 3, 1778, entries in *Valley Forge Orderly Book*, 173, 177–78; Bodle and Thibaut, *Valley Forge Research Report*, 3:42–43.

46. May 20, 1776, entry in *Orderly Books of Henshaw*, 134.

47. GO, Jan. 16, 1777, in *AWP*, 8:78.

48. Maj. Gen. Israel Putnam to Washington, July 22, 1777, in *AWP*, 10:362; OB (McDougall), July 22, 1777, in *EAOB*, roll 4, no. 43.

49. Orders, Oct. 20, 1781, in *EAOB*, roll 15, no. 149.

50. OB, July 11, 1779, *Pennsylvania Archives*, 2d ser., vol. 11 (1896), 487; Apr. 17, 1778, entry in "Journal of Capt. William Beatty, 1776–1781," *Maryland Historical Magazine* 3 (1908): 115; GO, July 30, 1780, in *FWW*, 19:278; R. Wright, *Continental Army*, 39.

51. OB, Sept. 19, 1778, *Pennsylvania Archives*, 2d ser., vol. 11 (1896), 367.

52. Return of the Provost Marshal, S/William Marony, June 3, 1776, and Report of the Prisoners in the Court House at White Plains, Oct. 27, 1776, RWR, M246, #135.

53. GO, Aug. 9, 1777, in *AWP*, 10:561; Washington to Charles Scott, Oct. 18 and 25, 1778, in *FWW*, 13:103, 103n, 153–54, 154n.

54. GO, Jan. 24, 1777, in *AWP*, 10:80.

55. Orders, June 10, 1778, RWR, M853, roll 4, vol. 24. In early May 1778, the provost guardhouse at Valley Forge had thirty prisoners; May 5, 1778, entry in George Ewing, *The Military Journal of George Ewing* (Yonkers, N.Y.: Thomas Ewing, 1928), 53.

56. OB of First Virginia Regiment, Mar. 5, 1778, VHS; Orders, Mar. 5, 1778, RWR, M853, roll 3, vol. 21; Mar. 5, 1778, entry in *Valley Forge Orderly Book*, 249.

57. Orders, Sept. 25, 1781, RWR, M853, roll 8, vol. 52; GO, Aug. 1, 1781, in *FWW*, 22:444.

58. GO, Feb. 8, 1778, in *AWP*, 13:474; Neagles, *Summer Soldiers*, 237.

59. GO, Feb. 8, 1777, in *AWP*, 13:474; Neagles, *Summer Soldiers*, 96.

60. GO, Feb. 8, 1777, in *AWP*, 13:475; Neagles, *Summer Soldiers*, 128.

61. Adj. Gen. Timothy Pickering to William Livingston, June 11, 1777, in *AWP*, 10:249n.

62. Remarks for the Information of Maj. Gen. Gates, May 20, 1778, McDougall Papers, NYHS; Nov. 21, 1780, entry in Rice, *Travels in North America*, 1:88.

63. GO, Jan. 21, 1778, in *AWP*, 13:303; Neagles, *Summer Soldiers*, 90.

64. Washington to Maj. Gen. William Heath, Sept. 3, 1779, in *FWW*, 16:220.

65. Brigade Orders, Jan. 21, 1781, RWR, M853, roll 8, vol. 49.

66. GO, Aug. 16, 1780, in *EAOB*, roll 12, no. 123; Washington to Maj. Gen. Benedict Arnold, Aug. 13, 1780, in *FWW*, 19:370–71.

67. Moody, *Lieut. Moody's Narrative*, 29–34; Susan B. Shenstone, *So Obstinately Loyal: James Moody, 1744–1809* (Montreal: McGill-Queen's University Press, 2000), 87–89; Leiby, *Revolutionary War in the Hackensack Valley*, 279–80.

68. May 7, 1778, entry in "Orderly Book of the Second Pennsylvania," 278; Orders, May 7, 1778, RWR, M853, roll 4, vol. 24.

69. After Orders, Oct. 31, 1781, RWR, M853, roll 9, vol. 56.

70. Orders, Feb. 6, 1783, RWR, M853, roll 11, vol. 70.

13. The Maréchaussée Corps

1. *Harrap's Standard French and English Dictionary* (New York: Charles Scribner's Sons, 1970), 520, 611; William W. Kibber and Grover A. Zinn, eds., *Medieval France: An Encyclopedia* (New York: Garland, 1995), 593–94; Lynn, *Giant of the Grand Siäcle*, 402–3; Kennett, *French Armies in the Seven Years' War*, 84–85; "U.S. Provost History," <http://www.usprovost1778.org/history.htm>, Feb. 4, 2001.

2. Henry Emanuel Lutterloh to Adj. Gen. Timothy Pickering, Nov. 15, 1777, and Capt. Bartholomew Von Heer to Washington, Nov. 17, 1777, in *AWP*, 12:289–91, 291n.

3. GO, July 1, 1777, in *AWP*, 10:162; see also 9:535n, 12:291n, and 292n; *NG*, 2:308n, 313n.

4. Joseph Reed to the President of Congress, Sept. 20, 1776, and Petition of Von Heer to Congress, May 20, 1784, PCC, 1101, 178, 19:55, 156, 142, 8:59; Von Heer to Congress, Mar. 18, 1780, and Washington to Von Heer (Certificate of Service), Nov. 4, 1783, WP; Von Heer to Washington, Nov. 17, 1777, in *AWP*, 12:289–91, 291n; Mar. 19, 1777, entry in *JCC*, 7:186; Trussell, *Pennsylvania Line*, 197; Heitman, *Historical Register*, 422, 561; Albert B. Faust, *The German Element in the United States*, vol. 1 (Boston: Houghton Mifflin, 1909), 298.

5. Committee of Camp to Henry Laurens, Feb. 5, 1778, and Laurens to Washington, May 20, 1778, in *LD*, 9:29, 724–25; Washington to the Committee of Camp, Jan. 29, 1778, and Washington to Greene, June 6, 1778, in *FWW*, 10:374–76, 12:26. The table is found in *JCC* 11:541, May 27, 1778.

6. *AWP*, 12:291n.

7. Instructions on Duty of the Captain of the Maréchausseé, Oct. 1, 1778, in *Steuben Papers* (Gratz Collection, Historical Society of Pennsylvania, Philadelphia).

8. GO, and Instructions to Capt. Bartholomew Von Heer, Oct. 11, 1778, in *FWW*, 13:61–63, 68–70.

9. Roll and Muster of Capt. Von Heer's Independent Company of Light Dragoons for the Month of April 1782, Apr. 14, 1782, and Return of Troops of Light Horse Commanded by Capt. Bartholomew Von Heer, Apr. 16, 1783, RWR, M246, #116; Von Heer to Washington, Sept. 24, 1778, WP; Roll of Captain Von Heer's Dragoons, *Pennsylvania Archives*, 2d ser., vol. 11 (1896), 172–76; Nolan J. Bennett, *George Washington and the Town of Reading in Pennsylvania* (Reading: Chamber of Commerce, 1931), 142–43; "General Washington's Mounted Bodyguards Commanded by Von Heer," in Neal S. Smith, *Some German-American Participants in*

the American Revolution: The Ratterman Lists (McNeal, Ariz.: Westland, 1990), 5–7; Aaron S. Fogleman, *Hopeful Journeys: German Immigration, Settlement and Political Culture in Colonial America, 1717–1775* (Philadelphia: University of Pennsylvania Press, 1996), 80; Trussell, *Pennsylvania Line*, 230; Neimeyer, *America Goes to War*, 51. Officers who served at one time or another in the Maréchaussée included Bartholomew Von Heer, captain; Jacob Mytinger, first lieutenant; Philip Strubing, second lieutenant; Mathias Schneider, third lieutenant; Baron John Wolfen, first lieutenant; James Rutter (Nutter), second lieutenant; Bagge Christian, captain lieutenant; and John Stake, cornet.

10. E. James Ferguson et al., eds., *The Papers of Robert Morris*, 9 vols. (Pittsburgh: University of Pittsburgh Press, 1973–99), 5:91n; Washington to the President of Congress, Aug. 9, 1778, in *FWW*, 12:304–5.

11. At a Board of War, July 28, 1778, and A Return of the Maréchaussée Enlisted in Capt. Barth. Von Heer's Troop of Light Dragoons, July 29, 1778, PCC, r157, i147, 2:149, and r56, i42, 8:63; July 29, 1778, entry in *JCC*, 11:729; Edmund C. Burnett, ed., *Letters of Members of the Continental Congress*, vol. 6 (Washington, D.C.: Carnegie Institution, 1933), 129n.

12. Washington to Greene, June 6, 1778, in *FWW*, 12:26–27.

13. A Report of a Troop of Maréchaussée Light Dragoons Commanded by Bartholomew Von Heer, Sept. 18, 1778, WP.

14. Lesser, *Sinews of Independence*, 89, 102, 110, 129, 138, 169, 173, 181, 185, 232, 234, 240, 242, 244, 250; Monthly Report of a Troop of Light Dragoons Commanded by Capt. Von Heer, May 22, 1780, WP; Returns, Aug. 1780, and June 29, 1783, RWR, M246, #116.

15. Von Heer to Washington, May 7, 1779, Richard Peters to Washington, May 23, 1779, and R. K. Meade to Von Heer, June 1, 1779, WP; Richard Peters to James Duane, Dec. 9, 1780, in *Steuben Papers* (PCC); Dec. 21, 1780, entry in *JCC*, 18:1179–87.

16. "Military Dress, Company of Light Dragoons, 1778–1783," *Military Collector and Historian* 11 (1959): 80; Elting, *Military Uniforms*, 96; Peterson, *Book of the Continental Soldier*, 237–38.

17. Excerpt of letter of Samuel Miles to Von Heer, Mar. 26, 1781, in Nolan, *George Washington and Reading*, 100.

18. Washington to the Board of War, Dec. 19, 1780, in *FWW*, 20:499.

19. Washington to Von Heer, May 17, 1779, in *FWW*, 15:92–93.

20. Washington to the Board of War, Apr. 13, 1779, and Washington to Von Heer, June 1, 1781, in *FWW*, 14:373, 22:150; Impress Warrant for Teams, Apr. 10, 1781, WP.

21. Washington to Von Heer, June 1, 1781, in *FWW*, 22:149.

22. Washington to the Superintendent of Finance, Feb. 22, 1782, in *FWW*, 24:24–25.

23. Von Heer to the Board of War, May 15, 1781, WP; Von Heer to Congress, July 27, 1781, PCC, r104, i78, 23:185; Receipts of Members of the Maréchaussée, 1778–1782, RWR, M859, 59:18509–612.

24. Washington to President William Moore, Feb. 8, 1782, in *FWW*, 23:491–92; Robert Morris to President Moore, Mar. 1, 1782, in *Pennsylvania Archives*, 1st ser., vol. 9 (Philadelphia: Joseph Severns and Co., 1854), 505; "Diary," Feb. 7, 14, 25, and 27, 1782, Robert Morris to President Moore, Mar. 2, 1782, Morris to ———, Mar. 5, 1782, and Expenditures of the Paymaster General, Jan. 1–Mar. 31 and Oct. 1–Dec. 31, 1782, in Ferguson, *Papers of Morris*, 4:178–79, 179n, 234, 300, 315, 333, 348, 9:733, 788.

25. Washington to Von Heer, July 27, 1778, in *FWW*, 12:241.

26. Von Heer to Washington, Apr. 15, 1780, WP.

27. GO, Mar. 29 and Apr. 1, 1779, in *FWW*, 14:310, 324.

28. GO, Nov. 11, 1778, in *FWW*, 13:247.

29. GO, Feb. 11, 1779, in *FWW*, 14:100.

30. GO, Oct. 1, 1779, in *FWW*, 16:385.

31. GO, June 5, 1782, in *FWW*, 24:311.

32. Washington to William Livingston, Mar. 3, 1779, in *FWW*, 14:185; Livingston to Washington, Feb. 18, 1779, in Prince et al., *Papers of William Livingston*, 1:37; see also 1:42n.

33. Washington to Von Heer, Feb. 16, 1779, R. K. Meade to Von Heer, June 2, 1779, and Von Heer to Congress, Mar. 18, 1780, WP; Von Heer to Greene, Jan. 24, 1779, and Greene to Thomas Durie, Aug. 25, 1779, in *NG*, 3:179, 4:338; Washington to Brig. Gen. William Maxwell, Apr. 1, 1779, Washington to Maj. Gen. Arthur St. Clair, June 2, 1779, Washington to Von Heer, Aug. 23, 1779, and GO, After Orders, Aug. 22, 1780, in *FWW*, 14:319, 15:213, 16:159, 19:420; see also 15:215n; and Angelakos, "Army at Middlebrook," 113–14.

34. Von Heer to Steuben, Dec. 31, 1779, in *Steuben Papers* (NYHS).

35. Von Heer to Washington, Apr. 15, 1780, WP.

36. Washington to Col. Charles Armand-Tuffin, Feb. 6, 1780, and Washington to the Board of War, Feb. 18, 1780, in *FWW*, 17:497, 18:25; Berg, *Encyclopedia of Continental Army Units*, 10.

37. Washington to the President of Congress, Nov. 26, 1780, in *FWW*, 20:400; R. Wright, *Continental Army*, 157, 161.

38. Samuel Huntington to Greene, Dec. 6, 1780, in *LD*, 16:420, 420n; Dec. 4, 1780, entry in *JCC*, 18:1118.

39. Washington to Von Heer, Mar. 30, 1780, WP; Washington to the Board of War, Mar. 30, 1780, in *FWW*, 18:179.

40. Von Heer to Washington, Apr. 21, 1780, WP; Nolan, *George Washington and Reading*, 98.

41. Washington to Von Heer, May 11, 1780, and GO, May 28, 1780, in *FWW*, 18:344, 433.

42. Washington to Maj. Gen. Robert Howe, June 20, 1780, in *FWW*, 19:41.

43. Fleming, *Forgotten Victory*, 168–70; Freeman, *George Washington*, 5:172.

44. Tench Tilghman to Von Heer, Sept. 2, 1780, and Von Heer to Washington, Dec. 16, 1780, WP; After GO and Order of March, Oct. 6, 1780, and Brigade

Orders, Oct. 8, 1780, in *EAOB*, roll 13, nos. 126, 129; Washington to Col. Stephen Moylan, Nov. 21, 1780, and Washington to Lafayette, Nov. 23, 1780, in *FWW*, 20:382, 392.

45. GO, Oct. 15 and Nov. 10, 1780, in *FWW*, 20:187, 333; R. Wright, *Continental Army*, 348, 350.

46. Von Heer to Congress, May 20, 1784, PCC, r56, i42, 8:59.

47. Von Heer to the Board of War, May 16, 1781, PCC, r160, i147, 5:343; Von Heer to the Board of War, May 15, 1781, and Richard Peters to Von Heer, May 16, 1781, WP.

48. Washington to the Board of War, June 28 and July 9, 1781, in *FWW*, 22:281, 343.

49. Washington to the Board of War, July 9, 1781, in *FWW*, 22:343; Burnett, *Letters of Members*, 129n.

50. Washington to Von Heer, June 1, 1781, in *FWW*, 22:149–50.

51. Washington to Joseph Jones, July 10, 1781, and to Von Heer, July 13, 1781, in *FWW*, 22:352–53, 372.

52. Washington to Lt. Mytinger, Sept. 7, 1781, WP.

53. A Return of Men, Horses, Arms, Tents, and Several Other Articles Wanting to Complete a Troop of Marichosee Light Dragoons, Sept. 21, 1781, WP.

54. Von Heer to Washington, May 28, 1782, Washington to Von Heer, July 22 and Sept. 25, 1782, and D. Humphreys to Von Heer, Oct. 25, 1782, WP; Orders, Oct. 25, 1782, RWR, M853, roll 11, vol. 67; Washington to Von Heer, Mar. 14, 1782, and GO, Sept. 4, 1782, in *FWW*, 24:67, 25:120; see also 25:92n; and Lesser, *Sinews of Independence*, 222.

55. Berg, *Encyclopedia of Continental Army Units*, 133.

56. Benjamin Lincoln to Gov. John Rutledge, July 24, 1779, in *BL*; Mattern, *Benjamin Lincoln*, 92–93.

57. Greene to Col. William Hampton (abstract), July 29, 1781, Greene's Orders (abstract), Aug. 23 and 27, 1781, and Greene to James McCormack (abstract), Nov. 8, 1781, in *NG*, 9:100, 226, 226n, 260, 548; see also xvii.

58. Capt. Nathanael Pendleton to Col. Morton Wilkinson, Feb. 25, 1782 (abstract), in *NG*, 10:409, 459n.

59. May 26 and Oct. 18, 1783, entries in *JCC*, 24:364, 25:703.

60. Feb. 14, 1785, entry in *JCC*, 28:64; *FWW*, 27:231n; *Major Bartholomew von Heer, Patron of Unit Number 986, Steuben Society of America* (n.p., n.d.), 15–16; Heitman, *Historical Register*, 561.

61. Petition of Von Heer, Jan. 12, 1785, and Expenditure for the Payment of Old Accounts from Apr. 21 to June 20, 1785, PCC, r56, i42, 8:55–56, r154, i141, 2:271; June 18, 1781, Jan. 22, June 1, 1784, and Oct. 14, 1785, entries in *JCC*, 20:660, 26:43, 27:509, 28:65; List of Loan Office Certificates . . . Officers and Soldiers of Capt. Bartholomew Von Heer's Troop of Light Horse, RWR, M246, #116.

62. *Major Bartholomew Von Heer*, 18–19; Nolan, *George Washington and Reading*, 100.

63. Discharge of Lew Boyer, Dec. 10, 1783, in Richter, "General Washington's Body Guards," 23–24; Endorsement to Certificate, Dec. 24, 1783, in *AWP*, Confederation Series, 1:250n; Washington to the Superintendent of Finance, Oct. 3, 1783, in *FWW*, 27:177–78.

64. Freeman, *George Washington*, 6:469–72; Berg, *Encyclopedia of Continental Army Units*, 133.

14. Corporal Punishment

1. Quoted in H. de Watteville, *The British Solder: His Daily Life from Tudor to Modern Times* (London: J. M. Dent & Sons, 1954), 121.

2. Graeme Newman, *Just and Painful: A Case for the Corporal Punishment of Criminals* (London: Macmillan, 1983), 7.

3. OB of Maj. Gen. Robert Howe, Apr. 9, 1780, in *EAOB*, roll 10, no. 104.

4. GO, Jan. 1, 1776, in *AWP*, 3:1.

5. Washington to Col. William Woodford, Nov. 10, 1775, in *AWP*, 2:346.

6. Luther West, *They Call It Justice: Command Influence and the Court-Martial System* (New York: Viking, 1979), 22.

7. Christopher Duffy, *The Military Experience in the Age of Reason* (New York: Atheneum, 1988), 101.

8. Neimeyer, *America Goes to War*, 144.

9. GO, Sept. 3, 1777, in *AWP*, 11:133.

10. Edmonson, "Desertion," 334–35.

11. Artillery Orders (West Point), July 5, 1780, in *EAOB*, roll 12, no. 118.

12. Sept. 19, 1775, entry in Paul Lunt, "A Journal of Travels from Newburyport to Cambridge and in Camp," *MHSP* 12 (1871–73): 201; *NG*, 1:121n.

13. Winthrop, *Military Law*, 442.

14. F. Anderson, *Crucible of War*, 782n.

15. Dec. 30, 1776, entry in "Journal of Captain Charles S. Middleton," in Gibbes, *Documentary History*, 1:61.

16. Hanna, *History of Dewees*, 239.

17. Brigade Orders, Apr. 28, 1781, Regimental Orders, Feb. 26, 1782, and GO, Apr. 30, 1782, in *EAOB*, roll 13, no. 134, roll 15, no. 156, roll 16, no. 158; Orders, Oct. 2, 1779, RWR, M853, roll 5, vol. 32; Berlin, "Administration of Military Justice," 138; Alice M. Earle, *Curious Punishments of Bygone Days* (1896; reprint, New York: Book League of America, 1929), 133; C. Bolton, *Private Soldier*, 176.

18. Regimental Orders, Apr. 7, 20, and July 6, 1781, in *EAOB*, roll 13, no. 134.

19. GO, May 10 and June 9, 1776, in *AWP*, 4:251, 469; Lender and Martin, *Citizen Soldier*, May 10 and 15, 1776, 45–56.

20. GO, July 10, 1775, in *AWP*, 1:82–83n; George W. Chase and Henry B. Dawson, eds., *Diary of David How* (Cambridge, Mass.: H. O. Houghton, 1865), 32; Earle, *Curious Punishments*, 129–31; Applegate, "Constitutions like Iron," 149; F. Anderson, *Crucible of War*, 781n; Neagles, *Summer Soldiers*, 235, 252.

21. GO, Aug. 20, 1780, in *FWW*, 19:45; Oct. 2, 1778, entry in "Order Book of

John Faucheraud Grimké," *SCHGM* 13 (1912): 94; Mar. 9, 1778, entry in "Order Book of Samuel Elbert," 111; William Gibson pension application (1832), in Dann, *Revolution Remembered*, reference to an event of summer 1779, 188–89; Hanna, *History of Dewees*, 238; Sept. 30, 1779, entry in Bray and Bushnell, *Diary of Greenman*, 14; Randy Steffen, *The Horse Soldier, 1776–1943: The United States Cavalryman, His Uniform, Arms, Accoutrements, and Equipments*, vol. 1 (Norman: University of Oklahoma Press, 1977), 34; F. Anderson, *Crucible of War*, 781n; Grose, *Military Antiquities*, 2:200.

22. Steffen, *Horse Soldier*, 34; Applegate, "Constitutions like Iron," 149; Barker, *Redcoats*, 29; Scudieri, "Continentals," 135; Fisher-Fabian, *Prussia's Glory*, 83.

23. C. Bolton, *Private Soldier*, 175.

24. Greene's Orders (abstract), Apr. 13, 1782, in *NG*, 11:50.

25. Court Martial (Valley Forge), Mar. 11, 1778, RWR, M853, roll 3, vol. 21.

26. June 29, 1779, entry in "Journal of Thomas Roberts," in Cook, *Journals of Military Expedition*, 241.

27. Thacher, *Military Journal*, 187; Bradford, "Discipline in Morristown," 25.

28. Edmund F. Patrick pension application (1833), in Dann, *Revolution Remembered*, 375–76.

29. Hanna, *History of Dewees*, 240.

30. GO, Sept. 3, 1777, in *AWP*, 11:133.

31. GO, Jan. 4, 1780, in *FWW*, 17:345.

32. GO, Jan. 17, 1779, "Order Book of Grimké" (1913), 105; Greene's Orders, Mar. 5, 1782, in *NG*, 10:443.

33. Washington to Col. Richard Butler, July 31, 1782, in *FWW*, 24:449.

34. Brigade Orders, Mar. 20, 1781, in *EAOB*, roll 13, no. 135.

35. Washington to the Committee of Congress with the Army, Jan. 29, 1778, in *FWW*, 10:402.

36. Washington to the Council of General Officers, Aug. 20, 1778, in *FWW*, 12:344, 344n; Edmonson, "Desertion," 328–29.

37. GO, Mar. 10, 1778, Washington to Col. Thomas Hartley, May 29, 1778, and GO, Apr. 22, 1779, in *FWW*, 11:57, 480, 14:425; Jan. 28 and Mar. 10, 1778, entries in *Valley Forge Orderly Book*, 214, 253.

38. Lender, "Enlisted Line," 186.

39. Berlin, "Administration of Military Justice," 133–34.

40. July 21, 1779, entries in "Journal of Erkuries Beatty" and "Journal of William McKendry," in Cook, *Journals of Military Expedition*, 21, 200.

41. Proceedings of the Regimental Court Martial (Germantown), Oct. 5, 1777, in Turner, *Journal and Order Book of Kirkwood*, 217.

42. Nov. 17, 1780, entry in Henry Whiting, ed., *Revolutionary Orders of General Washington* (New York: Wiley and Putnam, 1844), 139.

43. GO, Apr. 22, 1779, in *FWW*, 14:425; Svejda, *Quartering, Disciplining*, 115.

44. General Court Martial, Aug. 1, 1779, in *BL*.

45. William B. Weeden, ed., "Diary of Enos Hitchcock," *Publications of the Rhode Island Historical Society* 7 (1899–1900): 111.

46. Regimental Orders, Oct. 29, 1780, and Mar. 7, 1781, in *EAOB*, roll 13, nos. 129, 134; Brigade Orders, Jan. 21 and June 18, 1782, RWR, M853, roll 9, vol. 57, roll 10, vol. 62; Hugh F. Rankin, *The North Carolina Continentals* (Chapel Hill: University of North Carolina Press, 1971), 146.

47. Regimental Orders, Mar. 11, 1781, in *EAOB*, roll 13, no. 134.

48. Oct. 5, 1781, entry in "Orderly Book of Lieutenant John Spear . . . 1781," *PNJHS*, n.s., 1 (1916): 140.

49. Brigade Orders, June 26, 1782, RWR, M853, roll 10, vol. 62; GO, Apr. 22, 1779, and July 29, 1780, in *FWW*, 14:424, 19:467.

50. GO, Apr. 22, 1779, in *FWW*, 14:424–25.

51. Garrison Orders, Sept. 15, 1781, in *EAOB*, roll 14, no. 144.

52. Artillery After Orders (West Point), July 8, 1780, in *EAOB*, roll 12, no. 118.

53. GO, Nov. 30, 1782, in *FWW*, 25:382.

54. Oct. 20, 1781, entry in "Orderly Book of John Spear," 140.

55. GO, Mar. 26, 1778, in *FWW*, 11:156; Krueger, "Troop Life at the Champlain Valley Forts," 200.

56. Egly, *History of First New York Regiment*, 251.

57. Proceedings of a Court Martial, May 1, 1777, in Turner, *Journal and Order Book of Kirkwood*, 56; Bradford, "Discipline in Morristown," 20.

58. Regimental Orders, Apr. 10, 1781, RWR, M853, roll 8, vol. 50.

59. Regimental Orders (Providence), July 24, 1779, RWR, M853, roll 5, vol. 32.

60. GO, Dec. 22, 1777, in *AWP*, 12:603.

61. For example, at Valley Forge, see Trussell, *Birthplace of an Army*, 74–75.

62. Division Orders, July 16, 1777, in Turner, *Journal and Order Book of Kirkwood*, 177; Mayer, *Belonging to the Army*, 241, 261.

63. Greene's Orders, Jan. 29, 1778, in *Valley Forge Orderly Book*, 215; Trussell, *Birthplace of an Army*, 75.

64. Regimental Court Martial, Mar. 13, 1783, in Egly, *History of First New York Regiment*, 258.

65. Brigade Orders, Sept. 29, 1781, in *EAOB*, roll 12, no. 118.1.

66. GO, Sept. 18, 1776, in *AWP*, 6:328.

67. GO, Nov. 19, 1782, in *FWW*, 25:354–55.

68. Rankin, *North Carolina Continentals*, 179; Bodle and Thibaut, *Valley Forge Research Report*, 3:62; Robert G. Albion and Leonidas Dodson, eds., *Philip Vickers Fithian: Journal, 1775–1776* (Princeton: Princeton University Press, 1934), 202n; Thomas G. Tousey, *Military History of Carlisle and Carlisle Barracks* (Richmond, Va.: Dietz, 1939), 154; Hanna, *History of Dewees*, 236.

69. GO, July 23, Sept. 22, 1775, Apr. 20, and Sept. 7, 1776, in *AWP*, 1:158, 2:35, 4:93, 6:240; GO, Mar. 26, May 29–30, 1778, Apr. 14, Aug. 18, 1779, and Aug. 29, 1780, in *FWW*, 11:156, 487, 489, 14:377, 16:126–27, 19:468; "Orderly Book of Livermore's Company," 232; Regimental Orders, Mar. 14, 1782, in *EAOB*, roll 16, no. 159; Apr. 4, 1776, entry in "Journal of a Connecticut Officer: Camp Life in 1776—Siege of Boston," *Historical Magazine* 8 (1864): 332.

70. Sept. 11, 1776, entry in *Orderly Books of Henshaw*, 23; Berlin, "Administration of Military Justice," 130; Bernath, "George Washington and Military Discipline," 89; John E. Ferling, *A Wilderness of Miseries: War and Warriors in Early America* (Westport, Conn.: Greenwood, 1980), 116–17.

71. July 27, 1776, entry in Lender and Martin, *Citizen Soldier*, 90.

72. Hanna, *History of Dewees*, 203–4; Royster, *Revolutionary People*, 78.

73. GO, Maj. Gen. Gates, Dec. 11, 1782, in *GP*; Garrison Orders (West Point), Feb. 6, 1783, in *EAOB*, roll 16, no. 168.

74. Thacher, *Military Journal*, 186; Berlin, "Administration of Military Justice," 131.

75. GO, Feb. 8, 1778, in *AWP*, 13:475.

76. Charles J. Napier, *Remarks on Military Law and the Punishment of Flogging* (London: T. and W. Boone, 1837), 163. Corporal punishment was abolished in the British army in 1881; Frey, *British Soldier in America*, 93.

77. GO, Mar. 25, 1778, in *FWW*, 11:143.

78. Hanna, *History of Dewees*, 203.

79. Bowman, *Morale of American Revolutionary Army*, 72; Richard L. Blanco, "Desertion in the Continental Army," in Blanco, *American Revolution*, 1:464–65.

80. David Cobb to Col. Henry Jackson, June 8, 1780, in Gaillard Hunt, *Fragments of Revolutionary History* (Brooklyn, N.Y.: Historical Printing Club, 1892), 150.

81. Thacher, *Military Journal*, 187.

82. Benjamin Rush, "Inquiry into the Effects of Public Punishments . . .," in *Essays, Literary, Moral, and Philosophical* (Philadelphia: T. and W. Bradford, 1806), 138–39; Carl Binger, *Revolutionary Doctor: Benjamin Rush* (New York: W. W. Norton, 1966), 173.

83. Napier, *Remarks on Military Law*, 150–180.

84. J. Jackson, *Valley Forge*, 177; Apr. 14 and May 6, 1778, entries in John J. Stoudt, *Ordeal at Valley Forge: A Day-by-Day Chronicle from December 17, 1777, to June 18, 1778, Compiled from Original Sources* (Philadelphia: University of Pennsylvania Press, 1963), 232, 272.

85. Nov. 8, 1781, entry in "A Recollection of the American Revolution by a British Officer," *Virginia Historical Register* 6 (1853): 211; Don Higginbotham, "Daniel Morgan: Guerrilla Fighter," in George A. Billias, ed., *George Washington's Generals* (New York: William Morrow, 1964), 293; James Graham, *The Life of General Daniel Morgan . . .* (New York: Derby & Jackson, 1856), 199–200.

86. GO, Nov. 12, 1782, in *FWW*, 25:332.

15. Drummers and Fifers

1. Arthur B. Tourtellot, *William Diamond's Drum: The Beginning of the American Revolution* (Garden City, N.Y.: Doubleday, 1959), 19–20.

2. Brig. Gen. William Woodford to Washington, Oct. 2, 1777, in *AWP*, 11:371; Kenneth Silverman, *A Cultural History of the American Revolution* (New York: Columbia University Press, 1987), 353; Herbert Aptheker, *The American Revolution, 1763–1783* (New York: International, 1960), 221; William C. Nell, *The Colored Patriots*

of the American Revolution (1855; reprint, New York: Arno, 1968), 128; Harry E. Wildes, *Valley Forge* (New York: Macmillan, 1938), 232; Simon V. Anderson, "American Music During the War for Independence, 1775–1783" (Ph.D. diss., University of Michigan, 1965), 51–54.

3. Quotation from Bennett Cuthbertson, *A System for the Complete Interior Management and Oeconomy of a Battalion of Infantry* (1768), in Raoul F. Camus, *Military Music of the American Revolution* (Chapel Hill: University of North Carolina Press, 1976), 9.

4. GO, Aug. 27, 1779, in *FWW*, 15:163; Camus, *Military Music*, 72; Quaife, "Boy Soldier," 549, 553; Regimental Orders, Apr. 29, 1780, in Lauber, *Order Books of New York Regiments*, 334.

5. John C. Fitzpatrick, *The Spirit of the Revolution* (Boston: Houghton Mifflin, 1924), 171.

6. William C. White, *A History of Military Music in America* (1944; reprint, Westport, Conn.: Greenwood, 1975), 27.

7. Order to Capt. William Scott, Jan. 14, 1777, in *AWP*, 8:69; Rosters in Saffell, *Records of the Revolutionary War*, 190–203, 210–15, 230–31, 266–67, 274–77; William S. Cramer, "From Hessian Drummer to Maryland Ironmaker," *Journal of the Johann Schalm Historical Association* 3 (1985): 24; Grose, *Military Antiquities*, 2:314.

8. GO, Nov. 1, 1780, in *EAOB*, roll 13, no. 126; Resolution of Congress, May 27, 1778, and Washington to the President of Congress, Oct. 11, 1780, in *FWW*, 12:308, 20:162.

9. Return of Christian Febiger, Second Virginia Regiment, May 25, 1779, and Return of Second Pennsylvania Regiment of Foot, May 16, 1779, in *Steuben Papers* (National Archives); Return of Third New Jersey Regiment, May 7, 1780, in "Some Unpublished Revolutionary Manuscripts," 79; Return of Gen. Sullivan's Division, June 1, 1777, in O. Hammond, *Letters and Papers of Sullivan*, 354; Silverman, *Cultural History of the American Revolution*, 353; Herbert T. Wade and Robert A. Lively, *This Glorious Cause . . . : The Adventures of Two Company Officers in Washington's Army* (Princeton: Princeton University Press, 1958), 132.

10. John C. Moon, *Musick of the Fifes and Drums*, 4 vols. (Williamsburg: Colonial Williamsburg Foundation, 1976–81), 2:v.

11. "Pay of a Battalion in the Continental Service," *Pennsylvania Gazette*, Aug. 14, 1776; In Congress, May 27, 1778, in *FWW*, 12:30–31; Silverman, *Cultural History of the American Revolution*, 353.

12. June 18, 1776, entry in *Orderly Books of Henshaw*, 157.

13. Eric A. Chandler, "A History of Rudimental Drumming in America from the Revolutionary War to the Present" (DMA diss., Louisiana State University, 1990), 35; Fitzpatrick, *Spirit of the Revolution*, 132; Hanna, *History of Dewees*, 277; John F. Murphy, "Military Music," in Blanco, *American Revolution*, 2:1140.

14. GO, June 4, 1777, in *AWP*, 9:603; GO, Feb. 8, 1778, in *FWW*, 10:433–34; George B. Bruce, *The Drummer's and Fifer's Guide, or Self-Instructor* (1885; facsimile ed., Austin, Tex.: Book Lab, 1996), 9.

15. W. White, *Military Music in America*, 21. For Steuben's directions for musical signals, see Riling, *Baron Von Steuben*, 91–93.

16. Bruce, *Drummer's and Fifer's Guide*, 37; W. White, *Military Music in America*, 24.

17. Bruce, *Drummer's and Fifer's Guide*, 42; Camus, *Military Music*, 80–101; Hanna, *History of Dewees*, 163, 165, 169.

18. Camus, *Military Music*, 8, 85, 87; Fitzpatrick, *Spirit of the Revolution*, 165–69; Hanna, *History of Dewees*, 271; Michael Olmert, "Military Music in the Eighteenth Century," *Colonial Williamsburg: Journal of the Colonial Williamsburg Foundation* 11, no. 4 (1989): 8.

19. General Instructions for the Colonels and Commanding Officers of Regiments in the Continental Service, —— 1777, in *FWW*, 10:242.

20. John W. Molnar, *Songs from the Williamsburg Theater . . . in the Eighteenth Century* (Williamsburg: Colonial Williamsburg Foundation, 1972), 31–33.

21. GO, Aug. 23, 1777, in *AWP*, 11:57.

22. John Adams to Abigail Adams, Aug. 24, 1777, in Charles F. Adams, ed., *Familiar Letters of John Adams and His Wife, Abigail Adams, During the Revolution* (New York: Hurd and Houghton, 1876), 298.

23. Aug. 1, 1776, entry in Albion and Dodson, *Journal of Fithian*, 202; June 23 and 29, 1779, entries in "Journal of William Rogers," 249, 254; Bruce, *Drummer's and Fifer's Guide*, 50; Camus, *Military Music*, 115–16; W. White, *Military Music in America*, 51.

24. Greene's Orders, Aug. 26, 1782, in *NG*, 11:576.

25. GO, July 8, 1775, and Oct. 30, 1776, in *AWP*, 1:75, 7:57.

26. Sept. 15, 1776, entry in Albion and Dodson, *Journal of Fithian*, 232.

27. Camus, *Military Music*, 96.

28. Camus, *Military Music*, 96.

29. Quotation from Samuel Potter, *The Art of Beating the Drum* (1815), in Chandler, "History of Rudimental Drumming in America," 18.

30. W. White, *Military Music in America*, 25–26; Fitzpatrick, *Spirit of the Revolution*, 160; Moon, *Musick of the Fifes and Drums*, 1:iv.

31. GO, June 4, 1777, in *AWP*, 9:603.

32. Aug. 31, 1779, entry in "Orderly Book of Gamble," 236.

33. Dec. 9, 1776, entry in Louise Rau, ed., "Sergeant John Smith's Diary of 1776," *Mississippi Valley Historical Review* 20 (1933–34): 268.

34. GO, Oct. 27, 1776, in *AWP*, 7:36; GO, July 20, 1778, in *FWW*, 12:194.

35. GO, May 9, 1778, June 30, 1779, and June 18, 1780, in *FWW*, 11:366, 15:342, 19:22.

36. Regimental Orders, Apr. 4, 1781, in *EAOB*, roll 13, no. 138.

37. GO, May 9, 1778, in *FWW*, 11:366.

38. Quaife, "Boy Soldier," 559.

39. Washington to the Board of War, July 9, 1776, and GO, July 25, 1776, in *AWP*, 5:247, 559; Regimental Orders, Jan. 28, 1782, in *EAOB*, roll 15, no. 157; "Orderly Book of the Fourth Pennsylvania Battalion . . . ," *PMHB* 30 (1906): 211; Feb.

3, 1776, entry in Salsig, *Parole, Quebec*, 50. Occasionally, brigade drum and fife majors were appointed to instruct field musicians.

40. Hanna, *History of Dewees*, 205–6.

41. July 17, 1776, entry in "Orderly Book of Captain Sharp Delany," *PMHB* 32 (1908): 303; June 6, 1778, entry in "An Orderly Book of the First Regiment, South Carolina Line, Continental Establishment," *SCHM* 7 (1906): 135; GO (Anthony Wayne), Jan. 5, 1778, in Ford, *General Orders of Heath*, 110.

42. Thomas Crafts to William Heath, Aug. 24, 1778, in *The Heath Papers, Collections of the Massachusetts Historical Society*, 7th ser., no. 4 (1904): 265.

43. J. Jackson, *Valley Forge*, 175; Camus, *Military Music*, 132; Silverman, *Cultural History of the American Revolution*, 355–58; Kenneth E. Olson, *Music and Muskets: Bands and Bandsmen of the American Civil War* (Westport, Conn.: Greenwood, 1981), 6.

44. Camus, *Military Music*, 149; Rice, *Travels in North America*, 2:107–8, 279–80.

45. Bradford, "Discipline in Morristown," 22.

46. GO, Sept. 9, 1778, in *FWW*, 12:415; Jan. 4, 1780, entry in Lauber, *Order Books of New York Regiments*, 217; Neagles, *Summer Soldiers*, 263; Rankin, *North Carolina Continentals*, 162.

47. Sept. 27 and Oct. 1, 1776, entries in Chase and Dawson, *Diary of How*, 30.

48. Division Orders, Aug. 7, 1777, in Turner, *Journal and Order Book of Kirkwood*, 133–34; Neagles, *Summer Soldiers*, 168.

49. Washington (by David Humphreys) to John Hiwell, May 5, 1782, WP; GO, Sept. 11, 1778, and July 20, 27, 1781, in *FWW*, 12:429, 22:398, 425; Camus, *Military Music*, 129–33.

50. GO, Aug. 8, 1782, in *FWW*, 24:489.

51. GO, Feb. 16, and Apr. 2, 1783, in *FWW*, 26:138, 282; Egly, *History of First New York Regiment*, 248.

52. Oct. 9, 1775, entry in Samuel Haws, "A Journal for 1775," in Abraham Tomlinson, comp., *Journals of Two Private Soldiers* (Poughkeepsie, N.Y.: A. Tomlinson, 1855), 76; Oct. 8, 1775, entry in Jabez Fitch, "A Journal . . . 1775," *MHSP*, 2d ser., 9 (1894–95): 66.

53. J. Wright, "Some Notes on the Continental Army" (1933), 89; Camus, *Military Music*, 113.

54. Brigade Orders (McDougall), Apr. 13, 1777, in *EAOB*, roll 4, no. 113.

55. Jan. 23, 1776, entry in *Orderly Books of Henshaw*, 76.

56. Washington to Maj. Gen. William Heath, Feb. 6, 1781, in *FWW*, 21:233–34.

57. GO, Jan. 5, 1778, in *FWW*, 10:266.

58. GO, May 11, 1783, in *FWW*, 26:424.

59. Dec. 1, 1779, entry in Field, *Diary of Angell*, 99.

60. Greene's Orders, Jan. 29, 1778, in *Valley Forge Orderly Book*, 215.

61. June 5, 1778, entry in Symmes, *Citizen Soldier*, 32; Hanna, *History of Dewees*, 165; Mayer, *Belonging to the Army*, 112.

62. William Barton to ———, Nov. 17, 1778, in Robert Fridlington, "A 'Diversion'

in Newark: A Letter from the New Jersey Continental Line, 1778," *New Jersey History* 105 (1987): 77–78.

63. GO, Mar. 14, 1778, and Nov. 3, 1779, in *FWW*, 11:83, 17:66; Mar. 14, 1778, entry in *Valley Forge Orderly Book*, 257–58; Mar. 18, 1778, entry in "Diary of McMichael," 157; Mar. 18, 1778, entry in Stoudt, *Ordeal at Valley Forge*, 183; Camus, *Military Music*, 113; J. Wright, "Some Notes on the Continental Army" (1931), 89.

64. Washington to John Hancock, Jan. 26, 1777, Washington to Col. Mordicai Buckner, Jan. 28, 1777, and GO, Feb. 9, 1777, in *AWP*, 8:161, 169, 282; see also 7:312n and 8:163n; Heitman, *Historical Register*, 130; and H. Ward, *Major General Adam Stephen*, 201–11.

65. Quoted from Rev. Andrew Hunter's Diary, Sept. 1775, in Albion and Dodson, *Journal of Fithian*, 238n.

66. Hanna, *History of Dewees*, 179.

67. Hanna, *History of Dewees*, 220; July 22, 1776, entry in "Diary of Oliver Hart" (typescript; mimeographed copy at the Southern Baptist Theological Seminary, Louisville, Ky., 1949), 11.

68. GO, Feb. 18, 1780, in *FWW*, 18:23.

69. Benét, *Treatise on Military Law*, 166–67.

70. Hanna, *History of Dewees*, 240, 260.

71. GO (Heath), Sept. 5, 1777, RWR, M853, roll 3, vol. 16; May 8, 1778, entry in "The Military Journal of Colonel Icabod Goodwin," *Collections and Proceedings of the Maine Historical Society*, 2d ser., 5 (1894): 49; Thacher, *Military Journal*, 186; Regimental Orders, June 29, 1777, in Turner, *Journal and Order Book of Kirkwood*, 94; Hanna, *History of Dewees*, 203; Olmert, "Military Music in the Eighteenth Century," 8; Bradford, "Discipline in Morristown," 5; Barker, *Redcoats*, 28; de Watteville, *British Soldier*, 113.

72. Napier, *Remarks on Military Law*, 151, 172.

73. Orders (McDougall), Oct. 24, 1777, in *EAOB*, roll 5, no. 49.

74. Aug. 3, 1776, entry in Elmer, "Journal of an Expedition to Canada," 172; Winthrop, *Military Law*, 43.

75. GO, Aug. 11, 1776, in *AWP*, 5:663.

76. Israel Trask pension application (1845), in Dann, *Revolution Remembered*, 410–11; Heitman, *Historical Register*, 455; Tousey, *Military History of Carlisle*, 154.

77. "An Anecdote," *New-Jersey Gazette*, Jan. 21, 1778.

78. Proceedings of a Regimental Court Martial, July 2, 1777, in Turner, *Journal and Order Book of Kirkwood*, 95–96.

79. Regimental Orders, Aug. 5, 1781, in *EAOB*, roll 14, no. 143.

80. GO, Jan. 28, 1778, in *AWP*, 13:369–70.

81. OB of Marinus Willett, and GO, Jan. 3, 1778 (Fort Schuyler), in *EAOB*, roll 4, no. 42.

82. Regimental Court Martial, Mar. 10, 1780, RWR, M853, roll 5, vol. 33.

83. Oct. 19, 1776, entry in Rau, "Sergeant John Smith's Diary," 256.

84. Fairfax Downey, *Fife, Drum and Bugle* (Fort Collins, Colo.: Old Army, 1971), 30.

85. Quaife, "Boy Soldier," 555–56.

86. Col. Armand to Washington, Sept. 2, 1777, in *AWP*, 11:232.

87. Quaife, "Boy Soldier," 553–55; Oct. 1780 entry in "Orderly Book of Livermore's Company," 234.

88. Hanna, *History of Dewees*, 135, 138–41, 226–27.

89. Hanna, *History of Dewees*, 271.

90. Hanna, *History of Dewees*, 236–38.

91. Garrison Orders, Jan. 14, 1782, in *EAOB*, roll 15, no. 156.

92. Heath to Washington, Jan. 10, 1782, WP; Camus, *Military Music*, 168.

93. Benjamin Lincoln to the President of Congress, Dec. 21, 1781, in *JCC*, 21:1182–83.

94. Dec. 24, 1781, entry in *JCC*, 21:1183.

95. Apr. 23, 1783, entry in *JCC*, 24:270; Washington to Maj. Gen. Henry Knox, June 8, 1783, in *FWW*, 26:482.

16. The Executioners

1. See Stuart Banner, *The Death Penalty: An American History* (Cambridge: Harvard University Press, 2002), 36–37.

2. May 20, 1778, entry in "Order Book of Samuel Elbert," 148; Maj. James Moore to Greene, Feb. 25, 1783 (abstract), in *NG*, 12:470n.

3. Washington to Maj. Gen. Joseph Spencer, Apr. 3, 1777, in *AWP*, 9:56.

4. Washington to Brig. Gen. George Clinton, May 5, 1777, in *AWP*, 9:348; Washington to Brig. Gen. Alexander McDougall, June 25, 1779, in *FWW*, 15:317. For a similar view, see Maj. Gen. Henry Knox to Alexander Hamilton, July 24, 1782, in Syrett, *Papers of Hamilton*, 3:118.

5. Articles of War, Sept. 20, 1776, in *JCC*, 5:798–800.

6. GO, Aug. 11, 1782, RWR, M853, roll 10, vol. 66; GO, July 22, 1780, in *FWW*, 19:221, 224 (After Orders); "Journal of William Beatty," 80; Jan. 4, 1780, entry in Lauber, *Order Books of New York Regiments*, 217; Applegate, "Constitutions like Iron," 150.

7. GO, Oct. 12, 1777, in *AWP*, 11:490, 492n; Edward W. Hocker, "Spies, Hangings, and Other Crimes During Winter at Valley Forge," *Picket Post*, no. 21 (Apr. 1948): 6; Trussell, *Pennsylvania Line*, 125, 125n; June 4, 1778, entry in Stoudt, *Ordeal at Valley Forge*, 321.

8. Sept. 2, 1778, entry in William Duane, ed., *Extracts from the Diary [of Christopher Marshall] Kept in Philadelphia and Lancaster . . . 1774–1781* (Albany: J. Munsell, 1877), 198; Sept. 2, 1778, entry in Elaine C. Crane, ed., *Diary of Elizabeth Drinker*, vol. 1 (Boston: Northeastern University Press, 1991), 324.

9. GO, May 2, 1779, in *FWW*, 14:474; Maj. Gen. Heath to Washington, May 19, 1777, in *AWP*, 9:472–73; Sept. 11, 1777, entry in Ford, *General Orders of Heath*, 78–79; GO (Greene), Aug. 21, 1781, in *NG*, 9:218.

10. Greene to Col. John Jameson, Oct. 15, 1780, in *NG*, 6:390.

11. Washington to Col. Goose Van Schaick, Oct. 27, 1778, and GO, Oct. 28, 1778, in *FWW*, 13:167, 171–72; Bradford, "Discipline in Morristown," 26.

12. Bernath, "George Washington and Military Discipline," 91; Berlin, "Administration of Military Justice," 157–58; GO, June 10, 1777, in *AWP*, 9:659; GO, May 6, 1778, and June 4, 1779, in *FWW*, 11:356, 15:363–64.

13. Heath to Washington, Jan. 9, 1777, Washington to Heath, Jan. 12, 1777, Heath to Washington, Jan. 19, 1777, Gates to Washington, Feb. 15, 1777, Washington to Gates, Feb. 23, 1777, Maj. Gen. Putnam to Washington, May 10, 1777, Washington to Putnam, May 12, 1777, Maj. Gen. John Sullivan to Washington, May 23, 1777, and Brig. Gen. Francis Nash to Washington, Aug. 14, 1777, in *AWP*, 8:26, 27n, 48, 105, 342, 422, 9:382, 403, 509, 10:611, 611n; Washington to Henry Knox, May 13, 1779, in *FWW*, 15:63–64; GO, Oct. 10, 1778, in "Orderly Book of the First Pennsylvania Regiment," 383; Gen. St. Clair to Gen. Irvine, Sept. 14, 1781, in William Smith, ed., *The St. Clair Papers . . .* , vol. 1 (Cincinnati: Robert Clarke, 1882), 557.

14. Washington to Preudhomme de Borre, Aug. 3, 1777, in *AWP*, 10:495.

15. Benedict Arnold to Washington, Aug. 23, 1780, in *Steuben Papers* (WP-LC).

16. Feb. 27, 1780, entry in *JCC*, 10:204–5.

17. See, for example, court-martial of Mar. 13, 1778, in Duane, *Extracts from the Diary*, 172.

18. Thacher, *Military Journal*, 216.

19. See, for example, the case of Edward Palmer, Aug. 8, 1777, in Ford, *Correspondence of Webb*, 1:227; and Neagles, *Summer Soldiers*, 216.

20. Bowman, *Morale of American Revolutionary Army*, 89; Bernath, "George Washington and Military Discipline," 88; Ferling, *Wilderness of Miseries*, 117; Edmonson, "Desertion," 345; Applegate, "Constitutions like Iron," 150.

21. GO, June 3, 1778, in *FWW*, 12:14; Washington to Maj. Gen. John Sullivan, July 22, 1777, in *AWP*, 10:367–68; June 3, 1778, entry in "Orderly Book, May–June 1778," *MHSP* 7 (1864): 135; Berlin, "Administration of Military Justice," 147.

22. See, for example, Sept. 9, 1777, entry in Ford, *Correspondence of Webb*, 1:288.

23. GO, Sept. 22, 1776, in *AWP*, 6:366; Mar. 4, 1777, entry in "Journal of William Beatty," 108; Bodle and Thibaut, *Valley Forge Research Report*, 3:62.

24. Woodman, *History of Valley Forge*, 80.

25. Angelakos, "Army at Middlebrook," 117; *NG*, 3:267n.

26. GO, July 18, 1779, in *FWW*, 15:436; Garrison Orders, Oct. 31, 1777, in Bray and Bushnell, *Diary of Greenman*, 97.

27. *AWP*, 8:422n.

28. GO, Oct. 31, 1776, in *AWP*, 7:59.

29. GO, Jan. 8 and 9, 1778, in *AWP*, 15:171, 185; GO, Sept. 12, 1780, in Field, *Diary of Angell*, 115–16n; Sept. 9, 1777, entry in Ford, *Correspondence of Webb*, 1:288; Bodle and Thibaut, *Valley Forge Research Report*, 3:62; Lender, "Enlisted Line," 183.

30. Garrison Orders, Feb. 14, 1782, in *EAOB*, roll 15, no. 157; After Orders, May 12, 1782, RWR, M853, roll 10, vol. 6.

31. June 12, 1779, entries in "Journal of Roberts" and "Journal of Major Daniel Livermore" in Cook, *Journals of Military Expedition*, 240, 180; June 6 and 11, 1779, entries in Ellis, "Order Book of Barber," 66, 69.

32. Thacher, *Military Journal*, 200.

33. Neagles, *Summer Soldiers*, 36.

34. Washington to Col. George Gibson, Mar. 11, 1778, in *FWW*, 11:65.

35. GO, Sept. 10, 1781, in *EAOB*, roll 14, no. 140.

36. Sheldon S. Cohen, "Alexander Scammell," in John A. Garraty and Mark C. Carnes, eds., *American National Biography*, vol. 19 (New York: Oxford University Press, 1999), 343.

37. GO (Heath), Sept. 4 and 30, 1777, RWR, M853, roll 3, vol. 16; Scheer, *Private Yankee Doodle*, 165.

38. Garrison Orders (West Point), Feb. 10, 1782, in *EAOB*, roll 15, no. 156.

39. Washington to Gates, Feb. 23, 1777, in *AWP*, 8:422.

40. Orders (Lancaster), Mar. 10, 1778, RWR, M853, roll 3, vol. 18; July 22, 1778, entry in "Diary of Oliver Hart," 11; Berlin, "Administration of Military Justice," 147.

41. Instructions to Capt. Bartholomew Von Heer, Oct. 11, 1778, in *FWW*, 13:70.

42. GO, After Orders, June 27, 1776, in *AWP*, 5:112.

43. GO, Feb. 18, 1780, in *FWW*, 18:22–23.

44. Oct. 2, 1780, entry in *Elijah Fisher's Journal*, 41.

45. Roy J. Honeywell, *Chaplains of the United States Army* (Washington, D.C.: Office of the Chief of Army Chaplains, 1958), 73; Parker C. Thompson, *From Its European Antecedents to 1791: The United States Army Chaplaincy*, vol. 1 (Washington, D.C.: Office of the Chief of Army Chaplains, 1978), xix, 218.

46. GO, Feb. 7 and July 9, 1776, Circular to the Brigade Commanders, May 26, 1777, David Roberdeau to Washington, May 26, 1777, and John Hancock to Washington, May 27, 1777, in *AWP*, 3:258, 5:246, 9:533, 540n, 540; Charles W. Heathcote, "Army Chaplains at Valley Forge Recognized for Their Leadership," *Picket Post*, no. 17 (Apr. 1947): 8.

47. GO, June 9, 1777, in *AWP*, 9:651.

48. Sept. 12, 1780, entry in Weeden, "Diary of Enos Hitchcock," 223; Howard L. Applegate, "Duties and Activities of Chaplains," *Picket Post*, no. 61 (July 1958): 13.

49. Mar. 20, 1776, entry in *Journal of the Rev. Ammi R. Robbins, a Chaplain in the American Army in the Northern Campaign of 1776* (New Haven: B. L. Hamlen, 1850), 3.

50. June 30, 1779, entry in "Journal of William Rogers," 249; P. Thompson, *From Its European Antecedents*, 255, 261.

51. Orders, Feb. 6 and 14, 1779, in Hall, *Life and Letters of Parsons*, 214–15.

52. Washington to Maj. Gen. Gates, Oct. 10, 1778, and Washington to Rev. Alexander McWhorter, Oct. 12, 1778, in *FWW*, 13:54, 71–72.

53. *AWP*, 2:556n; Jan. 10, 1777, entry in Alexander A. Lawrence, ed., "Journal of Major Raymond Demere," *Collections of the Georgia Historical Society* 52 (1968): 344; July 29, Aug. 8, 14, 17–18, 1778, and Oct. 13, 1779, entries in Reuben A. Guild, *Chaplain [Hezekiah] Smith and the Baptists* (Philadelphia: American Baptist Publications Society, 1885), 240–41, 263; Applegate, "Constitutions like Iron," 151–52.

54. July 1, 1776, entry in Elmer, "Journal of an Expedition to Canada," 45.

55. *Pennsylvania Evening Post*, Mar. 8, 1777, quoted in Frank Moore, comp., *Diary of the American Revolution* (New York: Washington Square, 1967), 210.

56. *AWP*, 10:55n; Jedediah Huntington to Jabez Huntington, July 29, 1777, in Bates, *Huntington Papers*, 357; Ebenezer David to Nicholas Brown, Aug. 2, 1777, in Jeanette D. Black and William B. Roelker, eds., *A Rhode Island Chaplain in the Revolution: Letters of Ebenezer David to Nicholas Brown, 1775–1778* (Providence: Rhode Island Society of the Cincinnati, 1949), 37; Royster, *Revolutionary People*, 170, 173–74.

57. "Personal Narrative of the Services of Lieut. John Shreve of the New Jersey Line of the Continental Army," *Magazine of American History* 3, pt. 2 (1879): 573.

58. William Abbatt, *The Crisis of the Revolution: Being the Story of Arnold and André* (1899; reprint, New York: Harbor Hill, 1967), 75.

59. Carl Van Doren, *Secret History of the American Revolution* (1942; reprint, New York: Viking, 1968), 371.

60. Hanna, *History of Dewees*, 241.

61. William Heath to Washington, Apr. 20, 1781, quoted in *FWW*, 21:482n.

62. Warrant for execution, July 29 and Aug. 10, 1781, in *NG*, 9:100, 100n, 158, 158n.

63. Abbatt, *Crisis of the Revolution*, 75 (quote); John E. Walsh, *The Execution of Major André* (New York: Palgrave, 2001), 144–45.

64. Hanna, *History of Dewees*, 201.

65. Hanna, *History of Dewees*, 260–63; summer 1782 entry in John R. Shaw, *A Narrative of the Life and Travels of John Robert Shaw, the Well-Digger* (1807; reprint, Louisville: George Fowler, 1930), 86–87.

66. Charles I. Bushnell, ed., *Memoirs of the Life of Samuel Smith . . . Extract from a Journal . . . 1776 to 1786*, in *Crumbs for Antiquarians* 1, no. 2 (privately printed, 1864), 16–19.

67. "Narrative of Henry Hollowell," 172.

68. Jan. 10, 1778, entry in "Journal of Wild," 106.

69. Scheer, *Private Yankee Doodle*, 164–65; John T. Hayes, *Connecticut's Revolutionary Cavalry, Sheldon's Horse* (Chester, Conn.: Pequot, 1975), 33.

70. Sept. 12, 1780, entry in Weeden, "Diary of Enos Hitchcock," 223.

71. June 13, 1779, entry in "Journal of Major David Livermore," *Collections of the New Hampshire Historical Society* 6 (1850): 314; June 12, 1779, entry in "Journal of Sergeant Thomas Roberts," 240; Banner, *Death Penalty*, 77–79.

72. GO, Aug. 25, 1776, and Oct. 2, 1777, in Ford, *General Orders of Heath*, 66, 89; Greene's Orders, Apr. 22, 1782, in *NG*, 11:87; Light Infantry Orders (Anthony Wayne), in "Orderly Book of Gamble," 241; Division Orders, Aug. 9, 1777, in Turner, *Journal and Order Book of Kirkwood*. 136; J. Thomas Scharf and Thompson Westcott, *History of Philadelphia*, vol. 1 (Philadelphia: L. H. Everts, 1884), 339; Scheer, *Private Yankee Doodle*, 46.

73. GO (Heath), Sept. 5, 1777, RWR, M853, roll 3, vol. 16; GO, Nov. 1, 1777, in *AWP*, 12:74; Aug. 25 and Oct. 2, 1777, entries in Ford, *General Orders of Heath*, 66, 89; Neagles, *Summer Soldiers*, 37.

74. See, for example, Greene to Sgt. Edward Boothe, Jan. 4, 1781, and Death Warrant for Sgt. John Radley (abstract), Aug. 6, 1781, in *NG*, 7:41, 9:13, 13n.

75. GO (Heath), Sept. 5, 1777, RWR, M853, roll 3, vol. 16; May 10, 1778, entry in "Order Book of Samuel Elbert," 147; Mar. 24, 1778, entry in "Order Book of the First Regiment, South Carolina Line," 79; Sept. 1776 entry in Bellas, *Personal Recollections of Enoch Anderson*, 22–23; Benét, *Treatise on Military Law*, 166–67.

76. Berlin, "Administration of Military Justice," 148–49; Robert I. Alotta, *Civil War Justice: Union Army Executions under Lincoln* (Shippensburg, Pa.: White Mane, 1989), 41.

77. Berlin, "Administration of Military Justice," 148–49. Camp colour-men dug the graves "under the direction of a Sergeant"; GO, May 25, 1780, in *FWW*, 18:422.

78. See, for example, May 21, 1778, entry in John F. Grimké, "Journal of the Campaign to the Southward . . . 1778," *SCHM* 12 (1911): 64; May 1, 1781, entry in William H. Denny, ed., "Military Journal of Major Ebenezer Denny," *Memoirs of the Historical Society of Pennsylvania* 7 (1860): 238; and Lawrence, "Journal of Demere," 344.

79. Hanna, *History of Dewees*, 23–31, 236.

80. Quaife, "Boy Soldier, 552n.

81. Quoted in William Gordon, *The History of the Rise, Progress, and Establishment of the Independence of the United States of America*, vol. 4 (1788; reprint, Freeport, N.Y.: Books for Libraries, 1969), 28.

82. Hanna, *History of Dewees*, 232.

83. June 24, 1779, entry in "Journal of Lieutenant Robert Parker of the Second Continental Artillery, 1779," *PMHB* 27 (1903): 406.

84. Greene's Orders (abstract), Aug. 6, 1781, in *NG*, 9:133.

85. Alotta, *Civil War Justice*, 9, 15. Col. Benjamin Cleveland, commander of North Carolina militia during the Revolution, was probably the most notorious user of drumhead courts-martial.

86. GO, Oct. 1, 1776, in *AWP*, 6:445.

87. Washington to Joseph Kirkbride, Apr. 20, 1778, in *FWW*, 11:284.

88. GO, Oct. 4, 1781, in *FWW*, 23:171.

89. July 31, 1777, entry in Turner, *Journal and Order Book of Kirkwood*, 127–28.

90. William H. Denny, "Soldier of the Republic: The Life of Major Ebenezer Denny" (Ph.D. diss., Miami University, 1978), 27.

91. Washington to Greene (abstract), Feb. 2, 1781, in *NG*, 7:240, 240n; Bennett and Lennon, *Quest for Glory*, 134–35.

92. Aug. 4, 1777, entry in "Journal of William Beatty," 108; Rankin, *North Carolina Continentals*, 314.

93. Hanna, *History of Dewees*, 201.

94. Henry Laurens to Washington, July 11, 1779, WP; Washington to Henry Laurens, July 9 and 10, 1779, in *FWW*, 15:388, 399; Peter Ten Broeck to his parents, July 9, 1779, in "News from Camp: Letters Received by Cornelius Ten Broeck . . . from his Sons . . . 1779–1780," *Magazine of American History* 1, pt. 2 (1878): 169; Royster, *Revolutionary People*, 81–82.

95. Maurer, "Military Justice under Washington," 65.

96. GO, June 10, 1777, in *AWP*, 9:659.

97. Washington to Brig. Gen. Hogun, Nov. 19, 1779, "Council of War," Mar. 27, 1780, in *FWW*, 17:133, 18:165; Greene to Clement Biddle (abstract), Sept. 30, 1779, in *NG*, 4:426, 426n; Feb. 23, 1780, entry in Walter Clark et al., eds., *The State Records of North Carolina*, 19 vols. (Goldsboro: Nash Brothers, 1895–1907), 16:1062; Carol L. Snow, *Volunteer Revolutionary War Soldiers from North Carolina* (Toast, N.C.: C and L Historical Publishers, 1963), 26; Samuel A. Ashe, *History of North Carolina*, vol. 1 (1925; reprint, Spartanburg, S.C.: Reprint, 1971), 599, 602; Samuel S. Smith, *Winter at Morristown, 1779–1780: The Darkest Hour* (Monmouth Beach, N.J.: Philip Freneau, 1979), 7; Rankin, *North Carolina Continentals*, 218–19; Royster, *Revolutionary People*, 296–97.

98. Petition of Ann Glover to the General Assembly, 1780, in Clark, *State Records of North Carolina*, 15:187–88; Royster, *Revolutionary People*, 298–99.

99. "Thoughts on the Present State of the Army, Addressed to the Military," signed "A Lieutenant Colonel," *New-Jersey Gazette*, Dec. 24, 1777.

100. OB of Maj. Gen. Gates, Jan. 30, 1783, in *GP* (NYPL). Brown (1663–1704) was known for his satirical verse.

Index

Harry M. Ward is the William Binford Vest Professor of History emeritus at the University of Richmond. A native of Illinois, he received his graduate degrees from Columbia University. He is the author of numerous works on Colonial and Revolutionary America, several of which have won national awards. His most recent books are *The War for Independence and the Transformation of American Society* and *Between the Lines: Banditti of the American Revolution*.